M000238760

RECOIL OFFGRID

PRESENTS

THE BUG OUT BOOK

BAGS, TOOLS, AND SURVIVAL SKILLS TO SAVE YOUR ASS IN AN EMERGENCY

Copyright ©2023 Caribou Media Group, LLC

All rights reserved. No portion of this publication may be reproduced or transmitted in any form or by any means, electronic or mechanical, including photocopy, recording, or any information storage and retrieval system, without permission in writing from the publisher, except by a reviewer who may quote brief passages in a critical article or review to be printed in a magazine or newspaper, or electronically transmitted on radio, television, or the Internet.

Published by

Recoil Offgrid Books, an imprint of Caribou Media Group, LLC
5600 W. Grande Market Drive, Suite 100
Appleton, WI 54913
offgridweb.com | gundigest.com

To order books or other products call 920.471.4522 ext.104
or visit us online at gundigeststore.com

DISCLAIMER: Prices and details for items featured in RECOIL are set by the manufacturers and retailers, and are subject to change without notice. Please read all local and federal laws carefully before attempting to purchase any products shown in this guide or building your own firearms. Laws change frequently and, although our text was accurate at the time it was originally published, it may have changed between then and what's currently legal.

ISBN-13: 978-1-951115-91-3

Edited and designed by Recoil Offgrid Staff

Printed in the United States of America

10 9 8 7 6 5 4 3 2 1

TABLE OF CONTENTS

Introduction

The expression "get out of Dodge" dates back to the late 1800s – when famous gunslingers like Wyatt Earp, Doc Holiday, and Bat Masterson walked the streets of the renown frontier town. Even according to Dodge City's own tourism website it was a place where "visiting cowboys and locals could get away with just about anything". This rough-and-tumble reputation, attractive to some, caused a lot of innocent people to uproot themselves and move...well...anywhere else. It may be one of the first well-known references to bugging out. The concept of relocating to get away from

trouble has since been branded, like a steer's hide, into the psyche of American preparedness culture.

The idea, like many emergency response plans, is scalable. If severe weather is passing through, "bugging out" may look like packing a bag and staying in a hotel, or on a family member's couch, until the storm blows over. If the crisis is more severe, large scale riots, supply shortages or long-term disruption of utilities, the answer might be taking a "tribe" of family and friends to a hunting property, or second bugout location you've pre-staged with supplies. Whatever worries you at night, we've got information on how to make you and your loved ones better prepared to cope with it. This book covers a wide array of how to pack and plan for bugging out.

Perhaps most eye-catching, we present an entire section on bugout bags – the quintessential building-block of preparedness. Bugout bags are like fingerprints: everyone has one (or should!) and they're all unique. We have a recurring column in RECOIL OFFGRID magazine where we feature a different bugout bag in every issue. They come from our editors, contributors, readers, and family members. Each bag, and its contents, are unique to the owner, who explains what the purpose of the bag is and how they selected its contents. If you don't have a bugout bag of your own, or haven't evaluated it in some time, we hope this section gives you some fresh inspiration or a place to start.

Of course, having a bugout bag filled with useless gadgets or poor-quality tools is more likely to cause another disaster on top of whatever one you're already up against. So we've also included a number of buyer's guides and product round-ups. Covering everything from flashlights and whistles to tourniquets and gun-maintenance tools, these buffet-style articles will give you a deeper dive into the pros and cons of various product types to help you make informed decisions as a preparedness product consumer.

The pivotal concept of bugging out is that you take this bag full of life-saving gear and physically take it somewhere other than your normal place of work or residence. So you can also find thorough explanations of the process of bugging out, or displacing from your routine surroundings. Long-term strategies like staging supply caches and selecting a bugout property are covered in-depth, as are more niche bugout considerations like how to escape your office, how to bug out with babies or dogs, and how to hide your tracks on the move. We also have an entire section on transportation options that run a wide gamut of possibilities from electric bikes and ATVs to canoes and helicopters.

Whatever your existing level of knowledge or preparedness planning goals, there is something for everyone in this encyclopedia of bugging out. As always, stay safe and stay ready.

*— **Tom Marshall***
Editor, RECOIL OFFGRID

You're Ready, But What About Your Best Friend?

You've Got Your Plans Mapped Out, Survival Essentials on High Stock and Everyone in the Family Is Pretty Much Covered, Right? What About Your Dog?

By John Jarasa
Photos by Jeff Chen

In a recent survey conducted by American Pet Products Association, studies have revealed that roughly 83 million dogs are owned in the United States. With numbers like that, it's no surprise that pets have become an increasingly important extension of our families — and for some, their only family. The smiles they bring and the personalities they share have made them an integral and intimate part of the new family household and further studies reveal just how important they have become.

Further investigation by Kelton Research also reveals that there are blurred lines when it comes to dogs and children. Although humorous (and disconcerting at the same time) the studies show that many consider their dogs as equally important as their children. Needless to say, we can all understand the love of a pet, but even more powerful is the passing of one. While pets are often at the forefront of our minds during our daily routines, in many cases, they are an afterthought when it comes to emergency preparation.

Having a contingency plan that includes your pets is crucial to any pet owner, and it would be most beneficial to include them in any plan ahead of time. That said, be prepared to handle any canine emergencies by studying this buyer's guide which was designed with your pets in mind.

From basic necessities like food and water, understanding the pedigree of your dog is crucial to determining the "hardiness zone" of your geographic area in order to truly understand what you'll need. Take for instance, dogs with thicker coats (think Pomeranians and Chow Chows); even in the coldest of winters in a location such as Southern California, they do NOT need jackets. Whereas you may be cold, the thicker fur coats on dogs within these breeds acts like insulation to keep them warm. As a matter of fact, you can actually "overheat" the dog and potentially cause death or seizures, so again, understanding the conditions you might be facing because of different pedigrees will require different attention.

Another thing to keep in mind is that these products will help increase the chances of your pets surviving and sustaining, but you will also need to plan strategically if you need to leave your home in a crisis. In the event of major catastrophes, many will be forced to flee in search of shelter, but you have to keep in mind (and understand) that some shelters may not allow your pets inside. So plan in advance, stock up on the supplies you feel necessary for your pets, and have a game plan. You don't want to have to plan that during the crisis itself, or even worse, after the crisis, when there will simply be no time or resources to be able to help your four-legged friend survive.

In addition to some of the topics we have discussed, as well as the many online resources you can peruse, you should also consider talking to your local veterinarian about pet needs in the event of an emergency. They can offer crucial advice on what supplies you should stock up on, as well as what unconventional methods you might be wise to use in treating a sick pet. The wealth of knowledge veterinarians have can truly be your best benefit when it comes to ascertaining the exact needs you'll need to meet for your pet in the event of an emergency. In fact, you'd be surprised to find out what you can find in you cupboards to help treat a dog and in the end, the most powerful resource is knowledge, so by all means ask questions and do your research.

U.S. DOG OWNERSHIP ESTIMATES

83.3 M – NUMBER OF OWNED DOGS
47% – Percentage of households that own at least one dog
70% – Percentage of owners with one dog
20% – Percentage of owners with two dogs
10% – Percentage of owners with three or more dogs
1.47 – Average number of owned dogs per household
20% – Percentage of owned dogs who were adopted from animal shelters
$231 – Average annual amount spent by dog owners on routine veterinary visits
83% – Percentage of owned dogs who are spayed or neutered
Even – Proportion of male to female owned dogs

Source: 2013-2014 statistics, contact the American Pet Products Association Pet Owners Survey

PROTECTION

Dog Survival Gear

There is plenty of gear on the market that can help you prepare and protect your dog from tough elements and unexpected events. Don't let your canine buddy get left out of your preparation plans. A few standouts of some dog-specific kit are presented in this guide.

	1	**2**	**3**	**4**
№ MAKE & MODEL	**ActiveDogs.com** Paw Mitts	**Top Paw** K9 Goggles	**Top Paw** Dog Boots	**21st Century Pet Health** Paw Pad Protector
SIZE	XS, Small (Pictured), Medium, Large, XL	XS, Small, Medium, Large (Pictured)	XS, Small, Medium, Large, XL (Pictured)	N/A
COLORWAY	Navy Blue, Black, Camo, Green, Orange, Purple, Red, Royal Blue, Wine, Yellow (Pictured)	N/A	Pink, Blue (Pictured)	N/A
$ MSRP	$32.99	$24.99	$14.99	$7.99
URL	www.activedogs.com	www.petsmart.com	www.petsmart.com	www.21stcenturypet.com
+ NOTES	Protect your dog's paws from broken glass and other dangerous debris. Paw Mitts have a water-resistant, 1000 denier nylon and urethane coated fabric outer layer. Its inner layer is a soft fleece and outside footpad is non-slip suede leather.	Sheild your dog's eyes from burning embers, heavy dust, and other air contaminants. Featuring 100-percent UV block lenses, these goggles for your dog are shatterproof, anti-fog, and come in multiple adjustable sizes.	These rubber soled Dog Boots are water resistant and non-slip. We wouldn't run around a disaster zone barefoot, why should your dog?	For dogs that don't like the feeling of boots on their feet, there is this alternative. It is a wax that can be applied to your dog's paw pads that creates a protective barrier between the skin and the ground.

1

2

3

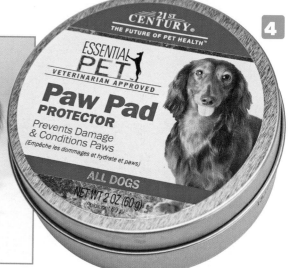

4

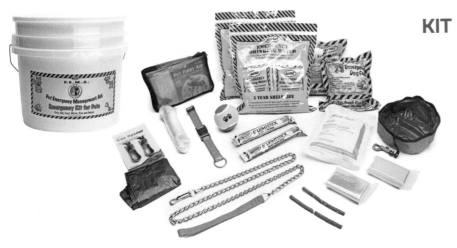

KIT

№

MAKE & MODEL
Mayday Industries
The 38 Piece "DogGoneIt PEMA" Kit For Dogs

$ **MSRP**
$87

URL
www.maydayindustries.com

+ **NOTES**
This "all-in-one" type kit covers many items of what you'll need to manage your dog. Everything from food, water, water bowl, first-aid kit, a leash, and more are included. We suggest supplementing this kit with more items to build a customized kit for your dog.

WEARABLES

	1	**2**	**3**	**4**
№	**MAKE & MODEL** **CQB K-9** Patrol/Tactical Harness	**MAKE & MODEL** **Top Paw** Backpack	**MAKE & MODEL** **Survival Straps** Wide Dog Collar	**MAKE & MODEL** **ThunderWorks** ThunderShirt
SIZE	Large, up to 30-inch girth	Medium, Large, XL (Pictured)	16 to 26 inches	XXS, XS (Pictured), S, M, L, XL, XXL
COLORWAY / COLORS	**COLORWAY** Tan	**COLORWAY** N/A	**COLORS** INSIDE: Various, Black (Pictured) Edge: Various, Blue, Royal (Pictured) DOG TAG OPTIONS: Center (Pictured), Left	**COLORS** Blue Polo, Green Polo, Heather Grey (Pictured), Holiday Red Limited Edition, Pink Polo
$ MSRP	$60	$34.99 to $44.99	$45.95	$39.95 to $44.95
URL	www.cqbk9.com	www.petsmart.com	www.survivalstraps.com	www.thundershirt.com
+ NOTES	The Patrol/Tactical Harness is a lightweight option over heavier dog packs. It features adjustable sizing straps, hook and loop surfaces along with a durable nylon leash attachment and zippered carry pouches.	Have your dog pull his or her own weight by putting survival supplies on their backs. This sturdy backpack is adjustable for a correct fit.	The Survival Straps Wide Dog Collar is made of 550 military-spec paracord and stainless-steel shackles. It's the ultimate survivalist dog collar.	Used to ease anxiety, the ThunderShirt provides your dog with a sense of security that could be important during stressful times.

MEDICAL

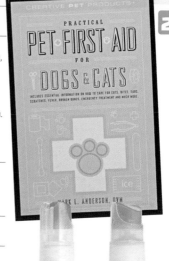

1

MAKE & MODEL
Creative Pet Products
Bow Ow First Aid Kit

MSRP
$39

URL
www.petfirstaidkits.com

NOTES
First-aid kit for your pets. This handy kit comes with a few essentials in a carry case, but will still probably need to be supplemented with other tools and medicines to suit your dog.

2

MAKE & MODEL
Creative Pet Products
Practical Pet First Aid For Dogs & Cats

MSRP
$14

URL
www.petfirstaidkits.com

NOTES
Because we can't all be veterinarians, having this guide with you can you help treat everything from fevers, bug bites, cuts, broken bones, and more.

3

MAKE & MODEL
GNC
Dog Aspirin

DOSES
All Small Dogs 120 mg (Pictured), All Large Dogs 300 mg

MSRP
$7.99 to $13.99

URL
www.gnc.com

NOTES
This is beef-flavored aspirin, what's not to love? Your buddy will not have a problem taking this tablet. The chewable tablets help with pain relief and inflammation.

4

MAKE & MODEL
Remedy+ Recovery
Medicated Antiseptic

MSRP
$7.99

URL
www.cardinalpet.com

NOTES
Much like antiseptic sprays you might have in your own first-aid kit, this spray kills germs, eases bug bites and scratches, and is formulated for your dog's skin and fur coats.

5

MAKE & MODEL
Remedy+ Recovery
Liquid Bandage

MSRP
$7.99

URL
www.cardinalpet.com

NOTES
This is a handy liquid bandage that dries quickly and keeps your pet's wound clean and dry so that it can heal quickly without complications from possible infection when applied correctly.

6

MAKE & MODEL
Remedy+ Recovery
Styptic Powder

MSRP
$10.99

URL
www.cardinalpet.com

NOTES
A blood-clotting agent for your dog, this powder can come in handy to stop the flow of small cuts and scrapes.

7

MAKE & MODEL
21st Century Pet Health
Flexible Bandage – Bandage Self-Adhering

SIZE
2-inch, 4-inch (Pictured)

COLORWAY
2-inch Blue, Pink, Purple | 4-inch Black (Pictured), Purple

MSRP
$0.97 to $1.97

URL
www.21stcenturypet.com

NOTES
Like their human counterparts, pets may require bandages to help treatment from cuts or even sprained or broken limbs. This self-adhering bandage is specifically made for pets.

8

MAKE & MODEL
21st Century Pet Health
Oral Syringe

SIZE
15cc (Pictured), 30cc

MSRP
$3.99

URL
www.21stcenturypet.com

NOTES
Any easy way to administer medicine for pets, this oral syringe is reusable and can hold up to 15cc's of liquid. In a disaster kit, it can be used for other pet and human purposes such as flushing out eyes with water.

9

MAKE & MODEL
21st Century Pet Health
Anti Diarrhea Liquid with Kaolin & Pectin

MSRP
$13.99

URL
www.21stcenturypet.com

NOTES
This item is self-explanatory. Pack one in your dog's kit and you'll be thankful that you have it.

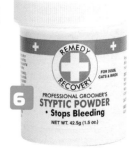

REAL-WORLD STRATEGIES FOR CONFRONTING YOUR WORST NIGHTMARES

From natural disasters to terrorism to grid-down chaos, the number of life-threatening nightmares we all need to prepare for is staggering.

WHAT IF? is based on **OFFGRID MAGAZINE**'s longest-running and most popular column. It's a scenario-based guide with insights from a panel of more than 40 actual survival experts to help you plan for and confront worst-case situations.

These pros include trainers for U.S. military special operations, the Department of Defense (DoD) and law enforcement SWAT. There are no keyboard warriors here; these are people who have made a living learning and teaching how to survive threats and then stay alive in nearly any conceivable scenario.

No matter what you're preparing for, *WHAT IF?* has the answers.

RECOIL OFFGRID PRESENTS

WHAT IF?

Experts' Survival Strategies for Natural Disasters, Urban Threats, and Other Deadly Emergencies

COMPILED BY THE EDITORS OF **OFFGRID** MAGAZINE

ORDER TODAY AT
GUNDIGESTSTORE.COM OR CALL 920.471.4522

Product No. R8155
ISBN 9781951115791

CARTRIDGES FOR WEAPONS,
INERT PROJECTILE, UN 0328

1315-01-369-6612-C784

1-CARTRIDGE, 120MM TP-T: M831A1

LOT MHM97C156H002

75.4 LB

OFM JIC M500CR

SURVIVAL KIT

Caching,
A Necessary Evil?

Stashing Essential Gear, Just in Case

By Erik Lund
Photography by Michael Grey

here are a few things in life that are just necessary evils — things that we all recognize are necessary, but hate doing just the same. Things like going to the dentist, purchasing life insurance, or preparing our last will and testament come to mind. Another necessary evil I find quite objectionable is the concept of caching a firearm. The idea of spending hard-earned money on a firearm whose only purpose is to be secured in a secret location, never to be used or enjoyed except in the most dire of circumstances is one such evil. But the real question becomes, is it necessary?

The practice of caching dates back to when man first walked on two feet. Quite simply, caching is the act of secretly hiding provisions or supplies for use at a later time. Caches can be as small as a candy bar and a bottle of water or they can occupy an entire warehouse. The size of a cache depends entirely on its purpose and your ability to properly secure it. The concept of saving supplies for use at a later date does not work very well if those supplies are either stolen or eaten prior to their retrieval. Let's review three critical aspects of a creating a successful cache: preparation, security, and accessibility.

Preparation is Key

First and foremost, preparation of the items to be cached is of utmost importance. Food items must be selected based upon their ability to be stored for long periods of time. Prepackaged items that are specifically designed for long-term storage such as military-style Meals Ready-to-Eat (MRE) or commercially available freeze-dried emergency food supplies are perfect for any food cache. The convenience of using prepackaged meals for small to midsized caches outweighs the preparation and cost savings of preparing canned food oneself.

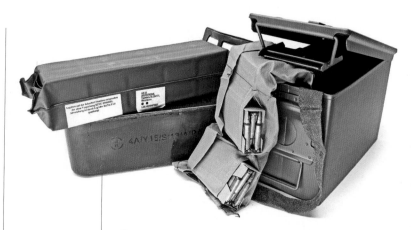

Larger caches that are designed to sustain several people over long periods of time will benefit from a combination of prepackaged emergency food supplies, store-bought canned food, and provisions prepared by the individual. As new canned food supplies are acquired or produced, older supplies can be used to ensure a periodic rotation of supplies. This practice keeps supplies from getting too old and verifies that one's canning processes are being performed properly — so the food is not spoiled after being stored for a long period of time. [For more about this topic, see "For a Limited Time Only" elsewhere in this issue.]

Care must be taken to ensure that all food supplies are carefully packed without compromising the integrity of the vacuum-sealed packages or containers. If the seal is damaged, the food will spoil over time and become inedible. One small piece of advice if you do choose to can your own food for a cache: include a couple of small can openers taped to the cans. Little things like this will make life immeasurably easier should the time ever come that you need to access your cache.

If you decide to include a firearm and ammunition in your cache, additional preparations are needed. While ammunition is by definition a self-contained item, it will corrode if exposed to moisture over long periods of time. Any type of corrosion will reduce the reliability of ammunition, causing misfires and, in extreme cases, failure to properly chamber in your firearm. While any type of ammunition can be properly prepared for long-term storage, a quicker alternative is to consider using surplus military ammunition. Most ammunition produced for the military is required to be packaged for long-term storage regardless of its anticipated use.

Military ammunition containers are constructed of metal with a convenient carry handle and a rubber gasket to seal out moisture and dirt. Additionally, small arms containers are designed to be stacked upon one another for more efficient use of available space. Surplus military containers come in different shapes and sizes and, due to their weatherproofing, are easily adapted to fill the roll of a cache container. Many types are available for purchase cheaply online as well as at your local military surplus store.

Another storage option is the MTM Case-Gard Survival Ammo Can (SAC). The SAC is a three-piece storage container, purpose built for being buried underground. It uses a double O-ring sealed lid and protective cap to secure items inside the bucket-shaped container, sized to hold around 500 rounds of ammunition (but any items that fit into the SAC can be safely stored). A Vapor Corrosion Inhibitor plastic bag and desiccant pack is included with every SAC. Should you choose to use a different container, ensure it has a good vacuum seal and consider the addition of silica gel packs. They will ensure that any moisture trapped inside the container when sealed will be absorbed.

OFF GRID Tip

Silica Gel Desiccant Packs

Be careful reusing silica gel packs that you've pulled out of other packaging – they may have already become saturated and no longer functional. It's easiest to use fresh packets, but you can also reactivate silica gel by heating them in your oven. Many packs can be recharged at 250 degrees for a couple of hours. Depending on the size of the packs to be recharged, the time and temperature will differ. A quick search online will net you more detailed instructions.

Similarly, when preparing firearms, the elimination of moisture is a critical step. The last thing one wants to see when retrieving a cached firearm is a rust-covered piece of junk that will not function. In addition to a properly sealed container with silica gel packs, you should consider a moderate coating of grease on all exposed metal parts and inside the bore of the barrel as an additional barrier against rust and corrosion.

Secure it Now or Lose it Forever

In real estate, there is a saying — "Location, location, location." The same advice can be applied to securing a cache. The location is the second critical part of a successful cache. Before we can select a secure spot for it, we need to understand the intended purpose of the cache. Is it designed to fully resupply our provisions, or is it just a pit stop on the way to a larger cache or bug-out location? Is access to the cache needed relatively quickly, or is there time to retrieve a more securely prepared one? Smaller caches meant for quick resupply may require a less secure location in exchange for quicker access. Larger caches that contain the bulk of your supplies may require more effort to secure, increasing the time needed to access them.

Once we have defined the purpose of our cache, our next chore is to choose a suitable location. The desired speed of access to our cache will determine how securely it is hidden. Quick access may require something simple like a camouflage tarp mixed with some foliage or a shallow hole dug into the ground. Sinking a watertight container with a cinderblock and a retrieval cord is another effective method for securing a small cache for quick retrieval, provided you can secure the cord!

Larger or more substantial caches may require a larger, deeper hole or a secure underground container. Regardless of the size of our cache, it must be secured not only from humans, but also from any four-legged (or creepy crawly) raiders. With any type of food provisions, care must taken to ensure no scent traces are left on the container or can escape from it. Failure to do so will result in quite a nice meal for Yogi Bear.

Access Denied

The final part of a successful cache is access. Having the best location in the history of caches does one no good if you can't access it when needed. A cache along a riverbank is a great hiding location, until the river floods and sweeps your container away or your access road to the river is flooded. A hidden location at the base of a remote mountain is a great choice until winter snows cause closure of the access roads or torrential rains turn the roads into an impassible muddy mess.

Another consideration is who actually owns the land you select for a cache? If the property does not belong to you, will you still have access to it when needed? Stashing supplies on remote private property may seem like a good idea until the landowner blocks access to the property — or worse yet, in your time of need, you discover the land was sold and a new shopping mall sits on top of your carefully hidden cache,

> With any type of food provisions, care must taken to ensure no scent traces are left on the container or can escape from it.

Enter Mossberg's JIC

Recognizing the wisdom in the concept of preparing a cache, Mossberg introduced the Mossberg Just in Case (JIC) series. The JIC series consists of a Mossberg 500, 12-gauge shotgun outfitted with only a pistol grip and no shoulder stock to reduce the overall size for storage. All JIC shotguns are capable of handling up to 3-inch shotgun shells and have either a six- or eight-round magazine tube, depending upon the model.

As part of the JIC series, several JIC shotguns are packaged in a waterproof storage tube with carrying strap. They are available in the Mariner, Cruiser, Sandstorm, and Patriot. A survival kit-in-a-can is included with the Cruiser, and a multitool and knife are included with the Mariner, which features a tough Marinecote finish. The Sandstorm is finished in a desert camo pattern, and the Patriot's storage tube proudly displays the American flag.

Combining a Mossberg JIC series shotgun with a MTM Caseguard SAC stuffed with ammunition, emergency food supplies, and water makes for a small cache that can effectively deal with a variety of emergency situations.

The concept of caching provisions and supplies is nothing more than insurance. It's the ultimate solution to the ultimate "what if" question. What if a situation arises and you are completely cut off from retrieving any supplies from your home? What if a flash forest fire has burned your home down to the foundation, or a tornado

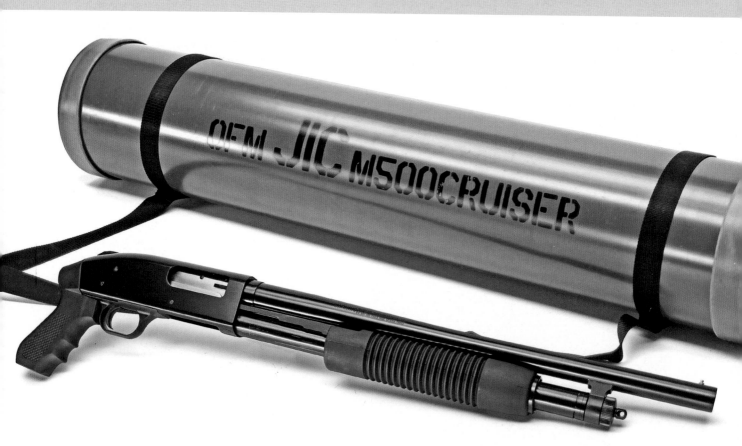

has spread your home over the next three counties? What if the only things you possess are literally the clothes on your back and the vehicle under your butt? When facing the possibility of this type of crisis, does the practice of caching firearms, supplies, and provisions become necessary? Absolutely. ▓

MAKE & MODEL
Mossberg
JIC Cruiser

CALIBER
12 gauge

BARREL LENGTH
18.5 inches

OVERALL LENGTH
31 inches

MAGAZINE CAPACITY
6

WEIGHT UNLOADED
5 lbs, 8 oz

MSRP
$494

URL
www.mossberg.com

FEATURES
❯ Water-resistant tube with carry strap
❯ Survival kit in a can
❯ Resealable plastic storage pouch

MAKE & MODEL
MTM Case-Gard
Survivor Ammo Can

CAPACITY
423.5 cubic inches
(same as a 50-cal. ammo can)

OUTSIDE DIMENSIONS
10-inch diameter, 13.5-inch height

INSIDE DIMENSIONS
7-inch diameter, 12.4-inch height

WEIGHT
3 lbs, 6.5 oz

MSRP
$30

URL
www.mtmcase-gard.com

FEATURES
❯ Double O-ring sealed lid
❯ Vapor corrosion inhibitor plastic bag
❯ Desiccant pack

SOURCE & ITEM
Tacti-Cool Guns & Gear, Inc.
120mm Ammo Tube

OUTSIDE DIMENSIONS
8-inch diameter, 44.5-inch height

INSIDE DIMENSIONS
6.25-inch diameter, 38.5-inch height (approx.)

WEIGHT
21 lbs

URL
www.facebook.com/TactiCoolGunsGearInc

OFFGRID Tip

When Packing a Firearm in Your Cache

Here's another little hint — pack some cloth, a bore snake, and a small bottle of lubricant along with the firearm to wipe off the grease and to quickly clean out the bore of the barrel. Once you've done this, a few drops of oil and a function check will ensure your firearm is ready for use.

SPONGEBOB
SQUARED AWAY

Integrate Kids' Bug-Out Bags with Your Family Emergency Plan

By Gordon Meehl
Photography by Michael Grey

Y ou can never be 100-percent prepared for what may come your way. Natural or manmade, crisis events have a Sun Tzu-like way of hitting us where we're weakest. A lot of us spend countless hours trying to recognize our shortcomings and beef them up. Practice, preparation, and some proactive thinking keep us prepared (hopefully) for any disaster that rolls our way. And when it does, we all want to think that we'll be a superman or superwoman, deflecting danger away from our kids and keeping them secure under our wings. Yet, the best way to be a superhero is to be a super teacher. Train your progeny to not only follow the family's SHTF plan, but also to be as self-reliant as possible if that plan fails in the face of overwhelming disaster.

So, does your survive-and-thrive plan fully involve your kids? What means and methods have you provided them with? Do they know what to do when you need to get the hell out of Dodge? More importantly, do they have their own bug-out bags specifically tailored to their needs? If you shrugged your shoulders at any of these questions, then you are woefully underprepared.

Educating your kids on how to prepare for and handle a crisis event can be a complex and detailed endeavor. So let's address one of the most essential pieces of your kid's plan for when the loaded diapers hit the fan — the bug-out bag (BOB). Just like the big boy go-bags, there are many different takes on the must-haves, should-haves, and nice-to-haves. The difference is that while our BOBs may remain relatively constant over time, your kids' bag and its contents will change as their bodies grow and their needs evolve.

Your child at 4 years of age will have very different survival needs than when he or she is 12 years old — and at every point in between. Following is a brief overview of what you should consider as you prepare bug-out bags for your children. In every age group, keep in mind that you'll need to periodically check the contents to make sure your little human weed hasn't outgrown everything you packed.

Newborns and Crawlers

Though the least self-sufficient, a newborn has pretty straightforward needs, even in an emergency. Keep them dry, fed, and in your arms. There's no need to run out to find a specialized pack for them; you essentially are their bug-out bag. They are totally dependent on your skills and supplies to keep them alive.

First and foremost is ensuring your infant stays hydrated and fed, and that means milk. Hopefully your little prepper is being breastfed. Without going into depth on lactation, there's little doubt in the medical community that breast-feeding is the ideal method for nourishing your baby — but in a crisis event, the practicality of breastfeeding alone trumps any other plan. As long as mom stays fed and hydrated, she can offer her child a near endless supply of nutrition. Ain't nature cool? If mom is no longer part of the family or has been separated from your clan, you'll have to consider packing formula milk as a backup food source.

Next, let's focus on creating your little booger's gear list. It's as easy as looking at what's in your everyday carry (EDC) diaper bag — various changes of clothes, comfort items, creams, ointments, and salves. Perhaps the most essential is the means to keep your tyke's poop in a group — AKA diapers, crap-catchers, a blanket for the brown bunnies, etc. Unlike the use-it-and-lose-it Pampers you currently keep in your EDC quiver, you'll want to have cloth nappies in your bag.

Why go old-school to cover your baby's assets? When it's the end of the world as we know it (TEOTWAWKI), the chances that you'll be able to replenish your stash of disposables will be very slim. Even if you have a good stock of the plastic poop pouches, better not to leave behind a telltale trail of white stink bombs marking your path. Cloth diapers worked for thousands of years before Huggies burst on to the scene, and they'll work for long-term survival situations.

Preschoolers and K-5 Kids

Children have a habit of growing up fast. As they grow, their needs become increasingly more complex as well. The good news is that they can start contributing more to the family emergency plan.

When your kid is in the 3-to-5-year-old range, the fun really starts. Children in this age range can carry lightweight bags. Work with your child to pick one that not only fits, but is also practical. While that Hello Kitty messenger bag might be exciting for your 5-year-old daughter, it's most definitely not the most practical choice if you want to teach her about creating an ergonomic and organized bug-out bag. You'll want to look for more purpose-built packs that allow for proper sizing and contain organizational systems, accessory options, and integral hydration systems (a 5-year-old needs about 1.3 liters [or 5.5 cups] of water a day). Finding a small pack doesn't mean you have to sacrifice functionality.

For the smaller kids in this range, CamelBak's Scout is a reasonably priced bag. It has all the key features you need

The CamelBak Trail-blazer 15 is great for older grade-school kids. Sized just right, it has lots of pockets, a hydration bladder, and an integrated safety whistle.

What to Pack

Here is a list of some suggested items to load in your kid's bug-out bag from the team at TinHatRanch.com. Using this as a base, you will want to customize this list for your kid's particular needs.

> Extra clothes (update regularly to make sure they fit)
> 3 pairs of socks
> 3 pairs of underwear
> Gloves
> Hat
> Extra pair of shoes
> Bar of soap in a plastic bag
> Deodorant
> Tooth brush and tooth paste
> Wet wipes (for washing and a toilet paper substitute)
> An area map
> Identification and family picture
> Refillable water bottle
> Water filtration supplies (teach kids to use them properly)
> Packable food and snacks (nuts, granola bars, etc.)
> Hard candy (no gum)

> Glow sticks
> Headlamp
> Flashlight with extra batteries
> Whistle
> Pocket knife
> Emergency blanket
> String
> Small first-aid kit
> N95 mask that fits your child properly
> Paper and pen
> Cards and dice
> A bag of dryer lint (teach your kids how to make a fire on their own)
> Fire starter (steel and flint)

For the very young, consider including:

> Coloring books and crayons
> A favorite blanket
> A stuffed animal

The Scout is tailor made for young school kids, comes with adjustable straps, and features a 1.5-liter water bladder.

in a kids' BOB — appropriately sized hydration bladder (1.5 liters), plenty of pockets, highly adjustable straps, and a safety whistle built into the safety strap. For the bigger kids in this age group, we like the CamelBak Trailblazer 15, which has all the features mentioned above, but on a slightly larger scale.

The fun part is working with your child to pick out what goes into their bag. Involving them in stocking their BOBs allows them to take real ownership of their place in the family's overall plan. Work with your child to fill the bag with warm clothes, glow sticks, and an emergency blanket. Along with the practical items there should be comfort items like a

stuffed animal — something that could give them a sense of normalcy when it's TEOTWAWKI.

The Survival Mom blog (www.thesurvivalmom.com) also suggests that you prepare for the possibility of getting separated from your child. She wisely suggests that you also put in your child's pack an updated family photo with parents' names, contact information, and an alternate person to contact. Fit all this on a single 3x5-inch card, and laminate them together. This is not static information, so you should teach your child how to use this info and, more importantly, who to safely share it with (remember the stranger-danger tips).

Adolescents and Older

Depending on your child's maturity and capabilities, it's around ages 10 to 12 that the real teaching begins. Now you can really start explaining and drilling the why's of being prepared and planning for a crisis. Preparing go-bags can (and should) be a family event. Don't pack the bag for them this time — they need to do it themselves so they know where everything is. Your role is to teach them why certain items are must-haves and how to use everything they pack. At this age children can take a great deal of responsibility in making their own plan that conforms to the family's overall SHTF plan. They can contribute to the group almost as much as the adults.

In choosing bags for middle-schoolers and pre-growth-spurt teens, you're essentially picking out the same types of bags you'd choose for yourself, just a little more size appropriate. Again, key features are hydration, storage, and flexibility in fit and function. Two recommended bags are the CamelBak Helena 22 and The North Face's Terra 55. The

Helena, designed specifically to fit a woman's frame, is full of all the essential features. The Terra 55 by The North Face is a full-fledged expedition-worthy BOB at about three-quarters the scale.

As your kids mature to high-school age, they should be able to carry a full-size BOB, which means they can carry more gear and supplies that can be shared by the whole tribe. They become an essential part of the family's bug-out plan, because hopefully you've taught them well enough that they can execute said plans even if you've been separated from them or, heaven forbid, been injured or killed.

Remember, when the chaos erupts, your family will be the only constant in a mixed up and crazy world. Each member of the family unit is vital to the survival of the whole. So in the words of Crosby, Stills, Nash & Young, "Teach your children well." ⠿

The Terra 55 is a hardcore expedition pack at three-quarters the size, making it ideal for high schoolers.

With a short torso length, the Helena 22 is made for women, but works great for teens. It's adjustable, comfortable, and functional.

How to Measure Your Kid's Back Height and Back Width

Back Width =
Shoulder Blade to Shoulder Blade

Back Height =
Top of Shoulder to Waist Line
+ 2 Inches

Average Back Sizes for Kids Backpacks

Age	Back Height	Back Width
4	11 inches	6 inches
5	12 inches	6.5 inches
6	12.5 inches	7 inches
7	13 inches	7 inches
8	14 inches	7.5 inches
9	14.5 inches	8 inches
10	15 inches	8 inches
11	15.5 inches	8 inches
12	15.5 inches	8.5 inches
13	16.6 inches	9 inches
14	17 inches	9 inches
15	17.5 inches	9 inches
16	18 inches	9 inches
17	19 inches	9.5 inches
18	19 inches	9.5 inches

SOURCES

CamelBak > www.camelbak.com
The North Face > www.thenorthface.com
Tin Hat Ranch > www.tinhatranch.com
The Survival Mom > www.thesurvivalmom.com

GRAB BOB AND GO

Are Off-the-Shelf Bug-Out Bags Right For You?

By Martin Anders | Photos by Michael Grey

Life is hectic enough. Working, running errands, picking up the kids, fixing that leaky faucet — there's a never-ending to-do list. Try compounding that daily grind with formulating an emergency plan based on a to-be-determined, life-altering catastrophe of unknown origins can be overwhelming to say the least. But if you're reading this magazine, it means you're responsible enough and have enough foresight to make disaster preparedness a priority.

So, is there a way to balance everything going on in your life to find the time to get ready for what may come? Well, you're in luck. There's an entire industry dedicated to convenient preparedness.

You probably have already seen the products while surfing the Web, shopping at your local big-box store, or flipping through the advertisements in these pages. Readymade emergency supplies seem to be popping up everywhere, especially as of late. The concept of saving time and money by buying a prepackaged kit is one that we appreciate, but how do these products really stack up? Based on their persuasive packaging, all these kits sound convincingly useful, but are the kits full of things that you'll never need or packed with tools that don't work well — or at all?

Let's set the record straight. We at OFFGRID believe that the best kits, particularly go-bags or bug-out bags (BOBs), are the ones that you assemble yourself. You are the only one who knows best what your and your family's needs and preferences are. You know your terrain, climate, community, and what type of disasters that your area is prone to. Only you know your disaster plan, where you will bug out to, and other contingencies. Companies that offer prepackaged survival kits do not know any of these factors. They can only estimate what people will need.

We do, however, like the idea of readymade bags as a starting point because of the time saved on piecing one together from scratch. But for off-the-shelf BOBs to work, you'll need to further customize them to suit your needs. While they can save you time, it's a long shot if they'll save you money, as you'll no doubt need to dump some products to make room for personalized items like medications, extra batteries, your favorite tools, or specific foods (in case you have allergies or a certain palate).

And don't forget the bag itself. Will it hold up to the rigors of survival? How does it feel on your shoulders on a hike? If it won't last, ditch it and get a sturdier, more comfortable one. (See OFFGRID's premiere edition, the Summer 2013 issue, for more on how to select a survival backpack.)

Due to the vastness of the market and considering the limited pages allotted for this article, we examined a limited number of preassembled go-bags of varying budgets, sizes, and uses. Before spending your time and money, take a closer look at the following buyer's guide and see if there's a ready-made bug-out bag that could serve as a starting point for your own BOB build.

Nitro Pak
Executive 72-Hour Survival Kit

This survival kit covers the basic needs for two people for about three days. It has water, food (in the form of rations), basic tools (like a flashlight, radio, and multitool), work gloves, and even a tent. This Nitro Pak kit includes with a water filter straw — always handy in any survival situation. The nylon backpack itself comes in bright day-glow orange for easy spotting, which can be a good or bad thing depending on the situation. (Good if you're stranded and need to be rescued. Bad if there's lawlessness and marauders are looking for easy targets.)

The kit includes a large selection of compact-sized survival items that cover a variety of needs, from warmth and shelter to food and first aid. Most of the items seem to be from reputable companies or of standard or better quality. Our concerns are with the bag itself. The shoulder straps seem rather thin and spaced closely to one another, which doesn't seem to be a comfortable way to carry 17 pounds (plus what you add to it) on your shoulders.

This bag's interior is rather large and has plenty of space for you to add more stuff. It has a good selection of small items, especially in the basic needs categories. If we were to use this as a base to build our bag, we would add a more potent primary flashlight and use the one included as a backup. Same thing goes for the multitool, which doesn't seem as capable as others that we've handled before. We would also add a headlamp and some spare clothes. But if you need a secondary or tertiary bag, this might fit the bill left as is.

6 FEET

№	MAKE & MODEL
	Nitro Pak Executive 72-Hour Survival Kit (item #5808)
📏	**APPROXIMATE DIMENSIONS** 16 in. H x 16 in. W x 12 in. D
⚗	**WEIGHT** 17 lbs
$	**MSRP** $175
🌐	**URL** www.nitro-pak.com

2 - SPACE Brand Emergency Blankets
2 - Emergency rain/wind ponchos
2 - Hand/pocket warmers
1 - Frontier water filter straw
2 - Compact sanitation/toilet tissue packs
2 - Compact facial tissue packs
1 - Deluxe AM/FM radio with batteries
1 - Writing pad, pencil, and ink pen
1 - Deck of playing cards

1 - 60-item first-aid kit with instruction book
1 - Bag of hard candy
6 - Emergen-C vitamin packets

2 - 3,600-calorie cookie-flavored ration bars
24 - Purified drinking water pouches (4.2 oz. each)

1 - Deluxe heavy-duty tube tent
1 - 50-foot nylon cord
1 - Pair of leather gloves
1 - Box of waterproof matches (45 sticks)
1 - Industrial flashlight with batteries
1 - 12-hr. instant light-stick
1 - 36-hr. emergency candle with three wicks
2 - N95 hospital-grade dust masks
1 - Emergency survival whistle
2 - Disposable sanitation bags
1 - Trash bag
1 - Pocket knife
18 - Wet-wipe packets

Nitro Pak
Urban Survival-Pak Level 1

For those who require a smaller, less noticeable bug-out bag that packs a defensive punch, the Urban Survival-Pak (USP) is right up your alley. This over-the-shoulder bag conceals its true usage, which comes in handy when you don't want to broadcast to the world that you're carrying a whole stash of supplies. The bag comes with an interesting mix of gear, many of which lean heavily toward personal defense. It includes more than a few defensive tools, including pepper spray (where allowed by law), swimmer's goggles for tear gas eye protection, and two sets of handcuff keys. Carrying this theme further, the bag includes an ambidextrous holster hidden inside a special weapon compartment for concealed carry of a handgun.

The USP is on the smaller side, so it's only natural that the amount of supplies it carries is less than that of the larger bags in this guide. The point of this bag is to get you in and out of areas a bit more ninja-like with a certain level of protection at your disposal. Think less Bear Grylls and more Jason Bourne.

It is made of ballistic nylon with a comfortable, fully adjustable padded carrying strap. It has an oversized and adjustable center compartment with nylon drawstring and multiple exterior pockets, including one that can secure a water bottle.

That brings us to a few highlights, which include a McNett Tactical Aquamira Water Filter Bottle that treats up to 100 gallons and removes 99.9 percent of chlorine, bad taste, and cryptosporidium and giardia (parasites that cause "beaver fever"). It also includes a quality Gerber Suspension Multi-Tool, a couple of emergency food bars, and water packets. A rudimentary first-aid kit is included as is a radio and emergency blanket. Although one of the priciest in this guide and not built for sustained survival, for its size, the USP has the potential to get you out of a jam and to your rendezvous point quickly.

6 FEET

№	MAKE & MODEL
	Nitro Pak
	Urban Survival-Pak
	Level 1 (item #5800)

APPROXIMATE DIMENSIONS
13 in. H x 11 in. W x 7.5 in. D

WEIGHT
8 lbs.

MSRP
$328

URL
www.nitro-pak.com

1 - Gerber Suspension Multi-Tool
1 - 2-oz. pepper spray (substituted with a knife in states not allowing pepper spray)
1 - Swimmers goggles
2 - N95 respirators
1 - Sudecon tear gas decontamination wipe
1 - Dead On Tools Exhumer Multi-Function "Tool"
1 - Tactical Spiked Kubaton Self-Defensive Tool with writing pen and pocket clip
1 - Self-defense power-punch key holder "tool"
1 - Pair of nylon covert rubberized gloves
1 - Covert black six-way wearing balaclava/cap
1 - Personal alarm and door alarm attachment with 9-volt battery
2 - Handcuff keys (standard and covert)
4 - HD Black 16-in. zip-ties
1 - Rear-viewing covert "sunglasses"
1 - Single-side razor blade
1 - Pair of foam earplugs

1 - McNett Tactical Aquamira Water Filter Bottle
2 - Purified Water Pouches (4.2 oz.)
2 - 400-calorie emergency food bars
1 - Lifesavers roll
1 - U.S. Military Medic Wound Bandage
2 - Germ-X antibacterial wipes
2 - Antiseptic wipes
2 - Ibuprofen (200 mg)
1 - Triple antibiotic ointment
1 - Fabric knuckle bandage
2 - Fabric adhesive bandages (1 x 3 in.)
1 - Safety pin
1 - DryFlex waterproof pouch

1 - Survival Whistle with breakaway lanyard and SLIM Rescue Howler Whistle
1 - 6-foot folded duct tape
1 - AMK mini roll duct tape (2 x 26 in.)
1 - Liquid-filled button compass
1 - 550 paracord wristband (10 feet unfolded)
1 - Dental floss
1 - SOL Survival Instructions

1 - SOL tear-proof emergency blanket (56 x 84 in.)
1 - LED flashlight with battery
1 - Red flashlight plastic film with two rubber bands
2 - Hand warmers
1 - Scripto butane lighter
1 - Fire Lite Flint One-Handed Fire Starter
4 - Tinder-Quik Fire Starting Tabs
1 - Coby Compact AM/FM Radio with batteries
1 - Rite-in-the-Rain Waterproof Note Pad
1 - Writing pencil
3 - Wet wipe alcohol
1 - Compact toilet tissue roll

Echo-Sigma
Get-Home Bag

Echo-Sigma is a husband-and-wife team that got into making emergency kits because they couldn't find kits that suit their needs. Since starting up only four years ago, Echo-Sigma has quickly made a name for itself as a producer of quality disaster preparedness kits. A big draw for Echo-Sigma is its use of top-quality products and highly customizable options for most of its offerings. Its signature item, the Get-Home Bag, has made a splash in both the mainstream public and niche survival realms for allowing customers to select what they want in their bags so that they're not stuck with gear they'll just toss aside.

The Get-Home Bag is a mid-sized disaster-preparedness kit that features eye, mouth, and hand protection, as well as fire-starting and water-purification capabilities, and much more. The backpack is rugged and built to take abuse. It offers decent support with both sternum and hip support straps and a comfortable padded back. It's not very large so every cubic inch of it is used to carry gear and supplies. Our featured sample bag even has an axe hanging on its exterior. It can easily find a home under your desk at work or in the trunk of a small car.

If saving time is the main motivator in your decision to purchase a go-bag, you'll want to take a long, hard look at this pack. It may not be the cheapest one around, but it does allow you to choose what tools come with it.

The level of customization is uncommon in this genre: select from four kinds of multitools, five models of flashlights, multiple types of knives, and even a couple of pressurized hydration systems. The bags come ready to go; there is no need for removing packaging from individual items. All the included products are arranged, organized, and stowed for fast and easy access in case of an emergency.

6 FEET

№	**MAKE & MODEL** **Echo-Sigma** Get-Home Bag
	APPROXIMATE DIMENSIONS 18 in. H x 9 in. W x 13 in. D
	WEIGHT 15 lbs 14 oz.
$	**MSRP** $425 (as configured)
	URL www.echo-sigma.com

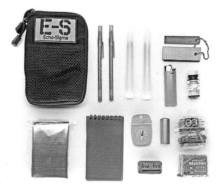

- 1 - Hydration System (2.5 liter)
- 1 - Echo-Sigma 1-3 Day Provision Pack with MRE (optional):
- > 1 - Meal Ready to Eat (MRE)
- > 3 - Food ration bars
- > 1 - Drinking water (1.75 liters)
- > 1 - Paper napkins

- 1 - Echo-Sigma Compact Survival Kit:
- > 1 - Compass
- > 1 - Emergency whistle
- > 1 - Emergency blanket
- > 1 - Butane disposable lighter
- > 1 - Magnesium fire-starter with flint striker
- > 1 - Duct tape (50 in.)
- > 1 - Bottle of water purification tablets
- > 2 - Chemical light sticks
- > 1 - Emergency fire-starter
- > 40 - Waterproof matches
- > 2 - Ballpoint pens
- > 1 - Pad of paper
- > 1 - Set of earplugs

- 1 - Echo-Sigma Compact First-Aid Kit
- 1 - SOG B63 Power Lock EOD Multi Tool (optional)
- 1 - Waterproof LED Flashlight by Fenix E25 (187 lumens)
- 1 - SOG FastHawk (optional)
- 1 - Midland ER200 Multi Power Radio (optional)
- 50 - Feet of military-grade 550 paracord
- 10 - Extra-large zip-ties

- 1 - Emergency tube tent
- 1 - Emergency Poncho
- 1 - Plexiglass mirror
- 1 - Thermal sleeping bag
- 6 - AA batteries
- 1 - Pair of leather work gloves
- 2 - N95-rated respirator masks
- 1 - Pair of Protective goggles
- 2 - Hand warmers

Ready America
4-Person Emergency Kit

It is recommended that we should be prepared to fend for ourselves for at least the first 72 hours after a disaster. The Ready America 4-Person Emergency Kit is a decent start to hit that goal. Compared to the other kits in this guide, this bag is bare bones, but it does have some of the basics covered. For sustenance, it includes four bricks of 2,400-calorie rations and four liters of water. Ponchos, goggles, and dust masks for four people are included, as is a 107-piece first-aid kit for very minor injuries.

The backpack that the kit comes in leaves a lot to be desired, however. It is rather flimsy and reminds us of backpacks we took to school — when we were 7 years old. On the positive end, this bag has a reflective strip on its front pouch, as well as a reinforced rubberized handle up top, which are nice touches. We do wish a higher-quality zipper were employed because the ones on this bag feel like they could fail at any time.

While this kit is not our first choice in disaster preparedness, its price tag makes it a solid fourth or fifth option. You can purchase one of these to have ready at locations that you don't frequent much (your mother-in-law's, for example), but would still like to have a kit ready just in case.

MAKE & MODEL
Ready America
4-Person Emergency Kit
(item #70380)

APPROXIMATE DIMENSIONS
18 in. H x 12 in. W x 9.5 in. D

WEIGHT
18 lbs 4 oz.

MSRP
$100

URL
www.readyamerica.com

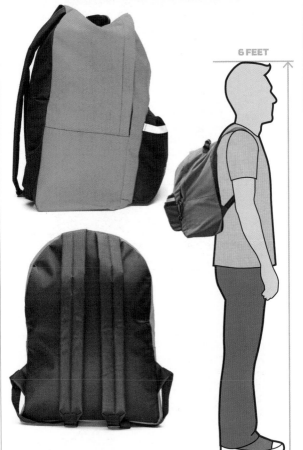

6 FEET

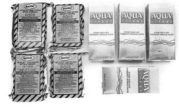

4 - Food ration bars
4 - Boxes of water (1 liter each)

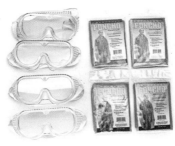

4 - Emergency ponchos
4 - Safety goggles
4 - Disposable dust masks
8 - Nitrile gloves

4 - Survival blankets
1 - First-Aid Kit (107 piece)
4 - Emergency light-sticks (12 hr.)
4 - Pocket tissue packs
1 - Pair of gloves
1 - Emergency whistle
3 - Biohazard bags
12 - Moist towelettes

Lansky Tactical
Apocalypse Survival Kit

Lansky's Tactical Apocalypse Survival Kit (or TASK) is a lightweight, no-nonsense bug-out bag that houses only the most essential of survival tools. There are neither provisions nor water to weigh this kit down. What it does have are tools that were carefully selected for their practicality and efficiency.

The TASK includes a multi-use axe, LED flashlight, multitool, combo-edge knife, a LifeStraw for on-the-fly water purification, and more. Everything is housed in a heavy-duty 20-liter nylon backpack, which features a padded back panel, a large main compartment and front pouch, both with organizational pockets, and compression straps that help keep everything held down in place. The back of the bag has a zippered compartment that can fit a hydration carrier in case you wanted to add one. Mesh and elastic water bottle pouches are found on both sides of the pack for additional storage. Its hip and sternum straps are adjustable to help you find the perfect fit and support. This bag is capable of carrying more than it comes with so although it is on the small side, it does have additional space to add your own selection of gear and supplies to it.

6 FEET

№	MAKE & MODEL
	Lansky Tactical Apocalypse Survival Kit
	APPROXIMATE DIMENSIONS 19 in. H x 10 in. W x 7 in. D
	WEIGHT 6 lbs 10 oz.
$	**MSRP** $200
	URL www.lansky.com

1- Multi-use battle axe
1- 20-Function multitool
1- LifeStraw water purifier
1- Tactical flashlight

1- Easy-Grip Knife
1- Blademedic Sharpener
1- The Puck (dual grit sharpener)

1- Firesteel Fire-starter
1- Button Compass (on the handle of the Firesteel)
1- 550 Paracord bracelet (8 feet)
1- Mini survival guide

Brownells
ESG Essentials All-In-One Kit

Brownells, a leading retailer of firearms parts, tools, and accessories, introduced its Emergency and Survival Gear (ESG) lineup just this past year. The ESG kits cover almost any kind of situation you might encounter, from being snowed in during a complete white-out to trying not to float away after a major flood. The ESG Essentials All-In-One Kit combines four ESG Kits into one all-inclusive package you can carry on your back.

Though it's the most expensive pack in this guide, it's priced at a discount when compared to trying to piecing the kit's parts together in-dividually. The array of tools, gear, and supplies in this kit should give you ample capacity to face most any emergency. The Power, Hygiene, Water Filtration, and Civil Unrest kits are orga-nized in their own separate organizer bags. The compact backpack the kit comes in fits about 22 liters of gear, is sturdy, and is made of thick nylon with heavy-duty zippers. It has hip and sternum straps to help you balance the go-bag on longer treks.

This kit allows you to do a whole host of key tasks: charge batteries and devices with a Goal Zero solar panel kit, keep your spirits and health levels up with toiletries in the hygiene kit, filter water and stay hydrated in a variety of ways, and plenty more.

Note: It doesn't include water, food, or per-sonal protection items such as gloves, goggles, and respirator masks, so you'll still need to add your own for a more complete bug-out bag. Brownells has other kits, such as its ESG Essen-tial Pandemic Kit, available that could comple-ment this kit if you have the inclination (and the cash) to add more gear.

№	**MAKE & MODEL**
	Brownells
	ESG Essentials All-In-One Kit
📏	**APPROXIMATE DIMENSIONS**
	18 in. H x 9 in. W x 8 in. D
⚖	**WEIGHT**
	8 lbs
$	**MSRP**
	$380
🌐	**URL**
	www.brownells.com

6 FEET

1- Goal Zero Guide 10 Kit
1- Goal Zero rechargeable AAA batteries
1- SureFire CR123 batteries (6 pack)
1- UST Volt XL
1- Organizer bag

1- United Spirit OK 72-Hour Kit
1- Adventure Medical Kits Adventure
   Medical Wipes
1- UST Survival Towel (2 pack)
1- Organizer bag

1- Sawyer Mini Water Filtration System
1- Potable Aqua Chlorine Dioxide Tablets
1- Camelbak 1L eddy
1- Oral I.V.
1- Organizer bag

1- Pro Mag Archangel Defense Pen
1- Top Cop 0.68-oz. Stream
1- ASP Baton
1- Ontario Knife Company JPT-3S Drop-
   Point Folding Knife
1- Organizer bag

OFFICE ESCAPE

Get-Home Bags Suitable for the Workplace or the End of the World

By Martin Anders
Photos by Michael Grey

It's a busy day for you at the office, and the last thing you needed was to get the Blue Screen of Death before you could generate your daily TPS reports. Frustrated, you get up to storm over to the IT department to demand an explanation. It's then that you look up and notice that not only is your computer on the fritz, but the entire floor looks like it has gone dark. Is it a blackout? Well, the backup systems didn't kick in like they should have. What's going on here?

The Situation

Regardless of what cut the power to your building, you realize by looking out the window that the power is out in every building in the surrounding area. The traffic lights aren't even flashing red. You're still hoping a run-of-the-mill power outage is the culprit when you see drivers exiting their cars in the middle of the street. That's when you get a sinking feeling that something more serious is going down. Perhaps it's the effects of a solar flare, or maybe even a hacker or terrorist attack? All you know is you need to get out while you can. While your office-mates are still trying to figure out if a circuit breaker was tripped, you're already on to the next step. You tell them about everything you've noticed, reach for the office-based get-home bag that you've kept under your desk, and head to the stairs to get to the ground floor.

On the Move

From the office, it's about 18 miles to home — it's already late afternoon, so you'd better get a move on. The supplies you stored in your bag are sufficient to keep you provisioned and geared up for the trek back home, even if it takes a couple of days. The average person can walk about 3 miles per hour, so you're looking at a six-hour walk at best without rest — and that's not taking into account obstacles natural or manmade (or man himself).

The Office-Based Bag

Since you're always prepared, you know the importance of stowing what you can where you can. You can never be too prepared, and it's not possible to anticipate where you'll be when a disaster strikes. What you do know is that you spend a good majority of your time either at home, at work, or traveling between the two. With that in mind, you've developed supply caches in the form of kits for places that you frequent the most. Keeping the mother lode of survival supplies at home is

less of an issue than keeping supplies in other places, such as at the office. At your workplace you opt for the less conspicuous, ever adaptable backpack.

Blending in

It's not hard to see why backpacks are the go-to bug-out supply carrier of choice. They're made to carry and to be carried. Slung on your back, packs keep your hands free and, depending on type, they can carry very large loads. They can also blend into their surroundings, perfect for an office environment. The less attention drawn to it, the better. In times of non-emergency, a boring-looking bag may be easier to hide in plain sight and less enticing to steal. When being used, it will draw a lot less attention on the streets than a bag finished in whatever spiffy new tactical pattern is the flavor of the month.

Inventory

What you may choose to carry in your office get-home bag will greatly differ based on your needs. Those who work just a stone's throw from home will require a very different loadout than those who have a long commute. It's easy to underestimate the difference between walking and driving, so be realistic and plan accordingly. We suggest packing as light as you can while carrying as much practical gear as you think you'll really need. Don't pack the kitchen sink. For example, if you think you might need to spend a night on the road, you're better off packing a $1 Mylar space blanket that weighs a few ounces than a $100 one-person tent that clocks in at 4 pounds.

Essentials such as water, a lighter, a first-aid kit, and high-calorie ration bars are a no-brainer. If you don't carry a knife on you every day, consider packing a quality fixed blade or folding knife. A hand-crank radio with an integrated flashlight could be a useful tool, too, as it can provide vital news updates as well as a source of light. Comfort items like a roll of toilet paper will go a long way. If you have room, an extra set of clothes and a couple pairs of socks are good to have. And because the apocalypse might not hit on casual Friday, a pair of sneakers or old boots wouldn't be a bad idea either. Nothing would suck more than having to hike back home while dodging meteor strikes in your Kenneth Cole wingtips.

Because backpacks come in so many different shapes, sizes, and looks, we've selected a few of our favorites in the following guide. Most can be hidden away under your desk and some look at home in the conference room as well as a backwoods trail. Take a look; your next pack might be among our survey of new and noteworthy packs on the next six pages.

BACKPACKS

Note: Measurements are approximate.

5.11 Tactical — Covrt Boxpack

 DIMENSIONS (VOLUME)
21 x 14.5 x 8 inches (30L)

 WEIGHT
2 pounds, 10 ounces

 COLORWAY
Black (shown), Storm, Tundra

 MSRP
$110

URL
www.511tactical.com

 NOTES
The Covrt Boxpack is a roll-top bag that features a slide-adjusting sternum strap and reinforced padded shoulder straps for a secure and comfortable carry while on the go. A stiff-faced covert front pocket hides any possible printing of a pistol and allows fast access when you need it. Internally, there are organizational dividers for small items as well as padded pockets for a laptop and a hydration carrier. The water-resistant finish keeps gear dry, while its dual side zip pockets are ideal for accessories and even big enough to carry a hydration bottle.

Pros: Thick ballistic nylon, high-quality build

Cons: Roll-top opening seems restrictive

Black Diamond — Magnum 20 Pack

 DIMENSIONS (VOLUME)
20 x 11 x 9 inches (20L)

 WEIGHT
1 pound, 2 ounces

 COLORWAY
Black, Laurel, Sulfur (shown)

 MSRP
$90

 URL
www.blackdiamondequipment.com

 NOTES
With a 20-liter storage capacity, the Black Diamond Magnum 20 features an internal stow pocket and an accessory loop perfect for a trekking pole or ice axe. Its side stretch pockets and front web compression can accommodate items of varying sizes. The Magnum 20 is smaller than the other packs in this guide, but its storage options are among the most flexible. Its contoured shoulder straps and ventilated back panel make it comfortable to wear. This pack is hydration-bladder compatible.

Pros: Lightweight, versatile, durable

Cons: Outer pockets don't have zippers

BLACKHAWK!
Diversion Wax Canvas Rucksack

BACKPACKS

 DIMENSIONS (VOLUME)
20 x 12.2 x 5.5 inches (25L)

WEIGHT
3 pounds, 12 ounces

COLORWAY
Earth (shown), Slate

MSRP
$256

URL
www.blackhawk.com

NOTES
Probably the most "undercover" and stylish bag of the bunch, the BLACKHAWK! Diversion Wax Canvas Rucksack is made of quality materials, including 10.10-ounce wax canvas, water-resistant zippers, and easy-to-use magnetic buckles. The top-loading ruck has a "cinchable" drawstring main compartment and a lid with a pass-through waterproof zipper for quick access. This well-conceived and executed bag also has a hidden, lockable, easy-access handgun compartment on the lower portion of its back panel. Inside, it has padded laptop and hydration-carrier compartments.

Pros: Build quality, materials

Cons: Price, weight

Camelbak
Skirmish

BACKPACKS

DIMENSIONS (VOLUME)
21 x 14.5 x 8 inches (33L)

WEIGHT
4 pounds, 14 ounces

COLORWAY
Coyote (shown)

MSRP
$315 to 345

URL
www.camelbak.com

NOTES
On the face of the Skirmish is a sleek, low-profile composite PALS panel that provides secure attachment for pouches and gear. The main compartment is accessed via a full clamshell opening for easy access. A lower access zipper at the bottom of the front of the pack provides direct access to the main compartment. There are multiple drink tube exit ports for routing the tube over the shoulder or under the arm. The backpack comes with a 100-ounce hydration bladder that is slung low in the pack and on your hips for a lower, more stable center of gravity with an easy-to-fill and clean wide-mouth opening.

Pros: Built-in hydration bladder, versatility

Cons: Price, weight

BACKPACKS

Condor
Frontier Outdoor Pack

DIMENSIONS (VOLUME)
18 x 11 x 7 inches (20L)

WEIGHT
3 pounds, 4 ounces

COLORWAY
Black, Brown, Grey (shown), MultiCam

MSRP
$125

URL
www.condoroutdoor.com

NOTES
The Condor Frontier Outdoor Pack is constructed with Mil-spec 500-denier Cordura fabric and high tensile-strength composite nylon thread, featuring a rugged, high abrasion-resistant rubber bottom for further reinforcement. This compact bag has plenty of compartments and even more pockets within the compartments. The main section can be accessed through two separate top zippers and contains large fleece-lined pockets that can hold a 2.5-liter hydration bladder and a 15-inch laptop. Other pockets can hold tablets and keep small items organized. The back panel is ventilated and side compression straps keep everything in place.

Pros: Number of pockets, ease of use

Cons: Small main compartment

BACKPACKS

FirstSpear
Comm Pack Large

DIMENSIONS (VOLUME)
18.5 x 13 x 7 inches (30L)

WEIGHT
2 pounds, 5 ounces

COLORWAY
Black, Blue/Silver, Light Grey Ripstop, Ranger/Coyote (shown)

MSRP
$208

URL
www.first-spear.com

NOTES
FirstSpear's Comm Pack is based on the company's ECP military assault pack, but has a toned-down urban appearance that allows you to blend into the crowd. It fits unnoticed in almost any urban scenario, from skateboarding to surveillance operations. In fact, this pack has discreetly placed access ports to facilitate ear buds for both entertainment and communications devices. Its low-key looks can get you out of the city and back home without being noticed. Featured here is the larger 1,800 cubic-inch version; a smaller 980 cubic-inch version is also available.

Pros: Well thought-out layout, quality build

Cons: Price

BACKPACKS

Grey Ghost Gear
Griff Pack

DIMENSIONS (VOLUME)	19 x 12 x 8 inches (30L)
WEIGHT	2 pounds, 10 ounces
COLORWAY	Black (shown), Grey
MSRP	$119
URL	www.greyghostgear.com

NOTES

At first glance, this looks like a fairly standard backpack that you'd find at any sporting goods store. Upon closer inspection, we noticed details such as a soft cloth-lined zippered compartment for safekeeping scratch-prone items and elastic loops that are capable of securely carrying pistol magazines. In its interior, you'll find plenty of loop panels to attach various hook-backed pouches and organizers. The large main compartment can swallow up to a 17-inch laptop in a built-in and well-padded sleeve. To each side of the main compartment are zippered pass-through doors for easy access to the interior, while carrying it on your back.

Pros: Interior space, customizable loop panels

Cons: Very little padding

BACKPACKS

Hazard 4
Clerk

DIMENSIONS (VOLUME)	18 x 11 x 6.2 inches (20L)
WEIGHT	3 pounds, 14 ounces
COLORWAY	Black (shown), Coyote, MultiCam (+$24)
MSRP	$240
URL	www.hazard4.com

NOTES

One look at the Hazard 4 Clerk, and we could tell that it's an extremely well-built pack. The two main compartments can be quickly unzipped and hinged open as you would a book, granting you full access to its interior without any fuss. On its front sits two hard cases that are good for protecting any sensitive equipment. The hidden back pocket can be fully unzipped across the top and to one side uncovering a padded and quilted compartment suitable for a 15-inch laptop or hydration bladder. The Clerk is nimble enough to be rotated from back to chest, allowing you on-the-go access to frequently used gear — perfect for tight quarters, such as in a vehicle interior.

Pros: Well thought-out details, craftsmanship

Cons: Price, weight

Tactical Tailor
Urban Operator Pack

DIMENSIONS (VOLUME)
18.5 x 12 x 6.25 inches (30L)

WEIGHT
2 pounds, 4 ounces

COLORWAY
Black (shown), Coyote Brown, MultiCam, Ranger Green

MSRP
$135

URL
www.tacticaltailor.com

NOTES
For those of us who are looking for a no-nonsense, no-frills backpack, this might be the one you're looking for. It doesn't play games with endless pockets and pouches and only has what you need. On the inside, there's a large main compartment with a high-visibility orange lining and a front pocket with a modest organizational panel for keys, pens, and cards. On one side of the bag is a zippered fold-out mesh pocket capable of holding a 1-liter bottle and modular webbing on the other for attaching additional pouches.

Pros: Basic layout, durability

Cons: No dedicated padded laptop pouch

Vanquest
Trident-20 Backpack

DIMENSIONS (VOLUME)
18.5 x 11 x 6 inches (20L)

WEIGHT
2 pounds, 15 ounces

COLORWAY
Black (-$10), Coyote Tan (-$10), MultiCam Black (shown), MultiCam, Wolf Grey (-$10)

MSRP
$165

URL
www.vanquest.com

NOTES
The Trident-20 backpack is worn with its two padded shoulder straps like a regular backpack, but also allows you the option of accessing its interior from its side zipper compartments for access in tight spaces. Its fully padded interior has hook-and-loop panels that allow its main compartment to become a multi-function storage system that is easily user-configured. The high-visibility orange 210-denier lightweight rip-stop nylon interior helps you find accessories in low-light conditions. It sports dual hydration bladder carrying capability, maximum 5-liter capacity.

Pros: Modular and padded interior

Cons: Not much space for a laptop

BACKPACKS

Vertx

EDC Gamut Bag

DIMENSIONS (VOLUME)
22 x 14 x 7 inches (28L)

WEIGHT
4 pounds, 2 ounces

COLORWAY
Black with Red Trim (shown),
Black, Smoke Grey

MSRP
$200

URL
www.wearvertx.com

NOTES
All business all the time, this pack was designed specifically to accommodate both a 15-inch laptop and a full-sized handgun simultaneously. That's what we call good times. The front of this pack opens wide for complete accessibility of its main compartment. In the back is a side-accessible, loop-lined concealment compartment that enables quick access to hook-attached accessories such as an optional pistol holster. Dual side pockets allow for additional storage capacity.

Pros: Easy access, modular interior

Cons: Price, weight

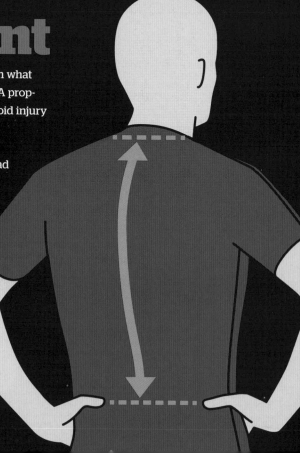

Proper Fitment

We stress that less is more, so pack lightly when possible. But depending on what your requirements are, a fully loaded pack can weigh 50 pounds or more. A properly fitted backpack can spread the weight evenly on your body to help avoid injury and ease fatigue.

To figure out what size backpack is right for you, you'll want to tilt your head down and feel for the bump where your shoulder meets your neck. This bump is called the C7 vertebra. When measuring torso length, the C7 is considered the upper most point and where you want to start your measurement.

Next, place your hands on your hip bones with four fingers facing forward and your thumbs toward the back. The imaginary line between your two thumbs is the bottom of your torso. It'll be easier if you have someone help you with this next step. Stand up straight (no slouching now!) and measure the length between the C7 vertebra and the imaginary line on your lower back. The length you come up with is your torso length and can be used to reference different backpack sizes. Taking the time to find a properly fitted bag is often overlooked, but is essential.

RECOIL OFFGRID

PRESENTS

DIY SURVIVAL

BEST HACKS FOR WORST-CASE SCENARIOS

ORDER TODAY AT
GUNDIGESTSTORE.COM
OR CALL 920.471.4522

TETRIS YOUR GO-BAG

Tips for Efficiently Packing Your Survival Backpack

Story By Martin Anders
Photos by Michael Grey

Whether you're preparing a bug-out, get-home, or general survival bag, much of the focus on assembling a survival pack is on *what* gear to pack. While there's little doubt that packing the right equipment (along with having survival skills) plays a big part in giving you an edge, there's another important factor that often gets overlooked: knowing *how* said gear should be packed. Anyone who has ever carried a heavy load can attest to this.

Packing a go-bag is a simple concept, but don't take its simplicity lightly. It's essential to properly organize the contents of your survival backpack — or any backpack for that matter — to help your body maintain peak performance, especially over long durations. We'll cover several rules of thumb that should be applied to any pack preparation.

Weight

Keep it lightweight! Weight is arguably the biggest enemy when it comes to outfitting a BOB. It's all too easy to shovel stuff into a backpack, causing it to almost burst at the seams. No matter how big or small you are, your goal should be to carry only what you need and what you can really use in a real-world situation. Carrying every little doohickey miracle survival gadget will probably hurt you more than it'll help you, so be mindful of what you choose to pack.

Gear that you can replace with knowledge and well-practiced skills will save you unwanted weight in your bag. For example, do you really need a folding knife, a fixed blade, a machete, and an axe all attached to your pack?

Also remember that tools that have multiple functions can save weight by replacing a few dedicated single-use tools. But be mindful that some single-use tools are better than multi-use ones, so you'll have to make the call.

Balance

The major rule of packing a BOB is to keep it balanced when it's on your back and hips. A balanced go-bag should feel stable, as if it were a part of your upper body. You want its contents to be packed tight, without any load shifting on its interior or exterior. To do this, cinch up its compression straps to keep everything in place and to help keep unexpected load shifts from throwing off your balance.

Bottoms Up

Obviously, you'll be packing from the bottom upward, but what items go where? A general rule of thumb is to

keep things you need to access often in easily accessed pockets or areas, while placing things you don't need to reach as much at the bottom. When not in your pockets, your flashlight, navigation tools, and self-defense weapons should be placed in quick-access pouches, while infrequently used items, such as a sleeping bag or extra clothing, are stowed in the bottom of the backpack.

Live hard for more than a few days and you'll likely reconsider stowing sleep gear and warming layers in the depths of your pack. This means dumping the gear above it and repacking a yard sale every morning. On longer outings, it's better to use the lash points on your pack and some webbing to secure sleep and snivel gear for easy, daily access.

Heavy Spine

We want to build a comfortable backpack to carry — a key to doing that is to have a BOB with a balanced center of gravity. Therefore, you'll want to situate the heaviest items, such as water, food, tools, and the like on top of the bottom layer, close to your spine. Placing the heaviest gear in the vertical center of your backpack helps it from feeling top or bottom heavy, allowing you to be more nimble.

Easy Access

Common sense will tell you that it's best to keep frequently used items at the top and on the outside pockets. Items that you might want to consider for top billing may include sunglasses, sunscreen, map, compass, flashlight, headlamp, snacks, a small first-aid kit, toilet paper, and rain gear. Bigger accessories that may not fit into a BOB very easily (think a machete, trekking poles, or a sleeping pad) should find their way into external pockets or be strapped on with your backpack's external loops or add-on compression straps.

Food For Thought

It's a good idea to lay out all of your contents before proceeding to organize them. This way you can visualize everything that's going in and piece together the puzzle in a deliberate way. It's also a good idea to keep the following tips in mind when organizing your gear:

Compartmentalize: All this preparation could be useless unless you can find what you need when you need it. A messy pack won't do you any favors when you're in survival mode. Stuff sacks are a great way to organize different "departments" into one location. You might have a

Check List

Cover your bases with the following categories of gear and supplies when outfitting your bug-out bag. Items from each category should be customized for your individual needs as well as region.

1. Hydration
2. Food
3. Fire-starter
4. Shelter
5. First aid
6. Tools
7. Navigation
8. Illumination
9. Clothing
10. Weapon
11. Protection from sun/rain
12. Communication

"kitchen" sack for your portable stove, fuel, and eating utensils and a "medical" sack for your medicines, for example.

Fill the Gaps: When packing your bag, look to see if any items have extra spaces you can fill up too. Perhaps a cooking pot or mug has extra space in it that you can stuff to save exterior space or to help protect fragile items.

Quality, Not Quantity: Make sure you have gear that you can depend on. High-quality gear goes a long way — we believe firmly in the "you get what you pay for" principle. After all, this gear is meant to save your life.

Practice Before Packing: Make sure you're familiar and comfortable with your chosen tools and equipment. Don't just buy something and stuff it in. Practice using it, and figure out if its effective for you before it makes the cut.

Two is One, and One is None: Invariably something will go wrong —after all, you're in a disaster situation. Spread out the risk that a single item might not perform its function when you need it by sourcing tools and gear that have overlapping capabilities. For instance, a hand-crank flashlight can provide light and be able to charge your electronic devices, while a solar-powered radio can act as a back-up charger.

Conclusion

You want to keep low-usage items at the bottom of your pack and heavier items close to your spine. High-use items should be kept up top or around the outside of the BOB. The pack's exterior and interior compression straps should be cinched tight to keep everything in its place.

If you find yourself on the move for hours or even days at a time, you'll be glad that you packed your bug-out bag properly. A balanced setup helps keep you on your feet and on the move, which can be a lifesaver in itself.

BETTER TO HAVE IT AND NOT NEED IT...

10 Must-Have Items for Survival in Hostile Regions

By **Molotov Mitchell**

Since 2001, the world has undergone a dramatic increase in travel risk, due to the ever-increasing surge of terrorism and international drug cartels. As one might expect, personal protection training has become increasingly popular for Westerners who work or vacation abroad.

As a combat instructor, I've traveled around the world providing that kind of training to people already working in hostile regions as well as preparing clients here in the U.S., with counter-abduction courses, escape-and-evasion seminars, and Krav Maga classes to help people stay above ground and out of gulags. This article outlines a handy-dandy list of things you'll need in sketchy countries — but before we get to that, just where the heck are you going?

These days, nobody wants to hurt anyone's feelings, so there's a lot of debate on how to de-fine a "hostile region." The most popular, super-sensitive way to gauge a nation's safety and threat level is to see if it has any travel warnings posted online. The U.K. Foreign Travel Department is a great resource: www.gov.uk/foreign-travel-advice. But if you just want a quick and dirty method, I call this an "ABC test" to keep it simple. When considering travel to another country, just ask the following:

A) Does the nation's government have a track record of physically oppressing people based on their beliefs or gender (executing apostates and dissidents, beating and/or stoning women, etc.)?

B) Does their army double as their police force (historically common in communist regimes)?

C) Does the region have a noticeable problem with vanishing visitors (cartel kidnappings, beheadings, and the like)?

If the answer was "yes" to any of those questions, then we can consider the region "hostile." And to be clear, "hostile" can range from "Go home, Yankee!" to "Slay the infidel wherever you find them." If that sounds like a place you're headed, prepare accordingly. But keep in mind that preparation doesn't equal safety; no one can guarantee your safety. Even with all the martial arts and counter-abduction training in the world, visiting a hostile region is always a roll of the dice in terms of personal security.

If Westerners would avoid some of these places, they'd really be much safer, and these oppressive regimes would have to clean up their act to preserve their tourist industry, which in many cases, is a huge part of their economy. However, the allure of ancient ruins and exotic islands draws waves of adventurers year after year, beheadings be damned! And in our global economy, many of us are required to conduct business in some dicey domains. Whatever your reason for treacherous travel, here's a list of 10 must-haves for hostile regions.

1. Trained Companion

While this isn't a piece of gear per se, selecting an appropriate travel companion is one of the best ways to minimize your risk when going abroad. For instance, I don't travel to hostile regions without someone who knows Krav Maga. If things get savage, I know that they'll fight (and fight well). Real talk? If you're traveling with someone who doesn't have your back, then you might as well be traveling alone.

2. Access to Firearms

Don't walk into any room that you don't know how to walk out of. The same goes for countries. In hostile countries, cities can spontaneously erupt in violence. So, if you can legally obtain a gun, do that immediately. When I was working in Egypt, the Muslim Brotherhood was gearing up to overthrow Mohamed Morsi. Tensions ran high. As you might suspect, I couldn't legally obtain a firearm. In hostile regions, guns are typically restricted to military/cartel/jihadi use. But hey, if bullets are coming your way, you'd really like the option to send some back.

So, one of the first things I did after arriving in Egypt was develop a relationship with a waiter who could get me and my colleague AK-47s within two hours. When I taught in Moldova, I found a villager who kept a pistol and shotgun ready for me, should I need them in a hurry. But developing these contacts and agreements isn't as easy as it may sound and requires strong social engineering skills, so neither I nor this magazine recommend that anyone do it unless their life dependeds on it. Try to buy from the wrong guy and you could wind up dead (or worse).

4. Hand-to-Hand Weapon
(ex. Delta Defense Ring, Benthic Butter Knife)

If you're being attacked or kidnapped, then the enemy probably has the element of surprise. The best way to level the playing field is to surprise them back with combat training and the augmented power of a hidden weapon. At Triangle Krav Maga, we make useful tools that pass through most security checkpoints without a problem. Take the Delta Defense Ring. This attractive piece of jewelry seems harmless, but it adds serious piercing and tearing damage to any punch or slap, depending on how you wear it.

Best of all, the Delta's always on your hand, so it's always ready. Another fan favorite, the Benthic Butter Knife, meets all the TSA travel regulations because it is, in fact, a butter knife. It's just a heavy, powdercoated butter knife with a retention ring and bottle cap jimping for enhanced grip. Whatever item you choose to carry, make sure it doesn't look scary; that would ruin the surprise, right? Check local laws to make sure any hand-to-hand weapons you bring are legal in your area of travel.

3. Covert Safe

Covert safes like a fake can of Pepsi or a can of shaving cream with a hidden compartment are perfect for protecting things like money, flash drives, and medicine. Sometimes you have to carry a larger amount of cash, especially if you're in a country where it's difficult to access ATMs or exchange offices. In those instances, don't carry money on your person, leave it in your bag, or hide it under a mattress. Thieves know to check those places. Keep your cash in a hollow toilet paper holder in your hotel room. Thieves will never look there, especially if you smudge some Nutella on the TP before you head out.

5. Fidget Toys/Puzzles/ Games

When I was working in Cuba this year, the communist government decided to stick it to Americans by cutting off all access to American bank accounts and blocking wire transfers from anywhere in the U.S. The timing couldn't have been worse. My travel partner and I had almost run out of cash and had just arrived in a new city. She started to lose it, but I managed to keep calm by simply playing with my small 3D puzzle as I concentrated on finding a solution.

After a few hours of creative calls and finding the right guy to bribe, we were able to get money through a back channel. But I was only able to remain calm and think clearly because of that silly little puzzle. Another great use for games and fidget toys is at-tracting local children. Kids fly under the radar; they can go to and fro on your behalf and no one bats an eye. And no matter where you go, kids love flashy little toys. If you ever need help but can't freely move through an area, let a kid play with your cool gizmo and then ask them to get you information, food, water, or whatever else you might need in a desperate situation in exchange for the toy. Works like a charm and is a cheap, easily replaceable bartering chip.

6. Handcuff Key

The best way to pick your way out of handcuffs is to use a key. Unlike doors, which have a different key for every lock, 90 percent of all handcuffs around the world can be opened with the exact same kind of key, and you can buy one at almost any military surplus store or law enforcement supply store. The nonmetallic variety is your best bet. Hide it in your shoe, sew it into your shirt, or stash it in your belt. Never leave home without it! Having a bobby pin or small metal hair barrette can also serve as an improvised lock pick or shim to free yourself from handcuffs.

7. Sat Phone

In hostile regions, cell coverage can be spotty. That's why it's a great idea to carry an Iridium satellite phone for emergencies. A decent model will set you back about $1,000, but if you're headed into shady situations, it's totally worth it. Don't forget to buy a pre-paid SIM card before you go. These days, you can purchase 50 minutes for around $100 online. After all, your cell phone may not have service in certain areas overseas, even if you're on an international plan.

8. Solar Panel

The first thing to fail on a mission is communications. Your sat phone battery may die, but the sun won't. No matter where you are, just set out your panel, kick back and allow nature to recharge that device. Note: I don't recommend rigid panels; they're too bulky and prone to damage. Bushnell's SolarWrap is a flexible panel that rolls up into a compact tube for easy travel.

9. Decoy Wallet

Carry a shiny decoy wallet in your front left pant pocket with a fake ID, a couple of random business cards, and petty cash for bribes. If you're being robbed, give them the decoy, not your real wallet (hidden elsewhere on your person). Absolutely never give up your passport. My decoy wallet has brushed nickel so it really catches the eye, a distracting feature that can set the thief up for a good sucker punch, kick, or elbow, if that's on the menu.

10. Smartphone Camera

A smartphone camera is surprisingly versatile. Aside from just taking pictures, you can covertly survey areas by pretending to shoot video or panoramic photos. You can act like you're taking a selfie to see if anyone's tailing you. Peek around corners without exposing yourself. And if you suspect that someone may go through your things while you're out and about, simply take pictures of your room beforehand. When you return, check the pics to see if anything is out of place. Hiding in plain sight, the smartphone can be your electronic Swiss Army knife.

About The Author

Molotov Mitchell is a black belt in Krav Maga, the head of Atlas Krav Maga, and a concealed carry handgun instructor through the North Carolina Department of Justice. Trained and certified by the Wingate Institute in Israel, he's trained groups around the world and invented weapons like the Benthic Knife and the patent-pending Hex Tool. When he's not standup paddle boarding with his daughter, Ivy, he serves on the Wake County Fitness Council in North Carolina. His favorite color is blue.

- www.atlaskravmaga.com
- www.trianglekravmaga.com

GET IN LINE

An Overview of "Line Gear" and Layered Preparedness

By **Tom Marshall**
Photos by **Patrick McCarthy**

There's discussion *ad nauseum* in preparedness circles about redundancy and layering. Like many survival concepts, grand-scale guidance is distilled down to a catchphrase that's then so beat-to-death that people lose track of what it actually means. One of our favorites is "two is one, one is none." It makes sense on the surface, but gets tossed around so much in forums and discussions that it becomes its own form of radio static. So, we thought we'd go down to brass tacks and talk about exactly why layering is important and how to do it. As always, what we present here is one way — not the only way. And, as a concept, layering is scalable to your own readiness needs. We'll provide some specific examples as a handrail for you. But the specific layers you create should be tailored to your daily routine and the contingencies you feel are most important to prep for.

One of the best layering strategies we've come across is known as the "Line Gear" concept. We can't verify for certain who coined the term or how exactly it started. We got it from an Army Special Forces veteran, and the anecdotal stories we've heard go something like this …

During the Vietnam War, U.S. Special Operations Forces adopted a methodology of using small, highly trained reconnaissance patrols to search the jungle for enemy forces and activity. These tiny teams, sometimes only four or six men strong, were able to move quietly and collect information about enemy movements. Many times, these teams would wind up in direct combat with forces vastly larger in size and firepower. In such cases, escape and evasion was the only effective way to survive the encounter. The ability to break away from a pursuing enemy and melt into the jungle became vital. In some cases, this meant shedding heavy rucksacks or jangling equipment vests to move faster and make less noise. But in the heat of the fight, it can be difficult to decide exactly what equipment to jettison and what to keep with you no matter what. So, the idea of organizing your gear into "lines," based on importance and where you store it in your load-out, became a simple and effective way to avoid rationing or decision-making on the fly while under fire. With some interpretation on our part, the basic concept broke down as follows:

First Line Gear was essential survival gear. This stuff was kept on your body — perhaps on your trouser belt or stuffed in your pockets — and was considered the bare minimum for successful escape, evasion, and survival. Nuts-and-bolts necessities like a compass, map, waterproof matches, emergency signaling devices, and some basic first-aid items were in this category.

Second Line Gear was what you needed to do your immediate job. In the case of a small jungle recon team, this was what they needed to shoot, move, and communicate — things like primary weapons, ammunition, grenades, and radios. These items normally go on a soldier's load bearing vest, chest rig, or plate carrier.

Third Line Gear provided long-term sustainment and comfort. Spare batteries, extra socks, rations, shelter half, Claymore mines, and anything needed for a 72-hour patrol were kept in a pack or rucksack for retrieval as needed.

The above lists are by no means comprehensive — they're generic examples of how to organize and classify your overall load by necessity. In the jungle war context, packing your equipment in this philosophy bears out that, if falling back under fire, the long-term-use gear in your rucksack could be dropped on the run to gain speed and reduce noise while still leaving you with the necessary equipment to fight the enemy and provide for basic survival needs. If, for some reason, you became separated from your weapon and fighting equipment, the items in your pockets and on your belt could still allow you to live long enough to return to friendly lines or be picked up under *in-extremis* circumstances.

Thankfully, very few of us will ever have to worry about sacrificing large amounts of equipment to evade an enemy force in direct pursuit. But this concept can still be adapted to help us better organize our EDC and bug-out bags in a succinct, prioritized manner. Odds are most of us do this already, to some extent. The idea of walking in and out of work every day with a rolling duffel bag of survival equipment is unrealistic. The things we deem essential to have at all times become our EDC, and everything else gets stashed or staged elsewhere for use as the situation dictates. What we like most about this method is that it forces us to sit down and truly assess what's important to have on us, right now, for immediate use, versus what can be packed, stowed, or stashed for retrieval if and when needed.

The approach is highly scalable and can be made your own, depending on what your routine requires. For soldiers deployed overseas, their rifle and body armor with attached ammunition pouches would be Second Line gear, as it's required to do their primary job. But for a prepared citizen, these same items would likely be relegated to Third Line since, especially in an urban setting, they're less likely to be used and more likely to be left behind if the immediate situation doesn't include contested gunfights at distance. (Contrast this with a defensive handgun that, for many, might be considered First Line Gear to be carried daily.) What follows are some examples we've put together to best illustrate the ideas, and to give you some inspiration to "line up" your own gear.

Example #1: "The Urbanite"

First Line: On-Body Carry (EDC)

Carbon Tactics Badger Strap Belt

The Badger Strap's double thickness makes it ideal for supporting holsters and holding up pants laden with the rest of the carry loadout.

SureFire G2X LE Flashlight with Thyrm "Switchback" Ring

The SureFire G2X series is lightweight and inexpensive, while still bringing 500 lumens to bear with a click of the tailcap. Adding the Thyrm Switchback ring provides both a pocket clip and a highly intuitive way to use the light while maintaining a two-hand grip on a pistol, if need be. The "LE" variant offers two outputs: 60 lumens and 500 lumens, but always offers 500 on the first button push. If you want to step down to 60 lumens for admin tasks, double tap the clicky tailcap. No programming, no extra switching, no twist-for-this, push-for-that.

Zero Tolerance 0566

The Zero Tolerance name is synonymous with hard use and high performance. Their now-discontinued 0566 line provides a slimmer, more discreet EDC option over some of their other offerings. (Pictured above is my previous EDC knife, a well-worn Emerson CQC-7BT.)

Casio G-Shock Watch

The G-Shock watch is bombproof and easy to oper-

Above: When all laid out for this photo, we realized just how much gear it's possible to carry comfortably and concealed in a well-broken-in pair of jeans and a loose T-shirt.

ate, no stranger to hard-use environments like war zone deployments. (This particular watch has been to Afghanistan a dozen times.) In addition to the quick-reference navigation aid of the Suunto Clipper compass, the Gearward A-K (Anti-Kidnapping) band allows you to carry some sneaky escape tools like a nonmetallic handcuff key and ceramic razor blade.

LAS Concealment Ronin 3.0

A lot of holsters come across our desks. But the Ronin 3.0 from LAS Concealment has quickly become one of our favorites. It includes both holster and spare mag carrier, joined together by a length of elastic cord. This gives the rig a degree of flexibility that allows it to move with your body without the shifting, tilting, and sliding we experience when running an IWB mag pouch that's entirely separate from the holster.

JB Knife Ditch Pik

A concealed, dedicated defensive fixed blade is typically faster and easier to bring to bear in a fight, versus having to pocket-draw and open a similar-sized folder. There are some excellent boutique knife makers specializing in sharp things for street fights. One of our favorites is the Ditch Pik from JB Knife & Tool in collaboration with our friend and colleague Ed Calderon. It's available in a number of different configurations. This one has G10 scales and a full-length double-edged blade. We tested this knife thoroughly in Ed's own Organic Medium Entry class — see "Sharp Edges and Dirty Tricks" in Issue 36 for more on that class — and found that it performed excellently, including stabbing through a standard-issue soft body armor vest without so much as slowing down. Depending on the circumstances, we carry our Ditch Pik instead of, or in conjunction with, our Glock 19.

LTC Pocket IFAK

The Live the Creed pocket IFAK is a drop-it-in-your-pocket way to carry some basic trauma supplies like gloves, anti-clotting agent, and chest seals.

"Scapular" E&E Necklace

This unassuming piece of jewelry came to us by way of a somewhat cryptic Instagram user known as @whoiscitizene. We got in touch with "E" through RECOIL OFFGRID alum William Echo. The necklaces are based heavily on the teachings of Ed Calderon. The Scapular consists of a Kevlar cord held together by small magnets, instead of a clasp. On the end of the Kevlar line is a small square pocket made of felt, adorned with Calderon's signature "Sneak Reaper" totem. The felt pocket is small, so whatever you keep in it must be micro-sized. Luckily, there are a number of companies producing specialty SERE tools with incredibly reduced footprints. We chose a handcuff shim and an ITS Tactical OSS Tool. The latter is a set that consists of a pint-sized tension wrench and several styles of lockpicking rakes on a small swivel bearing, allowing them to be fanned out like a poker hand without having to detach the individual tools to use them. The Scapular also has teeny-tiny elastic loops, which hold the smallest chemlight we've ever seen. Locked in a dark trunk or the back of a windowless panel van? Crack the chemlight, and you'll have just enough light to see, access, and use your tools.

Tuff Writer Carabiner

We've featured several Tuff Writer products before. Their Carabiner holds not only our keys, but a couple of other handy tools: namely the Carbon Tactics TiSlice box cutter and the Gearward Ranger BIC lighter carrier. The Ranger BIC sleeve provides a watertight seal around the head of a mini BIC lighter, and the bike tire inner tube it's made out of can be cut up (with the TiSlice!) and used as rainproof tinder.

This is a comprehensive First Line that includes an array of vital survival tools without forcing you to wear cargo pants, a fishing vest, and a fanny pack everywhere you go. This setup gives you the ability to:

❱ Defend yourself with force

❱ Handle small-to-medium cutting chores

Below: The Greyman Tactical Rigid Insert Panel has proven to be an excellent way to organize gear inside a pack. As an added bonus, if we want to use our 5.11 AMP 12 as carry-on luggage we simply remove the panel and store it while we're gone. Or pack it in our checked bag for use when we land.

❱ Make fire

❱ Escape restraints

❱ Treat traumatic wounds

❱ Dead reckon without electronics by tracking time and direction

… all with items that are worn or carried in pockets. With this EDC, if you had no other equipment or gear besides the clothes on your back and the contents of your pockets, you could still fulfill many of your basic survival needs — at least for a short-duration — through a spectrum of situations from a roadside breakdown to an active shooter. This is the essence of First Line Gear.

Second Line: 5.11 AMP 12 Backpack with Greyman Tactical Rigid Insert Panel

❱ *Laptop computer and charging cord*

❱ *Basic first-aid supplies (Band-Aids, Ibuprofen, antihistamines, etc.)*

❱ *Passport*

❱ *Thumb drive (with tie-on glow sprinkles cube from @whoiscitizene)*

❱ *Full-size compass*

❱ *Tactical Combat Casualty Care quick reference guide*

❱ *Tactical pen*

❱ *North American Rescue IFAK trauma kit*

The NAR trauma kit provides redundancy to the LTC pocket IFAK, plus a C-A-T tourniquet.

G-Code OSH holster on RTI mounting panel

G-Code is a top-notch purveyor of Kydex and nylon tactical gear. We've been duly impressed with everything we've seen from them. But, in particular, we like the RTI mounting system in this particular setup. The RTI "wheel" is a circular mounting disc that accepts the three-pronged triangular backing plate that the company attaches to the back of its holsters. Once mounted, the wheel has a locking mechanism that keeps the holster in place. Conversely, the RTI wheel can be unlocked, and the holster can be taken out of the pack and mounted onto any other piece of kit with another mounting wheel. For my daily grind as your Editor, I typically work from home or well-known local nooks like coffee shops and cigar lounges. In these environments, I don't typically find it necessary to have my gun on my person, but always have this bag in arm's reach when settled in behind my laptop. For unfamiliar environments and trips to more exciting locales, I switch to my LAS Concealment Ronin 3.0 holster (see above) to keep my weapon on me as needed.

Glock 19 with SureFire X300 Ultra and Holosun 508T optic

This Glock has a whole slew of performance-enhancing features, from the ported barrel/windowed slide combo by Southwest Precision Arms to the Sonoran Defense laser-stippled frame, KE Arms magwell, and Johnny Custom Glocks trigger. It's loaded with Hornady's 135-grain Critical Duty ammunition and equipped with a SureFire X300 Ultra weapon light for things that go sideways after sundown.

G-Code Scorpion Softshell Mag Pouch with Spare Magazine

G-Code Scorpion Softshell Mag Pouch with Leatherman F4 Free Multi-Tool

The Leatherman Free series offers some additional capabilities above and beyond the pocket knife.

5.11 Mini Operator Ax

5.11's Operator Ax was designed with input from former Special Forces operator and Viking Tactics owner Kyle Lamb. This is a shrunk-down version we were able to fit inside the AMP 12. The small hatchet blade and hammer on the reverse side offers limited ability for emergency breaching — whether trying to get into a wrecked car to help a trapped motorist or breaking through a door or window to escape a building fire.

The Redwire Gear Emergency Management Rack gets donned first, with the Eberlestock pack buckled on over top of it. If the pack needs to be jettisoned, simply unbuckle the waist and sternum straps and drop it without losing your Second Line Gear.

Below inset: The Firefly signal device is a lightweight, concealable way to mark your position. Carrying multiple markers could even allow you to leave "breadcrumbs" or mark a landing zone or shelter site.

Sport Smoke Sportsman
Smoke Grenade

Having the ability to signal for help is vital. Patrick McCarthy discussed the importance of this capability in his visual signals *Pocket Preps* column in Issue 37. We like the Sport Smoke grenade by Superior Signals for its emergency-ready design. These models are wax-sealed and have an advertised shelf life of five years, so you can pack 'em and forget 'em for a while without worrying about the smoke-producing agent degrading over time. When needed, simply peel off the wax cap and pull the ring ignitor. At only $12.50 per unit, they're a low-cost, long-lasting addition to any emergency kit.

Elastic Loop Velcro Panel with Mini Chemlights

As with smoke, keeping a couple spare chemlights in your pack is a great option to signal for help, read maps, or light your way when trying to conserve flashlight batteries — or when your batteries have already faltered.

Cobra Cuffs Flex Restraints

While we don't plan to detain anyone with flex cuffs any time soon, these are all-around useful accessories to have that can be pressed into service for multiple other uses. Two examples: They can be used to hold double doors closed if sheltering in place from an active shooter, and they can also be used to construct splints to immobilize injured limbs.

Third Line: Use What You've Got!

Most city-dwellers don't usually walk around with 72 hours' worth of sustainment supplies on their body. Nor should they, in our opinion. Instead, make use of the best two resupply points that almost everyone has built into their daily routine: your house and your car. If you live in a major metropolitan area, suburb, or even a small town or rural farm area, your Third Line will probably be in the bed of your pickup truck, the trunk of your hybrid smart-coupe, or a bin stashed in your pantry or garage. At the end of the day, the most effective and consistently practiced preps will be those that fold into your existing routines and lifestyle. Prep around your life; don't live around your preps.

If you don't already do so, consider keeping a duffel bag, suitcase, or plastic tub in your vehicle with enough supplies to sustain yourself and your party for 48 to 72 hours. Are you a nuclear family with three kids? That's three days' worth for everyone. Are you and your partner young professionals just starting out? Six days' worth total, then. What does three days of sustainment look like? In the end, you'll have to figure that out for yourself. We suggest keeping it sparse; don't pack an entire second home. Even if you normally eat three full meals and a couple snacks every day, you can easily last on half that

(if not less) for a short duration. Either way, the essentials probably include:

❱ Food

❱ Water

❱ Basic hygiene/sanitation (wet wipes, hand sanitizer, dry shampoo, some toilet paper or paper towels)

❱ Weather protection (sunscreen for desert dwellers, extra pairs of thermal underwear and hand warmers for northlanders)

❱ Emergency signaling (flares, strobe lights, smoke signals, whistles, etc.)

❱ One full pair of clean clothes (shirt, pants, socks, underwear, jacket/fleece)

❱ Chargers or battery packs for all electronic communications

If possible, include a store of emergency cash. This could be used for everything from paying for a tow truck or buying a couple gallons of gas, to tipping a stranger to hitch a ride or borrow their cell phone, to using it as "throwaway" money if confronted by opportunistic criminals.

For this particular scenario, we won't dive into a specific sample loadout for Line Three. Instead, we'll move into another example of how to array your "Line Gear" where a Third Line becomes much more succinct.

Above: Shoot, Move, Communicate, Medicate — those are the "Big 4" tasks you may be required to do in an emergency situation. The Redwire Gear chest rig allows you to carry enough gear to do all four in a footprint about the size of most T-shirt logos.

Our outdoors pack also contains the full-size version of the 5.11 Operator Axe. It's got a longer handle that features a pry bar at each end as well as a larger blade and hammer head.

Example #2: "Weekend Warrior"

While your Editor spends his day-to-day lounging around caffeine and tobacco wells, tapping away at a keyboard and scrolling through social media, short and sometimes spontaneous excursions into the surrounding mountainous desert are a welcome reprieve that can typically be planned and executed in about 30 minutes. Hitting the trail poses a new set of challenges and restrictions that require some retooling of the gear lines outlined above.

Line One, at least for us, doesn't change much. As the term EDC would imply, we carry those items and tools on us or with us, regardless of the ebb and flow of daily routine. So, for the sake of simplicity, we'll skip listing out a separate First Line and instead focus on what changes when you go from blacktop to backwoods.

Second Line: Redwire Gear Emergency Management Rack and Demo Pouch

The open carry of weapons and gear is more convenient and commonly accepted when traversing the great wide-open, whether for an afternoon or weekend. Initially developed by commandos in Asia and Africa for carrying spare ammo, the chest rig has evolved into a modular, utilitarian platform to carry all manner of survival sundries. We especially like chest rigs for hikes, as they can be worn in conjunction with a backpack and give us quick access to supplies without having to stop and drop ruck to reach them. The Redwire EMR is one of the slimmest, lightest chest rigs we've put hands on to date, carrying a Goldilocks "just right" amount of gear while keeping weight and bulk to minimum. We've set ours up with the following:

2x G-Code Scorpion Softshell Rifle Mag Carriers

The stretchy bungee retention and hybrid cloth/polymer construction of the Scorpion Softshell carriers allows them to be used for a variety of purposes. We have two on our chest rig — one for a spare 30-round carbine mag and one for our cell phone. (Since our Third Line pack has a waist belt, it can be tough digging into your pants pockets on the go.)

Blue Force Gear Tourniquet NOW Pouch

Tourniquets are one of those items that you'll probably never have to use but, if you do, you want it 10 minutes ago. Our First Line med kit doesn't include a hard tourniquet, so we mounted one on our Second Line. The Blue Force pouch holds one C-A-T or similar TQ in an easy-to-access, rip-open vertical caddy. Putting it almost dead center on the rack allows it to be accessed with either hand from almost any angle with minimal movement.

Emdom USA Multitasker Pouch

Just as with our urban-focused Second Line, we wanted to include a multi-tool of some kind. We used a Multitasker for several years and carried it all kinds of places, including overseas and around the country. It includes a bit set and several AR-specific features, like a front sight adjustment tool and a castle nut wrench. The Emdom pouch accommodates the tool itself and has a separate pocket for the bit set that comes with it.

Redwire Demo Pouch

Redwire Gear also makes the hanger/dangler/abdominal/subload pouch (whichever term you care to use). There are a number of these types of pouches on the market, and in the tactical duty world, they've become a popular addition to all manner of chest rigs and plate carriers to carry additional gear. We like the Demo Pouch in particular because the inside is lined with tennis-ball-green Velcro — soft side on the back wall of the pouch, hook side on the front wall. With a couple of strips of adhesive Velcro from the hardware store, you can make sure the items in your demo pouch are securely fastened and won't rattle around in there. We stowed the following items in ours:

Sportsmoke Sportsman's Smoke Grenade
Leupold Handheld Thermal Optic
Firefly Infrared Beacon

The search-and-rescue groups in our area regularly coordinate with both federal and local law enforcement air assets to find missing or distressed hikers, and both the federal and local agencies operating in our area have FLIR-equipped aircraft. Therefore, an IR beacon is a legitimate, excellent way to signal potential rescuers without drawing unwanted attention from animals or criminal elements. We like the Firefly because it's so small and simple to operate. Just snap the beacon directly onto the leads of a household 9-volt battery and wait for the cavalry. To store it, flip the beacon upside down and tape it to the battery. They're small enough that you can carry several to mark a large campsite or landing zone, or drop them along a trail like IR breadcrumbs if you have to move. They can also be attached to packs, helmets, and hats, or left in trees. According to the manufacturer, the signal is so bright that the Firefly can be placed in your pocket and still be detected by IR goggles and cameras.

Explosive Ops Gear MOD 1 Chem Light Panel

One of the other things we like about the Redwire

Building in redundancy is always a good idea. For example: smoke signals, chemlights, and ammo are included in both our Second and Third lines. Even if you're required to ditch an entire line, you retain certain critical capabilities no matter what.

Demo pouch is that the front of it has a huge field of Velcro to accept patches or panels. We chose the MOD 1 Chem Light Panel from Explosive Ops Gear. EOG is a tiny gear company based on the East Coast and, like Redwire, composed of current and former Explosive Ordnance Disposal specialists. The MOD 1 is designed to hold up to five full-size chemlights or 10 miniature ones. We set it up with the latter, allowing us to have both visible and IR lights on hand, depending on the situation and how "loud" we want our distress signal to be.

Third Line: Eberlestock Lo Drag II

With the infinite number of day packs and hiking packs on the market today, there's bound to be one out there that fits your wants and needs exactly, or comes pretty damn close. We settled on the Lo Drag II by Eberlestock. We knew the application would be for a short-range pack meant for day hikes and trail use. We also knew we wanted something that wasn't excessively large — a bag that allows you to over pack can be just as bad as one that's too small to hold what you need. We packed ours with the following:

On waistbelt:

- ❱ Gerber fixed blade knife
- ❱ Military-style white light/IR dual-use beacon Leatherman multi-tool
- ❱ 30-round carbine magazine
- ❱ Military-style lensatic compass
- ❱ Fire-starting kit including Fiber Light tinder and ferro rod
- ❱ SureFire G2 Nitrolon flashlight with Malkoff Devices drop-in conversion head (The Malkoff lamp assembly uses a fully potted LED bulb and improved reflector. While the original G2 Nitrolon had a meager 60-lumen output, the Malkoff add-on bumps that to 250 lumens.)

Inside the pack:

- ❱ 3 stripped-down/disassembled MREs

This leads us to our only gripe about the Eberlestock Lo Drag. Its main compartment features two full-sized laptop sleeves that are sewn into the bag and can't be removed. For a bag that otherwise seems geared toward outdoor and field use, this seems like an odd feature. However, we cut open a couple of MREs and used the laptop sleeves like an accordion file to sort the various main dishes, sides, snacks, and ancillary components of the MREs.

- ❱ 300-ounce water bladder
- ❱ Shemagh/head scarf

The Eberlestock Lo Drag II is a medium-sized pack that works well for all-day outings with enough room for the supplies you'll need if your day hike turns into an unscheduled overnight.

- ❱ Microfiber camping towel
- ❱ General first-aid kit
- ❱ Collapsible entrenching tool/shovel
- ❱ Military "VS-17" signal panel
- ❱ Emergency space blanket
- ❱ 550 cord
- ❱ Butane lighter
- ❱ Carbine

This is our favorite part of the Lo Drag II — it comes with a built-in sleeve for a carbine. The sleeve can be unrolled to its full length, causing it to hang down below the rest of the pack, to hold a carbine up to 36 inches in overall length. Or you can keep the bottom portion rolled up tight and still fit a 24-inch gun. We chose the latter option and are running a 12.5-inch Sage Dynamics "K9" upper from Rosco Manufacturing. It's set up with a Vortex Razor 1-10x optic and Trijicon RMR red dot in an Arisaka Defense offset mount. The 12.5-inch barrel is match grade, made of 416R stainless, and finished in black nitride. The Rosco upper is mated to an American Defense Manufacturing lower with fully ambi controls and a Gear Head Works pistol brace. This setup allows us to carry a sub-30-inch gun that's capable of hitting targets out to 500 meters with the right ammunition. It fits into the Lo Drag's weapon sleeve with only the brace and the end of the lower sticking out.

The Last Line

Our hiking setup falls a little more in line with the original Special Forces paradigm of Line Gear. If we were on the run through the mountains from some hypothetical pursuing enemy and needed to drop the Eberlestock pack, we could remove the rifle, take the 30-round mag off the waist belt and load it into the "cell phone pouch" on our Redwire EMR, and get moving again with 90 rounds of 5.56mm, as well as some signaling and medical capability. If, for some reason, I had to shed the carbine and chest rig, I would still have a knife, light, fire-starting ability, mini IFAK, and some E&E tools.

Is this a likely scenario for any of us to encounter? No, but it illustrates the practical lessons of the Line Gear philosophy. Note how it incorporates the guiding principles of redundancy and prioritization. Once you understand the purpose of each "line" in your total preparedness strategy, you can scale the system in any way necessary to meet your needs. So, if you have mountains of gear stored in the shed or stuffed into old laundry bags, maybe it's time to get your gear in line. ⠿

WHAT TO DO?

Survival Situation Versus Natural Disaster Versus Bug-Out Scenario. Know What to Do and When.

By Shane "Whitefeather" Hobel

In our modern world, we're constantly presented with new concepts and theories for survival, gear, and gadgets, as well as new terminology that seems to pair nicely with all your cool new stuff. From "rolling gear" and "BOBs" (bug-out bags) to "caching" at rendezvous points, all this survival lingo can get a bit convoluted. As you have undoubtedly heard and read from likeminded people, both online and even in this very magazine, there are many labels for particular situations as well.

But what are the differences among a "survival situation," a "disaster situation," and a "bug-out situation?" Potentially horrific events flood the airwaves, the Web, newspapers, and lunchtime conversations. But what does it all mean? Are all these situations the same?

It all sounds a bit confusing. So to help decipher these now commonly used terms, we'll boil them down to a few major categories. Let's take a look at the major topics in this world of survival and all things disastrous/apocalyptic/zombie/end-of-the-world.

First, there is the known. What has happened on our planet thus far in history? Of what we know that has occurred, what incidents would be considered a threat? Big storms, earthquakes, acts of war, pandemics, forest fires, droughts, famine … sadly, the list can go on and on. Not to mention all the potential unknowns.

In the modern practice of "prepping" — we like to say, "being prepared is being responsible" — we have to define some basic scenarios and clarify the differences between them. There are three key scenarios that we need to understand and prepare for:

1 Disaster Situation	**2** Survival Situation	**3** Bug-Out/In Situation

We must understand that these three can overlap one another — or one can turn into another at a moment's notice. Depending on the particular scenario, and whether or not you have been a proactive planner, your position in a disaster situation may quickly turn into a bug-out situation. Then depending on your survival skills and available resources, it might remain at a manageable level or devolve into a survival situation.

A Disaster Situation

"Disaster" or "natural disaster" are two of the most commonly used terms. But what should really be classified as a disaster? To generalize a bit, most of the time it is related to a localized disruption due to any number of reasons. Let's examine natural disasters first.

Natural disasters occur regularly all over the planet, and have besieged the human race throughout the ages — hurricanes, tornados, typhoons, and now super storms, blizzards, ice storms, heat waves, and droughts. These types of disasters can happen swiftly with very little warning, like a tornado. Earthquakes are a prime example of a natural disaster that can completely disrupt, destroy, and kill in an instant and without any warning at all. On the other hand, your local weather anchor might be warning you all week that a pending storm is on the way and that you should expect serious amounts of damage.

It is in this type of pending potential disaster that we can actually choose to "bug in" or "bug out." The reality is that if you have an opportunity to leave in advance, choose not to, and then suddenly it turns out worse than anyone had expected, are you really equipped to deal with it? Or are you just placing yourself in harm's way no matter how proactively you've prepared? Are you risking your life or other lives by choosing to stay? Before something like an approaching storm, you have the ability to leave the area. After the fact, it may be impossible to go anywhere due to massive damage and losses to the

infrastructure in your area. This in turn affects the ability of emergency agencies to help you.

All this can happen if you choose to stay when you should have simply left — Super Storm Sandy, for example. We had plenty of warning, yet folks ended up dying in that storm. There was no reason for that to happen. So when it comes to storms and other forms of localized disasters, please use your best judgment — be rational and pragmatic.

Another type of disaster is, sadly, the man-made kind. These really piss me off. Think of all the oil spills, chemical leaks, preventable forest fires, nuclear catastrophes — the list seems endless. Though they may not always put your life in immediate danger, they are disastrous to all the animals in the region, to the waters we depend on, and to the world in general.

A Survival Situation

In certain cases, a disaster situation can develop into a full-fledged survival situation. Think loss of the power grid due to a solar flare (see "Blackout Preparations" in the Summer 2013 issue of OFFGRID). How about the sinking of a cruise ship? A crashed plane?

Or picture this: A huge storm hits your area, and you become trapped by raging flood waters. You are cut off from any outside help. What are your resources? What do you have with you? Who is with you? Do they have skills? What time of year is it? Is it safe to stay where you are or do you have to move? Many more questions should be asked. Survival situations can develop instantly or over a period of time.

In a major storm, for example, you may prep your home with extra food, water, pharmaceuticals, and any other personal provisions that your family may need. You've done your due diligence and have everything organized. You're ready. Then the storm hits, and it's a big one. Nervous, you sit and wait it out. It can go several ways — if you're just dealing with the inconvenience of temporary power loss, hopefully you have what you need to last you until it returns.

But it might become so bad that your area is declared a disaster area. You might become completely stranded from any outside help whatsoever. Your house and all your carefully prepared supplies are now floating away in the huge flood that followed the storm. You now have to rely on your wits, skills, and available material resources.

Now, you need to follow the order of survival:

STEP 1: Secure shelter

STEP 2: Find water (or utilize appropriate filtration)

STEP 3: Build a fire

STEP 4: Procure food

More than 70 percent of the U.S. population lives in areas with 50,000 people or more.

All the while, you need to keep in mind your safety and security. Perhaps you're on a road trip in the middle of nowhere. Your car suddenly breaks down. Perhaps you simply forgot to stash supplies and gear in your own car, or you're on a business trip in a rental car. You have just entered a potentially dangerous situation. The difference is whether or not you have skills that will mitigate your lack of gear.

Survival situations can also be so raw that you may only have what's literally on your person at the time of the event or what you can find in the environment around you. This might not fit into your overall master plan of preparedness. But guess what? Tough shit! You have to make do with the situation and adapt.

A Bug-Out Situation

What if the situation dictates that you must leave the area immediately? Bugging out is a method of action that can potentially save yourself and others. Understand that most Americans live in and around major cities — according to the last census, more than 70 percent of the U.S. population lives in areas with 50,000 people or more.

For example, you may need to bug out if your area has become too dangerous to be in or has been simply cut off from any and all support. Making a decision on whether or not you should leave is something that you alone will need to determine. Sometimes you may have to make that determination within moments of a particular event.

When it comes to actually bugging out, your preplanning comes into play. How far and how fast do you need to travel? How well are you practiced? How heavy is your BOB? What is inside your bag? Have you ever tried to walk for more than 5 miles with it fully loaded on your back? Did you even have the time to grab it? If not, we hope that you and your loved ones, friends, and coworkers know how to survive without your go-bags. Remember, a BOB is something that essentially represents what we know and what we don't know. In other words, are you so dependent on the bag and its contents to save yourself? If you can't survive without it, then what are you missing?

When discussing bugging out, many folks often focus on their bags. But there are so many factors that can influence your response and that you should consider in advance.

A bug-out response should be part of your overall emergency action plan. (See "Bug Out 101" in the Summer 2013 issue of OFFGRID.) It should be preplanned with rendezvous points, communication options, and predetermined paths of travel, as well as safety and security. There is much to consider in creating a bug-out plan. And all of these skills can be learned.

The More You Know

We have heard many folks in our programs talk about these various factors and how they impact their survival plans. When addressing these three different types of situations, it becomes clear how easily one can overlap or transition into another.

The first step is to build your foundation. So, start with the basic explanations in this article and understand the fundamental differences between these types of situations. As we have mentioned in past articles, honestly assess your own skills and abilities and start applying those skill sets to your overall plan. We can plan until the cows come home, but none of it matters unless you practice.

Then take it upon yourself to learn more and further your knowledge and experience base. Take notes from world disasters throughout history. From local disasters. And from individuals recounting their own personal survival stories.

As we have learned in the past, no matter the scenario — whether a disaster, survival, or bug-out situation — it's a matter of clearly recognizing what truly lies before you and acting accordingly. The more skills you possess, the more risk factors that you can mitigate. Think about the skill sets that require no gear and make sure you have them covered. For instance, learn basic first-aid and CPR — these skills are invaluable and give you the ability to help not just yourself, but others as well. Find a school near you that offers primitive and urban survival skills. Skills always remain with you, even if all you have is the shirt on your back.

As you move forward in becoming more self-sufficient, you will develop a greater appreciation of your own potential. And you will begin to realize that you are more and more equipped to handle any of these types of scenarios.

Stay in the now, be present. This will help you recognize the subtle changes that occur during times like these. Train hard and share with others. ✷

About The Author: Shane Hobel, also known as "White Feather," is the founder and head instructor of Mountain Scout Survival School, based in New York. He's been featured on numerous TV networks, including FOX News, History, National Geographic, and NBC. Specializing in wilderness primitive skills and urban emergency preparedness (among other programs), his company is the only one allowed to teach in the middle of Manhattan's Central Park and was named one of the top 12 survival schools in the country by *USA Today*. Also, Hobel is one of five elite members of the Tracker Search and Forensic Investigation Team, which is called upon to track and find fugitives, lost children, hunters, and hikers.
> www.mtnscoutsurvival.com

SAFE HAVEN

How to Locate and Buy Your Ideal Bug-Out Property

By Phil Schwartze

 ank Williams Jr. wrote and sang a song called "A Country Boy Can Survive." The song spotlights the skills and abilities of people who can survive on their own, with a little backwoods knowhow common in rural America. You can improve your survivability by having backcountry property that's able to sustain life when given the opportunity and a little preparation.

The problem for many of us, though, is that we're city dwellers living in a concrete jungle of skyscrapers, surrounded by a sea of suburban sprawl. And even if you don't live in a large metropolis like New York or Los Angeles, all it would take is one solid catastrophe to have your town go to pot. Owning land in the middle of nowhere — or at least isolated enough — will ensure you have a relatively safer destination to evacuate to in an emergency. A bug-out property can serve as a rally point for your family to reunite, a resupply depot (if you've dug a hidden cache) before moving to a safer region, or a place to set up your underground bunker (see sidebar for more).

Selection of a great rural bug-out location begins by determining the distance you think you can travel when SHTF. Draw an arc on a map with that distance, and your search for a bug-out location can begin.

Determining Land Ownership

All real estate is owned by someone. It may be privately held or owned by some governmental agency, but rest assured it has an owner. Property in private ownership will tend to be urbanized in some form, even if it is a fishing cabin 10 miles from a paved road. Property owned by a government entity will most likely be rural. That governmental agency may be a utility district or a city, county, or state government. In fact, the federal government owns approximately 27 million rural acres. But just because property is owned by a governmental agency doesn't mean it cannot be purchased or leased. For instance, you can obtain a leasehold interest in state and federal property, even in a national or state forest. (Visit www.fs.fed.us/land/staff/disposal.shtml to learn more.)

Most truly rural properties are located in unincorporated areas, meaning they are outside of a city's jurisdiction and therefore only subject to development rules of the county or the state. County building and rural development rules tend to be much less restrictive than those of an urbanized city and far less scrutinized by governmental officials. Once an ideal bug-out location is found, ownership of the land, no matter how rural, can be determined relatively easily. Using a common smartphone app or a geodetic map, determine the exact longitude and latitude of the property in question. If the property actually has an address, present either the longitude/latitude or address to your local title insurance company.

Title insurance companies have access to the historical ownership data of every piece of property in the United States, according to Rick Fortunato, senior vice president for Chicago Title Company. You can even check on properties in other states from your local title insurance company; they all have nationwide data search capabilities. Historical property data may date back hundreds of years and may include photographs. For a very small fee, the title insurance company can give you the name and contact information for any property owner as well as provide important data such as existing taxes, recorded easements, guaranteed access rights, and, most importantly, water rights. You will want to make sure you have the right to access the property and build on it if you so desire. It's also important to know if anyone else has any rights on your property before you acquire it. Those rights of others might include underground pipe easements and rights to access other adjacent properties.

Bomb Shelter Tax Breaks

In the early 1960s, a number of states, not the federal government, passed legislation that gave homeowners a tax break for money spent building a bomb shelter. In a few states and some cities, those tax break rules from the '60s have been overlooked and forgotten, but are still on the books. Your tax expert should check the regulations before taking the exemption on your returns for a preexisting bomb shelter on your property or building one that qualifies for exemption.

Drop-In Bunker

Now that you have acquired your bug-out land, you may choose to build your shelter yourself or hire someone else to do it for you. Another alternative is to buy a prefabricated bunker. Many of these premade bunkers can be customized to your specifications. They are constructed in a factory then brought your to your location, assembled, and professionally installed. There are many choices available; here are a few to check out.

Atlas Survival Shelters: This company makes underground cabins with patented "undetectable escape hatches" and plenty of amenities.
www.atlassurvivalshelters.com

Custom Survival Bunkers: This firm builds assorted custom bunkers and safe rooms to fit your specific property and needs.
www.customsurvivalbunkers.com

Ultimate Bunker: This family-owned business builds underground bunkers, gun vaults, and storm shelters for various disasters.
www.ultimatebunker.com

Easements/Building Regulations

The ability to build on a property is controlled by the zoning of the governmental jurisdiction. Rural properties will most likely be governed by a county or parish, depending on the location. Once a property location is known, zoning and development standards for the property can be found online, in most cases, by contacting the governmental jurisdiction. The development standards may include a required minimum parcel size, maximum building height, selection of building materials, grading maximums, and other important regulations. Those other regulations might include permits needed for tree removal, stream alteration, habitat modification, and endangered species locations that may impact your ability to build. It's important to know all of the regulations — even if you later choose to ignore them.

Most properties don't have mineral or hydrocarbon rights. Those rights may have been acquired from previous property owners by large oil or mining companies many decades ago. It's uncommon to have mining or oil-drilling rights, so don't be surprised if your bug-out site doesn't have them. Having easements on your property, for items such as underground piping, means that the easement holder usually has the right to come onto your property and repair the buried facilities at their discretion, not yours. The same would be true for mineral or hydrocarbon extraction. Theoretically, oil drilling and mining could occur at any time on your property although numerous governmental permits are required that often take years to obtain so it shouldn't be a surprise. Large oil and mining companies, for public relations purposes, typically negotiate with nearby landowners to eliminate confrontation prior to initiating construction activities. Additionally, mining companies may not even need to set foot on your property, accessing those precious underground goodies from afar.

Water is a primary need for a long-term stay at any location. If permanent running water or a lake is not available, then a well can supply your water needs, assuming a well doesn't already exist. Many properties don't have the right to drill a new well, so a careful review of title insurance company data can determine water rights of any property. The cost of drilling a well varies greatly due to soils and geographical conditions. A call to a local drilling company near the intended property can give you a reasonable estimate of the cost of a new well. Electricity may be required to run a pump.

Homesteading

Under Abraham Lincoln in 1862, the federal government passed legislation to promote westward expansion and agricultural development, basically known as the

Homesteading Act. This act provided 160 acres of free federal government land to persons wishing to start farming. Virgil Earp, Wyatt's older brother, was a noted homesteader and, although decades ago homesteading was once a popular style of acquiring free ownership of rural property, it's not a viable alternative in today's world due to changes in the laws. During the peak of free land homesteading the federal government gave out over 270 million free acres of land. In 1986, congress amended the old federal law and eliminated that free land alternative. Only Alaska still offers a form of homesteading to promote recreational cabin development.

Financial Incentives

The federal government and all states have dozens of agricultural and farming assistance programs that offer both tax breaks and financial incentives for new farmers. You must substantially farm the land to achieve any meaningful tax break or development grant. A quick check of your state's farmer assistance program will demonstrate ways of obtaining farmland. See the sidebar for additional resources that provide info on various other financial benefits you can qualify for.

Location, Location, Location

A quick search of the Internet using search terms like "bug-out properties" and "off-grid land" will produce hundreds of available, but certainly publically known, properties. While searching, you might find excess state or federal property for sale, lease, or even trade. The federal government often auctions off excess land that even includes former military missile silos and hardened bunkers. Acquiring excess federal government land is as easy as checking their website at www.govsales.gov and looking in your geographical area of interest. Excess-land sales occur all the time.

A proper bug-out property can often be acquired with a minimum amount of money utilizing a variety of financing mechanisms and depending on how much you want to spend. Some government land leases are free. A lease of private or government land is the cheapest, quickest, and easiest way of obtaining use of a safe haven property, but it is subject to their rules. Such land — acquired under the radar, away from the Internet, and not financed — is the logical choice if you wish to maintain maximum security.

A title insurance company, along with a licensed real estate broker/agent, can provide you with important property data with a minimal cost. The title company agents can assist you in interpreting all of the necessary information on any property no matter its location.

A country boy can certainly survive on a cheap lease.

Additional Resources

There are a variety of grants, subsidies, tax breaks, and other financial incentives your bug-out location may qualify for. Here is a brief list of the many resources available that can provide more information — but, as always, be sure to do your research first before soliciting any service for help.

Benefits.gov: A federal online guide to loans and grants for very low-income homeowners to repair and improve rural dwellings. www.benefits.gov/benefits/benefit-details/402

Eartheasy: A small family business that provides information on the establishment of land trusts and products for sustainable living. www.eartheasy.com

Federal Grants Wire: This is a directory for various federal grants and loans available from several hundred governmental departments and agencies. www.federalgrantswire.com

Land Trust Alliance: This organization assists in establishing land trusts for maintaining open land and conserving resources. www.landtrustalliance.org/policy/public-funding/state-funding

Public Lands Title: A private company that will assist anyone over 18, for a small fee, in acquiring rural land in 18 states. www.governmentland.com

The Center for Rural Affairs: This nonprofit corporation focuses on rural community development and family farm and ranch policy, among other issues. www.cfra.org/renewrural/freeland

The Houston Chronicle: Provides data on ways of utilizing loans and grants from the U.S. Small Business Administration to buy farms, start businesses, and even start beekeeping. http://smallbusiness.chron.com/grants-buying-farm-land-13924.html

USA.gov: The U.S. government's official web portal contains a directory for federal and state government surplus and seized properties, as well as surplus land sales. www.usa.gov/shopping/shopping.shtml

USDA Rural Development: A program from the U.S. Department of Agriculture to establish eligibility for obtaining rural housing. http://eligibility.sc.egov.usda.gov/eligibility/welcomeAction.do

About The Author:

Phil Schwartze is president of The PRS Group, a Southern California land-planning and entitlement-to-use company that specializes in obtaining governmental approvals for unique projects. He has a master's degree from Cal State Los Angeles and is the former mayor of San Juan Capistrano, California.

STORMPROOF SACKS

A Buyer's Guide for Bug-Out Bags That Can Endure Extreme Weather

By **Patrick Vuong**

ny prepper worth their weight in MREs will have SHTF packs set up in several locations for any number of potential disasters. A bug-out bag at home, a get-home pack at the office, and an emergency kit in the vehicle.

But what if the bags themselves don't hold up? What if they fall apart under a heavy load or get ruined in a torrential downpour paired with gale-force winds? Now your precious three-day cache is soaked, useless, or strewn across the muddy forest floor.

With spring showers approaching, we're taking a closer look at durable bags available today that will both increase your daily carry capacity and endure punishing weather.

For the sake of argument, we're calling them "stormproof" backpacks. Note: This is not a buyer's guide exclusively on waterproof bags, also known as dry bags. Because they tend to have just one large compartment and look like sacks made out of inflatable swimming pools, dry bags aren't as versatile for preppers and may stick out in urban settings. Though there are two dry bags among the six models we've tested here, we also got hands on with a duffel, a lumbar pack, a campus-style knapsack, and a true trail pack.

Each one fits a particular niche, but are adaptable enough for use in other situations — all with an eye toward keeping your vital supplies safe and dry. But how do you go about choosing?

What to Look For

For recommendations that hold water, we went to two subject-matter experts (SMEs) with almost a half century of combined experience making gear for outdoor adventurers: Patrick York Ma, the CEO and chief designer of Prometheus

Patrick York Ma
of Prometheus
Design Werx
recommends
avoiding packs
with PALS
webbing, as the
stitching are
tiny holes where
water gets in.
Photo courtesy of
Patrick York Ma

Design Werx and Mel Terkla, an independent designer who's worked for a variety of companies, including Kifaru. Here are some things they suggest you watch out for in a weatherproof pack.

Rain Cover: This is essentially a bag for your bag, and can turn any backpack (even your favorite Jansport) into a stormproof sack. "Rain covers are 'seamless' covers with ample interior coatings — typically polyurethane (P.U.) — that are sized to wrap and cover your entire pack, except for the suspension," Ma says.

Durable Fabric: "If I were looking for a stormproof pack, my first priority would be durability," Terkla says. After all, what good is a stormproof pack if it's just gonna rip and let moisture in?

Interior Coating: "Cordura can be had with a waterproof coating on the inside layer of the fabric," Terkla says. "Even without sealed seams or waterproof zippers, this makes the pack extremely water resistant."

Exterior Coating: Ma recommends getting a pack with a good durable water repellent (DWR) coating on the outside, too. DWR causes H_2O to pool into beads on the fabric's surface, making it easier to shed the droplets.

Seams: Try to look for bags with welded or taped seams. "This type of pack construction will be the best at blocking water penetration," Ma says, adding that packs with these types of seams usually come with coated interiors.

Zippers: Both SMEs recommend looking for zippers covered with an external flap.

Top-Load Design: Top-load backpacks feature a main compartment that opens at, well, the top — think Santa's toy sack, but with an large flap that covers the opening. Meanwhile, front-load backpacks feature a main compartment that unzips in the shape of an "n" and unfolds like a briefcase. While the latter design is easier to pack and compartmentalizes your gear, the former is the way to go if you want to keep your survival supplies dry, Ma says: "Top loaders with single or double quick-release buckles generally block rain better than full-zip front-panel loaders."

What to Avoid

On the flipside, our SMEs warned us to steer clear of these attributes when shopping for a stormproof sack:

Lightweight Fabrics: Terkla says the priority of any stormproof pack should always be durable materials. Even with DWR, thin fabrics can fray against rocks or snag on tree branches, allowing moisture to seep in. Likewise, Ma says to skip "any hipster cotton canvas," waxed or not.

P.U.-Coated Reverse-Coil Zippers: Not all zippers are created equal. Both SMEs agree that the recent trend of "waterproof" P.U.-coated reverse-coil zippers should be avoided, ironically enough. A regular zipper has its teeth, slider, and puller visible on the exterior. These new reverse-coil zippers have its teeth on the interior (hence the name) so that the backside of the teeth (on the exterior) can be laminated with water-resistant P.U. The problem is that P.U. gradually wears out, and even more so with hard use. "These just become more points of entry for rain as they wear out over time," Ma says. "A DWR-treated reverse-coil zipper is actually better at repelling rain ... but it's not common, though."

PALS Webbing: A MOLLE-style pack with PALS webbing stitched on it is full of needle holes, Ma says, all of which are tiny doorways for moisture to get in.

Also, survival expert and longtime RECOIL OFFGRID contributor Tim MacWelch advocates avoiding go-bags covered with PALS webbing in general, as they will attract a lot more unwanted attention from the desperate and the unprepared once SHTF.

Holes: It's common sense not to select any stormproof bags with drain holes or unprotected openings for wired earphones or hydration bladders. "Any drain holes on the bottom of a pack will let water in if you set it down on saturated ground or a puddle," Ma says.

Weathering the Test

With these tips in mind, we put the backpacks in this buyer's guide to the test. But since we're not Halle Berry in an *X-Men* movie, we couldn't conjure up a storm with our mutant powers.

To simulate a downpour and assess each bag's ability to shut out H_2O, we stuffed each pack full of newsprint paper as a substitute for our survival gear. Why? Newsprint turns to mush when wet, so we'd know right away if water got inside a pack. Next, we stuck each bag under a running showerhead for 10 minutes. Then we wiped down the exteriors before unzipping each model, noting whether (and where) any of the paper got soaked.

However, repelling water isn't the only measure of a great bug-out bag (BOB). We also looked at each pack's cargo capacity, internal storage organization, and comfort level during use.

Whether you expect hail and showers in the coming weeks, you live in a region prone to tornadoes in the spring season, or you're gonna hit the lake or river once the snow melts, there's no doubt a backpack option that can help you weather the storm. Read on to see if one of the following six bags is right for you.

Arc'teryx
Carrier Duffle 55

Canadian company Arc'teryx has an international reputation for making top-notch climbing, skiing, and hiking gear. So, it shouldn't surprise anyone that its Carrier Duffle 55 is one tough, technical SOB. The P.U.-coated nylon fabric combined with sealed seams and Arc'teryx's trademarked WaterTight Zipper shrug off rain, snow, and hail like nobody's business. In fact, in our testing, not a single drop of water got to the interior.

But how does it perform as a go-bag? This duffel is definitely durable. Designed for a variety of uses (commuting, traveling, winter sports, etc.), the Carrier Duffle 55 can withstand rigorous daily use in assorted environments. From the materials and hardware to the straps and stitching, everything spells sturdy. The quick-release shoulder straps are both removable and adjustable, so you can carry the bag as if it's a backpack, sling pack, or briefcase (thanks in part to four grab handles, which also work as lash points). The interior is white, allowing greater visibility inside.

On the flipside, most duffels have only one compartment, and this Arc'teryx model is no exception. So, if you're bugging out, the contents might slosh around inside. Oh, and minor complaint: When packed full, it looks like a big shiny black pillow on our backs. Not exactly indiscreet nor aesthetically pleasing.

Overall, a hard-core pack that's highly weather resistant and versatile enough for various duties ... but its lack of interior divisions might give preppers pause.

PROS:
> Impressive weatherproofing construction
> Storm flap helps keep rain and wind out
> Can be carried like a backpack, sling pack, or briefcase
> When not in use, it can be stowed compactly in the included mesh bag. When in use, the mesh bag can double as a travel organizer and be thrown inside the duffel.

CONS:
> Just one large compartment; no dividers or pockets to keep your gear organized.
> It's not the coolest looking nor the most discreet duffel on the market.

 BODY FABRIC
Polyurethane-coated NC400r-AC² nylon

 CAPACITY
55 liters (3,356 cubic inches)

 DIMENSIONS
31 by 17 by 18 inches

 WEIGHT
1.3 pounds

 COLORS
Black (shown), Cardinal, Pilot

 MSRP
$199

URL
www.arcteryx.com

Aquapac
Wet & Dry Backpack 35L

Aquapac set sail in 1983 when three British friends had the idea of making a case for a Sony Walkman (which was like, you know, an old-school MP3 player) so they could listen to music while windsurfing. Now the company produces waterproof protection for everything from tablets and cameras to maps and insulin pumps.

Aquapac's Wet & Dry Backpack is a stormproof bag with the standards rating to prove it. It has an IPX6 rating, meaning it can withstand rain, splashing, and rough sea conditions. It's no surprise, then, that the Wet & Dry Backpack had no problems passing our shower test.

Unlike most dry bags, the Wet & Dry Backpack has more than one compartment. It lives up to its name with a sizeable internal waterproof bag for separating clean clothes from dirty ones. Furthermore, this yellow bag has a clear pocket attached to it so you can quickly find your keys, smartphone, and other small objects without having to dig around.

On the outside, the padded back support can be removed to dry out, be substituted with a hydration bladder, or act as an improvised seat cushion on rocky terrain. Mesh pockets can hold water bottles or other items. And there are multiple lash points so you can clip on carabiners, lights, or other equipment.

At 35 liters, the Wet & Dry Backpack isn't large, but it can serve as a stellar daypack in turbulent conditions.

PROS:
> Truly stormproof thanks to its coated nylon, taped seams, and roll-top closure
> Ability to separate clean and dirty gear
> Waist strap, breathable mesh shoulder straps, and a sternum strap that slides
> Interior bag is bright yellow for greater visibility.

CONS:
> This medium-sized pack won't fit a lot of gear and supplies, so pack judiciously.

 BODY FABRIC
Polyurethane-coated 210-denier Taslan, 500-denier Oxford polyester

 CAPACITY
35 liters (2,135 cubic inches)

 DIMENSIONS
23.6 by 15.7 by 8.7 inches

 WEIGHT
1 pound, 14 ounces

 COLORS
Black

 MSRP
$110

 URL
www.aquapacusa.com

Granite Gear
Talus

The Talus is a part of Granite Gear's Barrier lineup, which has proprietary technology (including water-resistant zippers, Tarpaulite material, and Repelweave fabric) that aims to provide protection from the elements.

Prior to our shower test, we expected the Talus to fail because it has no external zipper flaps. We were surprised to find that the zippers and the Repelweave fabric stayed true, deterring water for seeping through its teeth and weave, respectively. Unfortunately, the seams betrayed Granite Gear's Barrier technology. While newsprint at the top and middle of the pack were bone dry, we found that our newsprint was damp where moisture had gotten through the bottom corner seams

As a campus-style knapsack, this bag has a padded, Tricot-lined sleeve that fits most 17-inch laptops, as well as a Tri-cot lined pocket for valuables like eyewear, smartphone, or wallet – all of which stayed dry during our tests.

However, you gotta take the pros with the cons. The Talus' tall-and-slim design is meant to keep the weight of your load as close to your back as possible, easing the strain on your spine and maintaining a better center of gravity. This means stacking your items on top of each other in the main compartment; not inherently a bad thing in and of itself. But the odd thing is that the zipper on this front-loading pack doesn't go past halfway, meaning you can't access stuff at the bottom of the pack unless you remove the items at the top first.

PROS:
> Divided sections, laptop sleeve, and mesh pockets help keep contents organized
> Sliding sternum strap, adjustable shoulder straps, and "hideable" waist strap
> Tri-cot lined pocket for valuables
> Affordable price tag

CONS:
> Zipper on main compartment doesn't extend down far enough, making it awkward to get items from the bottom of the pack.
> Water seeped through the seams at the bottom corners.

 BODY FABRIC
Repelweave

CAPACITY
33 liters (2,015 cubic inches)

DIMENSIONS
20 by 12.75 by 9.25 inches

WEIGHT
2 pounds, 8 ounces

 COLORS
Black (shown), Ember Orange, Enamel Blue, Flint, Midnight Blue, Rodin, Verbena

MSRP
$45

URL
www.granitegear.com

Kelty
Revol 65

Asher "Dick" Kelty is considered by many to be the inventor of the aluminum-framed backpack, among many other innovations. The Revol 65 carries on Kelty's legacy, offering an ergonomic pack that lets you lug around a poopload of life-sustaining cargo.

The aluminum and HDPE plastic frame combined with Kelty's brilliant PerfectFIT adjustable suspension system keep the cargo weight on your hips and shoulders instead of your lower back. Plus, the lumbar support is adjustable and the Kinesis hip belt actually moves with your every step to increase stability. If that weren't enough, there's also a trapdoor compartment at the bottom where you can access a sleeping bag (or other gear) without unloading the entire pack.

All this comes at a cost: weight. It's more than 4 pounds, the heaviest pack in this buyer's guide. If you load up the Revol to its 65-liter capacity, your three days' worth of supplies can easily weigh north of 50 pounds. On paper, adding 4 pounds doesn't seem like much, but after a few hours they'll feel like an extra 40.

The Revol 65 is a top-loader with two quick-release buckles, meaning the main section is virtually shielded from any drizzle or snow. However, in our shower testing, we were shocked to find that the bottom of the pack got damp. It appeared some moisture slipped into the trapdoor compartment through the stitching. Still, it's a technical trail pack that's crazy comfortable and highly functional.

PROS:
> Padded back panels, adjustable suspension system, and Kinesis hip belt
> Trap-door compartment
> Three-day pack that doesn't scream "bug-out bag!"
> It's packed (pun intended) with subtle smart features, including an external hydration sleeve, zippered pockets in the hip belt, dual grab handles, loops for trekking poles or ice axes, and a top stash pocket to keep phone and sunglasses from getting crushed.

CONS:
> At more than 4 pounds, it's about a pound heavier than we'd like.
> While the main section stayed dry, the trapdoor compartment got damp during our shower test.

RECOIL **OFFGRID** BEST BUG-OUT OPTION

 BODY FABRIC
210-denier Robic nylon ripstop

CAPACITY
65 liters (3,950 cubic inches)

DIMENSIONS
30 by 12 by 10 inches

WEIGHT
4 pounds, 3 ounces

 COLORS
Forest Green (shown), Raven

 MSRP
$220

 URL
www.kelty.com

Mountainsmith
Tanack 10L Lumbar Pack

Founded almost four decades ago by mountaineering guide Patrick Smith, Mountainsmith has been a staple among trailblazers because of its many ground-breaking patents. In recent years, the company has teamed up with photographer Chris Burkard to create a series of photography-focused packs. One of the latest collaborations is the Tanack 10 – the most hard-core fanny pack you'll ever see.

The Tanack 10's Cordura fabric is ridiculously tough, the zippers are guarded by external flaps, and there's a removable rain cover hidden in the base panel pocket. When encased in said rain cover, this lumbar pack is virtually waterproof. So naturally, we took the rain cover off to see how the lumbar pack would do naked. The results? Not ideal. Water managed to slip through, turning newsprint at the top and bottom damp.

Still, the Tanack 10 has numerous features to keep it as comfortable and convenient as possible: removable padded shoulder strap, two side pock-

ets for water bottles or other items, detachable interior bag for accessories that can be attached to the exterior, and a quick-release padded waist belt (which is compatible with the Mountainsmith Tanack 40 backpack).

Despite its name, the Tanack 10 actually has a 15-liter capacity – not a whole lot. However, it can be used as an improvised go-bag if feces suddenly meets fan or as a daypack on a hiking adventure. Of course, if you're into photography, it works best for those who want to stay mobile in challenging environments yet need quick access to their camera. (Though you'll need to pony up an extra $60 if you want padded dividers for your equipment.)

PROS:
❯ Durable materials combined with quality craftsmanship
❯ Included rain cover provides maximum protection from inclement weather
❯ Interior accessories pouch can transform into additional external storage

❯ Delta Compression System helps you adjust for different loads, cinching up as needed.

CONS:
❯ Too small to hold a substantial amount of survival supplies, yet weighs almost 2 pounds.
❯ Without the rain cover, the interior got wet while the exterior stayed damp the longest of all the packs tested.

BODY FABRIC
610-denier Cordura HP, 210-denier nylon liner

CAPACITY
15 liters (900 cubic inches)

DIMENSIONS
11.75 by 12.25 by 5.5 inches

WEIGHT
1 pound 13 ounces

COLORS
Barley (shown), Black

MSRP
$100

URL
www.mountainsmith.com

Is Budget Waterproofing Feasible?

Testing all the bags for our storm-proof backpack buyer's guide got us thinking: Is it feasible and possible to make a weather-resistant knapsack on the cheap? After all, not everyone has a hundred bucks lying around to spend on a brand-new dry bag. But a bottle of waterproofing wax runs for only $10.

To craft our own DIY stormproof backpack, we looked for a backpack that wasn't just affordable but also common (to approximate what one might find in an average household). Anyone who's ever attended high school in the past 50 years has owned or seen a JanSport bag, so we selected the Trans by JanSport SuperMax. It features a 15-inch padded laptop sleeve, four zippered compartments, and a lifetime guarantee. Price tag? Anywhere between $25 to $35 online.

Next came selecting the waterproof coating. There are all sorts or protectants available today, from silicone aerosols to durable water repellents (DWR) made of fluoropolymers. We chose a $9 bottle of Nikwax Tent & Gear SolarProof. Aside from being a water-based formula that's non-aerosol, non-flammable, and non-hazardous, it provides both H_2O repellency and shielding against UV damage.

Following the directions, we sprayed an even coat of Nikwax on the SuperMax, waited two minutes, and wiped excess liquid with a damp cloth. We let the pack dry overnight. The next day we performed our in-house rain simulation: stuffed it full of newsprint paper, closed all the zippers, and put it under a running showerhead for 10 minutes. Then we

wiped off the droplets on the pack's exterior.

So how did our DIY stormproof pack do? Like a drunk celebrity at a police checkpoint, it failed miserably. While the Nikwax did indeed help water bead up and stay on the surface of the polyester fabric, the coating couldn't stop H_2O from flowing through the seams or zippers, where our newsprint paper was most mush-like.

The lesson? You can paint a dinghy to look like a submarine, but that won't stop it from taking on water when you hit rough seas. If you're looking for a truly weatherproof pack for your next bug-out bag, make sure it was manufactured with weather-resistant properties in the first place, because a waterproof coating can only do so much.

Scrubba
Stealth Pack

Certainly the most unique entry in this buyer's guide, the Scrubba Stealth Pack is a four-in-one solution: a weatherproof backpack, a compression dry bag, a camp shower, and a portable washing machine. Yes, you read those last two functions correctly.

This invention came about when Scrubba founder Ash Newland of Australia and a friend were planning to climb Tanzania's Mount Kilimanjaro in 2010. They realized their cold-weather apparel and camping gear would take up most of the cargo space, leaving them room for just a few changes of casual clothes. Soon enough the first Scrubba bag was born.

The Stealth Pack version combines a waterproof roll-top bag, a flexible integrated washboard, and a multifunctional valve in one durable package. To use it as a washer, place your dirty clothes with some water and detergent inside the bag, close the roll-top closure, then scrub the garments for up to 3 minutes.

If you're in need of a shower after mucking around in the backcountry, just fill this dry bag with water, hang it from a tree, and let its black nylon soak up some sunrays. Then turn the valve and get a warm rinse in. If you're traveling, this Scrubba can act as compression bag. Fill it with clothes, squeeze out all the air, and tighten the valve. It'll stay compact, saving you luggage space.

As a dry bag, the Stealth Pack effortlessly passed our shower test with flying colors.

For serious survivalists, the Stealth Pack won't suffice as a primary BOB, but would shine as a valuable add-on thanks to its multipurpose design.

PROS:
› Can quadruple as a dry bag, compression bag, portable washer, and camp shower
› Weatherproof design and construction
› Outside-the-box design
› Excellent as a supplemental pack

CONS:
› Limited 21-liter capacity
› Like most dry bags, there's just one compartment; no internal or external pockets or pouches.

BODY FABRIC
Waterproof 40-denier nylon fabric, 210-denier nylon back panel

CAPACITY
21 liters (1,281 cubic inches)

DIMENSIONS
21 by 13 by 7 inches

WEIGHT
1 pound

COLORS
Black

MSRP
$100

URL
www.thescrubba.com

RECOIL OFFGRID BEST VALUE

H₂O Hack

As is the case with most survival gear, the higher the standards of quality and functionality we demand of our stormproof packs, the higher the price tags. So how can you keep your supplies dry if you can't afford an expensive dry bag?

If you're prepping on a budget, backpack designer Mel Terkla recommends two economical strategies.

"A built-in waterproof pack rain cover or a standalone one is the easiest way to keep the rain at bay," says Terkla, an independent designer who's worked for a variety of companies including Kifaru. "The other option is to separate all your gear into waterproof bags" before placing them in your backpack.

By "waterproof bags," he's referring to airtight plastic pouches made by companies such as Loksak. They look like zippered sandwich bags but are 100-percent waterproof, far more durable, and come in a variety of sizes. For example, Loksak's OPSAK can be as small as 7 by 7 inches or as large as 28 by 20 inches and start at $9.49 for a two-pack. If you're really pinching pennies, Terkla says, then use that money to get a box of Ziploc freezer bags and separate your survival gear accordingly.

As for rain covers, if your backpack doesn't come with one, you can find generic models for as little as $5 or quality brand covers starting at about $15, depending on size and compatibility.

"These two simple solutions will make your bag absolutely stormproof without any loss of durability," Terkla says.

Relocation Strategies

Safer Places in a Dangerous World

By Richard Duarte

 e've all heard the saying, "location, location, location." Real estate professionals commonly employ this phrase to emphasize how the value of similar properties can differ substantially, depending on where those properties are located. In other words, with all else being equal, location can (and usually will) dictate the appeal and value of a structure or a parcel of land. To many people, desirable locations often have certain traditional characteristics, including scenic views, stable neighborhoods, top-rated schools, proximity to quality healthcare, public transportation, entertainment, and shopping. Oth-

ers might consider more practical things, such as safety, economic development, jobs, population density, taxes, personal freedoms, elevation, and maybe even the ability to live a sustainable, self-sufficient life.

When it comes to surviving a natural or man-made crisis, however, location becomes even more significant, and there are many more factors to consider. Some of these elements can help you gauge if a particular location is desirable, and whether moving there can actually help you tip the scales of survivability in your favor.

In this article, we review some of the factors to consider when assessing locations for livability and survivability. We also review some of the ways to you manage

A rural parcel of land with a spring, lake, or pond ensures a stable and reliable water source, and tremendously increases the land's value.

a process that can at times seem completely unmanageable and overwhelming: evaluating all the variables for relocating to a safer and more "survivable" location.

Playing the Odds

When it comes to survival, where you choose to live, work, and play can make a huge difference. A preferred location can tip the odds heavily in your favor. A poor location, on the other hand, will most certainly have the opposite effect. The truth is, all locations come with some level of risk, and all will require some degree of adjustment and compromise.

Life holds absolutely no guarantees for any of us. The very best any of us can hope for is to take steps that afford us every possible advantage. We are, in effect, playing the odds and hoping that those odds come out in our favor as much as possible. This isn't rolling the dice; it's more like "loading the dice." While there are many things that you'll never be able to control, there are also many other areas where you actually have options; and here's where you should focus the majority of your attention.

Due Diligence

All important decisions should begin with thorough research, and an accurate assessment of the facts. In order to make solid, well-reasoned decisions, you'll need not only information, but accurate, well-researched information. This process will help you gather, study, weigh, and consider as many of the variables as possible.

For purposes of this article, here are some factors to consider:

Patience: Give yourself sufficient time to do solid research on a location, and to digest and analyze your findings. There will be lots of unknowns that gradually reveal themselves as you conduct your research. This is probably the most significant part of the process. If you rush it, you'll short-change yourself.

Objectives and priorities: If you don't clearly define what you're looking for, you're not likely to get it. Outline your objectives/priorities and keep that list front and center.

Keep an open mind: Never begin your research with bias, or preconceived notions of what you think, or hearsay. Look at everything with a "fresh set of eyes" and with absolutely no prejudgment.

Test your information: Throughout the course of your research, you may run across conflicting and contradictory information. Treat all this data, regardless of its source, with a healthy dose of skepticism.

Document your findings and keep good records: Start a file for each state or area that you're con-

sidering, and organize your findings in an easy-to-access spreadsheet/folder. You'll likely go back to the same information many times. It'll be far more effective and efficient if you organized your findings from the very start.

The Basics

What's the best location for increasing your chances of surviving a natural or man-made crisis? The simple truth is that there's no "best" location. Every place, no matter how attractive it may seem at first, will have its pros and cons. What you choose will depend largely on your particular needs and circumstances. A location that might be ideal for one person, could end up being the worst possible choice for someone else.

Coastal regions offer beaches, boating, and fishing. Access to a boat may also provide options for leaving an area quickly and without having to deal with the usual traffic. However, these regions may also be prone to storms and flooding.

Below are some of the more important categories that you should consider in your overall search parameters:

Population density: This is very significant. No matter the crisis, being close to a largely populated city center has the potential to make things much worse. The larger the population, the larger the chance of man-made problems arriving at your doorstep. (See "The Big Three" sidebar.)

Weather/climate: Cold or hot, humid or dry, windy or calm, quality air or pollution. All of these things matter, and oftentimes may even affect your overall health. Look for areas with mild to moderate climate, and try to avoid extremes. Also consider the length of the growing season, rainfall, flooding, and overall weather patterns, especially if you plan on growing your own food.

Jobs: No matter how self-sufficient you may be, you'll most likely still need some income. Traditional jobs are the most common source of income, but also consider working from home, or operating your own business — maybe even a home business. Research local regulations before you dive head-first into a business venture, since some states require all sorts of licenses and permits.

Economy: A thriving, growing and diverse economy offers the best chances for financial success no matter your particular circumstances. But a thriving economy will also attract people from far and wide, and can usually result in higher real estate prices, traffic, congestion, and an overall higher cost of living.

Hospitals and healthcare: Access to quality hospitals, physicians, specialists, dentists, and other medical facilities is often overlooked. Depending on your age and overall medical condition, this may or may not be high on your list of priorities, but remember, emergencies happen whether you plan for them or not.

Shopping: We're all consumers, and no matter how self-sufficient and independent we may be, we all need to shop. Do you mind driving long distances to pick up groceries, or do you need more convenient options? Also, the further goods have to travel to get to you, the more expensive they will be. Consider visiting some of the nearby shopping centers. It's amazing what you can learn by looking around and interacting with locals.

Public services: Having a wide array of public services can be a convenience to some and a burden to others. Remember, everything comes at a cost. The more services you get, the more taxes you'll pay. Finding

Many areas around the country offer mountain views and the possibility for remote living. But mountains also offer protection, security, and opportunities for harvesting natural resources like wood and game.

a balance is key. In some rural areas you'll need to plow your own roads, pay monthly subscription fees for fire department and EMS services, and you can forget about public transportation. Also, find out how reliable the grid power is, how often it's down, and if there are any alternatives.

Environment: Usually this refers to the natural environment and its overall health. Lots of areas in the U.S. have suffered tremendous damage at the hands of irresponsible corporate entities who have disposed of toxic waste into public waterways or landfills that eventually leak and contaminate the land. Also consider soil quality and study the type of crops that thrive in the area.

Education: Unless you plan to homeschool your kids, or grandchildren, the quality of the local schools is most likely very important, especially to young families. Research the local school districts, class sizes, technology use, percentage of certified teachers, grades, and rankings.

Cost of living: The overall cost of living will vary widely from one area to another. This should never be overlooked. If you expect your income to remain the same, or even decline, factoring in the anticipated cost of living is critical. Look at how your target location compares to neighboring states, and other comparable locations in similar cities or states. Fuel, heating, cooling, taxes, food, insurance, utilities, education, etc. — all these things add up. Start a spreadsheet and compare to other locations you might be considering. Do a cost benefit analysis; one area may have higher taxes, but may offer better schools, more public services, etc.

Taxes: Taxes represent a large chunk of most family budgets. Considering that just about everything we do is taxed, you'll want to determine the overall tax burden.

For example, some states like Florida, Wyoming, and Texas, have no state income tax, while others like New York, New Jersey, and California impose substantial state income taxes on top of the federal income taxes. Make sure to also consider sales tax, property taxes, and local taxes. (Tip: Research bordering states when considering a location. This will sometimes yield unexpected benefits, such as tax-free shopping a short drive across the state border.)

Homestead exemptions: Some states offer homeowners homestead exemptions on their primary residence. This represents a major advantage in two ways: (1) it may save you on property taxes; (2) it protects and shields your primary residence from some creditors. Certain states provide an exemption for the full value of the home, while others provide little to nothing.

Debtor rights: While all U.S. consumers have somewhat equal rights under federal law regarding debt collection, most states also have their own laws. Some states actually provide stronger protections. These

A free-flowing river or stream can often provide many options including a reliable water supply, and opportunities for fishing and hunting, since water usually attracts game.

protections are important and can often shield you, and your family, against overzealous collection efforts. Some states make it very easy for a potential creditor to levy against all your assets, including your home. Other states have laws that protect you and your assets, especially your primary residence.

Sustainability and self-reliance: Living a life of sustainability and self-reliance requires knowledge, skills, and having access to the proper resources. Geography, climate, and natural resources all play a role. Look for locations that provide an abundance of natural resources, including wood, water, and game.

Crime, security, and safety: Crime imposes an extremely high cost on society and its individual citizens. Few factors affect the quality of life in a community more than crime. Think increased police presence, increased security expenses, higher home and auto insurance rates, but also the physiological and emotional toll of living in fear. Note: True crime sometimes hides in the shadows. At first glance, a community may look nice, but the

Large urban areas are heavily congested, and have an extraordinarily high cost of living. Because of the population density, many of these urban areas have become very dangerous, especially during or after a natural or man-made crisis.

The Big Three:

The People Problem

Population density can become one of the biggest dangers to your safety and wellbeing, before, during, and in the aftermath of a crisis or public emergency. There's a very simple reason for this — during a crisis, these areas are likely to experience the most severe and extensive eruptions of violence, looting, rioting, and overall civil unrest. This isn't mere speculation; history has confirmed this sad reality time and again — when the SHTF, many people will be at their worst. Add to this a finely tuned infrastructure and supply chain that may be unable to keep pace with sudden changes to demand for food, water, sanitation, and public services. The more people there are in a given geographical area, the more precarious the situation will be. And as a disaster accelerates, trying to escape a high-density population center will become extremely difficult, if not impossible, unless you were able to get a jump on everybody else.

Personal Freedom

Where you choose to live can make a tremendous difference in how you live your life. Government regulations, limits on how you can use your property, how you can teach and educate your children, how you can make a living, and how you can feed yourself — all these things matter.

Some states seem to regulate even the smallest activities, while others tend to leave citizens alone to make their own choices and live their own lives. An intrusive government will always have a tendency to desire more power over you, and often even abuse its power. When considering your options, focus on locations with local and state governments that put a high value on personal responsibility, self-sufficiency, and freedom.

Risks – Natural and Man-Made

When considering the potential risks, people often focus on natural disasters, while ignoring or downplaying man-made disasters. Yet both are dangerous, and both can kill. Consider that no state is free from natural disasters, and that you'll usually trade one set of dangers for another. While the coastal states can suffer flooding, hurricanes, and other offshore hazards, many interior states are affected by tornadoes, wildfires, earthquakes, mudslides, or even volcanoes. No matter where you live, there'll always be risks. Avoid power plants, superfund sites, and areas affected by toxic contamination. Hazardous waste sites are scattered throughout the country. There are more than 1,300 of these "Superfund Sites" where toxic chemicals and other contaminants were dumped for years, polluting soil, water, and air.

The Great Migration

While there have always been patterns of migration throughout the United States, according to a U.S. Migration Report from North American Moving Services, 2020 saw Americans moving in record numbers. While some moves may have been influenced by COVID-19 and the fallout from lockdowns, job losses, and failing businesses, Americans continue actively leaving big cities for more rural locations as they've done in previous years.

This annual study tracked nearly all interstate and cross-border household relocations from January 1, 2020, to December 11, 2020. Here's a breakdown of the top states that Americans were moving to and leaving in 2020.

Top Inbound States:

Idaho (70%)

Arizona (64%)

South Carolina (63%)

Tennessee (63%)

North Carolina (61%)

Top Outbound States:

Illinois (69%)

New York (65%)

California (64%)

New Jersey (64%)

Maryland (61%)

In general, Americans are leaving the Northeast and Midwest in favor of the warmer climates, and the lower cost of living typically found in the Southeast and Southwest. Florida, Texas, and Colorado round out the top eight states for inbound moves. The full report, including an interactive map of the U.S., and a downloadable version of the report is available at www.northamerican.com/migration-map.

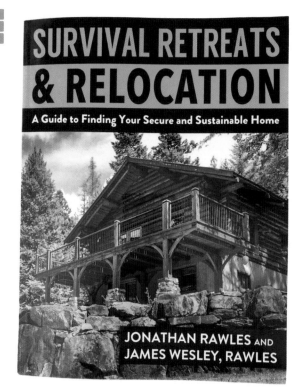

Survival Retreats & Relocation – A Guide to Finding Your Secure and Sustainable Home by Jonathan Rawles and James Wesley Rawles is an excellent resource for starting your research. It's also good for fine-tuning your search parameters using in-depth analysis and data specifically targeted for folks interested in the preparedness lifestyle, freedom, and self-sufficiency.

Strategic Relocation, North American Guide to Safe Places, 4th Edition by Joel M. Skousen and Andrew Skousen has long been a go-to resource for relocation research. In the 4th Edition, the authors have updated the state-by-state reviews to reflect demographics and other significant changes.

well-manicured lawns and picturesque downtown may not tell the full story. Research actual crime statistics, and look for specifics like the percentage of violent and property crimes, crimes per square mile, and how these measure up against national statistics. You can also call the non-emergency police number and request recent police call logs and crimes in a given area.

Self-defense and gun laws: Your ability to protect and defend yourself and your family is, and should always be, a top priority. Avoid, at all costs, states that restrict your ability to protect yourself and your loved ones. Also consider the laws that dictate when and where you may deploy a firearm in self-defense, and what your legal duties may be when using that firearm.

Water: Will you be relying on the public water system, your own private well, a river or stream, or rainwater collection? Where does public water come from? Are those

Rural areas will usually offer an abundance of solitude, privacy, and many opportunities for living a self-sufficient lifestyle.

sources safe and reliable? If the public water system fails, or is somehow compromised, would there be a reasonable alternative? It's important to know that some states have laws strictly regulating rainwater harvesting, while other states encourage and incentivize it.

Traffic: Look beyond commute times, and also research roads and road conditions, traffic patterns, traffic enforcement, and how drivers in the area are rated. Some states/cities are notorious for bad drivers, horrific accidents, and to no one's surprise – exorbitant auto insurance rates.

Insurance costs: Auto insurance, homeowner's insurance, even life and health insurance can vary depending on where you live. In areas with high likelihood of natural disasters (think hurricanes in Florida), you'll pay a premium for homeowner's coverage.

Air travel/airports: Being close to an airport can bring enormous advantages, but it comes at a cost — noise, traffic, congestion, pollution, and even potential aviation accidents. But if you're forced to travel often, this may be a trade-off you're willing to consider.

Overall wellbeing and livability: Certain locations feed the soul. For some, the mountains provide a deep calming connection to nature; others prefer being close to the ocean or a lake. The practical aspects of survival are very important, but so is being happy.

There are, of course, many other factors to consider. Entire books have been written on this topic, and we recommend that you read some of these books. Two of the most popular are *Survival Retreats & Relocation – A Guide to Finding Your Secure and Sustainable Home* by Jonathan Rawles and James Wesley Rawles, and *Strategic Relocation – North American Guide to Safe Places,*

4th Edition by Joel M. Skousen and Andrew Skousen. Both of these are excellent choices and will provide you with a wealth of material to consider, as well as insights, ideas, and suggestions on how to expand your research.

Wrap-Up

While there's no such thing as a "perfect" survival location, there are many safer locations to consider. Doing your research and taking advantage of existing resources can not only save you time and money, but can substantially increase your chances of success in finding a location that not only addresses your needs, but also provides an increased level of safety, security, and protection from both natural and man-made hazards. ⁘

SOURCES
> www.survivalreality.com
> www.joelskousen.com
> www.census.gov
> www.northamerican.com (2020 Migration Report)

BOOKS
Survival Retreats & Relocation by Jonathan Rawles & James Wesley Rawles
Strategic Relocation, North America by Joel Skousen

About the Author

Richard Duarte is an urban survival consultant, writer, and firearms enthusiast. He's the author of *Surviving Doomsday: A Guide for Surviving an Urban Disaster* and *The Quick Start Guide for Urban Preparedness.*

HYDRATION PACK
BUYER'S GUIDE

Water, Water Everywhere and Not a Drop to Drink...Unless You're Wearing it

Story by Martin Anders
Photos by Michael Grey

It's been almost a full day now and still, there's no one in sight. You estimate that you've been walking for about three hours since your last break and you're just about out of water. The two small bottles of water you carried got you this far, but you've got further to go. Three hours on your feet, and there hasn't been a sign of another living soul. There's got to be someone down this next stretch, you say to yourself.

Regardless if the above scenario played out on a nature hike or during a disaster, a lack of hydration can still be fatal. We won't belabor the reason why you'd need as much clean drinking water as possible. If you're reading this magazine, you already know why.

With space already limited in your pack and on your person, what's the best way to carry a large amount of water? Sure, you can carry a few half-liter bottles in a backpack or on a belt, but it can get mighty cumbersome and be an inefficient use of precious space. In this buyer's guide, we take a look at backpacks that are made to carry hydration reservoirs. Also called hydration packs, these backpacks have compartments for water bladders and furnishings that help route drinking tubes through and around the pack to keep them in place for ease of drinking.

What to Look For

Purpose: When buying a hydration pack, it's good to start out by deciding how much cargo space you need first. What's the purpose of this pack? Is it for a single-day hike? A multi-day camping trip? A get-home bag from the office in case all hell breaks loose? Pick the size of your bag accordingly.

Weight: Also be mindful of the overall weight after your gear and water is loaded into it. The great thing about a hydration pack is that it uses a refillable water reservoir that usually is positioned vertically on the back of the backpack. This helps with the overall balance of the bag, even when full with other gear.

Ease of Use: Consider how easy (or difficult) it is to access the reservoir for refilling and cleaning. Look at the hydration tube and make sure it's easy to access and stow while on the move. As with all gear considerations, these are personal choices that require some in-person fiddling

Frame Size: When buying a backpack, make sure the bag's size is suitable for your body's frame. An over- or undersized pack can reduce your stamina and create back problems you simply don't need to deal with while contending with the Apocalypse.

You wouldn't hike with an ill-fitting boot would you? A properly fitted pack can enhance your endurance and reduce fatigue. A reputable retailer should be able to help you choose the correct size backpack.

Bladder: A key factor to consider is the hydration bladders themselves. There are many different variations, so shop around. Investigate how easy or difficult each is to clean. Also examine how they're secured inside your pack of choice.

Yes, water is a heavy commodity to carry, but the difficulties of storing and carrying water is greatly reduced with the use of a hydration pack. Which one is right for you? Let's examine some of the newest models out now.

CAMELBAK®

RIM RUNNER
22

HYDRATION PACK

5.11
TRIAB 18 Backpack

Reservoir not included

DIMENSIONS
20 x 13 x 7 inches

WEIGHT
3 pounds, 4 ounces

COLORWAY
Midnight Ash (shown), Sandstone

MSRP
$140

URL
www.511tactical.com

NOTES
The TRIAB 18 is designed as a one-strap sling bag that can be used for a wide range of applications. For those who like a traditional-style pack, a second strap is also included for two-shoulder carry configuration. It's rugged and accommodates a hydration bladder in a slot pocket at the rear. It has hydration tube routing provisions at the top of the bag as well as on the shoulder straps. A unique feature is that the TRIAB 18's large main compartment is accessed through the bottom, requiring the user to set the bag down to open it up completely. For those who like access to the entire interior of the bag this is a good thing since, when unzipped, it opens up completely. It has MOLLE on the front and sides and has plenty of hidden zippered compartments throughout.

Pros:
> Modularity up the yin-yang
> Hidden compartments galore
> Sling bag that can be converted into a two-strap backpack

Cons:
> Access to main compartment is only through the bottom
> No reservoir included (it's shown here for demonstration purposes)

Black Diamond

Nitro 22 Pack

Reservoir not included

DIMENSIONS
19 x 10 x 7.5 inches

WEIGHT
2 pounds

COLORWAY
Moroccan Blue (shown), Deep Torch, Black

MSRP
$120

URL
www.blackdiamondequipment.com

NOTES
The Nitro 22 is a highly capable daypack with an external-access hydration sleeve that can accommodate reservoirs of varying sizes. Its right shoulder strap is fitted with several elasticized bands that are great for routing your reservoir's hydration tube. As its name suggests, it can fit 22 liters worth of gear and has plenty of pockets and compartments with which to do it. It's outfitted with a breathable backpanel and Black Diamond's reACTIV suspension to keep your back, arms, and shoulders cool and comfortable. The pack comes in two sizes to better fit the user for optimal long-term carry comfort. Zippered panels provide easy access to gear, while front, side, and hipbelt stretch pockets house need-to-reach essentials. A larger, 26-liter size of the Nitro is also available for those who need even more carrying capacity.

Pros:
> Good hydration management
> Zippered pocket on hip belt

Cons:
> Hip belt is not removable
> No reservoir included (it's shown here for demonstration purposes)

HYDRATION PACK

CamelBak
Rim Runner 22

DIMENSIONS
19.25 x 12.62 x 10.43 inches

WEIGHT
2 pounds, 1 ounce (with reservoir)

COLORWAY
Fallen Rock/Orchid Orange (shown), Sienna Red/Gunmetal, Charcoal/Chili Pepper

MSRP
$100

URL
shop.camelbak.com

NOTES
The Rim Runner is a good example of what CamelBak does best — make products with hydration as its central focus. This pack comes with its fantastic 3-liter capacity Antidote Reservoir, which also includes a quick-detachable hydration tube and bite valve. A zippered compartment at the rear of the pack has mounting points for the reservoir. Purpose-built tube routing hardware and straps keep the hydration tube neatly stored until needed. The Rim Runner's generous main compartment is accessed via an asymmetrical zipper that enables easy access and prevents cargo from spilling out when fully open. There is also a front organizer pocket for small items, two gear loops, and stretch mesh side pockets. A removable stability waist belt and four-point compression straps will keep your pack stable under any load. A CamelBak Air Channel back panel features center-channel ventilation and wicking mesh pods will keep you cool even on difficult terrain.

Pros:
> Comes with reservoir
> Easy access to compartments
> Good hydration management

Cons:
> It's hard to come up with a con for this pack

HYDRATION PACK

Elite Survival Systems
Pulse - 24-Hour Backpack

DIMENSIONS
19 x 11 x 8 inches

WEIGHT
3 pound, 12 ounces

COLORWAY
Coyote Tan (shown), Black

MSRP
$160 ($180 with 3L reservoir)

URL
www.elitesurvival.com

NOTES
Elite Survival System's Pulse is a feature-rich, hydration-ready pack that is constructed of 1,000-denier nylon and incorporates heavy-duty zippers that feature covered zipper chains to help prevent moisture seepage. The two rearmost compartments can both accommodate 3-liter hydration reservoirs with a simultaneous tube-routing system, giving you a total capacity of 6 liters of water. Its Hydrapak reservoirs are sold as add-ons to this pack for $20 each. It has three large, padded primary compartments with compression straps, and ample room for gear. Because liquids and gear can be heavy, a vented back panel is stiffened with an internal, aluminum spine to provide consistent support, added stability, and reduce load strain. A low-profile laser-cut PALS panel allows for plenty of customization opportunities and the paracord handle carry handle is quick detachable.

Pros:
> Large
> Rugged
> Plenty of organizational space
> Quick-detach paracord handle

Cons:
> Somewhat heavy
> The hydration compartment is a little undersized

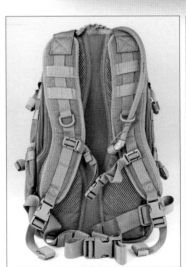
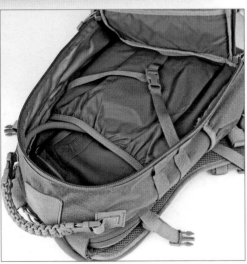

HYDRATION PACK

Condor Outdoor

Solveig Assault Pack

DIMENSIONS
20 x 11 x 6 inches

WEIGHT
3 pounds, 3 ounces

COLORWAY
Tan (shown), Black, Olive Drab

MSRP
$95

URL
www.condoroutdoor.com

NOTES
The Condor Solveig was originally conceived as a discreet assault pack and is jammed full of features. It has a padded pocket inside the main compartment that can be home to a hydration reservoir or a laptop. It has several hanger tabs to help secure the reservoir in place as well as a port for routing a hydration tube. At the back of the pack is a new airflow system for additional comfort and a drag handle that's reinforced with Hypalon for easier grip and durability. Its internal compartmentalization allows for plenty of organized storage space.

Pros:
› Rugged
› Wide mouth opening for interior
› Many options for add-ons

Cons:
› Hydration compartment is small
› No reservoir included (it's shown here for demonstration purposes)

Reservoir not included

HYDRATION PACK

Grey Ghost Gear
Stealth Operator Pack

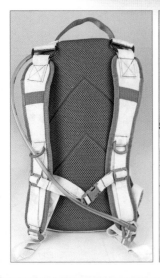

 DIMENSIONS
17 x 9 x 4 inches

 WEIGHT
1 pound, 5 ounces

 COLORWAY
14 colorways including, Kryptek Yeti (shown)

 MSRP
$109

URL
www.greyghostgear.com

NOTES
Grey Ghost Gear's Stealth Operator Pack is designed to blend into the crowd. The pack features a hydration pocket big enough to swallow up a 3-liter reservoir. Its main compartment has covered mesh compartments to keep smaller items in place. A center zip accessory pocket is easily accessible and contains admin and organizational pockets as well as a concealed holster to covertly carry a handgun. It also features a water-resistant coating on the backside of the fabric and a water-repellant coating on the face to keep everything inside dry. Heavy-duty zippers, grab handle, and a sternum strap round out this useful pack.

Pros:
› Easy-to-access front and main compartments
› Organized interior
› Lightweight

Cons:
› Bladder compartment is small, not very deep
› No reservoir included (it's shown here for demonstration purposes)

Reservoir not included

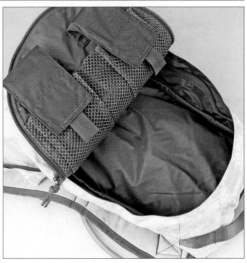

Tactical Tailor

Removable Operator Pack

Reservoir not included

DIMENSIONS
16.5 x 10 x 7 inches

WEIGHT
2 pounds, 3 ounces

COLORWAY
7 colors including Foliage Green (shown)

MSRP
$115 (as shown) to $135

URL
www.tacticaltailor.com

NOTES
The Removable Operator Pack is designed as a quick attach assault pack that attaches directly to Tactical Tailor's line of modular vests or larger packs. Think of it as a backpack for a backpack that can be used by itself. A separate hydration pocket accepts 2- or 3- liter bladders. Its shoulder straps have elastic straps that keep the hydration tube from flailing about. The Removable Operator Pack also features a large main compartment that is lined with high-visibility orange. This feature is nice to have in case you need to be seen by rescuers — and it makes it easier to find objects in its interior. For small items, a side entry front pocket is easy to get to. Because this can act as an add-on pack to larger packs, all hardware needed to attach the pack to other gear is also included.

Pros:
› Quality workmanship
› Bright interior is a good emergency signal

Cons:
› Overall size is limiting
› No reservoir included (it's shown here for demonstration purposes)

RECOIL

SUBSCRIPTIONS ARE NOW SAFE AND SECURE

SUBSCRIBE TODAY:
WWW.RECOILWEB.COM

ORDER TODAY

AND YOUR MAGAZINES
WILL BE SHIPPED TO
YOU IN A #4 LDPE 100%
RECYCLABLE POLYBAG
ALONG WITH A PROTECTIVE
PRIVACY INSERT TO KEEP
YOUR INVESTMENT SAFE.

**WE HEARD YOU LOUD AND CLEAR:
YOU DEMANDED MAGAZINE
SUBSCRIPTIONS AND WE'RE DELIVERING.**

RECOIL
P.O. Box 433229
Palm Coast, FL 32142-3229
ELECTRONIC SERVICE REQUESTED

Periodicals

RENEW ONLINE:
renew.recoilweb.com

RECOIL is now available for home-delivery and digital subscriptions.
A one-year subscription gets you six issues for $49.95. Unlike other magazines with thinner paper and dull covers,
the RECOIL issues sent to your door will retain all the same features that set us apart on the newsstands: thick
cover with gritty texture, high-quality paper stock throughout, and in-depth coverage of the gun lifestyle.

PREDATOR'S PACK

How to Assemble Tools to Fish, Trap, and Hunt in a Survival Situation

By **Kevin Estela**

 port fishing and hunting isn't the same as survival fishing and hunting. "Sport" implies there is an element of chance and fair play. To a survivor, the concept of rules and regulations should seem ridiculous. After all, why would a survivor or someone in an emergency consider the confines of sport fishing and hunting if they're starving? In a real disaster, there is no such thing as a bag limit, minimum length, or poaching.

As majestic as they are, in the absence of wildlife protection, even the bald eagle might be on the dinner table if you're hungry enough. We've been field tested and we know the frustration of watching supper run, swim, or fly away. We've also learned that with the right tools and a few no-nonsense ways of fishing and trapping, it's easy to make sure your dinner plate isn't empty at the end of the day.

The differentiator between frustrated and fed is preparing like a predator and casting aside socially acceptable methods of food procurement. We're not going to apologize for telling you how to kill prey and feed yourself with the gear and methods that follow. It's been said Chuck Norris doesn't hunt or fish because there's a chance for failure in those sports — he just kills sh*t. Follow our lead and you too can be like Chuck.

DISCLAIMER:
This article is meant to be a brief overview and not a detailed guide on improvised fishing, hunting, and trapping in survival situation. Check local regulations before attempting to use any tools or techniques discussed in this story.

10 Essentials
of the Predator Pack:

1. **Mosquito Head Net:** For use as a dip net
2. **Kevlar Thread:** Combined with gaff hooks for turtles
3. **Rat Traps:** Two to four for small game
4. **Gil Net:** Helps in catching larger fish
5. **Automatic Fisherman:** Great triggers for fishing or for small game
6. **Rabbit Snares:** Commercial grade (eight weigh approximately 1 pound)
7. **Sling Shot with Spare Bands:** For use as-is, or to rig up a Hawaiian sling
8. **Treble Hooks:** For predators or weight with split shot for snagging
9. **Flashlight:** Use with firearm for jacking or for frogging
10. **Frog Gigs:** for spearing frogs, fish, lizards, etc.

Luxury Items if Space Allows:

1. Extra fire-starter
2. Salt, pepper, oil, balsamic vinegar, and various spices to offset food boredom
3. Edible plant reference cards — no, one can't live on meat alone
4. Game processing blades, such as a small fillet and skinning blade
5. 110 Conibear: This trap is king, but each is heavy and bulky
6. .22 Pistol: Minimum 4-inch barrel.

Fishing

Sport fishing rules and regulation books may define fishing as a single baited hook attached to a pole held by an angler. This is meant to protect a species from overfishing. A lone survivor should not be limited. Some basic equipment provides an advantage over a single hook, line, and sinker setup.

Gill Net: Anyone who has seen the History Channel show *Alone* knows the concept of a gill net. Designed to capture fish by the gills, these nets work wonders if they're constructed to match the fish in your area. A gill net can be used in a stationary location, or it can be anchored on one side and walked through the water in an arc by holding the other side. A gill net can be set discretely underwater as well, if traveling unnoticed is a concern. It can also be fashioned into a scoop net or a net supported by a frame, and raised in and out of the water by a central point.

A gill net can be set above water or below water. When used with two poles, it can be moved through the water by two survivors. It's a versatile survival tool worth its weight in fish fillets. Just make sure to use the right size net for the fish you intend to catch.

Frog Spear: Made from steel and used for nighttime frog hunting, a good 3- to 5-prong frog spear will outperform any wooden spear crafted in the bush. Frog spears can be used on reptiles, amphibians, and small fish. They work exceptionally well when paired with a flashlight to temporarily blind your prey. Inexpensive Eagle Claw brand gigs are widely available and custom spears made from higher-quality steel ensure you have the right point for your spear.

Hawaiian Sling: A Hawaiian sling is a long thin-shafted spear with an elastic band attached to one end and a pointed barbed end on the other. The elastic band is looped around the hand, stretched, and the spear is held holding the energy back until the hand is relaxed and the spear is launched forward. These are highly effective as they don't require easily telegraphed body motions to thrust. The Mako 3-in-1 Take Down Pole Spear is an excellent choice if space allows. Otherwise, the survivor can pack surgical tubing, spear head, and lashing twine to make his own.

Hacking: This method of fishing involves using the back of a machete in a chopping motion against a fish spine in order to break it, making easy retrieval of your fish. The back of the blade is used to avoid accidentally cutting your leg. While blood works great as chum, using your own blood isn't advised. Attract fish with a lantern, LED headlamp, or a torch made from folded birch bark.

Long Line: Imagine a length of paracord with pieces of fishing line hanging off of it at different intervals and depths. These lines are just short enough to avoid tangling with one another, and since they're attached to a single long line, multiple fish can be caught with a single retrieve. The long line works well — so well that it's on the

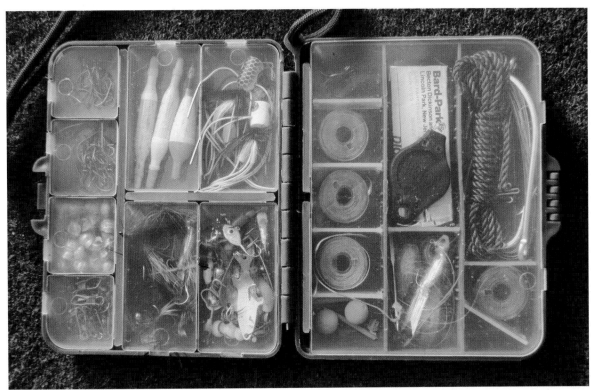

A well-stocked small fishing kit will take up very little space. A combination of dry fly poppers for bass, nymphs for trout, and jigs for panfish are all contained within the author's fishing kit.

radar of the humane society. That's good for you if you need to indiscriminately catch to put on your plate.

Automatic Fisherman Reels: Operated by a spring, these lightweight fishing reels automatically retrieve your fish after they swim away and trigger the mechanism. These reels do your work while you tend to other survival needs. They can work above water or underwater in iced-over conditions. The constant spring tension "plays" the fish and your prey will be tired when it's time to retrieve the unit from the water.

Collapsible Fishing Rod: Sometimes, you still need a good fishing rod to reach out to the fish biting just outside your reach. Three-piece (or more) fishing rods break down to less than 24 inches and are easily packable on the outside of a small ruck. From the inexpensive and durable Ugly Stick brand to higher-priced St. Croix Rods, there's an option for everyone. If space allows, it can't hurt to pack a small, ultra-light fishing rod and reel with some basic tackle. This combination this author used while in Alaska to feed himself for two weeks in the bush.

Trapping

A survivor should consider trapping before he considers hunting. It's easier to fashion traps than it is to make projectiles. A properly constructed trap can be just as effective as (or even more effective than) a hunter seeking out prey while burning calories and launching a projectile with questionable accuracy at a target, which may be situated in an awkward position.

5 Ways of
Stacking the Odds in Your Favor

Hunt at morning/night: Animals are most active during the early morning and late hours of the day. They tend to hunker down during the brightest hours of the day. To be more effective, avoid hunting and fishing when the sun is high. Spend your time building your kit and planning your predation during these hours.

Camouflage: Animals aren't foolish. Unless one is injured or ill, you probably won't be able to walk right up to it. Camouflage yourself to the environment. Use natural concealment to hide your presence. Minimize your footprint and blend in.

Bait/chum: Baiting or chumming animals is often illegal in many jurisdictions, but fair game for survival.. Don't discard, burn, or bury the entrails of an animal. Use the unwanted bits for scavenger bait. Raccoons and catfish are fond of scraps and both are edible.

Overset (quantity of traps): There's no such thing as too many traps. If you're capable of setting 10, set 10. If you can set 15, set 15. Set as many as possible and learn to set them correctly. Assume some of your traps will be triggered, but won't harvest game. Even a 20-percent chance of success out of 10 traps is better than 100-percent success on one.

Ambush (driving game): Many survival scenarios involve a single person. With a team of two or more stuck in an emergency, a team can be coordinated to drive animals into nets or toward an ambushing member with a club or spear. Utilize natural choke points and create a strategy. Work like a pack of wolves and be lethally efficient.

Rat Traps: Inexpensive, lightweight, and crazy effective against small rodents — do you need more reason to pack these? Oh that's right, if you have special skills, they work well to close circuits and make other traps for bigger threats. They can be baited with camp scraps or wild edibles gathered on the move.

Braided Picture Wire: The same wire you used to hang that painting of dogs playing cards is the kind you can use for creating snares. Braided wire is much tougher to break than solid copper or stainless wire of equal strength. The braid also grabs onto animal hair as your prey fights for its life. Depending where you are, the braided wire can also serve as fishing leader for fish with sharp teeth that would otherwise cut through your line.

Commercial Rabbit Snares: If space allows, carry real snares. They are often equipped with locking cams that prevent the snare from loosening after the animal realizes it's caught. These snares also have hardware designed to swivel to prevent the wire from kinking and breaking. If space allows, you can't beat a half dozen or more real snares. Just learn where and how to place them.

Flashlight: A high-intensity flashlight can help you confuse animals like ... well, a deer in headlights. There's a reason why hunting some game with a flashlight is often illegal — it's simply effective. A good flashlight can help the survivor catch animals by hiding behind the wall of light. Paired with a spear, club, firearm, or other hunting tool, a flashlight is a game-changer.

Build a Better Mousetrap: Litter is found in the most remote places around the globe and some of the best

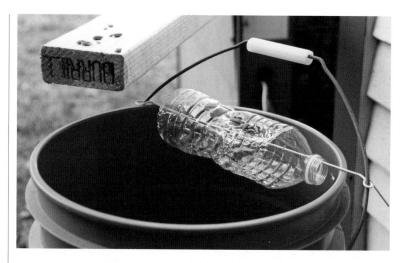

traps are repurposed garbage. An easy but highly effective mousetrap requires a bucket, a piece of wire, and a bottle. The wire is inserted through the bottle and poked through the bottom. The wire is extended over the top of the bucket and you're left with a roller like those found on *American Ninja Warrior*. The bottle is baited with seeds, nuts, or scraps of leftover food. When the mouse stands on the bottle, it rolls off into the bucket. If you fill the bucket with water, the mouse drowns. These traps have been used in farmhouses and barns for years and for good reason.

With a few scavenged materials, a survivor can create a highly effective rodent trap. Rodents are numerous, nutritious, and easily caught with a roller-bottle bucket trap.

Hunting

We've all known that one guy in our camp who takes the nearest piece of wood and sharpens it to a point for "bear protection." An equally comical explanation may be given about how he'll use that spear to get dinner. Aside

When Manuals Get it Wrong, Get it Right

Too many survival manuals are butchered and doctored from their original source. Once information leaves the author's control, editors and art layout folks have the potential to tweak a factually correct point into something foreign that's more pleasing to the eye than it is effective in the field. Here are a couple common mistakes leading to misconceptions we've found in the survival manuals in many bookstores today.

Spearing a fish: Have you ever tried hooking a minnow through the body with a steel hook? It isn't easy, and this is when you have one hand on the fish and one on the hook. How many survival manuals show a single pencil-point-style wooden spear going through a fish floating in the water? The best type of fish spear is a forked spear that pins the fish to the underwater bottom.

Complicated trap triggers: Some of the best trap triggers can be learned from classic poorly drawn survival manuals from true outdoorsmen. Many survival manuals today feature traps

we've never seen a single person construct and set on their own (though it may be possible with a steady-handed team of two or more). Intimate knowledge of a handful of triggers is better than limited knowledge of many. Don't try constructing anything that looks like the boulder Wile E. Coyote balanced upon a sharp point in the cartoon world to kill the Road Runner.

"M"-shaped fish trap: We've all seen that sketch in manuals. A set of sticks is driven into the ground to create a trap that resembles the letter "M." Sometimes the back of the trap is also cordoned off with a "C" shape to create a pen. This trap works as long as the conditions are right. It doesn't work in rocky creeks, or when the fish sought are able to wiggle through the gates (weave some horizontal branches between the vertical), and it sucks when fish won't swim into it. In rocky conditions, build a trap out of rocks and to get the fish to swim into the trap, beat the water with evergreen boughs as you walk from upstream down.

from scratching his ass, that "spear" won't work nearly as well as some of the hunting implements that'll put meat in the pot with a little practice. As previously mentioned, hunting does require energy and it burns calories, but this doesn't mean you should leave the hunting tools at home. Sometimes, shots present themselves, and you'll kick yourself if you could have taken it with any of the following.

Slingshot: Unless you grew up in a sheltered household with overbearing parents, you probably had a slingshot as a kid. At some point, you probably noticed how well it worked on soda cans, or managed to scare off the neighborhood cat or the birds that cat was chasing. Since your childhood, slingshots have come a long way and are now equipped with more powerful bands cut from Theraband Gold. As long as you practice, you can become extremely proficient with one, and it's possible to kill squirrels, rabbits, snakes, ducks, and other small game. Keep a spare set of bands in an airtight bag and use marbles, steel or lead shot, or small pebbles as ammo.

Bow and Arrow: While the slingshot works well and operates quietly enough for discreet hunting and undisturbed follow-up shots, the bow and arrow is the right tool for larger game and greater impact. The survivor can select field points, broadheads, or bludgeon points, depending on what animal is hunted. A good takedown bow that needs little maintenance along with a few arrows is easily packed opposite of the takedown fishing rod to balance out your pack.

.22 Pistol: If you're legally able to pack a quality .22 pistol, do it. In our experience, the .22 pistol is the king of compact survival firearms. Not quite rifle accurate, but accurate enough, the .22 is capable (with the right shot placement, of course) of putting food in your belly. A 4-inch barrel cuts velocity down, but not to a point it becomes impotent. Of course, if you can carry a longer barrel, do it. The increased sight radius will help you if you aren't running a micro red-dot.

Conclusion

There's no such thing as *fair* in the animal kingdom. Lions don't discriminate and will eat any easy meal they can sink their claws into. Wolves gang up and seek out the weaker animals, and sharks will hunt out the source of blood in the water even if it comes from one of their own. When a survivor takes on a predator mindset, he or she must be willing to accept the psychological conflict of killing immature or undersized game, destroying a nest for eggs, or maiming a cute and fuzzy animal and hearing it sound off in pain.

One must be willing to break sport hunting and fishing rules and regs if they want real results. From our experience, hunger is a great remedy for the guilt associated with *cheating*, and hunger can motivate the average person to unlock their primal self. Primal man existed long before sporting fair play. Next time you venture out, be prepared with your predator pack when you need to fill your belly at any cost.

Slingshots are not just kids' toys. When powered with modern bands, they're capable of dropping small game quietly with lead rounds, steel shot, or small pebbles.

Broadheads, field points, and bludgeon points can all be used from the same bow and arrow. If you have the room, a takedown bow and arrow makes a great addition to the predator pack.

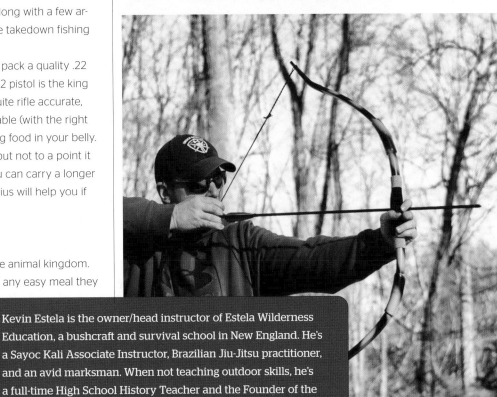

About The Author

Kevin Estela is the owner/head instructor of Estela Wilderness Education, a bushcraft and survival school in New England. He's a Sayoc Kali Associate Instructor, Brazilian Jiu-Jitsu practitioner, and an avid marksman. When not teaching outdoor skills, he's a full-time High School History Teacher and the Founder of the Estela Wilderness Education Fund. **www.kevinestela.com**

BUILD OR BUY?

Evaluating Premade Survival Backpacks for Kids

By Bernie Carr
Photos by Bernie Carr and RECOIL OFFGRID Staff

Despite parents' best efforts, large-scale disasters often result in kids getting separated from families. During Hurricane Katrina, more than 5,000 children were displaced. Fortunately, nearly all of them were later reunited with their families, but the search process took several days. There's always a chance you won't be with your kids when an emergency happens, which underscores the importance of equipping your children with a survival backpack and teaching them how to use its contents.

In this modern era of off-the-shelf conveniences, there's the temptation of letting someone else do the work and assuming that careful deliberation went into

the selection of products. Way back in RECOIL OFF-GRID Issue 6, we reviewed a few premade bug-out bags with mixed results. Now we turn our attention to three premade survival backpacks geared toward children. We evaluated each of them for quality, price, practicality, and a few other key criteria. We also assembled our own DIY survival pack to show how you can build custom load-outs for your kids based on your budget and their needs.

Why Buy a Premade Survival Back-pack?

The main reason to buy a premade survival kit is convenience. Many parents — especially those who aren't experienced preppers — may not have the time, energy,

or understanding of how to build a survival kit. This quick purchase is intended to cover a child's basic needs for a set amount of time, such as 72 hours.

Prepackaged survival kits are designed to cover basic requirements like respiration, water, food, light, shelter or warmth, and communication. They'll save you time and help eliminate the guesswork on what to include. In some cases, manufacturers buy the items in bulk and are able to pass the savings on to you. By ordering one survival kit for each child, you can check it off your to-do list in a matter of days.

On the other hand, a prepackaged survival kit is by definition "one size fits all." We all know every child is different and has unique preferences and abilities. For

Large-scale disasters often result in kids getting separated from families. **During Hurricane Katrina, more than 5,000 children were displaced.**

just a few of the points you must consider before deciding if a premade kit is sufficient for your kid.

What Should a Child's Survival Backpack Include?

In general, a child's survival kit should include the basics:

Water: Most preparedness sites, including Ready.gov, recommend a gallon of water per person per day for drinking and sanitation. However, for a portable survival kit, that amount of water would be too heavy for a child to carry. Include at least six 4-ounce water bottles for children under 11 years of age.

Food: Food in the survival backpack should have a long shelf life, be lightweight, and easy to consume without much (if any) preparation.

Respiration: At least one disposable mask should be included to offer some protection against smoke, dust, contaminants, or debris in the air.

Lighting: A basic flashlight or some glowsticks would be easy to operate, even for little hands.

Communication: A way to signal for help, such as a whistle and mirror, would ensure your child will have a way to communicate.

Hygiene: Include a few personal care supplies such as toothbrush, travel-sized toothpaste, tissues, soap, shampoo, and anti-bacterial gel.

Warmth: A blanket will help keep your child warm in case temperatures drop and there's no heat. A poncho will help them stay dry in the rain.

First aid: Even small kids know they need an adhesive bandage if they a get a cut. A simple first-aid kit containing disinfecting wipes and adhesive bandages will help them deal with small wounds or insect bites.

Entertainment/comfort items: There can be a lot of downtime while being stuck indoors during a storm, especially in a power outage. Kids can get more anxious if they have no way to keep their minds occupied. Include a few items for entertainment, such as a small game or activity book. A small plush toy can also provide comfort.

Considerations

When building your child's survival backpack, you'll need to be mindful of your child's size, age, strength, and ability to understand how to use the included contents. Smaller children may not be able to carry a larger pack, so the weight of the backpack is a consideration. Another factor is ease of use. While an adult survival kit may have several compartments and pockets, the child's backpack should be simple and clearly organized so they can readily find what they need.

example, some children may not like the taste of the food bars provided, but in a survival situation, some food is better than no food at all. You also have a baseline of included products you won't have to hunt down, but you can also embellish these with your own personal changes if desired. Would your child refuse to eat the food bars, be too young to use some of the tools, or leave the pack behind because it's too heavy? These are

Personalize Your Child's Survival Backpack

》 Include a family photo.

》 Add a letter to your child assuring them you'll do everything you can to get to them as soon as possible. I also added a few little jokes of my own to cheer them up.

》 For older children, consider adding $20 in cash.

》 If your child uses an inhaler or has other medical conditions, consider including a supply of what they'll need in the kit. However, if the kit is being used at school, you may need to clear it with the school authorities.

》 Include an "In Case of Emergency" (ICE) card and tuck the card into the backpack in case your child is separated from you. Fill in your name, address, and phone number so emergency personnel can contact you.

Introducing Your Child to the Survival Backpack

As soon as you receive your child's survival backpack, inspect the contents and determine their appropriateness to your child's age and maturity. Examine each item and decide whether or not your child can or will be able to use it. For example, would your child be able to purify water using chlorine tablets? If you determine your child wouldn't understand how to use purification tablets correctly, then omit them.

Each of the survival backpacks included in this guide has items still in the packaging, as well as batteries needing to be installed in the radios and flashlights. You'll need to set up the items so they're ready for your child to use.

Once you've examined the kit, show it to your child and discuss the contents together. Go over situations that they may face and how the kit can help them during events where you may be separated from them for an extended period, such as an earthquake during school hours, power outage, storms and associated flooding, or a tornado/hurricane where children are evacuated to a shelter.

Reassurance is part of the process in getting them comfortable with the idea of the pack's purpose. It's important to remind your child that if they're thrust into a situation where they have to use it, it doesn't mean you're not coming to pick them up — it's just something they can use while they're waiting for you. Make it a fun learning experience, but be sure to keep your discussion grounded in reality so they know it's not just make-believe.

Unless your child is already familiar with basic survival skills, they may not know what each item is for. Talk about each item's purpose and how and when they'd use it.

Maintenance

Buying or building your child's survival backpack is not a one-time task. There is some maintenance involved. The kit will need to change as they grow and their needs evolve. You'll also need to replace any clothes in the survival kit when the seasons change or when your child outgrows them. Check expiration dates annually and replace items that have expired. Check and replace the batteries in electronic devices such as radios and flashlights periodically to ensure they still work properly and haven't corroded. If you make it a habit to go through your own survival pack periodically, it'll be easy to check your family's packs at the same time.

Premade Survival Backpacks

MAKE & MODEL
The Cure Inc.
Children's Survival Kit

COLORS
red, white, and black

DIMENSIONS
15 by 12 by 6 inches

WEIGHT
8.5 pounds

MSRP
$80

URL
www.thecuresafety.com

FOOD
》 Pack of 6 400-calorie Mainstay food bars

WATER
》 12 4-ounce water pouches
》 10 water purification tablets
》 1 straw

LIGHT
》 1 LED rechargeable flashlight – recharges by squeezing the handle which generates and stores power
》 3 12-hour light sticks

SHELTER/WARMTH
》 1 fleece blanket
》 1 plastic poncho
》 1 16-hour hand/body warmer
》 1 small pair of winter gloves

RESPIRATION
》 1 N95 dust mask

COMMUNICATION
》 5-in-1 survival whistle (includes signaling mirror, whistle, mini compass, fire-starter flint, and storage container)
》 1 pocket AM/FM radio with earbuds

HYGIENE
》 1 toothbrush
》 1 tube of toothpaste
》 1 mini bar of soap
》 9 packets wet wipes
》 3 pocket tissue packs

FIRST AID
》 37-piece portable first aid kit includes:
》 10 plastic adhesive bandages 3/4 x 3
》 10 plastic adhesive bandages 3/8 x 1/2
》 2 gauze pads
》 3 alcohol cleansing pads
》 1 butterfly closure
》 10 cotton tips in a reusable case

ENTERTAINMENT
》 1 activity coloring book
》 4 crayons
》 1 children's fishing toy

MAKE & MODEL
Stealth Angel Survival
1 Person Survival Kit for Children (72 Hours)

COLORS
camo; red, white, and blue. Waterproof dry bag and duffel bag versions are available as well.

DIMENSIONS
15 by 12 by 6 inches

WEIGHT
8.5 pounds

MSRP
$88

URL
www.stealthangelsurvival.com

FOOD
》 Pack of 6 400-calorie Mainstay food bars

WATER
》 12 4-ounce water pouches
》 10 water purification tablets
》 1 straw

LIGHT
》 1 LED rechargeable flashlight – recharges by squeezing the handle which generates and stores power
》 3 12-hour light sticks

SHELTER/WARMTH
》 1 fleece blanket
》 1 plastic poncho
》 1 16-hour hand/body warmer
》 1 small pair of winter gloves

RESPIRATION
》 1 N95 dust mask

COMMUNICATION
》 5-in-1 survival whistle (includes signaling mirror, whistle, mini compass, fire-starter flint, and storage container)
》 1 pocket AM/FM radio with earbuds

HYGIENE
》 1 toothbrush
》 1 tube of toothpaste
》 1 mini bar of soap
》 9 packets wet wipes
》 3 pocket tissue packs

FIRST AID
》 37-piece portable first aid kit includes:
》 10 plastic adhesive bandages 3/4 x 3
》 10 plastic adhesive bandages 3/8 x 1/2
》 2 gauze pads
》 3 alcohol cleansing pads
》 1 butterfly closure
》 10 cotton tips in a reusable case

ENTERTAINMENT
》 1 activity coloring book
》 4 crayons
》 1 children's fishing toy

3 MAKE & MODEL
Emergency Zone
Keep-Me-Safe Children's
72 Hour Survival Kit

COLORS
Black, navy, pink, purple, red, or royal blue

DIMENSIONS
18 by 9 by 12 inches

WEIGHT
6.5 pounds

MSRP
$60

URL
www.emergencyzone.com

FOOD
» Pack of 6 400-calorie SOS Emergency Food Rations
» 2 energy bars

WATER
» 6 4-ounce water pouches
» 1 plastic sports water bottle

LIGHT
» 1 rubber flashlight with 2 AA batteries
» 1 light stick

SHELTER/WARMTH
» 1 reflective blanket
» 1 plastic poncho
» 1 mylar blanket
» 3 hand warmers

RESPIRATION
» 1 N95 dust mask

COMMUNICATION
» 1 whistle

HYGIENE
» 1 toothbrush
» 1 tube of toothpaste
» 1 mini bar of soap
» 6 packets wet wipes
» 1 packet conditioning shampoo
» 1 mini comb
» washcloth

FIRST AID
» Pack of 10 children's bandages

ENTERTAINMENT
» 1 small plush bear
» 2 activity books
» 4 crayons
» 1 pad of paper and mini pencil

Visit us online at
offgridweb.com
for more
information on
each survival bag

Findings

It was very interesting to examine each item included in these survival backpacks. Here are my findings, as well as some retrospective tips:

Compare the itemized list to the photo: I noticed the written description doesn't always match up with the photo. For example, The Cure Inc. didn't have the pocket radio and earbuds included in the description, but these items appear in the photo. The actual kit I received did include the pocket radio and earbuds. The description for Stealth Angel's 1 Person Survival Kit for Children listed a "16 Function Tool, safety goggles, and sewing kit" in the description, but they don't appear in the photo, nor were they included in the kit I received. The Keep Me Safe description didn't itemize every item, but provided a general description of the contents. The photo on the website did match the actual items received. If you're not sure whether an item is included or not, call the customer service number to clarify exactly what's included.

Compare prices: The Cure Inc. Children's Survival Kit and Stealth Angel 1 Person Survival Kit for Children have identical contents. At the time of purchase, The Cure Inc. Children's Survival Kit was listed at $56.95 and Stealth Angel 1 Person Survival Kit for Children at $77.95, although these prices have since changed. The only

difference was that Stealth Angel offers a few different styles to choose from: a backpack in red, white, and blue; a camo backpack; a waterproof sack; or a red duffel-style bag. These style and color changes also affect the price by a few dollars. The Cure Inc. only offers the backpack in red, white, and black. Does this warrant the difference in price? The choice is yours, but this is an example of *caveat emptor.*

Food: All three backpacks contained a good amount of food for a child. Mainstay and SOS both contain high calories and nutrition, and are filling. The Cure Inc. and Stealth Angel Survival both included six Mainstay bars — the child can eat two bars per day. Keep Me Safe Children's 72-Hour Kit included six SOS Bars, which are also high nutrition and high-calorie bars, and they also included two extra energy bars.

Water: Both The Cure Inc. and Stealth Angel Survival packs included 12 4-ounce water pouches; 10 water purification tables, and one straw. The purification tablets would be appropriate for older children who have learned about water purification. Keep Me Safe included six 4-ounce water pouches and one plastic sports water bottle.

Light: All three provided flashlights that worked just fine. The Cure Inc. and Stealth Angel provided three light sticks, while Keep Me Safe only provided one.

Money-Saving Tips for Creating a Survival Backpack for Children

)) Reuse or recycle items you already have around the house. You can use last school year's backpack as an emergency kit. As long as it's clean and undamaged, you can repurpose it as a survival backpack.

)) Collect freebies, such as the toothbrush and travel toothpaste your dentist gives at your dental checkup, samples from your doctor's office, complimentary hotel soaps, shampoo etc.

)) If your child receives a surplus of toys and stocking-stuffers at Christmas, reserve a couple of toys they may have overlooked and stash them in the survival backpack.

)) Buy some of the items in bulk such as food bars, water pouches, etc. and split the cost and quantities with other family members. You can all get more prepared at the same time!

)) As of this writing, first-aid kits and sunscreen can be purchased using a flexible spending account (FSA) or health savings account (HSA). Check your employee benefit package and see what your FSA or HSA covers.

Warmth: All three provided adequate warming items in the pack. Both The Cure Inc. and Stealth Angel included a pair of children's gloves, which was a nice touch.

Communication: All three provided whistles, but Keep Me Safe's whistle was a basic one, while the other two brands provided a 5-in-1 survival whistle that also included a small mirror, which can be used for signaling.

Respiration: All three included the same N-95 mask.

Hygiene: They all provided good items to help with hygiene; however, the tissue packs included by The Cure Inc. and Stealth Angel are easier for a child to use than the washcloth.

First Aid: The pack of 10 children's bandages provided by Keep Me Safe wasn't as robust as the 37-piece portable first-aid kit included with The Cure Inc. and Stealth Angel, as theirs included alcohol cleansing pads as well as various sizes of bandages and gauze pads.

Entertainment: They all had adequate entertainment options, with Keep Me Safe having a slight edge since they included a pad and pencil, along with a small plush toy younger children would appreciate.

Conclusion

After comparing all the contents, I would have to say that The Cure Inc., with contents identical to the Keep Me Safe kit at a lower price, came out ahead. ⁂

DIY Survival Backpack

After deciding what I wanted to see in a child's survival backpack, I went ahead and assembled one myself. First, I collected items I already had in the house. Then, I shopped for a child's backpack at our local Goodwill store. I soon found one that was the right size. Better yet, it looked new and still had store tags. I also purchased a few items at the .99 Only Store.

It took me about a day to search for items around the house, and another couple of days to order and shop for the rest of the items. I included six mini

THE COMPONENTS

CONTAINER	School backpack	Goodwill	$6.99
FOOD	Pack of 12: Soft granola bars	Grocery store	$3.99
WATER	6 4-ounce water pouches	.99 Only Store	$0.99
	LifeStraw	Amazon	$14.89
	Sports bottle	Previously owned	N/A
LIGHT	Flashlight	Previously owned	N/A
	Light sticks	.99 Only Store	$.99
SHELTER AND WARMTH	Fleece blanket	Previously owned	N/A
	Plastic poncho	Previously owned	N/A
	Small pair of winter gloves	Goodwill	$0.99
AIR	N95 dust mask	.99 Only Store	$0.99
COMMUNICATION	5-in-one survival whistle (includes signaling mirror, whistle, mini compass, firestarter flint and storage container)	Previously owned	N/A
HYGIENE	Toothbrush	Previously owned	N/A
	Toothpaste	Previously owned	N/A
	Mini bar of soap	Previously owned	N/A
	Pack of wet wipes	.99 Only Store	$0.99
	2 tissue packs	.99 Only Store	$0.99
	Antibacterial gel	.99 Only Store	$0.99
FIRST AID	12-piece portable first aid kit-includes 2 plastic adhesive bandages 3/4 x 3 in; 4 plastic adhesive bandages 5/8 x ¼ in; 4 gauze pads; 2 cleansing wipes	.99 Only Store	$0.99
PERSONAL CARE	Lip balm	Previously owned	N/A
	Sunscreen stick	Previously owned	N/A
	Natrapel 12-hour insect repellent (DEET free) wipes	Previously owned	N/A
ENTERTAINMENT	1 activity coloring book, 4 crayons, 1 children's fishing toy	.99 Only Store	$0.99

water bottles to save on weight, but I included a sport bottle along with a LifeStraw, which removes bacteria such as E. coli and salmonella and parasites such as giardia and cryptosporidium from water. During the initial stage of a disaster, water still runs from the tap but may have to be filtered for safety. The LifeStraw will serve as a good water filter and can be used with the sport bottle. I'd also go over how to use the LifeStraw with my child ahead of time.

Another area I deviated from the commercial backpacks was in the personal care area. I included sunscreen, lip balm, and insect repellent. These are optional items that you may want to consider.

Although my DIY survival backpack total cost less than my top pick from The Cure Inc., I have to consider that not everyone may have an extra flashlight, plastic poncho, or survival whistle. In addition, The Cure Inc. Children's Survival Kit also included Mainstay Bars, which are higher calorie than your average granola bar, and a mini radio that I didn't include. The prices for these items could add around $20 more to my cost, to total closer to $55. Factoring in the fuel I used picking up items and the time I spent assembling the kit, the decision isn't as clear-cut as you might've expected.

Whether you decide to buy a pre-made survival kit or create it yourself, you'll have taken an important step to help your child stay safe in the event of a disaster.

PURE HYDRATION

Comparing Three Portable, High-Output Water Purifiers

By **Patrick McCarthy**

ater is one of the fundamental elements required for human life. If you're completely cut off from any form of drinking water, you could die in as little as three days, depending on environmental factors and your level of physical exertion. However, a total absence of water usually isn't the problem — it's much more likely that you'll be able to find a lake, pond, creek, or a puddle somewhere in the vicinity. Even if these natural water sources look clean, they can be teeming with dangerous bacteria (such as Cholera and E. coli) that would only be visible through a microscope. Even if they smell clean, they can contain dormant parasites (such as cryptosporidium and giardia) and viruses (such as hepatitis A and norovirus). Even if they're not shallow or stagnant, they might be carrying the remnants of a rotting animal corpse or raw sewage from further upstream. Instead of rolling the dice and hoping you don't end up puking your guts out in a few hours, you should always have a plan to purify water in the field.

Narrowing Down the Options

Boiling is a tried-and-true method of killing invisible pathogens in water, but it's far from convenient. You'll need to set up camp, start a fire, gather water in a heat-resistant vessel (assuming you have one), wait for it to reach a rolling boil, and wait some more for it to cool enough to drink. Chemical purifier tablets or droplets don't require a heat source, but most need at least half an hour to take effect, and many leave an unpleasant aftertaste. You might also recall one of the numerous improvised water-purification techniques we've discussed in previous issues, such as a solar still. All of these are valuable techniques to know, but we wouldn't rely on any of them as a primary means of purifying water. They also won't help to strain out the unappealing muck and floaties that are swirling in your cup.

As usual, humans have solved this problem by using our brains and opposable thumbs to craft tools. Portable water purifiers allow us to produce safe, drinkable water in seconds rather than minutes or hours, without using up our consumable resources. Inexpensive, compact straw-style filters such as the LifeStraw are good for occasional use or emergencies, but they have some downsides. First, they're powered by suction, so it's tiring to gather more than a few gulps of water. Second — with a few exceptions such as the Sawyer Squeeze — they must be used on-site at a body of water, rather than offering a means of portable hydration. There's a reason our ancestors started carrying water in animal hides, gourds, and other vessels thousands of years ago — it allowed us to venture further from the rivers and coastlines.

With all of this in mind, we rounded up three water purifiers that share some of our key criteria for backpacking, camping, or survival outdoors. Each of them uses pressure to rapidly push water through a filter, instead of forcing the user to go blue in the face sucking gallons through a tiny straw. All three also feature ways to help you carry water on the move — either an integrated bottle, an output hose to fill your reservoir of choice, or both. These purifiers are small and light enough to easily fit into a backpack, and most importantly, they offer high-level protection against the most common waterborne pathogens: bacteria, protozoan cysts, and viruses. They'll also filter out sediment, certain dissolved chemicals, and heavy metals, thereby improving the taste, odor, and clarity of even the grimiest water source you can track down.

Setting the Bar

How pure should water be before you can consider it safe to drink? Two major safety certification organizations, NSF International and ANSI, joined forces to create a standard called NSF/ANSI P231 that answers that question. Based on data from a U.S. Environmental Protection Agency report titled "Guide Standard and Protocol for Testing Microbiological Water Purifiers," they concluded that at a minimum, water purifiers should remove 99.9999 percent of bacteria, 99.9 percent of protozoan cysts, and 99.99 percent of viruses from water.

Before you say this sounds like splitting hairs, let's look at an example. Say you have a cup of water that contains exactly 1,000,000 illness-causing microbes. Basic math tells us that eliminating 99 percent of those microbes would leave 10,000 in the cup — more than enough to make you sick. A 99.9 percent reduction rating would remove all but 1,000, 99.99 percent would remove all but 100, and so on. No water purifier can promise 100-percent effectiveness, but each one of these decimal places offers extra assurance against serious illness.

Much like body armor and tourniquets, water purifiers can be considered life-saving emergency equipment. You don't want to trust your life to something that will probably be good enough; you want something that has been proven to meet the highest standards. Choose carefully.

In the chart below, each • represents one decimal place after 99 percent.

	Bacteria	Protozoan Cysts	Viruses	Conclusion
NSF/ANSI P231 Standard	••••	•	••	
GRAYL	••••	•	••	Meets standard in all categories.
LifeSaver	••••	•••	••	Meets standard for bacteria and viruses. Exceeds standard for protozoan cysts.
Survivor Filter	•••*	•••	•••	May not meet standard* for bacteria. Exceeds standard in other categories.

*See our notes on the Survivor Filter for more details.

GRAYL GeoPress

DIMENSIONS: 3.4 by 10.4 inches

WEIGHT: 1 pound

LIFESPAN: 250 liters / 350 refills per replaceable cartridge ($30 each)

MSRP: $90

URL: grayl.com

WHAT CAN IT DO?

We weren't able to find a PDF of test results for the GeoPress on Grayl's site. However, the company clearly states that it was "independently tested by a certified laboratory" and shown to remove 99.9999 percent of bacteria, 99.9 percent of protozoan cysts, and 99.99 percent of viruses. This claim meets the NSF/ANSI P231 standard.

HOW DOES IT WORK?

1. Pull apart to separate outer sleeve from purifier.

2. Fill sleeve with dirty water to indicated maximum line.

3. Loosen "Simplevent" spout cap by a half turn to allow air to escape. Then, press purifier firmly into sleeve, forcing water up through the purifier cartridge.

NOTES:

Back in our "H2O Hygiene" buyer's guide in Issue 15, we reviewed the predecessor to this purifier, the Grayl Ultralight, and awarded it our "Top Pick" above seven other competitors. The GeoPress is essentially a larger version of the same concept, but with a few notable improvements. Its capacity is now 24 fluid ounces, allowing the user to filter more water per press and travel further between refills. The styling is more appealing, with rubberized Topogrip accents and a variety of color combinations to choose from. But the most important upgrades are found on the cap. While it can be unscrewed and removed like the Ultralight, it also has a small pour spout with a second protective cap. This makes it more convenient to drink from, and greatly reduces the risk of cross-contamination while pressing on the purifier. There's even a loop for carrying it or clipping it to gear. As much as we liked the Ultralight, the GeoPress outshines it in every way, as long as you can accept that it's a tiny bit heavier (5 ounces, to be exact).

PROS:

❭ Wonderfully fast and convenient — just scoop, press down for 8 seconds, and drink

❭ 24-ounce capacity makes this a good stand-alone bottle

❭ This cap design is a huge improvement compared to the old Ultralight. It protects the spout from contamination and allows air to vent without exposing the clean water.

CONS:

❭ Grayl repeatedly states that the GeoPress meets the NSF/ANSI P231 standard, and the listed reduction specs match this claim. However, we'd have a little more peace of mind if we could validate the reduction ratings by viewing the test results firsthand.

❭ Relatively short cartridge lifespan leads to a higher long-term operating cost

LifeSaver Liberty

DIMENSIONS: 3.2 by 10 inches

WEIGHT: 1.2 pounds / 1.4 pounds with accessories

LIFESPAN: 2,000 liters / 5,000 refills per replaceable cartridge ($55 each)

MSRP: $140

URL: iconlifesaver.com

WHAT CAN IT DO?

Independently tested by BCS Laboratories in Gainesville, Florida. A summary of test results is available in PDF format on the manufacturer's website. This purifier was shown to remove more than 99.9999 percent of bacteria, 99.999 percent of protozoan cysts, and more than 99.99 percent of viruses. These results exceed the NSF/ANSI P231 standard.

HOW DOES IT WORK?

BOTTLE MODE

1. Unscrew base of purifier, and scoop dirty water into the reservoir.

2. Tightly screw on base, then twist bottom cap a half turn to unlock pump handle. Pump three times.

3. Unscrew top cap and rotate white flow valve 90 degrees to release pressurized water from nozzle. Continue pumping to maintain flow rate as needed.

PUMP MODE

Attach scavenger hose to inlet on bottom cap. Place float in dirty water source. Open lid and water flow valve, then pump continuously to maintain flow rate.

NOTES:

Much like the Grayl GeoPress improved upon the Ultralight, the LifeSaver Liberty is an evolution of this UK-based company's previous purifier, the original LifeSaver Bottle. We also reviewed that purifier back in Issue 15. The Liberty condenses LifeSaver's ultra-filtration technology into a smaller package. The durable body is available in five different colors, each with black rubberized accents and clear windows to show the water level inside its 400-milliliter (13.5 fluid ounces) container. Twisting the top cap a half turn reveals an output nozzle surrounded by a sports-drink-style rubber bite protector. An optional hose can be connected here to pipe clean water into a bottle or bladder, or the entire purifier can be inverted and screwed onto a wide-mouth bottle. Our favorite feature is the scavenger hose attachment, which comes in a drawstring carry bag. Hooking it up converts this bottle into an in-line pump that can process 1.2 liters of clean water per minute. For quick fill-ups on the trail, it can be used in bottle mode, but pump mode is our first choice for use on longer treks or at a campsite.

PROS:

> Extremely versatile — can be used as a stand-alone bottle, threaded onto a wide-mouth Nalgene, or installed in-line on a CamelBak with the optional hydration tube adapter ($22)

> Pressurized water stream is useful for washing hands or dishes

> Bottle mode works well for individuals; pump mode is great for families and small groups

CONS:

> Immersing the container to fill its reservoir immerses the output side of the purifier in dirty water. If the protective cap isn't fully tightened, this could lead to cross-contamination of the purified water nozzle.

> The white plastic flow valve lever is thin and seems like it might snap off easily. We would've preferred a larger, sturdier knob for this critical control.

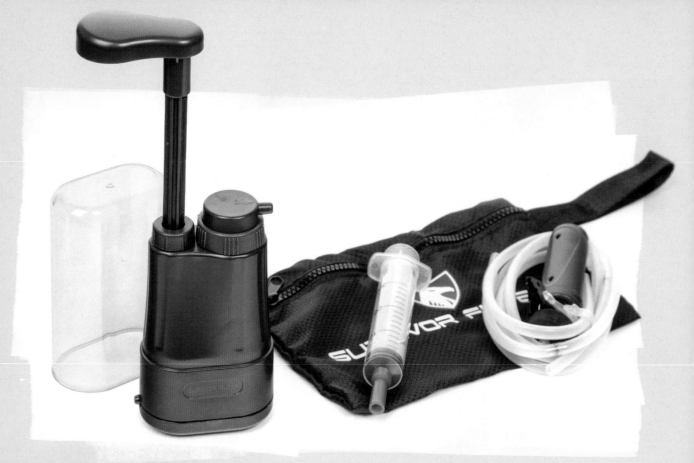

Survivor Filter Pro

DIMENSIONS: 4.5 by 7.5 by 3 inches

WEIGHT: 1.2 pounds

LIFESPAN: 100,000 liters for replaceable pre-filter and ultra-filter ($30 for both); 2,000 liters for replaceable carbon filter ($15 each)

MSRP: $70

URL: survivorfilter.com

WHAT CAN IT DO?

Independently tested by Intertek in Columbus, Ohio, for bacteria and virus reduction; independently tested by BCS Laboratories in Gainesville, Florida, for protozoan cyst reduction. Both test results are available in PDF format on the manufacturer's website. This purifier was shown to remove more than 99.999 percent of bacteria, more than 99.999 percent of protozoan cysts, and more than 99.999 percent of viruses.

HOW DOES IT WORK?

Connect inlet hose to lower nozzle, and place float in dirty water source. Remove clear plastic cap from unit and connect outlet hose to upper nozzle (marked "OUT"). Place end of outlet hose in the clear plastic cap, or a clean water reservoir of your choice, using the included clip to hold it in place if necessary. Pump handle to maintain flow rate.

NOTES:

The most compact purifier of our trio, the Survivor Filter Pro exclusively functions as a pump device. It can't carry water internally like the other two, but it does have a clear plastic cover that doubles as a cup in a pinch. Otherwise, just stick the outlet hose into your favorite bottle, canteen, or hydration bladder. Working the manual pump produces approximately 500 milliliters of clean water per minute. Much like straw filters, flow rate will gradually decrease over time as the filter becomes clogged. A backflush syringe is included to push clean water back through the filter, which will restore original flow rate in less than a minute. For those who don't want to lift a finger, an electric-powered Pro X version ($125) is also available and uses two AA batteries to produce the same flow rate with the press of a button.

PROS:

❯ Packs away neatly into the included carrying case, and doesn't occupy much space in your ruck

❯ Low price and long-lasting, user-serviceable filter make this a budget-friendly choice

CONS:

❯ The results don't *conclusively* prove that it meets the P231 standard for bacteria, since "more than 99.999%" is not necessarily the same as "99.9999% or more." Despite this technicality, it seems very likely that it would pass.

❯ Its flow rate is the slowest of any of the purifiers we tested — less than half that of the LifeSaver, and 1/10th that of the Grayl.

❯ Packing recently used clean and dirty water hoses in the same carrying case could lead to cross-contamination. A larger plastic cover would've allowed the output hose to be stored safely inside.

BLADESHOW

BLADESHOW West

BLADESHOW Texas

FOR DETAILS ON ALL THREE EVENTS, GO TO

BLADESHOW.COM

CONNECT WITH US AT #BLADESHOW

Preps Of The Pros

Tom Marshall

Current Occupation: Editor, RECOIL OFF-GRID Magazine

Part I: EDC

What is your general approach/philosophy for everyday-carry tools? What do you see as the most likely threats/issues you might deal with in your daily routine, and what items are necessary to address these issues?

I believe that equipment selection is a form of mission analysis. In simpler terms, it's impossible to carry every piece of gear for every single possibility. So, select tools for EDC that fit most seamlessly into your daily wardrobe and routine, and those which will be the most helpful in the most likely problems you might face.

Please outline the gear you carry on a daily basis. Include specific brands/models, and why you chose each.

A sturdy belt is the foundation of a solid EDC setup. I use a Mastermind Tactics Specialist Pro belt, which features medical-grade, high-cycle hook-and-loop, a chemically dipped stiffened tail end, and an almost non-existent

steel loop in lieu of a larger buckle to help reduce printing when carrying appendix inside the waistband (AIWB). In my pants pockets, I have a Zero Tolerance 0566 folding knife, a Cloud Defensive MCH flashlight, pocket trauma kit from Live The Creed, and a small keychain with Glow Rhino prybar, Carbon Tactics TiSlice razor blade, and two tools from Gearward: their Ranger Bic waterproof lighter sleeve and keychain duct tape roll. I keep this on a second key ring, completely separate from my car and house keys. This way, if I lose my daily life keys, or hand them off to someone, I still have the emergency tools. My Suunto Traverse Alpha watch also wears the Gearward A-K band, which conceals some escape tools. If the situation dictates, I'll add my custom Glock 48 MOS pistol and a spare mag in my LAS Concealment Ronin-L holster, and/or the JB Knife Ditch Pik fixed-blade defensive knife.

What is one underrated piece of EDC gear that more people should strongly consider carrying, if they don't already?

I always go by the rule of "The Big 4:" Defend, Move, Communicate, Medicate. Your EDC should include tools that enable you to defend yourself, navigate your daily world (urban or rural), call or signal for help, and treat likely medical issues (boo-boo level or trauma).

What was the most recent change you made to your EDC kit?

I recently swapped my smartphone into a Juggernaut IMPCT case. In addition to offering military-grade bump and drop protection, the IMPCT is compatible with Juggernaut's line of mounts and brackets. Now I can pop my phone off my belt and directly onto my plate carrier, hiking pack, or dashboard vehicle bracket.

Part II: Go Bag

Which make/model of bag did you choose, and why?

I use a 5.11 AMP12. This bag is large enough to hold not only my daily work supplies (laptop, chargers, cords, snacks, paperwork, etc.) but is also augmented by a Grey Man Tactical Rigid Insert Panel, sized specifically for this bag.

Where is this bag staged (or carried) and what specific purpose does it fulfill in your daily preparedness plan?

I carry this bag almost every single day — to the coffee shop or cigar lounge while working on articles, to business luncheons, and on road trips. If I need to fly, I can remove the Grey Man panel with weapons and pyro on it, without having to disassemble each individual pouch and tool, and still have all my administrative gear in a carry-on bag that fits under an airline seat.

Please outline some of the most important items you have in this bag, to include brands/models where possible. Discuss why you chose these items and how they complement and expand upon your EDC gear from Part I.

I augment the main compartment of this bag with a Rigid Insert Panel from Grey Man Tactical. This is a single polymer panel that I can permanently mount gear on, that can be removed as a single piece without having to dismantle all the individual pouches. The RIP holds a customized Glock 17 in a QVO Tactical holster on a G-Code RTI mount, one spare magazine, a multi-tool, smoke signal, 5.11 compact Operator Axe, and North American Rescue IFAK with full trauma kit and hard tourniquet. This supplements my EDC by providing medical and self-defense redundancy with the addition of a hard tourniquet (which I don't carry on-body) and a larger, more capable handgun. The ax can be used for everything from cutting brush or small trees for shelter or fire-starting to emergency egress from a building or vehicle (smashing a window or breaching residential-grade doors).

The rest of the bag holds general-use first aid supplies (Band-Aids, pain relievers, cold/flu meds, etc.) as well as a compass, NATO issue TCCC reference cards, pens/pencils, business cards, etc.

What is one extra item you've considered including in this bag? Briefly explain why you haven't added it yet (space, weight, cost, likelihood it'll be needed, etc.).

I've gone back and forth about adding some food to this bag — even something quick like meal bars or dried fruit or granola. Whether it's for snacking during a day full of meetings, getting stuck on the side of the road, or on an airport layover, extra calories become a priority quickly as stress levels rise. I haven't really stuck with it due to a combination of not having much physical space left in this bag, and that sometimes finding food that's edible on the go but holds stable in the desert heat can be a difficult task, especially if the bag is left in my truck or sits at my feet outdoors for any length of time.

The AMP's zip-pouches hold important paperwork, pens and pencils, and some basic travel meds like cough drops, analgesics, and gastrointestinal remedies.

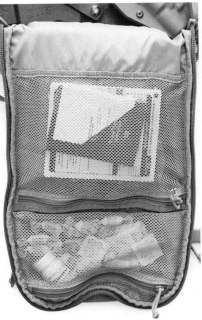
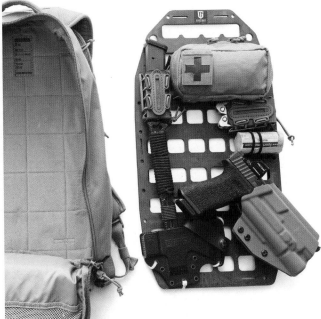

Patrick Diedrich

Residence: Hancock, Upper Michigan
Occupation: Writer and amateur blade/
blacksmith

Part I: EDC

What is your general approach/philosophy for everyday carry tools? What do you see as the most likely threats/issues you might deal with in your daily routine, and what items are necessary to address these issues?

If I were to sum up my approach to EDC, it would be "versatile redundancy." Every item carried should have more than one function and should complement each other. Since I live in a remote area, finding myself stranded due to unforeseen circumstances is a very real possibility. So, being able to signal for help, create a fire for warmth, or improvise my way to safety governs what I leave the house with.

In my region, crime is low, so I usually do not feel the need to carry a firearm. The exception is when I purposefully head into the wilderness to recreate or hunt, where there are large predatory mammals that do pose a potential danger. A Walther PDP accompanies me in a G-Code Drop Leg rig via a Kydex holster from T-Rex Arms. The PDP is fitted with a Leupold DeltaPoint Pro and a Streamlight TLR-7 light.

Please outline the gear you carry on a daily basis. Include specific brands/models, and why you chose each.

Having a well-made knife is a crucial part of my EDC. If I am out and about in town, I like to bring the WESN Micro Blade. If I am spending time in the great outdoors, I like to have a multi-tool as well as a fixed blade like the Corvus Survival Carrion. My key ring has become part of my EDC kit, and includes a Griffin pocket tool, as well as a CPR face shield in case I find myself needing to give life-saving support to someone.

I almost never leave without a Wazoo Cache belt. The belt is packed with the Wazoo Adventure Kit, which provides 23 tools including several tools for fire-starting and water purification, a button compass, high-quality cordage and wire, a fishing kit, a whistle, and a signal mirror. If I'm on the road for a few days, I'll put some extra cash in the belt. The Tasmanian Tiger wallet shields the chips in my debit card, driver's license, and passport from being scanned and exploited remotely.

What is one underrated piece of EDC gear that more people should strongly consider carrying, if they don't already?

There are two things that I think are always overlooked. One is a dedicated light source. Having a light has been useful on so many occasions. The Wazoo button light doesn't have the bulk or awkwardness of larger lights and can be stored in the cache belt or put on a key ring. It comes in handy when rummaging through bags when it's dark out, looking for items that were dropped in between seats, and can be used to attract attention as an emergency signal or as a light source for night tracking. The other thing that's overlooked, and should be a part of everyone's EDC, is physical fitness. All the gear in the world is never going to help if you do not have the physical strength or endurance to make it through a tough situation.

What was the most recent change you made to your EDC kit?

Last year, I had the pleasure of meeting survival expert Jerry Saunders of Corvus Survival. When we were talking about his EDC, it turns out that he also uses a Wazoo cache belt as well, and he mentioned lock picks. I had a lightbulb moment when I heard this, because if I lost my keys, needed to get into a building for shelter, or needed to open a medicine cabinet in an emergency, a set of lock picks would be extremely helpful. This led me to a company called Serepick. They have an array of picks to choose from, and even a see-through tumbler lock that you can practice with. At present, I am only mildly proficient, but my skills are improving. The set of picks I have fits easily in the cache belt along with everything else.

Part II: Go Bag

Which make/model of bag did you choose, and why?

Mystery Ranch makes a line of bags designed for cold weather environments in various volumes, but I use the Saddle Peak. Where I live, it seems like nine months of the year is nothing but cold temperatures and snow, and the Saddle Peak was designed to keep zippers from icing shut and the material from degrading due to frozen temperatures. The front pouch was specifically designed to house an avalanche kit. It also has straps on the outside for snow mobility tools like skis, snowboards, and snowshoes. Initially, I used it as a cold weather emergency bag, but it has evolved into my search and rescue (SAR) 24-hour Ready Pack, and I always have it prepped and handy.

Where is this bag staged (or carried) and what spe-

cific purpose does it fulfill in your daily preparedness plan?

The bag is always ready to go and sitting close to my front door. Normally, if I am called to a SAR operation, the only additional item I add is a freshly filled 3L CamelBak. When I return, I make it a priority to clean and restock what was used so that everything is ready again. Besides being a really useful SAR pack, it also makes a great bug-out bag, because it has everything I would need to sustain a small group for a few days. Also, if I know I'll be driving in inclement weather, I can toss it in the back of the truck in case of an emergency on the road.

Please outline some of the most important items you have in this bag, to include brands/models where possible. Discuss why you chose these items and how they complement and expand upon your EDC gear from Part I.

I usually adapt it based on the season and how long I expect to be wearing it. For example, if I think I'll be responding to a SAR operation that could last days, I will pack a camp stove, mess kit, and extra food. I may even bring a second bag with extra clothing to change and restock during the event. But, typically, it's just this one pack with as little as I can get away with. There are some who claim that a 24-hour pack should be at least 35 to 45 liters, but by keeping it around 25L, I force myself to pack only what's necessary and useful. Even so, when this pack is filled to the max, it can still weigh a little over 30 pounds.

During the winter months, the front pouch contains a Black Diamond avalanche kit with a collapsible snow shovel and probe. In the main compartment, I have:

- 3L CamelBak hydration pouch
- My handy military poncho, which doubles as a tarp or hasty shelter
- Blizzard EMS hypothermia blanket rated for cold weather

- Fire-starting kit, which includes SOL Fire cubes, UCO Stormproof Matches, an Exotac Ferro Rod, and a BIC lighter
- Silky Gomboy folding saw
- Several bungee cords and zip ties
- Small, waterproof first aid kit and large CPR mask
- Some Nutrient Survival food kits and SaltStick electrolyte chews

There is a smaller compartment on top where I keep a Fenix Raptor headlamp, a 5.11 Response hand flashlight, and extra high-visibility marking tape. In winter months, I also keep Oakley ski goggles and a neck gaiter in this pouch. On the hip straps, I keep an extra compass, a MOLLE pouch with 50 feet of 550 cord, an IFAK, and a Nalgene Survival Filter bottle if the windchill threatens to freeze the tube on my CamelBak. Lastly, on the shoulder straps, I hook several chemlights for trail marking or signaling, and a Varusteleka Terava Jaakaripuukko 110 knife.

What is one extra item you've considered including in this bag? Briefly explain why you haven't added it yet (space, weight, cost, likelihood it'll be needed, etc.).

Since this bag is quite minimalistic for what it's used for, all the gear prevents me from effectively storing a change of clothes, a more robust shelter, or room for extra layers if working in the cold starts generating too much sweat. I can strap extras to the outside, but there's the risk that nature will claim whatever isn't fastened securely enough. My hesitation to change to a pack with more volume comes from not wanting to fill that space with more stuff — which almost inevitably happens — and creating a pack that weighs more. I like to stay light on my feet so as not expend valuable calories as a pack-mule and being able to burn the energy when it matters. ▪

The Walther PDP is simple, reliable, affordable, and offers 18+1 rounds on tap in the full-size frame seen here.

On-Body IFAKs

By **Joey Nickischer**

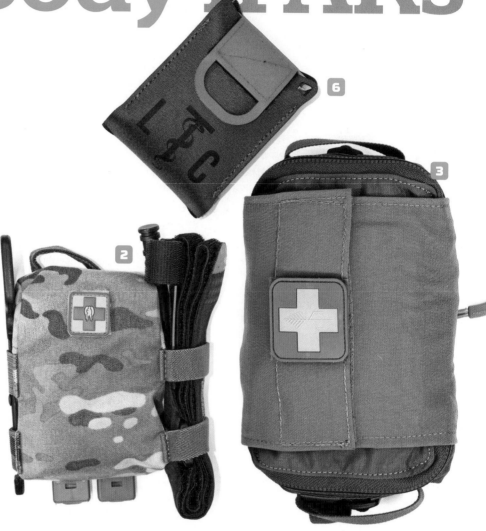

The on-body IFAK (Individual First-Aid Kit) has been a standard item in military kit for generations and has become common with police, fire, and other first responders. As the trend goes with smart ideas, it's now becoming common with hunters, hikers, and savvy moms at the playground.

Minor accidents and injuries happen all the time and it's nice to be able to just deal with the issue on the spot, rather than having to run home or dash off to the closest store for the needed equipment. But on top of that, some of the better-equipped IFAKs contain trauma dressings and tourniquets, for when the absolute worst happens and minutes or seconds can mean the difference between life, death, or long-term impairment, while waiting for a 9-1-1 response.

Naturally, your personal IFAK will vary depending on the level of your training, your destination, and even your outfit. It's not socially acceptable to wear a business suit and have a large, red IFAK worn on your belt. However, a pocket or ankle carry kit will likely go unnoticed to all but the most astute observer. Likewise, a larger kit could blend well with your backpack-style water carrier while you're hitting the trail or single-track forest path on your mountain bike. For whatever your social engagement, there's a kit that fits your needs.

---

1 Ryker Nylon Gear
4WS AFAK

DIMENSIONS:
6 H by 17 W by 2 D (full) inches

COLORS:
Black, Coyote Brown, Gray, Ranger Green

INCLUDES:
Pouch only

MSRP
$75

URL
rykernylongear.com

---

2 Dark Angel Medical
Every Day Carry (EDC) Trauma Kit

DIMENSIONS:
4.5 H by 3.25 W by 1.25 D inches

COLORS:
Black, Coyote Brown, MultiCam, Ranger Green, Red

INCLUDES:
Pouch, hemostatic gauze, nitrile gloves, mini compression bandage, pair of Hyfin Vent Compact chest seals

MSRP
$100

URL
darkangelmedical.com

---

3 Arbor Arms
Medical Nut Ruck Small

DIMENSIONS:
5.5 H by 7.5 W by 2 D inches

COLORS:
Black, Coyote Brown, Grey, MultiCam, MultiCam Black, Ranger Green

INCLUDES:
Pouch, 5x elastic bands, 1x wrap

MSRP
$60

URL
arborarmsusa.com

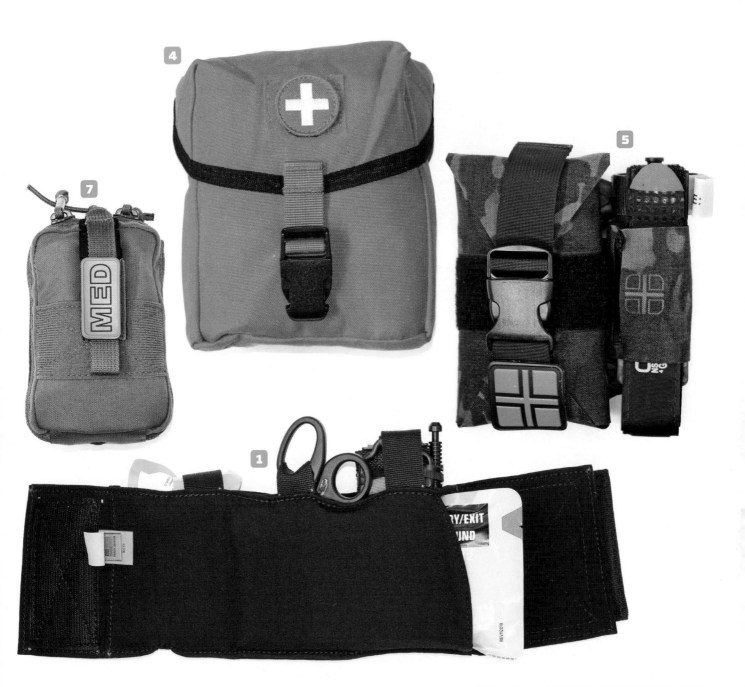

4 Doom and Bloom
Ultimate Compact First Aid Trauma Kit Grab N Go

📏 **DIMENSIONS:**
7 H by 6 W by 4.75 D inches

⭘ **COLORS:**
Black, Coyote, Digital Camo, Red

➕ **INCLUDES:**
A lot! (see notes)

$ **MSRP**
$99

🌐 **URL**
doomandbloom.net

5 Live the Creed
Responder IFAK

📏 **DIMENSIONS:**
7 H by 4.5 W by 1.5 D inches

⭘ **COLORS:**
Black, Coyote, MultiCam, MutiCam Black, Ranger Green, Wolf Grey

➕ **INCLUDES:**
Pouch, QuikClot Combat Gauze, NAR HyFin Vent Compact chest seal, nasopharyngeal airway, H&H Mini Israeli bandage, trauma shears, XL Bear Claw gloves

$ **MSRP**
$150

🌐 **URL**
ltcreed.com

6 Live the Creed
EDC Pocket Trauma Kit

📏 **DIMENSIONS:**
5.5 H by 3.5 W by 1.25 D inches

⭘ **COLORS:**
Black/Red, Coyote/Red, Grey, MutiCam Black/Wolf, Ranger Green/Black, Wolf Grey/Red

➕ **INCLUDES:**
Pouch, SWAT-Tourniquet, QuikClot Dressing, Tan XL nitrile gloves, bandages, wound closure strips, iodine wipe, alcohol wipe, bacitracin ointment

$ **MSRP**
$75

🌐 **URL**
ltcreed.com

7 North American Rescue
Enhanced Trauma Aid Kit (ETAK)

📏 **DIMENSIONS:**
5.75 H by 4 W by 1.75 D inches

⭘ **COLORS:**
Black, Coyote, MultiCam, Ranger Green

➕ **INCLUDES:**
HyFin Vent Twin Pack, wound packing gauze, 4-inch mini emergency trauma dressing, large black nitrile gloves, permanent marker

$ **MSRP**
$85

🌐 **URL**
ltcreed.com

Ryker Nylon Gear
4WS AFAK

A nice take on the IFAK, the Ryker Nylon Gear AFAK is an ankle worn kit, which keeps it discreetly out of the way when wearing a suit and tie, or keeping your tactical vest uncluttered. It features three vertical pockets with hook- and loop-style retention straps and one long horizontal pocket on the smooth back side. It's designed to hold their AFAK Medical Supply Kit (sold separately, $134), which includes an orange SOF Tactical Tourniquet, QuikCot Combat Gauze, HyFin Vent chest seal twin pack, trauma shear, and Black-Fire latex-free nitrile gloves. This will cover the basics of major trauma, like a sucking chest wound or arterial bleed. I found this kit to be more comfortable worn over a high-top boot, but love the ankle concealment aspect.

Pros:
❯ Discreet carry, keeps chest and waist free for other uses

Cons:
❯ Can be uncomfortable on skin for prolonged wear

Dark Angel Medical
Every Day Carry (EDC) Trauma Kit

Compact and lightweight, this pouch features a Hypalon panel on the back with cuts made for the included MALICE clips, and a belt channel that'll fit up to a 2-inch-wide belt. There are webbing loops on the right side that can hold a pair of reduced-size trauma shears (not included), and elastic loops on the left to hold a tourniquet (not included). I particularly like the design of the large loop pull handle on the top of the flap for fast, break-away style access in an emergency. You have to pull this flap away from you, not toward your body as on common pouches. There's even a loop square on the front of the pouch for the included red cross identifier, or your 1-inch patch of choice. This kit comes standard with QuikClot Bleeding Control Dressing, but ChitoGauze XR Pro is available for a small upcharge.

Pros:
❯ Size, excellent top opening, quick access to tourniquet and shears

Cons:
❯ Tourniquet windlass juts out a bit

Arbor Arms
Medical Nut Ruck Small

The Arbor Arms Medical Nut Ruck Small is a very versatile and customizable pouch. It can be worn as a traditional fanny pack with its stowable/removable waist strap, which can be either side-release or G-hook. You could also attach it directly to their SALT belt system or similar MOLLE gun belt via snap-on side-release buckles or the built-in Velcro flap, or to a plate carrier with their First Spear Tube Hanger (not included). The Check-Mate panel on the inner back wall of the pouch offers a ton of versatility for a customizable setup. The Medical Nut Ruck Small is 80 percent of the size of the slightly larger Standard Ruck ($80), which is designed to hold the contents of the U.S. Army issue IFAK, while the even larger Plus variation ($90) is designed to hold the contents of the USMC IFAK.

Pros:
❯ Duty-grade construction, numerous mounting options, modularity, fanny pack strap is standard

Cons:
❯ Sold as an empty bag with no medical supplies available, most options are extra cost

Doom and Bloom
Ultimate Compact First Aid Trauma Kit Grab N Go

If you're looking for the most comprehensive IFAK assortment for your journey to the local trail, you may have found your kit. This kit includes: pouch, CPR instruction booklet, tourniquet, "how to stop bleeding" instructions on waterproof paper, surgical face mask, hand sanitizer packets, 4-inch Israeli bandage, Celox 2gm powder, organic cayenne pepper powder (35,000HU), raw unprocessed honey packets, 6-inch gauze, 4-inch ACE bandage, stainless steel Mayo scissors, four nitrile gloves, 3M Steri Strips, super glue, 4x3-inch Moleskin, 3x4-inch gauze, Burn Jel packets, insect repellent packets, Bacitracin packets, 4x4-inch gauze, ABD 5x8-inch dressing pads, 2x4-inch Band-Aids, 1x3-inch Band-Aids, triangular bandage, medical tape, iodine wipes, alcohol wipes, ibuprofen tablets, and a 12-hour glowstick. The pouch features a hook-and-loop first-aid patch, high-quality quick-release buckle, and MOLLE attachment system.

Pros:
❯ Contains a little of everything, can effectively deal with many minor issues

Cons:
❯ Big, bulky, better suited to minor injuries than major trauma

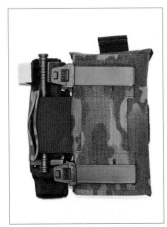

Live The Creed
Responder IFAK

Live The Creed
EDC Pocket Trauma Kit

North American Rescue
Enhanced Trauma Aid Kit (ETAK)

This is a strong, compact, and very well-secured IFAK. It's made from laser-cut laminated Cordura and secured with a medium-sized 1.5-inch quick-release buckle. The narrow profile has a different design than most other pouches. It has both top and bottom pass-through openings (or left and right, depending on the pouch orientation), so supplies can be removed from either side. And the included trauma supplies fit nice and snug, no wasted space and no frills. The Responder IFAK can be mounted horizontally to any MOLLE platform or belts up to 2.5 inches, or vertically to any belt up to 2.5 inches. There's also two Tac Tie polymer mounting clips and a 2-inch PVC medical identifier patch included. Tourniquet and tourniquet holder sold separately. This IFAK, with optional tourniquet holder, now lives on my rope rescue harness.

Pros:
> Convenient size and shape, excellent closure, mounting options

Cons:
> Most expensive of the reviewed kits

This kit is more like an "IFAK lite," but rather than that being a weakness, that is its strength. The compact nature of this kit allows it to fit into the breast pocket of most coats and many lighter jackets. It's really about the size of a very, very fat wallet, but easily fits into the rear pocket of a pair of jeans. You can also MOLLE mount it or clip it onto a belt. It certainly lives up to its EDC name.

Pros:
> Fits into most pockets for everyday carry

Cons:
> Bulky despite its small size, limited capacity

This nicely sized kit holds the bare essentials. Sized to fit on a standard belt, duty belt, or MOLLE system, this kit has a tearaway back panel to assist with stowage options or rapid deployment. There's also a convenient carry/grab handle on the rear. The main retention buckle is well designed. It stays closed securely, even when the pull tab is grabbed, ensuring it doesn't accidentally detach until you consciously open the flip-up buckle. But if you rip the pouch off in an upward rotation manner, it detaches nicely. The pull tab also has a 1x2-inch MED (medical) patch for easy identification.

Pros:
> Size, retention buckle, modularity, solid construction

Cons:
> You need to add a tourniquet to make it a complete kit

FIRE-STARTERS & TINDER

By **Kevin Estela**

Man's obsession with fire dates back thousands of years. You can imagine the fascination of those who first realized their ability to harness it. We're sure it caused conflict between those who had it and those who wanted it. Whether that looked like a scene from *Quest for Fire* is debatable. Fire was and still is primal, and in the survival space, fire is just as important now as it was back then. It's a technology that lets us treat water, heat our shelters, harden our tools, signal for help, and more. To those who've ever spent a cold and wet night in the woods, you've probably wished you could trade places with those sitting comfortably by a roaring fire.

You're only as good as your skillset and the tools you carry. You should have strong fundamental knowledge of how to build fire paired with the best modern tools you can afford. Primitive friction-fire starting skills are invaluable if you have nothing else but compact, reliable, and durable tools that shorten the time you need to prep and start your fire are the better option if you remembered to pack them before you left home. While the traditional skills earn you cool points, making fire by any means is the goal and there's absolutely no such thing as cheating. If you need to use the butane torch from your garage to get the backyard fire going or a road flare in the middle of the wilderness, as long as you survive, don't worry about what others will say.

We've come a long way from the primitive technology that caught our attention generations ago. There's a long lineup of modern fire-starters available today that pack serious capability in the palm of your hand. We've assembled a collection of fire-starters that early man would've clubbed someone over the head for. ✖

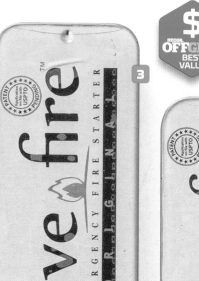

---

1 **EXOTAC**
TinderZIP

📏 **DIMENSIONS:**
3 inches long

⚖ **WEIGHT**
0.1 ounce

💲 **MSRP**
$9

🌐 **URL**
www.exotac.com

---

2 **Shomer-Tec**
Fire Buttons

📏 **DIMENSIONS:**
3/4-inch diameter, 5/32-inch thickness

⚖ **WEIGHT**
0.1 ounce

💲 **MSRP**
$10 magnesium, $16 ferrocerium

🌐 **URL**
shomer-tec.com

---

3 **Live Fire Gear**
Live Fire Original / Sport

📏 **DIMENSIONS:**
3.11 inches (original) / 1.89 inches (sport)

⚖ **WEIGHT**
0.9 ounce (original) / 0.5 ounce (sport)

💲 **MSRP**
$10 (original) / $7 (sport)

🌐 **URL**
www.livefiregear.com

4 Zippo
Emergency Fire Kit

DIMENSIONS:
4 inches by 1.13 inches

WEIGHT
0.1 pound

MSRP
$13

URL
www.zippo.com

5 UCO Gear
Titan Stormproof Match Kit

DIMENSIONS:
4.125 inches long

WEIGHT
2.9 ounces

MSRP
$11

URL
www.ucogear.com

6 S.O.L.
Fire Lite Fuel Cubes

DIMENSIONS:
6.29 inches by 8 inches by 1.77 inches

WEIGHT
0.2 ounce per cube, total weight per package 6.88 ounces

MSRP
$8

URL
www.surviveoutdoorslonger.com

7 Prometheus Design Werx
Ti-Fire Steel MK2

DIMENSIONS:
5.325 inches overall, 4-inch Ferrocerium, handle diameter 0.618 inches

WEIGHT
2.5 ounces

MSRP
$49

URL
prometheusdesignwerx.com

EXOTAC
TinderZIP

Shomer-Tec
Fire Buttons

Live Fire Gear
Live Fire Original/ Sport

Zippo
Emergency Fire Kit

We love multi-purpose gear. Swiss Army Knives, duct tape, peanut butter ... some things work well in multiple roles. The boys over at EXOTAC came up with an ingenious way to carry tinder in the TinderZIP. At first glance, this looks like a normal zipper pull with a plastic cord lock at the end. TinderZIP can attach to your zipper pulls and help you open or close your jacket, to your pocketknives as a fob for easy retrieval, or it can be used in its alternate role — fire-starting. All you have to do is free the cord from the plastic endpiece, pull out the tinder found inside the outer braid of the cordage, and fluff the end with the spine of your knife. It'll take a spark or a flame and once it lights, it'll burn for about a minute. TinderZIP burns like a candlewick and can save the fuel of your lighter. Each package comes with five units that'll let you replace the main zipper and hand warmer pockets, leaving you with a couple to practice with.

Pros:
> 1-minute burn time
> Easily forgotten until needed
> Water resistant

Cons:
> Clothing dependent
> Requires prep before use

You probably have owned a magnesium fire-starter bar at some point. You probably either wore through the ferro rod glued in place or the glue broke off. The magnesium bar has fallen out of popularity, but it's still an effective tinder if used correctly. Shomer-Tec Fire Buttons caught our eye for their ingenuity and innovation. These buttons can be sewn into your clothing and forgotten about. They scream *escape and evasion kit* since that was the idea behind their design. These buttons are made from magnesium and ferrocerium and work just like the traditional magnesium bar. Of course, you'll get a fire started better with both, but if you lose the mag button, you can still use the ferrocerium button on its own.

Pros:
> Easily forgotten about until they're needed
> Discreet design

Cons:
> Small size makes it difficult to use with cold hands
> Not easily transferred between garments
> Awkward scraping technique needed

Live Fire is a really interesting product that can be reused over and over. Instead of burning once or in a single way, Live Fire can be used with varying amounts of flame by regulating the amount of tinder exposed. All you have to do is open the container exposing the fabric inside that's impregnated with a proprietary blend of fuel. We like the fact it can be lit with just about anything including a paper match, butane lighter, or ferro rod. Once it's lit and used to ignite your natural tinder or kindling, you retrieve the Live Fire, close the lid, wait for it to cool, and throw it back into your kit. This lightweight little fire-starter fits perfectly in small emergency kits and can even be rubber-banded to a knife sheath for use with a ferro rod also carried there. Available in larger original size or smaller sport size.

Pros:
> Adjustable flame size
> Easily reusable
> Will ignite with flame or spark

Cons:
> Easily lost in a pocket
> Reusable after lighting but closing and pocketing too soon can burn the user

Zippo has a well-deserved reputation in the fire-starting community, thanks to generations of use by soldiers and outdoorsmen. In addition to its recognizable shape, the sound a Zippo makes when it opens immediately gives away its presence in the dark. Zippo has expanded their lineup beyond their classic and slimline series of lighters. The Zippo Emergency Fire Kit works much like the flint wheel of a traditional Zippo lighter. The paraffin wax-coated tinder is stored in a waterproof container to keep it dry; it ignites with the spark and burns long enough to get your campfire going. All you have to do is remove a small wrapper around the tin and unroll it. This fire-starter can be dummy corded with the molded-in lanyard hole, and it can be operated with a single hand.

Pros:
> This fire-starter floats on water!
> Up to a five-minute burn time per tinder piece

Cons:
> Flint wheel isn't protected if dropped
> Contains moving parts that may be fragile

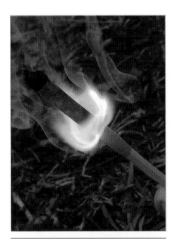

UCO Gear
Titan Stormproof
Match Kit

S.O.L.
Fire Lite Fuel Cubes

Prometheus Design Werx
Ti-Fire Steel MK2

Sometimes, it makes sense to carry a fire-starter most people know how to use. Since they can be found in most homes, matches fit the bill, but standard paper or box matches are flimsy and burn out fast. Titan Stormproof matches are not your average box matches. To reference the popular internet meme, if you're standard matches, Titan matches are the guy she tells you not to worry about. We're not kidding, these matches are about the diameter of a ballpoint pen, and they burn aggressively with large match heads. They're like miniature road flares, and they'll burn underwater if temporarily submerged. The name "stormproof" is appropriate, as they'll continue to burn in the strongest winds.

Pros:
❯ Up to 25-second burn time
❯ Easy to use just like standard-size matches
❯ Extremely wind and water resistant

Cons:
❯ Fragile match heads
❯ Each match is single use and takes up space quickly

S.O.L. Fire Lite Fuel Cubes are great multi-purpose fuel tabs. They burn exceptionally well, can be used in the campfire, or they can be used with solid fuel tablet stoves. They're made with an ethanol jelly that will actually burn on extremely damp surfaces. We like the ability to cut these down into smaller fire-starters to extend the number of fires you can make from a single package. Even the package the cubes come in can be used to carry tinder scavenged off the land, and it has enough capacity to house a ferro rod and lighter too.

Pros:
❯ 8-minute burn time
❯ Burns clean; nontoxic and odorless
❯ Works with most solid fuel folding stoves

Cons:
❯ Bulky
❯ Boil time listed on package is possible in ideal conditions, not all conditions

Prometheus Design Werx is always on the cutting edge of product designs. The Ti-Fire Steel MK2 takes fire steels to a new level. The handle of the Ti-Fire Steel MK2 is made from titanium, and the texture of it will remind you of a pineapple grenade. The inside of the handle is hollow and is revealed by a threaded cap. It can easily hold petroleum cotton balls or similar tinder until it's needed. Perhaps one of the best aspects of this fire rod is the threaded rod that can be replaced when it gets worn down. That said, a ½-inch ferro rod will last thousands of scrapes and even more if you use it sparingly.

Pros:
❯ ½-inch rod produces exceptional sparks.
❯ Handle texture offers great grip, even with cold and wet hands

Cons:
❯ Potential to lose the handle cap
❯ Doesn't come with a dedicated scraper

Sub-3-inch-Blade Folding Knives

By **Mike Searson**

hen most people think of survival knives, images of 1980s action films with muscle-bound heroes sporting massive Bowie knives with serrated spines, hollow handles to store fishing gear, and a mostly useless compass spring to mind. The fact is that more often than not, a sub-3-inch blade can take care of 95 percent of your cutting chores.

If you're in a rough and rugged setting where you need to baton up batches of firewood, clear massive amounts of brush, or perhaps skin a lot of game in a short period of time, you may need a better choice of tool. For most day-to-day uses, however, a short blade can make a lot more sense than tromping around with a Bowie knife or a Woodsman's Pal. These are the knives for opening boxes, letters, or cutting zip ties. Sometimes a sub-3-inch blade may be the only knife you're legally allowed to have in certain jurisdictions. Likewise,

if you're an extreme backpacker, skier, or climber and are looking at carry essentials in terms of ounces, one of these may be the right knife for you.

Blade styles may vary and one can see the real effectiveness of a Wharncliffe, reverse tanto, reverse-S curve, or recurve blade as these profiles tend to offer a more effective cutting edge in a shorter profile.

Any of the knives on this list are small enough to carry everywhere, and they can all fit inside an Altoids box. One model has been part of my personal EDC for close to 25 years. Chances are if you have a smallish knife like one of these, or are thinking of picking one up, it'll turn out to be the most-used knife out of your entire collection.

Most of us open more cardboard boxes and envelopes with our knives as opposed to hacking through the fuselage of a downed aircraft on a daily basis. Take a look at the attributes and design of each one of these and you're bound to find one that meets your needs.

1 Spyderco
Cricket

OAL:
4.75 inches

BLADE LENGTH:
2.75 inches

BLADE STEEL:
VG10

WEIGHT
1.75 ounces

MSRP
$127

URL
www.spyderco.com

2 Kershaw
Kapsule

OAL:
5 inches

BLADE LENGTH:
1.9 inches

BLADE STEEL:
8Cr13MoV

WEIGHT
2 ounces

MSRP
$54

URL
www.kershaw.kaiusa.com

3 CRKT
Razelcliffe Compact

OAL:
5.25 inches

BLADE LENGTH:
2.09 inches

BLADE STEEL:
8Cr13MoV

WEIGHT
3.3 ounces

MSRP
$40

URL
www.crkt.com

4 Cold Steel
Tuff Lite

OAL:
6 inches

BLADE LENGTH:
2.5 inches

BLADE STEEL:
AUS-8A

WEIGHT
2.5 ounces

MSRP
$51

URL
www.coldsteel.com

5 Benchmade
533 Mini Bugout

OAL:
6.49 inches

BLADE LENGTH:
2.82 inches

BLADE STEEL:
S30V

WEIGHT
1.5 ounces

MSRP
$140

URL
www.benchmade.com

6 Kizer Cutlery
Mini Begleiter

OAL:
6.61 inches

BLADE LENGTH:
2.87 inches

BLADE STEEL:
N690

WEIGHT
2.12 ounces

MSRP
$55

URL
www.kizerknives.com

7 Civivi Knives
Appalachian Drifter
Slip Joint

OAL:
6.8 inches

BLADE LENGTH:
2.96 inches

BLADE STEEL:
S35VN

WEIGHT
2.49 ounces

MSRP
$99

URL
www.civivi.com

Spyderco
Cricket

I have been carrying a Spyderco Cricket since 1995. Flat, unobtrusive, and it can perform double duty as a money clip or tie clasp if needed. The reverse-S blade design is very similar to the curvature of the Civilian and Matriarch defensive blades and the Cricket works well in that manner, too. I may carry other knives in addition to this one, but the Cricket handles most of the mundane tasks of the day. Ironically, at the time I got this, I was looking for another Spyderco called the Co-Pilot. I could never find one but found the Cricket instead, and it has served me well over the years.

Pros:
❭ The reverse-S blade has more cutting surface area in a shorter package.
❭ The edge is very easy to maintain.
❭ This knife can literally disappear into the folds of your clothing — always double check before you go through TSA.

Cons:
❭ We can live with tip-down carry on this model, but we feel bad for the southpaws. Could we get three holes on the other side?
❭ The stainless handles and frame lock may add strength, but the older FRN handles were more comfortable.

Kershaw
Kapsule

Kershaw's Kapsule is one of those designs I overlooked at first glance, but eventually grew to appreciate it. Designed by custom knifemaker Jens Anso, the Kapsule has a spearpoint blade and deploys out the front of the handle via a sliding button. The best part of this design is that when it's closed, it doesn't look very much like a knife. This is definitely one of those designs we see all too often that works well in its factory configuration, but could have much more potential if it were made with better materials and attention to detail. As it is, it's perfect for light cutting chores like opening boxes.

Pros:
❭ Its benign appearance when closed makes this the perfect blade to stash in an Altoids tin, spare pocket, etc.
❭ While not as sexy as an OTF automatic knife, the slider has a cool gadget factor.
❭ The clip placement and opening style make this ambidextrous.

Cons:
❭ Not very sharp out of the box, but took a keen edge in a matter of minutes
❭ There's a bit of blade play in the locked position.
❭ Although the design looks great, a different style of blade might make it more effective.

CRKT
Razelcliffe Compact

The CRKT Razelcliffe Compact is a recent design between Jon Graham and CRKT. Graham is usually known for his Razel designs, which are blades more profiled like a cleaver or straight razor. This one is styled as a Wharncliffe, but the sharpened front edge makes it more like a reverse tanto blade. It uses a frame lock construction with a finish giving it an ancient look. The pocket clip is removable but restricted to tip-up and right-hand use only. This is a stout little workhorse of a knife.

Pros:
❭ Small, compact, and equipped with a flipper for fast deployment
❭ Sharp and ready to go out of the box. The sharpened front edge turned out to be more useful than expected.
❭ The contour of the handle and placement of the checkering make this one very comfortable to use.

Cons:
❭ Limitations on clip placement may rule this one out for southpaws.
❭ The only option for a lanyard is through the body of the clip, which isn't ideal.
❭ While there were no problems flipping this one open due to the IKBS, we're a fan of backup opening methods, even if it's just a nail nick.

Cold Steel
Tuff Lite

The Cold Steel Tuff Lite illustrates all the virtues of the Wharncliffe blade, as a knife this small is packed full of cutting power all the way to the tip. The blade's profile transfers its energy into whatever you're cutting. Its small size ensures you can carry it comfortably almost anywhere. Other features include a very generously sized lanyard hole in the handle and a similar treatment on the opening hole in the blade. This particular model features a serrated edge with very usable serrations.

Pros:
❭ This is a very short knife that anyone should be able to carry regardless of wardrobe.
❭ The blade is AUS-8A stainless steel, which is sharp and corrosion resistant.
❭ Whether it's a knife this small or a hand and a half sword, Cold Steel builds tools that last.

Cons:
❭ It can be a tough knife to close due to its size and a stiff lockbar.
❭ Hard use can take a toll on AUS-8A, so you'll probably have to sharpen it more often than most other knives on this list.
❭ Clip position is ambidextrous but the only option for positioning the knife in your pocket for carry is tip-down.

Benchmade
533 Mini Bugout

Kizer
Vanguard
Begleiter

Civivi
Appalachian Drifter Slip Joint

The Benchmade Mini Bugout is aptly named, as this is a perfect lightweight pocket folder that can be stashed anywhere. Its light weight and short length are impressive. This is in large part due to the Grivory handles. Grivory is a thermoplastic synthetic nylon resin mostly used in the automotive trade for high-temp electrical connectors. An Axis lock secures the blade in the open position and imparts enough resistance to prevent unwanted openings. Unfortunately, you can't disengage the lock and flip the blade open as you might on a larger Benchmade. The lanyard hole is perfectly sized for attaching a lanyard, and the blade steel is S30V. The pocket clip is reversible for right- and left-handed use in the tip-up position.

Pros:
❯ The construction on this knife was very well-thought-out.
❯ Razor-sharp out of the box and a quality steel to boot
❯ Extremely lightweight and comfortable

Cons:
❯ At 1.5 ounces, this may take a bit of adjusting if you're used to heavier knives.
❯ We're not big fans of these minimalist-style clips.
❯ The blade's spine could use some jimping for the thumb.

I recently became aware of Kizer Cutlery over the past few years and have been growing more and more impressed with their offerings. The Vanguard represents a slimline series of folders with the touch of a gentleman's knife. The steel is N690, which is made in Austria and has properties similar to VG10. The linen Micarta handles provide for a sturdy hold. The pocket clip is removable, but restricted to tip-up and right-hand use only. Construction of the clip may be the weakest link on this one.

Pros:
❯ The reverse tanto blade shines in this size and configuration, this one is a keen slicer out of the box.
❯ There's a great deal of value packed into this little knife. Fit and finish is tight and the opening is extremely smooth.
❯ Razor-sharp out of the box, this knife cut like a scalpel.

Cons:
❯ Even though I'm right-handed and a tip-up carry kind of guy, there should at least be an option for lefties.
❯ The pocket clip feels flimsy, as if it could easily be unsprung.
❯ Although the design looks great, a different style of blade might make it more effective.

Civivi is a Chinese company that produces knives built to close tolerances with quality materials. The Appalachian Drifter is a slip-joint with a clip-point-style blade. Slip-joint knives don't have a lock like many other pocket knives. The blade is held under slight tension when the knife is in the open position. It normally takes a second hand to push the blade closed while the other hand holds the handle. Most pocketknives used by the Boy Scouts are of this type. The clip-point blade is razor sharp and this traditional profile is reminiscent of the Bowie style. The Micarta handles are grippy and the blade opens via front flipper or nail nick.

Pros:
❯ The blade fires with authority via front flipper.
❯ Quality steel with a razor-sharp edge
❯ Handles are well fitted, aesthetically pleasing, and make for a very comfortable hold

Cons:
❯ The lock is a bit loose for a slip joint. If you have a habit of placing your thumb on the spine of the blade, don't do it with this knife lest it prematurely close.
❯ The mounting point for the lanyard isn't the most intuitive.

EMERGENCY SIGNALING DEVICES

By **Patrick McCarthy**

Self-reliance is a term that gets thrown around a lot in the emergency preparedness community, but it's also a term that seems to be frequently misconstrued. A self-reliant individual takes every feasible step to avoid unnecessary dependence on outside resources. This means that if a problem arises, we should have a plan to solve it on our own, and backup plans in case Plan A falls through. However, that doesn't mean we should endanger ourselves by stubbornly refusing to call for help if a situation gets out of control.

Let's say you're out hiking when the ground underfoot gives way and sends you tumbling down a ravine. You're bruised and disoriented, and you think your leg might be broken. Would your first instinct be to crawl back to the trail, improvise a crutch, and hobble back to safety on your own? This might seem like the most self-reliant option, but it's hardly the safest one. We should never allow our pride or determined sense of independence to prevent us from accepting assistance, especially when going without it might mean putting yourself into an even more dangerous situation later.

Electronic communication devices such as cell phones, radios, satellite phones, and personal locator beacons are some good primary tools for calling for rescue. We've discussed each of them in previous issues of RECOIL OFF-GRID. But these devices can easily lose signal, malfunction, or run out of batteries. In that case, you'll want something analog to fall back on. Your best course of action may be to pop smoke and call for rescue — literally.

Today, we'll be covering six emergency signaling devices that can easily fit into a pocket or pack. We've specifically focused this guide on visual signals that can be used over long distances; these tools can be complemented by audible signals, such as a whistle or air horn. Just like fire-starters or any other critical survival tool, you should always have a variety of options to choose from in the event that things go awry. ⁑

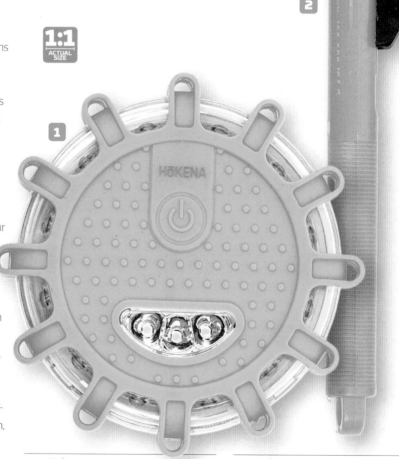

1 Hokena
LED Road Flares Emergency Kit

DIMENSIONS
4 by 4 by 1.3 inches

WEIGHT
5.5 ounces per light / 1 pound 3.7 ounces with 3-pack carrying case

MSRP
$33

URL
www.amazon.com

2 Orion
Compact Aerial Signal Kit

DIMENSIONS
7.5 by 1.5 inches

WEIGHT
4.2 ounces

MSRP
$28

URL
www.orionsignals.com

Remove film before use
Retirez avant d'utiliser

RECOIL OFFGRID TOP PICK

RECOIL OFFGRID BEST VALUE

3
PLOYMENT CCC
DEVICE
0589-P1-0706
PER UNIT
ANCE 5M
FER TO MSDS SHEET FOR
SAFETY INFORMATION
LIMIT 18 YEARS
POCKETS
UK by TLSFx Ltd.
www.tlsfx.co.uk
C€0589
TLSFX-M14

CAUTION: PRODUC
Keep away from spilled fuels
sparks or liquid as fir. Keep su
For outdoor use only. Stand
ALWAYS POINT FUSEE AWA
BODY WHEN IGNITING AND A
flares in sealed bag away fro
Failure to store in closed plas

HOLD BELOW L

ORION

Improved
Eco-Friendly
Formula

15 MINUTE RED EMERGENCY FLARE

3 **IWA International**
M14 Smoke Grenade

DIMENSIONS
4.8 by 2.6 by 1.8 inches

WEIGHT
5.4 ounces

MSRP
$34

URL
www.iwainternationalinc.com

4 **SOL**
Rescue Flash
Signal Mirror

DIMENSIONS
3 by 2 by 0.2 inches

WEIGHT
0.6 ounce

MSRP
$10

URL
www.kitfoxoutfitters.com

5 **Princeton Tec**
Meridian
Strobe/Constant
Light

DIMENSIONS
3.8 by 2.2 by 1.1 inches

WEIGHT
3.5 ounces

MSRP
$30

URL
www.princetontec.com

6 **Orion**
15-Minute
Road Flares

DIMENSIONS
9.2 by 1.1 inches

WEIGHT
6.6 ounces
per flare /
1 pound 5.6 ounces
per pack

MSRP
$20 for 2 packs of 3 flares

URL
www.orionsignals.com

Hokena
LED Road Flares Emergency Kit

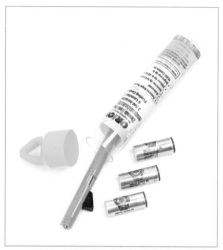

Orion
Compact Aerial
Signal Kit

IWA
International
M14 Smoke Grenade

We found this seven-piece road safety kit on Amazon as a "#1 Best Seller." It includes three hockey-puck-sized LED "flares" as well as a zippered carrying case, screwdrivers for changing batteries, two mylar emergency blankets, and an escape tool with glass breaker and seatbelt cutter. Each disc is made of clear plastic with a bright orange rubber overmold. One side has a power button that activates the 12 orange LEDs in a series of patterns including spinning, flashing, and constant-on. The final setting activates three white LEDs on the front as an emergency flashlight. The back of each disc includes a folding hang hook and rare earth magnet. The lights are powered by AAA batteries and are said to have an approximate maximum run time of 35 hours.

Pros:

❯ Strong magnet allows these lights to be stuck directly to your vehicle, greatly increasing its visibility on dark roads
❯ High-vis storage case fits nicely in a glove box or trunk
❯ Good value considering everything the kit includes

Cons:

❯ Visibility is excellent at night, but not very good on a sunny day
❯ The included escape tool and mounting bracket feel cheap and plasticky

When you think of aerial flares, you probably envision the classic orange flare guns found in life raft survival kits. The Compact Aerial Signal Kit serves a similar purpose in a much smaller package. It's housed in a floating plastic container and comes with a pen-shaped launcher and three red flare cartridges. To fire a flare, screw it tightly onto the launcher, then pull back the firing button to rest in the notch. Snapping the button out of the notch strikes the flare with a firing pin, launching it up to 300 feet as it burns for 6.5 seconds. We were unable to safely test-fire these flares due to the wildfire-prone conditions in our area, and this is a factor you must keep in mind as well. The last thing you want is for your signaling attempt to make you responsible for starting a devastating forest fire. Made in the USA.

Pros:

❯ Aerial flares can be seen in all directions, and can be used to reach above trees and other terrain obstructions
❯ Offers three attempts to get rescuers' attention in a pocket-sized container

Cons:

❯ Primarily designed for boating; not ideal for use in arid environments due to the risk of wildfires
❯ 6.5-second burn time means these can be easily overlooked if your target is distracted

Smoke grenades are widely used by military personnel for identifying extraction zones, hence the use of the term "pop smoke" to mean "let's get out of here." The M14 smoke grenade (or "Smoke Deployment Simulation Device" according to the label) is made in the UK by TLSFx; IWA International imported them to the U.S. and got them approved by the ATF. Operation is simple: Grip with the lever against the web of your hand, twist the ring to disengage the safety, pull the pin, and toss to release the lever. After a 3.5-second delay, the M14 will emit thick smoke for 60 seconds through a vent port in the bottom of the housing. The latest-generation M14 is currently in production and features dual vent ports for better smoke dispersal.

Pros:

❯ If you're attempting to get the attention of an aircraft overhead during the day, there are few better tools
❯ Available with white, red, green, or blue smoke, so you can select a color that will stand out in any terrain

Cons:

❯ Single-use item — you may want to carry an additional reusable signal device
❯ Windy conditions will cause smoke to disperse more quickly

SOL
Rescue Flash
Signal Mirror

Even if you also carry other items from this guide, a small signal mirror is a tool we believe no back-country emergency kit should be without. The SOL Rescue Flash mirror fits in the coin pocket on a pair of jeans, weighs next to nothing, and offers a powerful means of signaling over long distances (up to 30 miles according to the package). Instructions on the back side clearly explain how to aim the mirror using the central sight hole and an outstretched arm with "V" fingers to form a sight post. It's constructed from durable polycarbonate that won't break if dropped. We picked up our test sample from Kit Fox Outfitters, who also provided some cool stickers that show the basics of Morse code and ground-to-air signaling — two other valuable skills for sending a distress message.

Pros:
❯ Lightweight and compact enough to be forgotten until you need it
❯ Easy to use and aim precisely, even over very long distances

Cons:
❯ Can only be used on a clear day, and requires the sun to be on the same side of the sky as your target
❯ Once the protective film is removed, the mirror must be stored carefully to avoid scratches on its glossy surface.

Princeton Tec
Meridian Strobe/
Constant Light

Princeton Tec is a well-known supplier of lighting devices for law enforcement, military, and search-and-rescue personnel. The Meridian was designed as a locator light for use in these applications, as well as low-light industrial work and diving. It's powered by 3 AAA batteries and offers a maximum runtime of 100 hours. A large switch allows toggling between two modes, depending on the model you choose — white strobe and white constant, or white strobe and red beacon. We picked the former so it can be used as an emergency lantern or map-reading light. Each is available with a high-vis yellow or black housing and features low-profile clips that hook onto 1-inch PALS webbing, plus an included Velcro wrist strap. Made in the USA.

Pros:
❯ IPX8 rated as fully submersible — SCUBA diving is a recommended application
❯ Directly compatible with PALS webbing found on MOLLE-compatible packs
❯ Switch is designed to be activated with gloves.

Cons:
❯ Testing revealed the switch to be very touchy in strobe mode. A slight bump to the switch will deactivate the light, even if it doesn't click the lever fully to "off."
❯ Changing batteries requires a screwdriver.

Orion
15-Minute Road Flares

If you've witnessed a severe car crash, you've probably seen law enforcement personnel throwing down road flares or waving them to guide traffic around the obstruction. These simple devices send an immediate nonverbal message of "watch out!" This also makes them an effective means of signaling distress over short distances in other situations, such as flagging down a passing car. These Orion flares are available in 15- or 30-minute burn times; we chose the former due to its more packable size. Each of the three-packs we purchased comes with a protective bag, detailed deployment guide, and a free chemlight. Orion also offers detailed training resources on its website, so you can teach your family how to safely and effectively use flares. Made in the USA.

Pros:
❯ Ideal for roadside emergencies — every motorist is used to seeing them used at accident scenes to redirect traffic
❯ Waving a bright red flare makes you immediately visible, even during full daylight

Cons:
❯ Their size and weight make them better-suited to storage in a vehicle rather than a backpack
❯ Not the most effective means of long-range signaling during the day

KNIFE SHARPENERS

Story and Photos by **Patrick McCarthy**

 sharp knife is a safe knife — this saying may sound counterintuitive to some, but anyone who has ever struggled with a dull knife knows just how dangerous it can be. A razor-sharp blade glides effortlessly through materials with surgical precision, while a chipped and rolled edge tends to wander and snag with every slice. At best, this makes using your knife frustrating and tedious; at worst, it can lead to serious injury as you apply more force in an effort to persuade the tool to do its job.

Choosing a knife with appropriate edge geometry, durable steel, and properly applied heat treat will go a long way in keeping its edge sharp. It's also advisable to avoid abusing your knife by cutting against abrasive surfaces, pounding it through hard materials, or using it as a prybar. However, even if you follow every one of these best practices, all knives are bound to require maintenance eventually. This is where sharpeners come in.

You may already have a sharpening system in your kitchen, workshop, or garage, but these tools are generally far too large and elaborate to take into the field. For the times when you may not have access to your home sharpening system — whether that's during a normal workday or a long-term survival situation — it's wise to have a portable knife sharpener in your pocket or backpack. These compact tools can keep your knife cutting smoothly and safely, no matter where you are.

We collected seven pocket-sized sharpeners and evaluated each tool's effectiveness on a variety of blades. Read on to see if one of them can help your favorite cutting implements stay sharp.

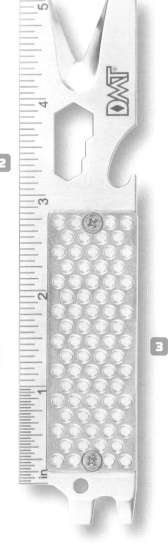

 OFFGRID BEST VALUE

1 CRKT
Knife Maintenance Tool

SHARPENING MATERIALS
Tungsten carbide & ceramic

DIMENSIONS
2.8 by 1.2 by 0.6 inches

WEIGHT
2.2 ounces

MSRP
$30

URL
www.crkt.com

2 DMT
EDC-Sharp

SHARPENING MATERIALS
600-grit diamond

DIMENSIONS
5.5 by 1.2 by 0.2 inches

WEIGHT
3.6 ounces

MSRP
$22

URL
www.dmtsharp.com

3 Lansky
Blademedic

SHARPENING MATERIALS
Tungsten carbide, 600-grit diamond, 1,000-grit ceramic

DIMENSIONS
4 by 1.2 by 0.5 inches

WEIGHT
3.5 ounces

MSRP
$16

URL
www.lansky.com

4 Mora
Diamond Sharpener S

SHARPENING MATERIAL
600-grit diamond

DIMENSIONS
4.1 by 0.4 by 0.3 inches

WEIGHT
0.4 ounces

MSRP
$25

URL
www.moraknivusa.com

5 Spyderco
Golden Stone

SHARPENING MATERIAL
Fine ceramic
(approx. 1,200 grit)

DIMENSIONS
7.2 by 3 by 0.3 inches

WEIGHT
8.8 ounces
including pouch

MSRP
$100

URL
www.spyderco.com

6 Victorinox
Dual-Knife Sharpener

SHARPENING MATERIAL
Medium stone, fine ceramic

DIMENSIONS
5.6 by 0.4 by 0.7 inches

WEIGHT
1 ounce

MSRP
$14

URL
www.swissarmy.com

7 Work Sharp
Guided Field Sharpener

SHARPENING MATERIAL
220-grit diamond surface,
600-grit diamond surface,
coarse and fine ceramic
rods, leather strop

DIMENSIONS
6.8 by 1.7 by 1 inches

WEIGHT
4.7 ounces

MSRP
$35

URL
www.worksharptools.com

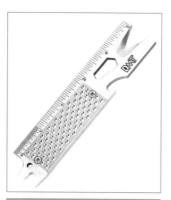

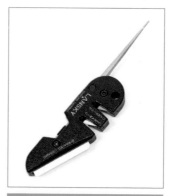

CRKT
Knife
Maintenance
Tool

DMT
EDC-Sharp

Lansky
Blademedic

Mora
Diamond
Sharpener S

As indicated by its name, the Knife Maintenance Tool is more than just a sharpener. It was designed by mechanical engineer Tom Stokes for CRKT, and features two draw-through notches for edge repair and maintenance: a tungsten carbide sharpener and a ceramic honing surface. CRKT doesn't advertise the angle of these notches, but they appear to be about 20 degrees. It also includes two flip-out bit drivers with T6 and T8 Torx bits — these are handy for adjusting a knife's pivot or tightening clip screws. The bits are removable and retained magnetically. The top of the tool has a bottle opener, flat screwdriver/pry bar, and key ring or lanyard hole.

Pros:
> Perfectly sized for a keychain accessory
> The bit drivers are very handy, but ...

Cons:
> ... the included hex bits are 0.9-inch long; standard bits are 1 inch. Replacement bits fit extremely tight unless filed down.
> Draw-through carbide sharpeners don't produce the cleanest edge and can be destructive if used excessively.

New from DMT, the EDC-Sharp is a multipurpose pocket tool with an integrated diamond sharpening surface. It's constructed from 1/8-inch-thick 5CR steel and features a 5-inch ruler on one side, a metric ruler on the other side, a wire stripper/cutter, bottle opener, two flat screwdrivers, and a small file edge. A cutaway in the center serves as a 7mm, 8mm, and 10mm wrench. A lanyard hole is also present, although this tool's size would be excessive for a keychain item. The sharpening plate is 1 by 2.7 inches and has a fine texture suitable for touching up slightly dull blades. This diamond sharpener is made in the USA; the rest of the tool is made in China.

Pros:
> Recessed holes in sharpener keep its surface clear and maintain abrasive performance
> All-metal construction feels solid

Cons:
> We like the multi-tool concept, but wish there was slightly more focus on the primary function. Adding features doesn't always add value.
> Flat surface isn't ideal for recurve blades

One of the most popular portable sharpeners on the market, the Blademedic fits easily on a keychain and includes four sharpening features in a metal case. The carbide and ceramic draw-through notches are set to 22.5 degrees on each side; instructions recommend three or four strokes through each to restore an edge. An additional ceramic section fits into serrations. Lastly, the tapered diamond rod can be used on serrations or for general sharpening. We'd favor this rod over the carbide notch as a starting point for sharpening, since it's much gentler. It's held in the open or closed position by strong magnets inside.

Pros:
> Good variety of tools in a small package
> Magnets ensure the diamond rod stays put while you work and doesn't rattle loose in transit

Cons:
> Surprisingly heavy for its size
> Be careful how often you use the carbide sharpener, since it aggressively removes steel.

Contained in a diminutive pen-shaped case, the Diamond Sharpener S can be carried almost anywhere. It features a small diamond rod with one flat side and a groove for fish hook sharpening. After close examination, we spotted something strange. The packaging says "Made in Mora Sweden," but the pocket clip says "EZE-LAP Carson City, Nevada." After some Googling, we found that this sharpener appears to be identical to an EZE-LAP Model S sharpener except for a Morakniv logo. Private-labeling is nothing new, but the EZE-LAP tool retails for $7. You could buy three of them for the price of one Mora-branded sharpener, and still have money left over.

Pros:
> Extremely small and lightweight, fits anywhere a pen would
> Grooved shaft can be used to sharpen fish hooks

Cons:
> Mora products usually offer excellent value, but not this time. You'd be better off buying an EZE-LAP Model S ... or three.

Spyderco
Golden Stone

Victorinox
Dual-Knife
Sharpener

Work Sharp
Guided Field
Sharpener

To use the Golden Stone, grab the narrow end with one hand and hold it upright. Then place the scalloped end of the stone against a flat surface and tilt it to the left or right. With your other hand, hold your knife blade vertical and draw it straight down along the edge of the stone. This creates an even 20-degree sharpening angle on either side. There's also a groove for sharpening fish hooks, as well as radiused and flat surfaces that can sharpen virtually any other blade. The included suede leather case doubles as a non-slip tabletop pad. We noticed that Spyderco's site lists this product (#308F) as a 1x5-inch stone, but it's substantially larger than that.

Pros:
❯ Easy to use while maintaining a consistent angle
❯ Leather case doubles as a strop to remove burrs
❯ Made in the USA

Cons:
❯ Must be used on a bench or other flat surface
❯ Ever dropped a plate and watched it explode into fragments? Dropping this slick ceramic stone would be equally disastrous.

Victorinox is known around the world for its multi-function Swiss Army knives, but the European company has a wide range of other products to offer, including a few different sharpeners. As you probably guessed from its name, the Dual-Knife Sharpener has two functions. An oval 3.2-inch stone serves to grind away larger edge imperfections; its narrower sides can be used on serrations, and its grooves can sharpen fish hooks. Opposite the stone, there's a V-shaped ceramic notch for refining a blade's edge. These items are packaged in a tough black polymer case with the Victorinox logo emblazoned on a bright red pocket clip. Made in Germany.

Pros:
❯ Oval stone makes it easy to sharpen a variety of blade and serration types
❯ Simple and durable case fits easily into a pocket

Cons:
❯ Using the ceramic hone necessitates working with the blade pointed down at the support hand. Most other tools avoid this by turning the notch 90 degrees.

This compact tool from Work Sharp offers an impressive array of five stages. First, the coarse and fine diamond surfaces are used to remove large imperfections and restore the edge. Next, turn the red knob to "C" or "F" to reveal coarse and fine ceramic honing surfaces. Each of these stages includes a 20-degree angle guide. Lastly, run the edge against the leather strop on the side to polish away burrs with the embedded micro-abrasive compound. There's also a ceramic rod for small serrations, a fish hook sharpening groove, and — after removing the diamond plates from their magnetic retainers — an arrow broadhead wrench and a small storage compartment for hex wrenches or other items.

Pros:
❯ Five-stage system can quickly revitalize even the dullest blades
❯ 20-degree guides help maintain edge geometry

Cons:
❯ Coarse plate is highly abrasive and should be used sparingly
❯ Thumb grip could be more comfortable

Tourniquets

By **Joey Nickischer**

On more than one occasion, I heard the story about a guy who was using a chainsaw in his backyard to clean up some storm debris. As he was cutting a few of the fallen branches, he lost his footing and the running chainsaw came down on his leg, causing a tremendous wound. While his wife quickly called 9-1-1 and helped apply direct pressure, the femoral artery was cut and he died before the ambulance arrived. A tourniquet would've likely saved his life.

Tourniquet use goes back to at least the 4th century BC, when Alexander the Great had troops using tourniquets of leather and bronze. There are other documented uses during the Middle Ages with battlefield tourniquets, which were simple garrotes. In 1785, Sir Gilbert Blane advocated that, in battle, each Royal Navy sailor should carry a tourniquet:

"It frequently happens that men bleed to death before assistance can be procured, or lose so much blood as not to be able to go through an operation. In order to prevent this, it has been proposed, and on some occasions practiced, to make each man carry about him a garter, or piece of rope yarn, in order to bind up a limb in case of profuse bleeding."

The use of tourniquets waned after World War II, with much documented misapplication, plus lag time between application and subsequent receiving of proper medical attention, causing them to fall out of favor. But their military use continued to rise through the Korean War, Vietnam, Iraq, and Afghanistan.

Today, after much scientific study, their use has become mainstream. A set of established clinical practice guidelines direct the appropriate use of tourniquets. The present doctrine used by the U.S. Military is that every soldier in the field has a tourniquet and knows how to use it. This has carried over to the civilian sector, where police officers, firefighters, and EMTs routinely carry them. There are also an untold number of schools and businesses across the country that have trauma kits stockpiled with numerous tourniquets in case of a dire emergency.

Understand this: Tourniquets are not just for soldiers and gunshot wounds. Automobile accidents, athletic events, and home improvement projects can all lead to unforeseen trauma where a tourniquet can mean the difference between life and death. Whether you're a soldier on the front lines or a well-prepared mom shuttling kids between activities, emergencies happen, and there's something you can do about it. Be prepared and enroll in a Stop the Bleed (stopthebleed. org) or Tactical Emergency Casualty Care (TECC) course to learn the proper way to control bleeding in a severely injured person.

Special thanks to Guardian Revival (guardianrevival.org) and Medicine in Bad Places (Medicine InBadPlaces.com) for their technical assistance with this article. ⁂

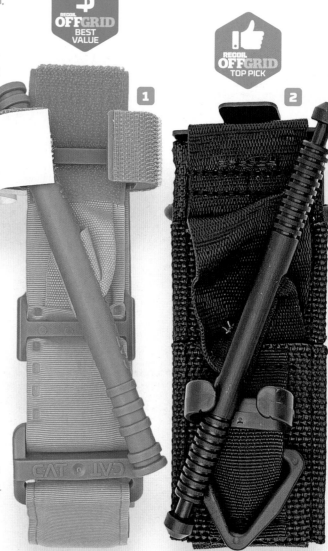

1 North American Rescue
Combat Application Tourniquet (C-A-T)

COLORS:
Black, Blue, Orange

SIZE:
Packaged L 6 by W 2.4 by D 1.5 inches; open length 37.5 inches

WEIGHT:
2.7 ounces

PRICE:
$30

URL:
narescue.com

2 TacMed Solutions
SOF Tourniquet

COLORS:
Black, Blue, Orange, Red, Tan

SIZE:
Packaged L 5.5 by W 2 by D 1.75 inches; open length 44 inches

WEIGHT:
3.7 ounces

PRICE:
$31

URL:
tacmedsolutions.com

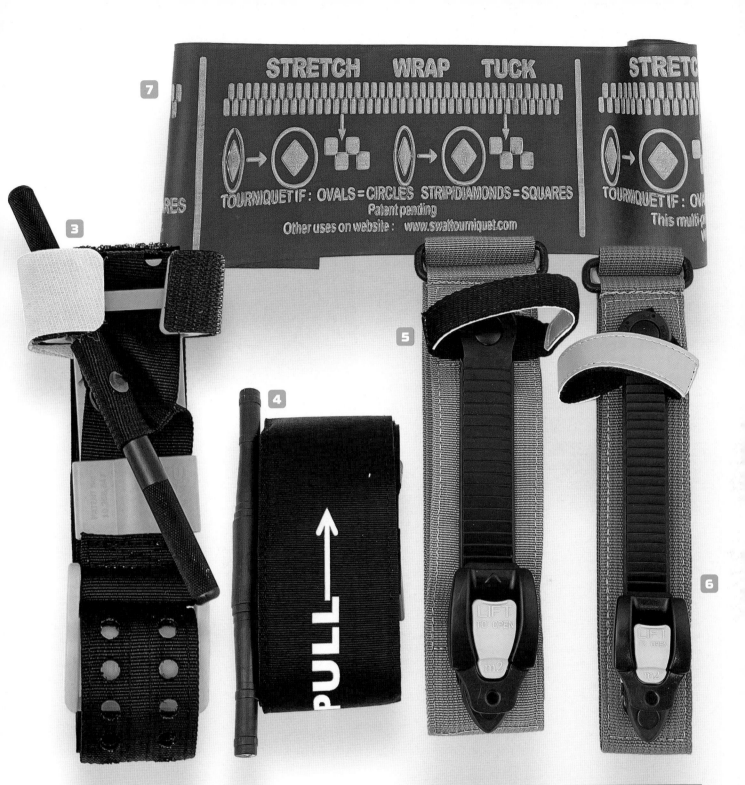

3 SAM Medical
SAM XT
Tourniquet

COLORS:
Black, Blue, Orange

SIZE:
Packaged L 7.25
by W 2.5 by D 1.5
inches; open length
36 inches

WEIGHT:
3.8 ounces

PRICE:
$38

URL:
sammedical.com

4 Combat Medical
TMT Tourniquet

COLORS:
Black

SIZE:
Packaged L 4.5 by W
2.5 by D 1.85 inches;
open length 38
inches

WEIGHT:
2.9 ounces

PRICE:
$30

URL:
combatmedical.com

5 RevMedx
TX2

COLORS:
Tan

SIZE:
Packaged L 8.5 by
W 2 by D 1.5 inches;
open length 39
inches

WEIGHT:
3.1 ounces

PRICE:
$39

URL:
revmedx.com

6 m2 inc.
Ratcheting Medical
Tourniquet (RMT)
Tactical

COLORS:
Black, Tan

SIZE:
Packaged L 8.5 by W
1.5 by D 1.25 inches;
open length 37.5 inches

WEIGHT:
3.6 ounces

PRICE:
$36

URL:
chinookmed.com

7 H&H Med Corp.
SWAT-T Tourniquet

COLORS:
Black, Blue, Orange

SIZE:
Packaged L 4.5 by W 3 by
D 0.75 inches; open length
37.5 inches

WEIGHT:
3.6 ounces

PRICE:
$19

URL:
store.doomandbloom.net

North American Rescue
Combat Application Tourniquet (C-A-T)

TacMed Solutions
SOF Tourniquet

SAM Medical
SAM XT Tourniquet

Combat Medical
TMT Tourniquet

As one of the first modern tourniquets on the market, this is the style the vast majority of people are familiar with. Noted as the best pre-hospital tourniquet in the February 2008 supplement of *The Journal of Trauma*, the patented C-A-T is a true one-handed tourniquet proven to be fully effective by the U.S. Army's Institute of Surgical Research. Currently in Gen 7, this is a windlass system where you use the stick to wind up or tighten the tourniquet. The rotation tightening of the windlass gives you a mechanical advantage to apply more pressure. Once the blood flow is occluded, the windlass is pressed into a retaining clip to maintain pressure. Be sure to buy the genuine C-A-T product from a trusted retailer (not a third-party Amazon reseller). There are a lot of dangerous counterfeits on the market. The C-A-T is approved by the Committee on Tactical Combat Casualty Care (CoTCCC) and carries NSN 6515-01-521-7976.

Pros:
> The de-facto standard in tourniquets
> Virtually all tourniquet users are trained on this model

Cons:
> Hook-and-loop attracts lint and can snag on other gear if left exposed

Designed by a Special Forces medic while on deployment to Afghanistan in 2003, the SOF-T is a well-refined tourniquet. This is a tried-and-true windlass design with several improved features. The first is that the windlass is made from aluminum, rather than polymer. It also has a buckle for fast application around a limb, using only gross motor functions, versus rethreading a strap through a buckle. I find it to be a little more supple than most of the other tourniquets, which gives it a nice feel and is quieter than the hook-and-loop types when carried. It has seen adoption by many large organizations including NYPD, LAPD, and the American Red Cross. I keep this tourniquet as part of my EDC. It's CoTCCC approved and is available for purchase by the Department of Defense under NSN 6515-01-696-4522.

Pros:
> Aluminum windlass
> Packs flat and lacks hook-and-loop, making it convenient for on-body carry

Cons:
> Time tag not on top

The SAM XT is a windlass design tourniquet with an obvious physical difference, as the hook-and-loop strap has two rows of holes in it. These holes work in conjunction with the unique TRUFORCE buckle that'll help lock the strap in place when a predetermined amount of force is applied. When you pull the strap hard enough, the buckle will lock into the holes. The tourniquet has a good feel to it, not too stiff and not too soft. I had no problem securing it one-handed. Anybody who has ever used the C-A-T or SOF-T will intuitively understand how to use this tourniquet. It's approved by the CoTCCC and carries NSN 6515-01-670-2240.

Pros:
> Aluminum windlass
> TRUFORCE buckle helps let you know when the strap is tight enough

Cons:
> The buckle makes it bulkier than most.

I found the TMT to be especially challenging to apply one-handed. On top of that, I found that if you twist the windlass counterclockwise, it's counter-intuitive to get it into the retaining clip. Instead of letting the windlass settle back into the clip, like on all the other windlass tourniquets, you actually have to push it forward. This counter-intuitiveness can cost you a lot of blood under pressure. Additionally, when tightening the windlass in a clockwise direction, you lose a little tightness. The Naval Medical Research Unit came to the same conclusion in 2015 on the clockwise tightening. The buckle is nice, though. I expected to have to thread the strap through it but found that's not possible. Instead, you simply unhook the buckle. These issues are easily remedied through proper training. It's approved by the CoTCCC and carries NSN 6515-01-656-6191.

Pros:
> Smooth windlass action
> Fast to apply once trained
> Wide 2-inch band

Cons:
> I found it to be slow and difficult to secure one-handed.
> Not intuitive to use

RevMedx
TX2

m2 inc.
Ratcheting Medical Tourniquet (RMT) Tactical

H&H Med Corp.
SWAT-T Tourniquet

A departure from the traditional windlass design, the RevMedx TX2, and its big brother the TX3, utilize a ratcheting mechanism to achieve the final tightening on the tourniquet. It's a lot like using a ratchet strap — simply wrap it around the limb, pull tight, and start ratcheting. Knowing how superbly tight a ratchet strap can get, I had high hopes, and this tourniquet didn't disappoint. The 1-inch-wide ratchet design works smoothly and the tourniquet can be left in service after using it for training. In fact, it's encouraged in the product literature. The 2-inch-wide strap allows for better bleeding control. The TX3 is another inch wider and 21 inches longer, fitting even the burliest of people. A Naval Medical Research Unit study found that the TX tourniquets outperformed the windlass-style tourniquets in multiple categories. Both are approved by the CoTCCC and carry NSN 6515-01-667-6027 and 6208.

Pros:
❭ Wide 2-inch strap allows for better bleeding control
❭ Convenient ratcheting mechanism

Cons:
❭ No time tag on top of mechanism

The Ratcheting Medical Tourniquet is made by m2 inc., a leading manufacturer of industrial-strength mechanical closure technologies. Besides this Thermo Plastic Ratcheting Buckle, they also make surgical, industrial, marine, and military items. The RMT is the cousin to the REV MED TX2 and TX3, but somewhat smaller. The buckle comes in at ¾ inch, allowing it to be readily used on narrow tourniquets. It also features a tactical loop that doubles as a bite loop for easier application with one hand or gloves. While this is the military tactical tan version, it also comes in three civilian versions of XL, greater than 120 pounds, and less than 120 pounds (pediatric), as well as three military versions of tactical, paramedic, and 2-inch, with various colors. It's approved by the CoTCCC and carries NSN 6515-01-527-3841.

Pros:
❭ Versatile with numerous application-specific variants
❭ Many color and size choices

Cons:
❭ No time tag on top of mechanism

The Stretch Wrap and Tuck Tourniquet is often disregarded because it has never gotten CoTCCC approval. That said, it does its job when properly applied. It's a rubber strap with instructions printed on one side. To apply it, stretch the band firmly until the printed oval and diamond shapes stretch into circles and squares. This is how you know you're applying it with enough force to occlude blood flow. Wrap as many times as you can and tuck the end in. For some, tucking the end in can be difficult. A big upside is it'll work just as well on children as adults. The SWAT-T can also be used to apply pressure to a packed wound, and can be used as a K9 tourniquet or sling. It truly is the multi-tool of the tourniquet world. The SWAT-T comes packaged in a plastic pouch, with pre-cut tear notches every 2 inches on each side. Even wet, it tears open readily with a two-handed grip or your teeth.

Pros:
❭ Very affordable
❭ Doubles as a pressure dressing or even a canine TQ

Cons:
❭ Not as easy to apply one-handed
❭ Not CoTCCC approved, making it more of an "honorable mention" than a top-tier contender

GUN MAINTENANCE MULTI-TOOLS

By **Chad McBroom**

Most firearm malfunctions are caused by a lack of proper maintenance. Like any other machine, firearms experience wear and tear after prolonged use. Dirt, rust, carbon buildup, and worn-out or broken parts can cause stoppages or even catastrophic failure. Regular cleaning, lubrication, and inspection of a firearm is necessary to keep it operating smoothly and ensuring early detection of damaged components.

Modern firearm platforms like the AR-15 require specialized tools for sighting, cleaning, and adjusting. Even the 100-year-old 1911 platform requires a special bushing wrench for disassembly. The most basic field armorer kit typically consists of enough punches, wrenches, drivers, bits, and other tools to fill a medium-sized tool bag.

The expense of a full maintenance kit is more than most gun owners will ever wish to invest. Those who have sacrificed their hard-earned cash to acquire these tools will frequently find themselves stuck at the range in want of a tool they left at home, because their tool kits were too heavy and cumbersome to haul with them.

One of the best ways to increase productivity at the range is to have all the tools needed to make sight adjustments, tighten loose accessories, and disassemble and clean your gun. A quality gun maintenance multi-tool can provide most of those tools in a compact package that can be conveniently stowed in a range bag.

In this edition of *Pocket Preps*, we'll examine some of the most versatile gun maintenance multi-tools on the market. As we look at the capabilities and limitations of each tool, we hope to provide the reader with the information needed to select the best multi-tool for the job. ⠿

 Multitasker
Twist

DIMENSIONS
5 by 9/16 inches

WEIGHT
1.8 ounces (3.7 ounces with included bits)

MSRP
$60

URL
www.multitaskertools.com

 Real Avid
AR15 Tool

DIMENSIONS
5 by 2 by 1 inches

WEIGHT
18.4 ounces

MSRP
$90

URL
www.realavid.com

 Real Avid
Gun Tool Amp – AR15

DIMENSIONS
5 1/2 by 2 by 1 5/8 inches

WEIGHT
13.3 ounces

MSRP
$70

URL
www.realavid.com

$
OFFGRID
RECOIL
BEST
VALUE

OFFGRID
RECOIL
TOP PICK

	Multitasker Nano		**Gerber** Short Stack		**Emissary Development** R2-0		**Fix It Sticks** The Works
4		**5**		**6**		**7**	
DIMENSIONS	1.2 by 0.5 inches	**DIMENSIONS**	3 by 1.25 by 5/8 inches	**DIMENSIONS**	3.5 by 11/8 by 5/16 inches	**DIMENSIONS**	7.25 by 3 by 4.25 inches
WEIGHT	0.1 ounce	**WEIGHT**	2.8 ounces	**WEIGHT**	0.5 ounce	**WEIGHT**	26.2 ounces
MSRP	$13	**MSRP**	$47	**MSRP**	TBD	**MSRP**	$280
URL	www.multitaskertools.com	**URL**	www.gerbergear.com	**URL**	www.emissarydevelopment.com	**URL**	www.fixitsticks.com

Multitasker
Twist

The Twist is nothing short of a pocket toolbox packed into the size and shape of a large permanent marker. The rear section of the double-ended, threaded housing holds a pick for scraping stubborn carbon deposits and pulling retainer pins, a ³⁄₃₂-inch pin punch, and a radial carbon scraper. These three tools attach to the 8-32 thread adapter located on the front cap. Underneath the front cap is a magnetic ¼-inch bit driver with an AR front sight tool installed. The Twist comes with a few Phillips, slotted, hex, and Torx bits, but any ¼ bit can be used with the driver. The rear cap has a two-prong Aimpoint micro sight turret adjuster on the end, making this tool invaluable to any Aimpoint shooter. When the rear cap is removed, the pocket clip becomes a field expedient, lightweight flathead driver.

Pros:
› Marker-style housing is easy to carry.
› Saves space and weight while offering essential tools
› Can be used in conjunction with pull-through cleaning kits

Cons:
› Small number of tools within the unit
› Aluminum housing doesn't allow the use of a hammer when using the pin punch

Real Avid
AR15 Tool

This 37-in-1 tactical gun multi-tool on a folding X-frame platform has everything necessary to remove carbon from bolt surfaces, make field repairs, add or remove accessories, and completely disassemble and reassemble a firearm. The AR15 Tool contains needle-nose pliers, carbide cutter, metal file, bolt carrier carbon scraper, 8-32 threaded receiver and post to attach all standard cleaning attachments, ³⁄₃₂-inch detachable pin punch, 10-function bolt carrier group scraper, cotter pin puller, serrated tanto blade, detachable hook pick, three-position locking ¼-inch bit driver with 12 bits, and a bolt override tool. The MOLLE-compatible nylon sheath has elastic bit storage loops and an A1 and A2 front sight tool storage pouch on the side. Although it's designed as an AR tool, this beefy device works for pistols too.

Pros:
› Full-featured multi-tool has everything needed for field maintenance.
› Convenient nylon case
› G-10 side-plates increase gripping surface.
› Very cost-effective

Cons:
› Heavy
› The overall size is a bit bulky and makes precise task work cumbersome.

Real Avid
Gun Tool Amp – AR15

The Gun Tool AMP is a series of compact multi-tools that come in three platform-specific versions, AR15, Pistol, and 1911. The AR15 version shown here contains a tanto-style knife blade, bolt override tool, takedown punch, retaining pin puller, multi-surface bolt carrier group scraper, carrier scraper, firing pin scraper, and tap hammer. All tools lock in place using a liner lock system. The holster has a fold-out, locking ¼-inch bit driver and a nine-function bit set. Bits include hex, Torx, Phillips, flat, and A2 Front Sight Adjuster. The folding driver arm locks into place with a quick release lever. The holster has a MOLLE-compatible, metal belt clip for convenient stowing and transport. The AMP is a specialized tool, so the user needs to choose the right platform.

Pros:
› Case with driver and primary tool separate, allowing the user to work with each independently
› Each AMP platform has everything needed to perform field maintenance and cleaning.
› Functional sheath reduces waisted space.

Cons:
› Specialized platform is weapon specific.
› Weight

Multitasker
Nano

The Multitasker Nano Tool is a tiny pocket tool intended for making optic adjustments. It's about the size of an aluminum can flip tab but packs a lot of practical utility despite its tiny footprint. The Nano features a dedicated Aimpoint T1/T2 turret adjuster on one end and a slotted screwdriver with radiused edges on the other. Although the Nano can be conveniently carried on a keychain using the built-in lanyard hole, the Nano has been specifically engineered with winglets on each side, which act as a dovetail for docking into the SpaceFrame storage slot found on the Gen3 MagPod. The Nano is compatible with a wide variety of popular optics and aiming lasers, including the Aimpoint M68 CCO, EOTech EXPS-3, Trijicon ACOG, Trijicon RMR, PEQ-15, and the B.E. Meyers & Co. MAWL.

Pros:
› Tiny and easy to carry
› Compatible with the Gen-3 MagPod SpaceFrame storage slot
› Works with the most popular optics and lasers

Cons:
› Functionality is mostly limited to aiming devices.
› Easy to misplace or lose due to its size

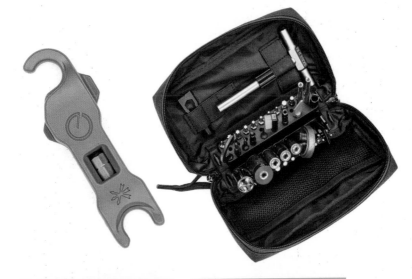

Gerber
Short Stack

The Gerber Short Stack uses a revolutionary three-piece magnetic design to form a compact, weapon-specific multi-tool. The Short Stack has everything needed to disassemble and maintain the AR rifle platform, including a front sight tool, firing pin scraper, bolt and bolt carrier scraper, cleaning cable pull-through handle, castle nut wrench, 4mm wrench/bit driver, 7mm wrench (fits M-LOK fasteners), ½-inch wrench, ⅜-inch wrench, ¾-inch wrench, curved slotted driver, and two double-sided Hex bits (#0 Cross Diver, T10, ⅛-inch Hex, 4mm Hex). This tiny, self-contained multi-tool can fit snugly into Magpul MOE and MIAD pistol grips so it's always close by when the rifle is in hand.

Pros:
❯ Extremely light and compact
❯ Can be stored inside the weapon
❯ Cost effective

Cons:
❯ Small size reduces leverage.
❯ AR-platform specific
❯ Doubles as a brain puzzle when returning the tool to its carry configuration

Emissary Development
R2-0

The R2-0 (Return 2 Zero) is a lightweight minimalist tool designed through a collaborative effort between Emissary Development and Unity Tactical. The R2-0 is designed to interface with Geissele Super Precision Scope Mounts and snaps in place between the mounting screws using a clamp/hook design. The tool houses a T15 Torx bit that fits into a ¼-inch socket on the undercarriage. An additional ½-inch socket fits standard scope mount nuts and can be used to tighten loosening mounts or make mounting adjustments. The lack of any torque limiter means the R2-0 isn't ideal for use with precision weapons; however, it's a handy tool for tightening a loose scope mount on the range or in the field.

Pros:
❯ Conveniently locks into the Geissele Scope Mount for convenient storage

Cons:
❯ User must have the Geissele Scope Mount for the tool to interface.
❯ The lack of torque limiter makes it impractical for precision use.

Fix It Sticks
The Works

This all-in-one gun maintenance kit contains a variety of tools that come in handy at the range or work bench, including an A2 front sight tool, castle nut wrench, bolt carrier scraper, 1911 bushing tool, Glock front sight bit, universal choke tube wrench, metal pin punch and a non-marring plastic pin punch, bronze scraper, steel pick, set of brass 8-32 thread cleaning rods, set of two 8-32 bit adapters, cleaning brush, and mini pry bar. There are four torque limiters (15, 25, 45, and 65 inch-pounds), a ½-inch socket, and 24 assorted ¼-inch bits for mounting scopes, tightening chassis, and zeroing optics. Every tool pairs with the accompanying ¼-inch T-handle wrench. The entire kit packs inside a compact, MOLLE-webbed soft case. A magnetic Velcro patch on the outside of the case helps keep track of loose screws and bits. The Works has it all.

Pros:
❯ Has virtually everything a shooter needs for field maintenance
❯ Multi-platform tools for a variety of firearms
❯ Standard ¼-inch bits and driver make this multi-tool highly customizable and adaptable.

Cons:
❯ Price

IDENTIFICATION LIGHTS

Story and Photos by **Patrick McCarthy**

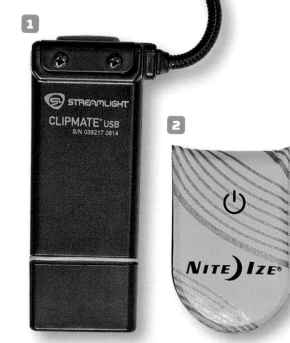

Compared to other members of the animal kingdom, humans have a major deficiency: poor night vision. As ambient light fades, our eyes struggle to perceive even the faintest outlines of objects in our immediate vicinity. This poses a safety risk during nighttime group activities such as hiking and cycling, since it's easy to get disoriented and separated when you can't clearly see your friends. It's also a hazard in urban environments, because motorists may struggle to see you from a distance. And in a SHTF situation, a persistent light source provides the means to signal for rescue after dark.

A flashlight or headlamp can illuminate your field of view, but these directional light sources aren't ideal tools for making others aware of your position (at least not without temporarily blinding them). Enter the identification light, a device designed to attach to your gear and provide a source of long-lasting, clearly visible light. Identification lights are typically compact, lightweight, and durable — some are even intended to be disposable one-time-use items.

The most commonly known ID light is the chemlight, also called a glowstick. These flexible plastic tubes contain a glass ampoule that can be snapped to mix two chemicals, inducing a reaction known as chemluminescence. This reaction can be calibrated by the manufacturer to glow dimly for a long period or brightly for a short while, but either way, the stick's light will gradually fade after a few hours. Chemlights are still commonly used today, but technological advancements have made ultra-compact LED lights a viable alternative. LED identification lights can be reused and often feature multiple output colors or modes.

We collected and evaluated seven compact lights that are ideal for nighttime identification, or for use in situations where only a small amount of diffuse light is needed, such as reading a map or illuminating the inside of a tent. Consider one of these lights as a supplement to your current flashlight or headlamp. ⁘

---

1 **Streamlight**
ClipMate USB

CLAIMED MAXIMUM BRIGHTNESS
70 lumens

CLAIMED MAXIMUM RUNTIME
65 hours

DIMENSIONS
3.1 by 2 by 0.7 inches

WEIGHT
1.9 ounces

BATTERY TYPE
Built-in lithium-polymer rechargeable

CONTROLS
Push-button switch

OUTPUT MODES
low/high red, low/high white

MSRP
$55

URL
streamlight.com

---

2 **Nite Ize**
TagLit

CLAIMED MAXIMUM BRIGHTNESS
Unlisted

CLAIMED MAXIMUM RUNTIME
70 hours

DIMENSIONS
2.2 by 1.6 by 0.5 inches (folded)

WEIGHT WITH BATTERY
0.5 ounces

BATTERY TYPE
CR2032 lithium (one, included)

CONTROLS
Push-button switch, press repeatedly to change modes

OUTPUT MODES
Green flashing or constant-on

MSRP
$10

URL
niteize.com

---

3 **Princeton Tec**
Amp 1L

CLAIMED MAXIMUM BRIGHTNESS
90 lumens

CLAIMED MAXIMUM RUNTIME
72 hours

DIMENSIONS
5.1 by 1.4 inches (including cone)

WEIGHT WITH BATTERY
2.2 ounces

BATTERY TYPE
AAA (two, included)

CONTROLS
Twist head

OUTPUT MODES
On-off only

MSRP
$20

URL
princetontec.com

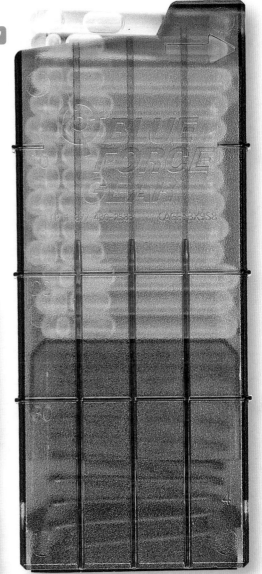

4 Nitecore
NU05

CLAIMED MAXIMUM BRIGHTNESS
35 lumens

CLAIMED MAXIMUM RUNTIME
20 hours

DIMENSIONS
1.2 by 1.2 by 0.6 inches

WEIGHT WITH BATTERY
0.4 ounces

BATTERY TYPE
3.7v 120mAh lithium-ion rechargeable

CONTROLS
Push-button switch, press repeatedly to change modes, press and hold for lockout

OUTPUT MODES
Red LED indicator, slow flash, or fast flash; white LED slow flash or constant-on

MSRP
$20 with headlamp/bike kit, $15 for light only

URL
nitecore.com

5 COAST
HX4 Cliplight

CLAIMED MAXIMUM BRIGHTNESS
80 lumens

CLAIMED MAXIMUM RUNTIME
3 hours 45 minutes

DIMENSIONS
3.1 by 1.8 by 1.2 inches

WEIGHT WITH BATTERY
1.8 ounces

BATTERY TYPE
AAA (two, included)

CONTROLS
Push-button switch, press repeatedly to cycle through modes

OUTPUT MODES
White constant-on, red constant-on

MSRP
$18

URL
coastportland.com

6 Fenix
CL09

CLAIMED MAXIMUM BRIGHTNESS
200 lumens

CLAIMED MAXIMUM RUNTIME
150 hours (90 with included battery)

DIMENSIONS
3.1 by 0.9 inches

WEIGHT WITH BATTERY
1.8 ounces

BATTERY TYPE
ARB-L16-700U rechargeable (one, included) or CR123A (not included)

CONTROLS
Twist tail cap, twist on and off repeatedly to cycle through modes

OUTPUT MODES
Low, medium, high, turbo, red, red flashing, green

MSRP
$45

URL
fenixlight.com

7 Blue Force Gear
MARCO Marking System

CLAIMED MAXIMUM BRIGHTNESS
Unlisted

CLAIMED MAXIMUM RUNTIME
4 hours at maximum intensity, more than 24 hours total glow time

DIMENSIONS
6 by 3 by 0.75 inches

WEIGHT
3.8 ounces

BATTERY TYPE
None

CONTROLS
Push forward to partially eject a marking stick, then bend upward to snap and activate light

OUTPUT MODES
Available in red, green, blue, or infrared

MSRP
$65

URL
blueforcegear.com

Streamlight
ClipMate USB

With a flexible neck and slim rectangular body, the ClipMate USB is just the right size for a shirt pocket. Its strong metal clip also fits nicely on PALS webbing loops, 1.5-inch belts, or a hat brim. When light is needed, the segmented neck can be aimed precisely in any direction, casting a dense spot beam. The ClipMate includes red and white output modes, which can be accessed by either a short-press or long-press of the top-mounted power button (short-press turns on the last-used mode). This light is also USB-rechargeable via a hidden charge tab that enables the user to plug it directly into any USB outlet or computer port. Streamlight says it can be fully charged in 2.5 hours, and it's rechargeable up to 300 times.

Pros:
❭ Flexible neck allows for targeted hands-free illumination
❭ Red light is directly accessible, preserving the user's night vision

Cons:
❭ Tight spotlight beam pattern is too focused for identification purposes
❭ Integrated charge tab hangs the light precariously on a USB port while charging and blocks nearby ports. Its cover is also easily dislodged, allowing for ingress of water and dust.

Nite Ize
TagLit

This magnetic LED marker light features a folding design with two strong neodymium magnets that can adhere to the edge of any shirt, jacket, hat, headlamp band, or even a dog collar. The TagLit is available in three high-visibility colors: red, pink, or neon yellow. The former two feature four red LEDs, and the latter features four green LEDs; all include stripes of reflective silver for an additional boost in visibility. A hidden pressure switch under the power symbol turns the light on and cycles between its two modes. Nite Ize doesn't advertise an exact lumen output for this light, but we'd guess it's around 5 — plenty to alert motorists of your position during a nighttime jog. Clipped to the brim of a ball cap, this light can also be used for map reading and other low-light tasks.

Pros:
❭ Magnetic clasp attaches securely to clothing and other gear
❭ Bright color and reflective accents increase visibility

Cons:
❭ Weather-resistant but not waterproof
❭ Slightly too wide to fit into PALS webbing loops

Princeton Tec
Amp 1L

The Maxbright LED in the Amp 1L produces 90 lumens and gradually ramps down brightness to yield a 72-hour run time from its AAA batteries. Twisting the rubberized bezel turns on the light, and pressing on the included cone diffuser attachment scatters the beam into a broad lantern-style pattern. The light can then be attached to a tent loop or ridgeline with a carabiner to illuminate your campsite, or used as an ordinary flashlight with the cone removed. Half of the light's polymer body is rubberized for extra grip, and it's fully O-ring-sealed for an impressive waterproof rating. The loop at the tail end of the Amp 1L also features a bottle opener tab in case you need a way to open a cold beverage. Made in the USA.

Pros:
❭ Bright, diffuse light works great as a mini-lantern
❭ With the cone removed, it works equally well as a spotlight
❭ IPX8 waterproof to 100 meters

Cons:
❭ Bottle opener seems like an afterthought, and can't be used when the light is attached to a carabiner
❭ The cone attachment is held in place by friction alone
❭ Single output mode limits versatility

Nitecore
NU05

Nitecore calls this tiny light a "headlamp mate" due to its ability to be used in tandem with a full-size headlamp, either clipped to the back of the head strap or worn elsewhere on the body. As a result, the NU05 is tailored to identification purposes. It features a total of five LEDs — two white, two red, and one low-output red indicator light — each of which includes a flashing mode. The NU05 also features one 35-lumen constant-on setting that can be paired with an optional head strap and bike mount bracket kit to provide emergency illumination. The built-in battery will last just one hour when used this way but can be quickly recharged via a micro-USB port. We noted that this light is the perfect size to clip onto a single loop of PALS webbing, making it a valuable accessory for nighttime hiking or backpacking.

Pros:
❭ Tiny size and light weight make it an ideal backup for emergency use
❭ For an extra $5, the head band and bike mount kit add versatility.
❭ IP66 waterproof

Cons:
❭ Short battery life when used in constant-on mode
❭ Lacks constant-on mode for red LEDs

COAST
HX4 Cliplight

Fenix
CL09

Blue Force Gear
MARCO Marking System

This new LED light is available in a variety of color configurations that include white plus red, blue, green, and/or ultraviolet. The HX4 features a spring-loaded pocket clip that allows the light to be easily attached to the hem of a pocket, PALS webbing on a MOLLE-compatible pack, or the brim of a hat. Four small magnets are also attached to the corners of the clip, providing more hands-free mounting options. COAST says the light's head rotates 180 degrees, but we'd say it's closer to 220. Combined with the wide flood beam, this makes the HX4 ideal for illuminating a workbench while mounted on your shirt pocket or lighting your path while mounted on your belt. Pressing the large rubberized power button turns it on in white mode; pressing again cycles through other colors.

Pros:
❭ Wide beam pattern provides a smooth wash of light for your work area
❭ Clips onto gear in a variety of locations, and can be aimed easily by rotating the head

Cons:
❭ White light must be turned on before other colors, potentially impacting night vision.
❭ An additional low-output mode would've been helpful to extend run time.

Serving as a hybrid between an identification light and a miniature lantern, the CL09 can sit upright on any flat surface, hang from a small carabiner, or slide securely into PALS webbing. There's also a magnet in its tail cap, making it a good hands-free work light. This light includes Fenix's ARB-L16-700U battery, which features a micro-USB charging port, but it also accepts more common rechargeable CR123A (aka 16340) and standard CR123A batteries. Twisting the tail cap repeatedly cycles through a total of seven modes, with a white light that ranges from 1 to 200 lumens, as well as 5-lumen red and green. The anodized aluminum body is available in either black or gray finish.

Pros:
❭ White setting works great as a mini-lantern for your campsite; red and green modes can be used for identification or signaling.
❭ Magnetic tail cap adds versatility
❭ IP68 waterproof to 2-meter immersion

Cons:
❭ Red and green light modes aren't directly accessible
❭ Included Fenix battery has a convenient charging port, but offers 40-percent shorter maximum run time than a standard CR123 (90 hours versus 150 hours).

This system was originally designed to identify cleared rooms inside a building. Instead of carrying a handful of loose chemlights, the MARCO enabled quick access to dozens of smaller marking lights. The system has many non-combat applications, such as marking a trail or tracking downed game animals. The MARCO's tough polycarbonate dispenser features a spring-loaded follower that feeds 30 2-inch sticks to the top one at a time. These sticks can be activated one-handed by bending them upward with your forefinger as they're dispensed. Various optional storage pouches are available. Made in the USA.

Pros:
❭ Easy to activate and deploy several light sticks with one hand
❭ Ideal for identifying multiple items or individuals
❭ Color options increase versatility

Cons:
❭ No built-in way to attach the sticks to gear, although we found sandwiching one behind the edge of a Velcro patch works well.
❭ You'll need to use all 30 lights in a short time frame, since the active chemicals begin degrading as soon as the dispenser is unwrapped.
❭ Each dispenser is designed as a single-use item.

MINI PRY BARS

By **Chad McBroom**

ew tools have as many practical applications as a pry bar. The mechanical advantages of the leverage that can be generated with a pry bar makes it the perfect tool for a variety of everyday tasks. Unfortunately, a standard crowbar isn't the most convenient tool to carry around. Not only is it heavy and cumbersome, but lugging around a crowbar can also give onlookers the wrong impression about your intentions.

Many a knife has been broken in the absence of the proper tool. Such blasphemous use of a blade can not only leave one frustrated and angry but also injured and bleeding. As the saying goes, "A knife is the most inefficient screwdriver and most expensive pry bar you'll ever own."

Thankfully, the advent and evolution of multi-tools has gradually led to the incorporation of miniature pry bars into a vast selection of everyday-carry tools. Although they're limited in scope compared to their big brothers, mini pry bars can be used to pry open windows and interior doors, break glass, force open security gates, wedge car doors, open cabinets and lock boxes, and pry containers. They can also be used to perform more mundane tasks like opening beer and soda cans, removing staples, lifting nails, and tightening screws. When integrated into a

multi-tool platform, their usefulness is expanded even further.

In this edition of Pocket Preps, we'll highlight some of the most versatile mini pry tools on the market and help you determine which tool might be the best choice for your personal needs. ✖

1 **Fix It Sticks** Mini Pry Bar	**2** **Gerber** Prybrid X	**3** **Elite Outfitting Solutions** TiShark
DIMENSIONS 2.14 by 0.64 by 0.7 inches	**DIMENSIONS** 4 by 0.875 inches	**DIMENSIONS** 4 by 1 by 0.14 inches
WEIGHT 0.4 ounce	**WEIGHT** 1.7 ounces	**WEIGHT** 1 ounce
MATERIAL S45C	**MATERIAL** 3Cr	**MATERIAL** 6Al-4V Titanium
MSRP $10 (Driver Sold Separately)	**MSRP** $23	**MSRP** $20
URL www.fixitsticks.com	**URL** www.gerbergear.com	**URL** www.eoscases.com

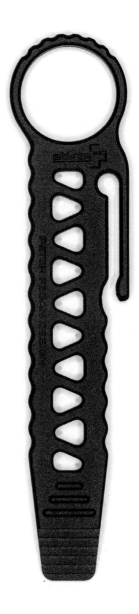

5 **Böker Plus**
Minibar Pro

DIMENSIONS
4.45 by 0.15 inches

WEIGHT
2.01 ounces

MATERIAL
8Cr13MoV

MSRP
$35

URL
www.bokerusa.com

6 **Prometheus Design Werx**
SFPB

DIMENSIONS
4.5 by 0.624 by 0.25 inches

WEIGHT
2.5 ounces

MATERIAL
D2

MSRP
$59

URL
www.prometheusdesignwerx.com

7 **WE Knife**
Gesila

DIMENSIONS
4.76 by 0.75 by 0.20 inches

WEIGHT
1.51 ounces

MATERIAL
6AL4V Titanium

MSRP
$56.50

URL
www.weknife.com

8 **Böker Plus**
Tango Bar

DIMENSIONS
5.71 by 0.15 inches

WEIGHT
2.1 ounces

MATERIAL
440C Stainless Steel

MSRP
$27

URL
www.bokerusa.com

Fix It Sticks
Mini Pry Bar

Unlike the other tools in the lineup, the Fix It Sticks Mini Pry Bar isn't a stand-alone tool, but an attachment designed to convert the Fix It Sticks or other ¼-inch bit driver into a mini pry tool. The bit has a small pry lever and nail puller for minor prying tasks. The inside cutouts allow the MPB to be used as a ¼-, ⁵⁄₁₆-, and ⅜-inch wrench. The MPB integrates perfectly with the Fix It Sticks Replaceable Version Kit, which includes 16 assorted bits and two Fix It Sticks that combine to form a T-handle, or the stand-alone Fix It Sticks T-Way Ratcheting Wrench (both shown here).

Pros:
❯ Quickly converts any ¼-inch driver into a min pry tool
❯ A convenient and inexpensive solution for solving many common prying tasks

Cons:
❯ Requires a separate driver
❯ The small pry head isn't suitable for heavy-duty levering.

Gerber
Prybrid X

This miniature hybrid pry bar multi-tool combines the precision blade of a hobby knife with a multifunctional pry bar. It contains a replaceable standard #11 hobby knife blade inside the housing. The blade is retracted using a push-button slide lock, which offers resistance to prevent accidental opening. The dual-ended design also incorporates a mini pry bar, wire stripper, nail puller, small and medium flathead drivers, and bottle opener. A 550 cord wrap and raised notches on the spine and belly provide additional grip. When attached to a key ring, this key-sized multi-tool becomes an everyday travel companion that's easily forgotten about but always within reach.

Pros:
❯ Perfect for fine tasks that require small, precise tools.
❯ Replaceable hobby knife blades are easy to find at any big-box, hardware, or craft store.
❯ Compact and easy to carry on a small keychain

Cons:
❯ The small tool design relegates this tool to basic tasks.
❯ Hobby knife isn't suitable for heavy-duty cutting.
❯ The smooth metal housing is a little slick, even with the raised notches.

Elite Outfitting Solutions
TiShark

The TiShark from Elite Outfitting Solutions is a simple but effective CNC-machined pry tool. The 6Al-4V Titanium construction and compact size makes the TiShark lightweight and easy to carry. Although the shark-mouth bottle opener is the drawing feature for most users, the pry bar/screwdriver is quite capable of handling daily tasks that involve prying, wedging, and tightening/loosening slotted screws. There's also a ¼-inch hex wrench for holding standard hex bits. The TiShark has an integrated pocket clip and lanyard hole to offer multiple carry options. The orange, blue, and purple hues generated by the flame-treated titanium and the unique shark-like features makes the TiShark a beautiful conversation piece when not in use. A 3x0.75-inch Mini TiShark is also available.

Pros:
❯ Light and compact
❯ Stylish shark-themed design makes the TiShark an instant conversation starter
❯ Available in an ultra-compact mini version
❯ Tucks neatly along the front pocket inseam with the pocket clip

Cons:
❯ Likely to be stolen by envious company if left unattended

Böker Plus
Minibar Pro

The Böker Plus Minibar Pro is a multifunctional leveraging tool designed by custom knifemaker Jim Burke. The pry end of the tool contains a dual-faced lever surface to accommodate a variety of levering tasks. The forward-facing portion of the lever head doubles as a flathead screwdriver. The pry end also contains a teardrop-shaped shackle opener. There's a ¼-inch hex driver situated at the upper portion of the handle. This driver works with standard ¼-inch bits when extra leverage is needed to break loose a stubborn screw. The beaked end is ideal for levering on flat surfaces. There's also a bottle opener located at the back of the beaked end. The tool has aggressive jimping on the sides for gripping and is equipped with a pocket clip and lanyard hole for convenient transport.

Pros:
❯ Offers six leveraging actions within a single tool
❯ Small, compact, and easy to carry

Cons:
❯ When clipped inside a pocket, the sharp, beaked head becomes a snagging point.

Prometheus Design Werx
SFPB

This multifunctional pocket pry tool is milled from D2 tool steel. The SFPB features a mini pry head, which can double as a screwdriver and a bottle opener. The SFPB also has an oxygen tank wrench located near the center of the tool, and a hex bit socket machined into the titanium pocket clip. The socket is located near the end of the tool to offer maximum leverage for overtightened screws. A Strikeback notch behind the pry head is designed to pair with just about any ferro rod to create sparks when starting campfires. The refined machined details of the SFPB, including the recessed hardware and chamfered edges are a testament of the quality craftsmanship and invested into this versatile pry tool.

Pros:
❯ Compact and sleek design makes the SFPB easy to carry.
❯ Perfect choice for wilderness rescue professionals
❯ High-quality materials and craftsmanship give this tool a high-end feel.

Cons:
❯ Upper tier pricing puts the SFPB out of reach for many would-be users.

WE Knife
Gesila

The Gesila from WE Knife is a simple but stylish mini pry bar with basic features. This tool, made from 6AL-4V Titanium, features a chisel-shaped pry end is also slotted and notched for pulling small nails. The back end has a bottle opener for busting open cold beverages. The overall design looks like it came straight out of a Star Wars movie. Fortunately, the same design features that give the Gesila a futuristic look also add a lot of function. The jimping located on both sides just behind the pry head adds just enough gripping surface to help with wedging the head into tight spaces. The tip-down pocket clip makes it easy to carry the Gesila in just about any pocket. This offering from WE Knife is a good choice for those who need serious prying capabilities in a small and simple package.

Pros:
❯ Small, light, and convenient to carry
❯ Can be used as an improvised impact weapon
❯ Aesthetically pleasing design

Cons:
❯ Limited function as a multi-tool

Böker Plus
Tango Bar

The Böker Plus Tango Bar, designed by Peter Fegan, combines the utility of a pry tool with the defensive proper-ties of a palm stick and the retention qualities of a karambit. Constructed of powdercoated 440C stainless steel, the Tango Bar is both sturdy and aes-thetically appealing. An integrated clip allows the tool to be worn on a pocket hem or attached to MOLLE loops. The pry end, which can also serve as a flathead screwdriver, is stepped up to provide more control. What makes this pry tool truly unique is its double function as an impact weapon. The karambit-style improves retention and makes the tool easy to draw, especially when combined with the ripple texture on the sides and the top jimping.

Pros:
❯ Flat and lightweight, perfect for EDC
❯ Offers excellent retention capabilities
❯ Doubles as an impact device
❯ Can be worn in a pocket or on MOLLE equipment

Cons:
❯ The location of the clip causes the tool to turn inward in pockets.

The Fighting Bag

By
Tom Marshall

MAKE & MODEL
Suarez International
Terrorist Interdiction/Active Shooter Bag (TIB)
MSRP
$55
URL
suarezinternational.com

or our inaugural installment of "Bag Drop," I'm going to talk about a bag that's been with me for years. It has literally travelled the world and was built for a clear purpose. I learned a long time ago that equipment selection is a form of mission analysis. In layman's terms — a well-packed bag should fill a specific need and do so with a minimum of bulk or excess. This particular bag can also be seen in "Trick Your Truck" in RECOIL OFFGRID Issue 33.

In a previous lifetime, I worked in Afghanistan as an independent contractor, providing facility security and close protection services to government personnel. Part of this job required driving or riding in armored SUVs, often as a single-truck element, in areas where IEDs and ambushes were a very real risk. In many cases, if a vehicle is blocked in or disabled during the course of an attack, you may have to bail out of it (possibly under fire) and leave the area on foot. Because of this, I wanted a lightweight low-profile bag to hold extra supplies I could bring with me if I was ever forced to exit my vehicle during a fight. This bag also stayed with me while manning static posts in the event of an active shooter or large-scale ground assault against our perimeter.

The bag itself is a Terrorist Interdiction Bag, from Suarez International. Measuring only 10 by 12.5 inches, the overall design is flat and lean. I found it perfectly sized to tuck under the driver seat of my vehicle or the drawer of my desk while working various duties in Afghanistan. The bag also includes a waist strap. With the shoulder strap slung across your chest like a seatbelt, and the waist strap clipped around your torso, you can fight directly from the bag with minimal bouncing or flopping while you move. In effect, this turns the TIB into an oversized holster, with all on-board supplies easily accessible on the go. On their website, the folks at Suarez International say this: "*The TIB is the answer for the man that needs to carry a full high intensity-short duration fighting kit 24/7/365, but in a very compact and ultra-discreet manner … We suggest you do not overfill it with non-essentials. Quick and dirty. Fill it with weapons, magazines, weapon accessories, and medical stuff. That is all.*"

To this end, my personal TIB would be a dedicated fighting bag. There would be no long-term survival provisions. I didn't keep any actual guns in this bag, as my duties required weapons be kept on my person while on duty. The main zip compartment includes a removable "kangaroo pouch" that holds three rifle magazine with bungee-cord top retention. I filled all three slots with spare 30-round magazines for my carbine. Behind the magazines is a large pocket, divided down the middle that I used for extra trauma medical supplies: hemostatic gauze, an Israeli bandage, and chest seals. Since the rifle mag pouch is covered with loop-side Velcro on the outside, I added a small placard with elastic loops that I filled with small chem lights for signaling or room-marking in a CQB scenario.

The front-flap of the bag is held closed with a fastex buckle and covers a shallow pocket lined with elastic loops. I used the loops in this compartment to hold a flashlight, tourniquet, folding knife, and multi-tool.

Finally, there are two small end pockets on either side of the bag. In one pocket, I kept "personnel control" supplies — flex cuffs and pepper spray, in the event that hostile or unknown personnel needed to be subdued or transported after the immediate fight. In a pinch, flex cuffs can also be used to help secure doors or gates. Opposite this, I kept fire-starting supplies. This is the closest I came to including actual survival gear. A Zippo lighter, bottle of lighter fluid, and several waterproof fire-starting wicks were just enough to fit in this pocket. The only things in this bag without a direct and immediate application in combat, this inclusion was simple personal preference. In retrospect, a personal GPS beacon or satellite phone would've been an excellent substitute. Most small-to-medium phones or pocket beacons would've fit perfectly in the same pocket.

That's it. I carried this bag, in this configuration, for several deployments. Fortunately, I never needed to use it. But I always felt better knowing I had the extra muscle in case I did. Even if Uncle Sam never sends you on that all-expense-paid trip to the Mid East, a dedicated fighting bag is a worthwhile consideration in any preparedness plan. Even if you can't — or don't want to — carry a firearm on you, this bag will hold even a full-sized handgun with ease. Stashing a government-sized 1911 or Glock 17 with several extended magazines gives you an all-inclusive solution to go from unarmed to fight ready. Having a bag like this cached in your trunk, hall closet, or desk drawer gives you a strong alternative to hiding and hoping for the best if faced with armed assailants. ⁂

The Commuter Pack

By **Patrick McCarthy**

doors, and tools and jumper cables under the trunk floor. But the bulk of my gear lives in a backpack that can be pulled out of the car and carried away at a moment's notice. Some might call it a get-home bag, but it's more aptly described as a general-purpose 24-hour emergency kit. The contents have helped me through numerous situations, from unexpected overnighters to a vehicle breakdown on a 116-degree F Arizona summer day.

The Pack

The basis for this kit is a Legion Day Pack from Cannae Pro Gear, which features a small 19.5x11.5x6-inch footprint and compact 21-liter capacity. It's an entry-level model, and that makes perfect sense for this sedentary application. There's not much sense in spending big bucks on a pack that's going to get worn so rarely. Despite the affordable price, it offers lots of organized storage compartments as well as a hidden waist belt — a feature that'll be helpful if I need to run while wearing it.

Exterior Pockets

I'll explain the contents starting from the outside. Two expansion straps at the base of the pack hold a rolled-up fleece pullover, which has proven its worth many times on cold evenings. The bottle pocket on the left side contains a 48-fluid-ounce Nalgene full of water — you can never have

---

With numerous pockets and pouches, this affordable pack offers organized storage for a variety of gear.

According to The AAA Foundation for Traffic Safety, the average American spends nearly an hour behind the wheel every day — for many, it's far more than that. A spokesperson for the Insurance Institute of Highway Safety said that driving is "probably the riskiest thing any of us do on any given day" from a purely statistical standpoint. This adds up to a simple conclusion: There's a high likelihood that you'll be in or near your vehicle when an emergency occurs. It's therefore critical to have some basic survival gear in your car or truck at all times.

Like many of you, I've stashed emergency gear throughout my vehicle. There's a glass-breaker on the sun visor, a flashlight in the center console, bottled water in all the

---

MAKE & MODEL
Cannae Pro Gear
Legion Day Pack

MSRP
$100

URL
cannaeprogear.com

enough in the desert. The green disc under the cap is a Pillid storage compartment that holds water purification tablets.

I also carry a Source Hydration Convertube adapter, which lets me drink from the Nalgene on the move. This item stays inside the pack, since I learned its rubber pressure-relief valve slowly leaks water when it isn't upright. If I'm heading out on foot, I'll swap it onto the bottle.

On the right side of the pack, there's a 5.11 Tactical 3x6 Med Kit pouch. It's solely for traumatic injuries and is shoved into the side pocket so I can pull it out immediately if I witness a car crash. It contains shears, a C-A-T tourniquet, hemostatic gauze, an Israeli bandage, gloves, and medical tape..

The front of the pack features two compartments — a sunglass pocket and an admin pouch. The former contains multipurpose items such as paracord, zip ties, superglue, a BIC Lighter wrapped in duct tape, and hand sanitizer. The admin pouch contents are as follows:

» Spare 8-round magazine for my Shield carry gun

» Mora Garberg Black Carbon knife

» SOG PowerAccess multitool

» Coast HP7 flashlight

» Streamlight Bandit rechargeable headlamp

» Chemlight

» UCO spork

» Signal whistle

» Compass

» Ironclad heavy-duty gloves

» Bandana

» Notepad, pen, and Sharpie marker

» Deck of playing cards

Main Compartment

The remainder of the gear is housed in the full-zip main compartment. A mesh pocket on the inside of the lid contains hygiene items, including deodorant, toothbrush, toothpaste, chewing gum, and wet wipes, as well as a trash bag for cleanup. Next are three pouches. The first contains energy-dense, travel-friendly foods such as Millennium bars and almond butter packets.

The rigid foam container has a tool I consider invaluable — a portable jumpstart box. There are many to choose from; this WinPlus 8000mAh lithium ion battery cost $76 on Amazon. It functions as a USB charger for small electronics, but can also deliver a high-output jolt through included jumper cable clamps to boost a weak car battery. This is the item that saved my ass on the aforementioned 116-degree day, when my car battery unexpectedly died at a rest stop in the middle of the desert. It allowed me to drive comfortably to the nearest

auto parts store, rather than begging other motorists for a jumpstart or waiting for roadside assistance. There's enough extra space for USB cables, a 12V car charger, and a small wall charger.

For a last-ditch charging solution, I slid an Enerplex Kickr IV folding solar panel into the laptop pocket. If all else fails, it'll give me enough juice to make a phone call or top off my headlamp.

Everyone will recognize the bright red first-aid pouch from Adventure Medical Kits. It includes basic supplies for cuts, scrapes, sprains, and other non-life-threatening injuries. I supplemented it with a few additional meds, such as 24-hour antihistamines, a Mylar blanket, and an additional hemostatic dressing.

The final items in the pack are clothing — pretty self-explanatory, and held in place using the pack's integrated elastic cinch straps. One notable item is an ultralight, water-repellent Pack-It Jacket from First Tactical. Made from a thin layer of ripstop nylon, it offers no insulation, but fits over the fleece to serve as a rain shell.

With the items in this backpack, I'm ready to deal with most everyday inconveniences as well as more serious situations. As I explain in my *On the Grid* column at the end of this issue, it's not a one-size-fits-all solution, but it provides for my immediate needs in the event of a vehicle-based emergency. ✥

Whether it's a natural disaster, breakdown, or short-notice road trip, a vehicle survival kit will help you cope with almost any challenging situation.

The Wildfire Bug-Out Bag

By **Eryn Chase**

I live in a mountain oasis — my little taste of heaven. My closest neighbors are three miles away. My little off-grid retreat is surrounded by pine, mahogany, and juniper. I'm relatively self-sufficient here — comfortable enough to survive the zombie apocalypse. However, my biggest threat every year is one that's not confined to the realm of fiction: wildfires.

Wildfire season in Nevada typically lasts from June through November, with seasons in surrounding states sometimes lasting through January. Dry weather combined with strong wind gusts could burn thousands of acres within hours. I know if a wildfire approaches, my best and safest bet is to grab my bag and evacuate to town. Ideally, this would mean notification during the day with ample time to get in my truck and drive the five miles of dirt road down the mountainside to the paved road that leads to civilization.

However, with unfavorable winds, I could be looking at a 0200 wake-up and sprint to the side-by-side because our only egress route is blocked. I have to be prepared for both scenarios. With this in mind, I chose a hiking pack to be my Wildfire Bug-Out Bag. After all, the situation could mandate I travel via truck, side-by-side, or on foot based on the fire location, thickness of the brush, and unfriendliness of the terrain.

The Bag

The bag itself is an Osprey Ariel 65. I've had this pack since 2013 and haven't been disappointed. While I could talk all day about the multitude of features and the Osprey's reputation for solid products, I'll focus on the final selling point for me: an adjustable, female-specific design. As a 5-foot-3 woman, it was imperative that I found a pack I could customize to my body shape. Like many vertically challenged people, my torso is quite short. Combine this fact with mother nature's birthing hips, and you can understand the challenge of finding a hiking pack that fits.

The Osprey Ariel 65 women's version has an adjustable harness system, curved shoulder straps for the female form, and a heat-moldable hip belt to ensure a snug fit around your unique body shape. There are many companies that currently offer female-specific packs. Not every pack fits every body shape well, so try on each brand until you find one that suits you.

Osprey no longer makes this particular model, but you can find the updated Ariel AG 65 version on the company's website.

The Contents

My intent is simple: get to safety and be prepared to rest in place for five to seven days until I'm cleared to go home or able to link up with friends or family. To me, this means probably spending a few days at an evacuation center or pop-up shelter. Do I still have long-term survival tools in my pack? Absolutely. I'm still prepared. However, they take up a small fraction of the space available, and these are items I'd rather have and not need than need and not have.

I've strategically placed items in the pack based on how quickly I need to reach them.

The outside hip pockets contain the items I want to use without having to take the pack off: knife, flashlight, female urination device, and RATS tourniquet.

The pack lid is completely removable. Inside, I've packed items I'd need to access rather quickly. These include welders' gloves in case I come across burning items that need to be removed, safety goggles to protect my eyes from ash, and other basic supplies — first-aid kit, LifeStraw, poncho, collapsible water bottle, and instant energy gels.

The first item inside the main compartment is my hygiene bag. This is a small Creek bag with pockets to keep supplies separate and easy to access. Under the secure flap, I hold my travel toothbrush and toothpaste, deodorant, wilderness wipes, pocket shampoo, and body wash leaves from Trek & Travel. In the zippered pocket, I carry a small microfiber hand towel, larger body bathing wipes, sunscreen, lip balm, and spare Colgate wisps. Again, the intent is to stay hygienic and healthy while displaced. Here, I also keep my "survivalist" gear: waterproof matches, compass, 550-cord, extra batteries, and multi-tool. I also keep a few hundred dollars in cash in the event I couldn't grab my wallet as I was leaving.

Inside the pack are items to use once I've reached a

Having a bag-within-a-bag, in the case of the author's hygiene supplies, can help compartmental-ize and prioritize survival needs if shedding excess gear becomes a necessity.

safe destination: a sleeping bag, small blanket, an extra set of clothes and Goretex layers I've vacuum-sealed, shower shoes, a set of hiking boots, and a few trash bags. Additionally, I have some freeze-dried food, just in case.

Closing Thoughts

I'm fortunate enough to have a fireproof vault where I keep all of my important documents. Otherwise, I'd be packing another bag to place inside this pack. But that's the beauty of this particular bag — it can fit a lot of stuff! It also still has plenty of room for me to shove those last-minute additions: wallet, phone, and pistol with extra mags. I hope I never need to use this bag, but knowing it's there makes me feel a lot better about the one threat that could force me from my refuge. Until then, I'll keep my ear on the scanner and watch for fire planes above. ⁑

MAKE & MODEL
Osprey
Ariel 65

MSRP
Original version seen here discontinued. Updated version $310.

URL
www.osprey.com

The Austere Environment Bag

By **Miles Vining**

Working in an austere environment brings with it a unique set of challenges when it comes to packing and maintaining a sustainment backpack that allows one to be independent and successful. The bag I'll be describing is a culmination of three separate trips to Syria with a relief group that focuses on casualty and humanitarian needs in conflict zones throughout the world. In order to support our team and our mission, I spent a good amount of time working out of my bag, and thus it was a very important addition to my gear selection.

Because we were vehicle-mounted, we had the liberty of bringing more personal items in a larger duffel-sized bag as well. But I needed something that would sustain me throughout varying weather conditions, in the front seat of our vehicles while on the road, and could be used to quickly bed down for the night. Due to the ever-changing circumstances of our relief work, sometimes we stayed in a single location for weeks, other times we were moving on a daily basis as needs and requirements fluctuated day to day. One day we could be sleeping in a comfortable hotel in the Syrian town of Qamishli, the next on ground mats in a rural field with our electronics powered by vehicles, power banks, and solar panels. Through much trial and error (which is never-ending), I settled on a combination and balance of items that allowed me to support our team's work.

Selection

I found an assault pack-sized backpack more useful than a waist-mounted or even a ruck option better for working in Syria for a number of reasons. An assault pack can be kept up front in a driver seat; it can be slung over the headrest out of the way; if you have to walk a long distance or transit via other vehicles, you can sustain yourself well. In the event that you need to fill it with mission-essential equipment (such as medical supplies and communications gear), it can support that aspect of a mission for an entire day or more.

Due to the nature of the threats abroad, a small measure of mitigating being targeted comes with maintaining a low profile. I often see products in the tactical gear world that bill themselves as low-profile/low-visibility but realistically fall short. If a bit of kit is Coyote tan or has some sort of MOLLE panel or Velcro sections, it screams tactical to even the most casual observer and will certainly raise eyebrows from those willing to do harm.

Contents

I made sure to always keep certain contents of the pack with it, while others would be constantly switched out depending on the mission tempo and daily rhythm of our team. Depending on the weather conditions and seasons, sometimes it'd include warming layers and appropriate jackets.

A very important note to be made here is the necessity of electronics and their accessories. Some of our most essential tasks depended on the ability to communicate, edit reports, power our phones, and top off our headlamps with rechargeable batteries. Even without a cellular connection, phones can be incredibly useful tools in an austere environment. Taking photographs of casualties, navigating offline with MapsMe, and sending documents and reports to team members in the field via a Bluetooth connection were all critical tasks that our phones permitted. In order to support these, I always carried the follow-

ing cables: MicroUSB, Apple Lightning, USB-C, and a 12V power port cable. On top of these electronics was a Goal Zero power bank that can support AC outlet charging or be hooked up to a solar panel, in addition to a smaller Goal Zero power bank to recharge my headlamp. Finally, I have my laptop (with hard case) and a Sandisk 2-Terabyte Solid State Drive — possibly one of the smallest on the commercial market that won't break a typical budget.

Other staple items were my first-aid kit (TQ, gauze, bandages, latex gloves), local scarf (can be used to cover face, hide sensitive items, clean or dry equipment, or function as a ground mat), flip-flops, international power adapter, pens, extra pair of socks, oral hygiene gear, raincoat, boonie hat, and textured gloves. During colder seasons, I made sure to pack a lightweight jacket and a beanie. If the weather got even worse I could put in thinner warming layers as well.

Closing Thoughts

The bag I chose and the items I packed in it were the result of constant trial and error over several mission trips, realizing what was truly important and what wasn't. But all of this could change overnight if I find a deficiency that needs to be fixed. More important than any of these items is an ability to always be thinking and finding a better way, realizing that there's usually no single solution to dynamic mission requirements that'll last. That's how we can get channeled into poor gear selection and is something we need to be considering when working in an austere environment. ⋕

When travelling through austere environments, it's important to pack light and efficiently.

MAKE & MODEL
Mountainsmith
Approach 25 Daypack

MSRP
$90 — This pack has been discontinued, but the Clear Creek 25 offers similar features and pricing.

URL
mountainsmith.com

The Amazon Gray Man Pack

Looking for Preps in All the Wrong Places

By **Brady Pesola**

By now, most people in self-defense or preparedness-oriented communities know what the term "gray man" signifies. It's the idea that you can walk around with all of your emergency tools at the ready without looking "tactical." This is funny because it's so easy to spot. Many of us are never truly gray, because we allow our preparedness to become a lifestyle or culture. To that end, many of us wear *something* that sends a signal to others and lets them know we are of this mindset, or culture. And believe it or not, there are characteristics of the gray man suit that are easy to profile by anyone who wants to do so, whether friend or foe. This means we're almost defeating ourselves.

However, there's still a large and legitimate market for low-profile gray man gear, and one of the biggest categories in this arena is packs. But sometimes the best sources for this kind of equipment are places that *don't* specialize in it. I've been recently looking for a different pack to carry for my day job working executive protection. I was on one of my favorite online tactical gear sites, Amazon, looking for my next ultimate gray man bag, when I stumbled upon DSLR camera bags. I was checking them out, and there's a wide variety to choose from. They have canvas and leather, bike messenger sling bags, sleek corporate bags, in all sorts of shapes and sizes.

Then I got to thinking, *these things are really well-built, padded to protect valuable equipment, and many are designed for quick access to a camera in the same way we like quick access to a firearm.* I also really took a keen interest in the organization compartments. I carry a lot of gear to keep clients and myself safe, and I hate having to dig through the bag to find stuff. The DLSR bags already come with a multitude of compartments, Velcro slots, quick-access zippers, and organizer pockets. All of them come with a compartment for computers and/or iPads. Finally, none of them looked at all tactical. Then it hit me: I don't think I've ever seen anyone make use of a camera bag for their EDC.

Shortly after making this realization, I'm on my second camera bag. I thought the first one was going to be great, but a couple months in the zipper broke — that's a no-go. Rather than buying sight unseen over the internet again, I went to Best Buy to check out their bags and found a winner. Let me introduce you to Lowepro camera bags — specifically, the Lowepro Flipside 300 AW II. This thing will run you about $120 but, in my opinion, it's well worth it. After having surfed their website, the company really has an outstanding selection of bags that, ironically enough, include some tactical and camo-looking ones — for the gray man who likes to print just a little. I'm really impressed by their selection of bags and applications. Some are more geared toward wilderness backpacking, some for urban carry, and some have a nice combo for both applications.

The Lowepro Flipside has a large compartment that takes up the whole bag. Some bags that I've found split the main compartment in half with an opening on the lower half, either in the front of the bag or in the back neck area, and the rest use up the whole length of the bag. I've decided after the first bag that had the split compartment, I like the full-length compartment more. It has more room and more Velcro slots for organization. What I really like when I open it up is how quickly I can access the compartments. The zippers move smoothly, and there's no protective material over the zipper to snag and impede access.

A slim admin pocket on the outside of the pack provides organized storage for small items, such as business cards, documents, and small electronic devices.

When the compartment opens, you're treated to a light gray contrasting color to the black, which makes it simple to find gear, along with five potential compartments and a small detachable zip compartment that's perfect for my gun when it's not on my hip. The rest of the compartments can be moved and modified to fit your needs and the gear you carry.

The size of the bag is important to me as well. In EP, I don't want a big cumbersome bag that I have to try to maneuver when on the move with the client. I like that the bag isn't very big to make it look like I have a bunch of stuff inside of it. The way the bag is designed makes it feel sturdy, easy to carry, and light. This is one of the better bags that I've carried. ⊞

MAKE & MODEL
Lowepro
Flipside 300 AW II

MSRP
$120

URL
www.lowepro.com

The "Office Escape" Bag

A Pack to Facilitate Leaving Work and Reuniting with Family in an Emergency

By **Alexander Crown**

Gamut's full zip/unzip feature allows supplies to be retrieved from anywhere in the main compartment without digging through everything else.

Unless you're one of the fortunate few who gets to work from home every day, you probably work in an office, out in the field, or at some other remote location. I work approximately 14 miles from my house, and am lucky that between myself and home is my wife's office and my children's school. I like to think of these places as "checkpoints" along my route. In the event of an emergency that doesn't allow me to drive to these places, I have the plan of walking or borrowing a bike.

The contents of this bag are designed to help me along the way, where I'll be traversing a multitude of environments that include large agriculture fields, trailer parks, subdivisions, and industrial complexes. All these spaces are taken into consideration for ease of movement, potential resupply points, and possible threats. Route planning became an important aspect of this with several alternate routes. The shortest distance is the last leg, where I'd have children in tow.

The Pack

The base of the kit is a Vertx Gamut 2.0 Backpack in gray to maintain a lower profile in the urban jungle. At 25 liters, the backpack is just the right size to not overload myself and to keep some maneuverability. The straps are comfortable for long-term wear, and there's a waist belt. The thin waist belt offers little in weight management, but will keep the pack from bouncing around during strenuous movements. I also prefer a pack that has a decent amount of internal organization, and this one delivers. Completed, this backpack kit weighs 22.2 pounds. Usually the pack sits in the back of my SUV, so its compact size is a plus for other cargo considerations.

The Contents

Externally, both sides contain water bottle pockets. These are left empty — instead, I use the pouch directly behind them to keep two 700ml Smartwater bottles (one per side). Keeping the bottles inside the pouch helps keep them from falling out and the backpack from being too wide. Within the back panel is an empty 50-ounce CamelBak bladder that can be filled along the way. The top pocket has quick-access items that include spare prescription glasses, wrist-mounted GPS, Gorilla tape, and a headlamp. Lastly, the front compartment has a small lightweight shelter kit containing a Bushcraft Outfitters 10x7-foot tarp, four aluminum tent stakes, and varying lengths of 550 cord.

Internally, the pack has a few zippered pockets and is mostly lined with loop Velcro. I affixed a Blue Force Gear Ten Speed Triple M4 Mag pouch to the top to keep more items close at hand without having to open up the entire bag. This includes a spare Glock 9mm 24-round magazine and a Yaesu FT-60R handheld ham radio (yes, I have my license). The radio has a small antenna and a large slim-jim antenna nearby. In the middle is a SOF-T tourniquet. Opposite in the pen pouches is a Leatherman tool, glass breaker, Sharpie marker, and lighter.

The inside portion has two small zipper pouches that include spare batteries, zip ties, ExoTac Rip Spool, sillcock key, small mirror, notebook, and a Southord PXS-14 lockpick set. The lower pocket has wet wipes and an Aquamira Frontier Pro water filter. This filter works in conjunction with the Smartwater bottles and CamelBak bladder to keep me hydrated while on the move and resupply from the river or using the Sillcock key at commercial buildings.

In the main bag compartment is:
> First aid kit (booboo kit)
> Vortex Solo R/T 8x36 monocular
> Snowpeak cook set with fuel, spork, and mini stove
> 1 serving Mountain House Mac & Cheese
> Compressed toilet paper in Ziploc bag
> Food bag (trail mix, granola bars, candy, etc.) — all contents are kid-friendly and can be eaten while on the move
> The bottom of the main compartment houses a waterproof bag with a hard-shell jacket, spare socks, shemagh, and work gloves.
> ESEE Knives PR4

Closing Thoughts

This bag is meant to sustain myself for movement to my wife, then to our children on an abnormal workday. It supplements my first line of gear carried on my body — Glock 19, pocketknife, bandanna, ankle trauma kit, and SureFire Stiletto flashlight. The radio is for the link-up between my wife and myself, as her bag has a similar one, as well as listening on the local stations for more information. The radio battery is checked weekly during the local net call.

The loaded bag is a comfortable weight for either my wife or myself to carry individually for the entire trek, in the event that we need to switch out the load. The purpose of three water storage items is to be able to drink on the move and have the ability to hand a bottle to my wife or the children without needing to stop. The included on-the-go snacks are mainly for the kids, but all are high in sugars, and Mountain House Mac & Cheese is their favorite in case we get stuck somewhere for an extended period of time and are able to boil some water with the small cook set. Having desirable snacks, such as candy, makes for a good bribe to keep the kids quiet and moving.

Overall, the contents are no-frills and are meant to sustain me, my wife, and two children for a day-ish-long hike, over not-so-difficult terrain. The children's school is the closest checkpoint to the house at 5.5 miles. It'll be slow moving with them in tow, but the gear we have will make it somewhat easier. Still, route planning, physical fitness, and family communications are the most important elements in our plan to make it home safely. ::

All buttoned up, the Vertx Gamut presents a nice clean look that blends well in modern suburbia.

MAKE & MODEL
Vertx
Gamut 2.0

MSRP
$215

URL
www.vertx.com

By **Joey Nickischer**

The Hard-Sided iM2950 Pelican Storm Case Offers Protection for Valuable Search & Rescue Gear

The First Responder Case

My introduction to Pelican cases came decades ago when I first started doing rescue work. I was arriving to a training class and spotted a pile of black, hard-sided boxes sitting outside, but there was a problem — it was starting to rain. Thinking that whatever was inside the cases must be valuable and could possibly be damaged by the rain, I quickly found one of the instructors and proclaimed that we needed to get the boxes moved to a dry location.

The instructor came outside and chuckled a little, realizing the equipment I was concerned about was already stored inside Pelican cases. He calmly explained that they

Pelican cases have a long-standing reputation for bomb-proof durability.

were waterproof. When I asked if he was sure the contents would be OK, the instructor said that everything would be fine. He proceeded to grab one of the cases, and deliberately threw it on the ground from chest height, very roughly. It thudded against the asphalt as it bounced and tumbled. He said that nothing short of a tank was going to hurt the contents of those cases. That was quite the eye-opener for me and set the bar for all my future equipment that needed a high level of protection.

Today, I'm talking about the iM2950 Pelican Storm Case. Measuring in at 31.3 by 20.4 by 12.2 inches on the outside, with the inside dimensions about 2 inches smaller, this 3.17-cubic-foot medium-sized case is ruggedly built to take the abuse and protect the contents. It'll keep water out, with its included EPDM O-ring seal, and offers a buoyancy of more than 200 pounds. This is enough to keep most things afloat, should the case end up in the drink. Heck, with that much flotation, you could probably use it as an improvised life raft.

As soon as you pick up this case, you can tell how ruggedly it's built. Weighing in at 20.8 pounds empty, it feels quite solid. The three main handles are chunky and rugged, providing a nice gripping surface that doesn't dig painfully into your hands. There's also an extendable handle and wheels so that you can roll this case like luggage.

There are a variety of interior configurations available directly from Pelican. You can have it completely empty to fill as your needs dictate, or do what is most commonly done — order it with the foam kit. That kit includes six lay-

ers of foam, four of which are 2-inch Pick N Pluck. One 2-inch piece is mated to the lid, and the final 0.63-inch pad sits at the bottom. There's also an excellent Trekpak Case Divider System that comes with 7/16-inch-thick rigid panels (walls), steel-locking pins, top and bottom foam, plus a cutting tool. The divider sections are manufactured from waterproof, closed-cell foam that's laminated to a rigid corrugated plastic panel. It's a pretty slick system that works well. With my case build, it uses both the Trekpak system to hold the tablet computer, and the foam kit to pad everything appropriately. If these options don't fit your needs, there's also a padded divider set and utility organizer with a variety of pockets, pen slots, and a business card holder.

With this case, we adapted it to hold 20 of the Grace Industries SuperCell SC500 SM GPS units in chargers, two repeaters, a tablet computer, and the ability to charge all of them with the case closed. The Grace Industries Supercell is a lone worker safety device. What that means is that these devices monitor a worker through a motion detector. If no motion is detected for a pre-selected period of time (ours are set for 5 minutes), the alarm will begin to sound and the other devices in the vicinity will also alert. This lets the other members of the team find and help the solo worker. The 900 MHz radio signal can also be sent to a computer monitoring system that can decode the latitude and longitude position and overlay it with an on-screen map. For my purposes doing technical rescue, which can include building collapse scenarios or lost person searches in a wilderness environment, it's an amazing way to keep tabs on everybody to help ensure their safety.

Most people purchasing a watertight storage box would never dream of doing exactly what we did: drilling a large hole in the side of it to accommodate a 120-volt household plug. But, with emergency services work, we need our equipment to be ready to operate on a moment's notice, and that means ensuring our equipment is fully charged all the time. But don't worry about the hole; it's a simple matter to add gasket sealant around the hole and fill the internals of the plug with silicone sealant, once you verify that everything is working as it should. The silicone will restore the original watertight condition.

The iM2950 Pelican Storm case has five latches to hold the lid securely shut — three on the front and one on each non-hinged side. You would think that these latches would be very tight and difficult to open, but Pelican has a unique Press and Pull latch that locks automatically and opens with the press of a button. I find it much nicer than their legacy latches that require a good slap to close and can take a bit of muscle to open. There are also two padlockable hasps if you need to further safeguard your equipment.

When you need a top-notch case to protect your investment in critical, expensive equipment, Pelican cases deserve your immediate consideration.

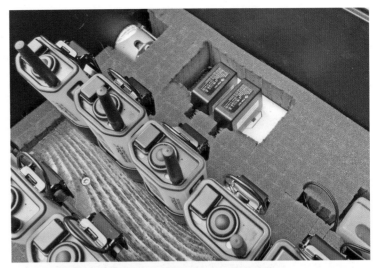

Above: The foam inserts can be plucked or cut to accommodate a wide variety of equipment.

Left: With just a drill and some silicone sealant, we were able to modify our case to charge the electronics inside without having to open it up.

MAKE & MODEL
Pelican
iM2950 Storm Travel Case

INTERIOR
29 by 18 by 10.5 inches

EXTERIOR
31.3 by 20.4 by 12.2 inches

WEIGHT (EMPTY)
20.80 pounds

PRICE
$253 (no foam); $300 (with foam)

URL
www.pelican.com/us/en/

ACCESSORIES
Pelican TrekPak Case Divider Kit: $208

The Escalated Threat Pack

By Patrick McCarthy

Active shooters, terrorists, and other mass-murderers have no uniform code of conduct. They carry out vicious attacks on a variety of targets, with little to no warning and a goal of generating carnage as quickly as possible. They select the most effective weapons they can get their hands on, and hope their victims are utterly defenseless.

The concealed pistol on your belt is an excellent tool for self-defense against these adversaries, but it's not the best possible tool for every situation. There's a reason law enforcement officers carry shotguns and/or carbines in their vehicles in addition to their duty pistols. If you're ever facing an opponent with multiple weapons, hundreds of rounds of ammo, and possibly even body armor, having those same tools at your disposal can even the odds. With this worst-case scenario in mind, I set out to build what I refer to as an "escalated threat" pack — a set of tools for situations that might require more than a handgun.

Before I proceed, I want to make something clear: This gear would only be used in a very narrow set of circumstances. If a mass shooting occurs, escaping safely with your loved ones (and anyone else you can help) should be priority number one. I'm not telling you to kit up, rush in, and try to stop the bad guy on your own. Doing so could lead to you being shot by the perpetrator or by confused first responders who think you are the perpetrator. But in an instance where you're trapped in the path of an oncoming, heavily armed enemy, and have at least a few seconds to prepare, these tools can give you a better way to defend yourself.

The Weapon

If you've flipped through this issue already, you'll recognize the Springfield Arms Saint Edge EVAC. Read my full review for all the details on this AR pistol. Suffice to say, it offers a whole lot of potency in a very small package. For this setup, I swapped the 20-round mag to a 30-rounder and left the detachable forend connected.

That allows me to keep a round chambered and shave several seconds off the time I'd need to get the gun into a fight — just unfold the brace, flip the safety, and go. Even with these adjustments, there's still room to spare in the pack. Speaking of which ...

The Pack

I wanted a high-quality, relatively plain-looking container for my gear, one that wouldn't appear out of place at the foot of a desk or on the front seat of a vehicle. These are the type of places it should be stored, under control at all times — it won't do any good five minutes away locked in a trunk. This led me to the Vertx Gamut 2.0, a 25-liter pack that's specifically designed to provide quick access to a personal defense weapon (PDW) or other mid-size concealed weapon. The exterior has no visible PALS webbing; instead, it hides it beneath a pull-down front flap. I used this to stash a C-A-T tourniquet and two 30-round mags in TYR Tactical pouches out of sight behind the flap.

The Gamut's large main compartment is lined with loop fabric that permits attachment of the removable laptop sleeve or Vertx Tactigami accessories. Instead, I opted for a Vertx SOCP rigid insert panel, which clips to the inside of the pack and serves as an organizer. Velcro strips and shock cord were used to retain a pair of Walker's active ear pro (a necessity for this blaster), one more 30-round mag, and an M14 smoke grenade from IWA International. In addition to its function as a rescue signal, the smoke grenade could be used to obscure an attacker's vision while you escape a dangerous area.

Admin pouches on the other side of the compartment contain general-purpose tools: a Pokka all-weather pen and Rite in the Rain notepad, Lionsteel glass breaker, Gerber Center-Drive multitool with bit set, Streamlight Bandit mini headlamp, Mylar emergency blanket, and heavy-duty latex gloves. A Hot-Pull Tab at the top of the main compartment can be secured between the two zipper pulls, allowing the main compartment to be ripped open with a single, fluid motion.

Concealed zippers behind the exterior water bottle pouches reveal two more organizer pockets. One contains a Baofeng UV-5R radio, which could be used to call for help or listen to news reports if you're engaged in a standoff, as well as some chem lights. The other has a TacMed Solutions Pocket Medical Kit with a tourniquet, Combat Gauze, compression bandage, chest seal, and gloves. There's also a WE Knife Stonefish fixed-blade knife in a Kydex belt sheath.

Ballistic Protection

Lastly, DFNDR Armor provided a hard armor plate that was made to fit perfectly into the zippered back panel of this pack. The American-made Level IIIA panel is constructed from Ultra High Molecular Weight Polyethylene (UHMWPE), and has been independently tested to defeat handgun rounds up to and including .44 Magnum. It wouldn't stop a high-velocity rifle round, but plates rated to that standard would be far heavier and more expensive. It's reassuring to know I have a substantial level of ballistic protection in the pack, which can be reversed and used as an improvised vest. Wearing it this way also gives me access to the spare mags and TQ on the concealed front panel.

If I someday come face-to-face with a heavily armed individual bent on mass murder, would I prefer to tell him to wait a sec, jog to my car, put on rifle plates and a helmet, prep my full-size AR-15, and enter the fight completely prepared? Of course. But I also know it doesn't work that way. Bearing in mind practicality, concealment, and accessibility, this escalated threat pack is a much more viable real-world defense kit. ▓

MAKE & MODEL
Vertx
Gamut 2.0

MSRP
$215

URL
www.vertx.com

MAKE & MODEL
DFNDR Armor
Level IIIA Handgun Rated Backpack Armor

MSRP
$215

URL
www.dfndrarmor.com

Gray Man EDC Bag

There's a Difference Between Trying to Look Discreet & Actually Being Discreet

By **Cody Martin**

This discontinued version of the Surge pack is more than a decade old, but still going strong.

s a federal agent for 12 years, I never knew if I'd be conducting surveillance, responding to a bomb threat, or meeting with a U.S. attorney. Defensive, medical, survival, and day-to-day gear had to be accounted for. My work has now shifted to consulting, but my desire to balance practicality and preparedness hasn't diminished.

The Backpack

When it comes to bags, I like something very low key. I want it to be able to blend in regardless of whether I'm at a college campus, urban area, rural area, or airport.

My current go-to bag is a 10-plus-year-old North Face Surge backpack. Weighing in at 3 pounds unloaded, it's slightly heavier than some alternatives, but the organization and comfort make up for the extra heft.

The capacity is just over 2,000 cubic inches (33L), which is smaller than some of my other bags, but still sufficient. The overall dimensions come in around 20 by 13.5 by 9.5 inches.

I find this bag to be very comfortable under heavy loads, which makes it easy to carry for longer periods of time. It has a waist belt that facilitates carry when on the move, but it can be hidden when not in use. It also has a pretty beefy grab handle, which is important when you have to grab and go.

Work Gear

As part of my job, I spend a lot of time online or on the phone. I need to be connected or have the ability to be connected to get work done while I'm on the move. I do a lot of work on my laptop and also my cell phone. Keeping these devices charged and functional is critical.

In order to support my electronics, there are certain things I need to carry, which include an assortment of cables, an Anker PowerCore 10000 power bank, and a set of AirPods.

I also carry a small canvas zippered bag with other peripheral items like an encrypted thumb drive, adapters, pens, pencils, and Nite Ize Gear Ties to keep small pieces of gear organized. If I need to go analog, a notepad and pocket-sized notebook are in there as well.

Medical

When it comes to medical gear, I always carry basic first-aid items. For normal everyday aches, pains, scrapes, and scratches, I carry an Adventure Medical Kits Ultralight .5, which I have supplemented with additional medication and bandages.

If I encounter more serious issues, I always have a tourniquet in my bag (and a second one on my body), as well as hemostatic gauze, chest seals, and so on. These are kept in a Maxpedition Moire pouch and stored for easy access.

When considering carrying medical gear, it's important to not just focus on shooting-related incidents. You're significantly more likely to encounter work-related accidents and vehicle-related accidents. Be prepared for all likely scenarios.

Self-Defense

In addition to the spare mag I carry on the body, I carry an extra magazine to support my primary carry weapon, in case I need it for an extended fight.

I also carry a less-lethal option in the form of OC spray. I prefer Sabre Red, and I keep this spare in my bag in case I forget my primary at home. I can grab it quickly and throw it in my pocket if I'm heading out into certain public areas or anywhere else that warrants extra attention.

A SureFire EDCL2-T flashlight is stored as a backup to my primary EDC light. To ensure it always has power, I carry a battery case with extra CR123 batteries.

One of the features I like about the Surge backpack is it has an extra interior compartment/sleeve on the back of the pack. I use it to house a Level 3A Hardwire Bulletproof Bag Insert.

This panel offers IIIA protection and measures 10 by 13 inches. It fits flat against my back and can also double as a dry erase board. This has proven to be an extra benefit several times when meeting with clients or teaching classes.

Survival

Like most of you, I store expanded survival kits in my home and my vehicle, so this bag is intended to supplement them. Most, but not all of these items, have multiple purposes, which is always a plus.

I have a pouch made by Tuff Possum Gear that houses fire-starting tools like a Bic butane lighter wrapped in duct tape, an EXOTAC titanLIGHT liquid-fuel lighter, a ferro rod, survival matches, and tinder tabs.

Water peripherals, like the Sawyer Mini Water Filter, are carried in the same pouch as my fire gear. I also have a GRAYL Ultralight Purifier Bottle that's used as a regular water bottle, but can also provide quick purification when needed. I have a Platypus collapsible water bladder to house purified water or extra water if the situation warrants. It sits with my fire gear and the Sawyer.

There's also 100 feet of paracord on a spool for those times when I need cordage. Outside of all the survival

benefits and uses of paracord, it can be used for a lot of everyday tasks as well. The spool helps keep the cordage neat and organized instead of ending up in a big knot.

Inside you'll also find a small E&E pouch containing various saws, blades, lock picks, handcuff keys, a signaling mirror, and other extras. You never know when you might lock yourself out of the house.

A pair of waterproof pants and a jacket from Mountain Hardwear are rolled up at the bottom of the main compartment in case I get caught out in a sudden downpour.

Additional Gear

In addition to the gear above, I've also stashed the following items in various compartments in my pack:

- ›Multi-tool
- ›Bandana
- ›Earplugs
- ›Headlamp
- ›Chemlights
- ›Clif Bars
- ›Spork
- ›Hand soap
- ›Cash
- ›Locking carabiner
- ›Gloves

There are more miscellaneous tools stuffed here and there, but you get the gist of the pack. Again, this is mainly for work and daily life, but I feel like there's a fine line between what's normal and the next major crisis. Being able to comfortably walk that line and having the ability to move in either direction is paramount. ⚏

My EDC bag loadout contains mundane office supplies as well as emergency survival tools.

MAKE & MODEL
North Face
Surge

MSRP
$129 (current version)

URL
wwwwww.thenorth face.com

Cold-Weather Survival Pack

A Loadout for Getting Stuck in Inclement Weather

By **Patrick Diedrich**

Feeling cold is a matter of perspective. Hot summer days can make the nights feel unbearably cool by comparison. This scenario is precluded by the fact that when 90 degrees F turns to 60, your health and wellbeing is usually not in immediate danger. Contrast this with a region which has harsh, or longer than average, winter seasons and this temperature change dynamic creates a new series of risks. For example, when temperatures dip into the negatives, even mild sustained winds can cause exposed skin to freeze solid in minutes. In the U.S., approximately 1,300 deaths occur each year due to cold-weather injures, about twice the number of fatalities incurred by heat.

Preparing for extreme winter conditions means preparing for the worst. As an avid outdoorsman in a region with extreme amounts of snowfall, I needed a pack that could accommodate spending a weekend snowshoeing, and just as easily be converted to a roadside emergency kit. In remote areas, if your vehicle gets stuck in a snowbank or you

25L storage capacity provides ample room for the essentials with room to spare.

MAKE & MODEL
Mystery Ranch
Saddle Peak

MSRP
$219

URL
www.mysteryranch.com

Saddle Peak's lightweight design and cold-weather durability make this the ideal bag when faced with formidable winter conditions.

become disoriented in a forest, you could be facing several days' worth of hiking to the nearest civilized outpost. Meeting my maker via cryogenesis never appealed to me, and the Saddle Peak backpack from Mystery Ranch is perfectly suited to prevent this, not only in weight and size, but also its functionality. It was designed for extended backcountry winter excursions and has versatility in droves, including gear-specific pockets and straps, a ridged yet comfortable synthetic frame, and zippers protected from snow and ice buildup.

One of the most important aspects for me was a balance of gear durability and loadout adaptability. When it comes to staying warm and thriving in a blizzard, I lean heavily on Varusteleka's Särmä products. Their thermal cloak is waterproof and lined with merino wool, a material that will stay warm even when wet and absorb odor. Another important aspect of Varusteleka's gear is that it was created as a higher-quality alternative to standard-issue Finnish military gear, which means it needs to withstand wear and tear in arctic conditions. Combine that with the fact that the Saddle Peak backpack has a front pocket specifically for this type of emergency gear, making it easily accessible when every second counts, and you have recipe for cold weather survival success.

I always have core gear available for first aid and fire-starting. The trauma kit has compression bandages, several Combat Application Tourniquets and an EMS blizzard blanket to treat hypothermia. It should also be noted that this is a modified version of the Individual First Aid Kit (IFAK) I carried on multiple deployments overseas. For rapid-snow-accumulation scenarios, Black Diamond has an avalanche kit which includes a metal alloy collapsible

shovel, avalanche probe, and GPS locator. The tools in this kit can be put to use in a variety of situations. The probe can be used as an impromptu shelter support and the shovel for digging a wind-blocking burrow or digging out a stuck vehicle. For fire, I pack some lighters and matches, a few emergency candles, and a heavy-duty puukko-style knife from Varusteleka, which can be used for cutting and chopping firewood, in addition to traditional knife uses. Being seen can be a matter of life or death, whether you're on the roadside or trying to get the attention of a rescuer. For this reason, I pack a Fenix HM65R SuperRaptor headlamp, also sourced through Varusteleka, which is rechargeable and has an output range between eight and 1,400 lumens.

Being active in the cold means more calories are being burned, so it's also important to have a high-calorie food source on hand. Food is even more important if you have to hunker down for a while. I prefer using a canteen and metal canteen cup over other water systems simply because I don't have to worry as much about damaging the vessel, freezing tubes, or puncturing a bag. Having a canteen cup makes heating food or melting snow for water much easier.

Lastly, one of the most important things to do to prepare for a cold weather emergency is something that won't fit in any bag — letting someone know your plan. Telling a trusted friend or relative exactly where you're going and how long you intend to be gone, could be the most important thing you can do to preserve your health and your life. If you think you're headed into inclement weather on the road, or if you only plan on spending an hour or two in the backcountry, tell someone, even if you're only sending a quick text message.

What gets packed in the bag is easily adapted to the situation I expect to find myself. How I pack when I have to be on the road during a snowstorm is slightly different than when I'm using it for recreation. Most people who live in cold regions are already wearing things like insulated jackets, boots, gloves, etc. But imagine driving to visit someone, only to find yourself in the middle of an ice storm or a blizzard with whiteout conditions. The vehicle you're in loses control or is struck by another vehicle. Now you're stranded on the side of the road; it's too dangerous to keep the engine running because of leaking fuel and help could be a long way off. The roadside emergency loadout is intended to be able to respond to trauma and stay warm until help arrives. Or picture being on a remote trek when an unexpected whiteout occurs, and now you must hunker down until the storm passes. Having the right equipment on hand can make all the difference in the world. ✖

Incognito Urban Messenger Bag

A Low-Profile EDC Gear Container

By **Boris Milinkovich**

The concept of Every Day Carry is to allow perpetual access to tools to increase resilience in times of need. Simply put, it's valuable to have gear readily accessible to deal with most situations I may come across in the course of my day. Aside from simply meeting my own immediate needs, it also allows me to help others.

Depending on the environment, context, and level of preparedness you're trying to achieve, you can tailor your EDC loadouts accordingly. For my purposes, I prefer a messenger bag while moving around an urban environment on foot, in a car, or on public transit.

Realistically, you can't be ready for everything all the time, especially when it's all carried in a smaller bag. So, I balance a mix of capability, cost, weight, and what's appropriate against what I'm preparing for. It's also important to note that you'll need adequate training to go with the tools you carry.

The J. Crew Harwick briefcase is the host for the majority of my urban EDC gear. It doesn't have an over-flap like some messenger bags, but it performs in the same way with direct access to the pockets. In this configuration, I can carry my EDC loadout and laptop without being too heavy or bulky. The only downside I have found is that, if overloaded and carried for a long period of time, the shoulder strap can dig into your neck or slide off your shoulder — an issue not as common with backpacks.

My main EDC goals are to have the following capabilities:

> Access to a multi-tool for common fixes (pliers, blade, scissors, screwdriver, pry tool, etc.)

> Deal with minor injuries, pain, and stop bleeding

> Have light and fire on command in the dark

> Access escape routes or life-saving items in exigent circumstances

> Render aid to self or others

> Facilitate travel during an emergency (to get home or to another relatively safe location)

As I live and work in Canada, any firearms are unfortunately a no-go to carry. Our laws differ greatly from those in the USA and the options available to us are far fewer, so I pack accordingly.

Compartmentalizing gear into pockets and pouches makes every item easy to locate quickly.

To meet the parameters I set for myself, I carry the following in my messenger bag, in addition to what I have on my person as first-line EDC:

› BIC lighter
› Leatherman Wingman multi-tool
› Nitecore E4K small flashlight
› Lock pick/bypass tools and escape tools (check your local laws)
› Personal Protective Equipment (PPE — mask, gloves, wipes, and sanitizer)
› First-aid basics (Band-Aids, Tylenol, dressings, Quik-Clot, tourniquet)
› Notepad, measuring tape, and pens
› Backup battery for phone or other devices, with various cables and adapters
› Duct tape, garbage bag, and paracord
› Some cash for transport or emergency purchases
› Business promo materials (cards, stickers, patches, etc.)

You may also consider adding a ballistic panel as a backer in your bag. They're usually very thin, light, and flexible, so they shouldn't affect your overall bag bulk. A panel can add protection against projectiles and shrapnel without being too obvious inside this type of discreet bag. Be sure to check your local laws in respect to this.

In the outside double pockets, I carry business promo materials and quick-access items (tourniquet and hand sanitizer). On the other outer-pocket, I carry a book. Inside, one pocket has two removable pouches — one holds some first-aid gear, a garbage bag, and PPE; the other pouch contains a battery, cables and adapters, lock pick tools, and duct tape. A final pocket houses a multi-tool, paracord, flashlight, notebook, pens, and wipes.

With the gear carried in this way, I keep everything organized, easily accessible, and streamlined. It also leaves the two sections of the main bag empty to carry my laptop and any other stuff I may need.

I really like the messenger bag/commuter briefcase setup. Regardless of what your loadout consists of, you're going to have to carry it in a convenient manner. All those pieces tend to add weight in your pockets and can impede movement. Nowadays, the messenger bag has gained a level of acceptance among the urban masses, and tends to stand out far less than backpacks. These bags can traverse a wider range of urban environments while still keeping your hands free and maintaining a lower-profile. Far more places will zero-in on backpacks as threats, while overlooking messenger bags as innocuous business accessories. ◫

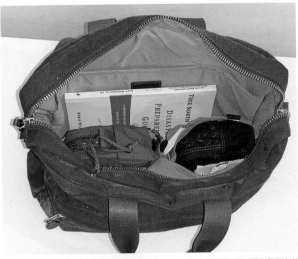

When the main compartment is open, there's no visible gear that would pique the interest of a bystander.

This bag blends seamlessly into an urban environment. It's surprisingly easy to walk, run, or climb with due to the adjustable strap and compact size.

MAKE & MODEL
J. Crew
Harwick Briefcase

MSRP
$120 (discontinued)

URL
www.jcrew.com

About the Author:

Boris Milinkovich, CD, CBCP, is a Canadian with a varied background of more than 20 years in military, law enforcement, and personal protection skillsets. He's the owner and training director at True North Tradecraft in Toronto, offering training and equipment to civilians and approved agencies in counter-custody, covert-entry, personal protection, and disaster preparedness. He can be reached through **www.truenorthtradecraft.ca**, **@truenorthtradecraft** (IG/FB/LinkedIn), and **@ttradecraft** on Twitter.

A Pack for Digital Preparedness

Urban Communication Kit

By **SoCal Offgrid**

As an electrical contractor with an interest in emergency preparedness, I've realized that there are a variety of events that could interfere with our normal communications infrastructure — if the internet and cell service go down, things can get chaotic quickly. If there's total loss of power, it's only going to get worse. As a result, I carry a kit that allows me to bypass these mainstream systems, and still stay in touch with those I care about.

MAKE & MODEL
Vertx
Commuter Sling 2.0

MSRP
$199

URL
www.vertx.com

The Backpack

I've carried $400 GoRucks, $100 REI bags, and a variety of CamelBaks on various adventures. You really have to try them all to get a sense of what feels good on your back. There seem to be two schools of thought regarding backpack choice — one group will remove their pack to go through the contents; the other will leave it attached to the shoulder while rummaging through it. The messenger-style backpack has some tactical advantages, since it leaves a smaller window of opportunity for a bag-snatcher and can give you better access to important items on the move.

This Vertx Commuter Sling 2.0 works exactly as designed. It has a rather large "Rapid Access" main storage compartment for a variety of tools. Whether it's a foldable rifle that requires a sling attachment point or your favorite handgun, the attachment possibilities are endless with the mounting systems Vertx offers. It also comes with retention G-hooks to prevent the bag from flopping open completely while surveying your environment. Its ballistic panel pocket easily accepts lightweight plates to give you a valuable layer of protection from projectiles and shrapnel flying in your direction.

This bag doesn't scream "tactical," so if you're trying to stay under the radar, it could be a great choice over some of the military-style bags out there.

Communication Equipment

GoTenna is a mesh network that can allow multiple devices to connect and chat offline. It offers a means of communicating silently within a small geographical area if there's no cellular or Wi-Fi service available (range will depend on the number of wireless devices in your vicinity).

Another alternative using the same LoRa Mesh technology is a stand-alone homebuilt communicator. This requires technical knowledge and soldering skills, but it's a stand-alone unit that doesn't require an Android/iPhone for communication. If placed in a familiar location, multiple devices can be linked to a repeater. A well-placed single repeater could potentially give you 10 miles of range. Buildings and trees obviously diminish these results. A "post office box" setting in this unit can save messages for when your device is in range.

A Baofeng ham radio is an excellent affordable device

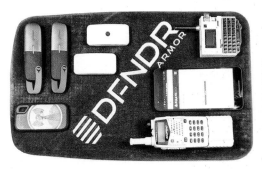

that's capable of communicating with other licensed ham radio operators within a decent range. They're also limited by terrain, and only travel from one to 10 miles under normal conditions. Maxing out at around 30 miles under ideal conditions would require a longer antenna and clear line of sight. It'd be a great portable way to communicate with someone in the event cell service wasn't an option — better yet, they're cheap enough that you can buy several for your family members and friends. If you need to extend that range to hundreds of miles, you need a high-powered, high-frequency (HF) radio and a general license.

The HackRF Portapack has a ton of features ranging from listening to/broadcasting a radio station, remote-starting your neighbor's car on a chilly morning for him, replacing a lost garage door opener, or chatting with a freight ship captain as he's coming into port. Although some features can be considered "nefarious" in nature, the all-in-one package is a very robust tool that can potentially reprogram traffic lights in your neighborhood or enable the restaurant buzzer to skip the long wait at your favorite diner. Use your powers responsibly and don't blame us if you get in trouble.

A Pirate Box is a small device that can broadcast your own LAN (Local Area Network). This can be a source to host a localized off-grid chat, share files, act as a "dead-drop" for digital information, or even provide an easy solution for an off-grid wireless camera setup. If you're tech-savvy, you can make one at home with less than $100 in materials, or you can purchase them pre-built.

Portable Power

Portable battery packs are vital to both power and recharge all the electronics discussed above. Mophie Powerstations have a track record of holding up to abuse. Extreme changes in climate and multiple charge/recharge events naturally wear out battery cells. Cheaper alternatives don't handle the wear and tear as well as some of the better brands, so do your research and get the most dependable unit you can afford.

18650 or Lithium-ion (Li-on) batteries pack a greater punch for some sensitive electronics, however, they have been known to spontaneously combust and can get you unwanted attention at TSA checkpoints. Keeping them safe and understanding their dangers is essential if you'll be using them for your equipment.

The CR123 batteries used in SureFire flashlights fall under the same category. Regular alkaline or nickel-metal hydride AA batteries just can't produce the power needed, and most rechargeable options tend to fizzle out rather quickly. Having a spare set of each type of disposable batteries in your bag is a requirement.

Solar chargers can be bulky and often don't perform as needed, but if you're in a pinch and all your resources are empty, an affordable foldup can serve as a last-ditch option for emergency power. Always keep a USB wall charger in your kit to borrow power from coffee shops and other local watering holes.

Having plenty of spare cables, both USB-C and Micro USB, can lead to tangles and clutter. Keeping them individually tied will help keep you organized and better prepared.

Medical

Being prepared for a fight is an automatic ticket to the "prepare to seal wounds" after-party. Tourniquets, chest seals, chito gauze, decompression needles, and Hello Kitty Band-Aids will take up very little room and invaluable space for any "What If" scenarios you may encounter. With the items contained in this pack and the everyday-carry gear in my pockets, I feel confident that I can weather any storm without being dependent on the power grid or established comms infrastructure.

For more info on the items in my kit, you can follow me on Instagram: @socal_offgrid.

Scoped Carbine Bag

A Perfect Pairing of Firearm, Pack, and Supplies

By **Kevin Estela**
Photos by **George Franek Photography**

The Scoped Carbine Class at Ridgeline Defense in New Hampshire has been on my to-do list for a long time. A scoped carbine is the Goldilocks porridge of choice, so to speak. Not dedicated for close-quarters or true long-range use, the scoped carbine can do most of it well, as long as you understand its realistic limitations. Configured with a Low Variable Power Optic (LVPO) and the right balance of bolt-on parts, this style of AR is a great contender for the "if I can only grab one" scenario.

Shortly after I signed up for the class, COVID-19 hit, along with ammo shortages and social unrest. This situation reinforced the value of a scoped carbine for protecting my family or traveling discreetly to help someone else. The class came at the perfect time to help me level up my skills on a platform that fits easily into a backpack.

Ridgeline Defense Instructor Rudy Gonsior demonstrating drills for students at the Scoped Carbine Course.

The Bag

The 5.11 RUSH100 is a large internal-frame backpack. The design is very straightforward with plenty of adjustment straps to keep the bag close to your body. The side pouches are removable, allowing the user to run the bag slicker, and they can be converted to a shoulder bag if necessary. A top pocket is fleece lined for eye pro, and the bottom pocket is compressible for a sleeping bag or, in my case, the forward and rear shooting rests. The bag comes with attachment straps at the bottom for a foam pad or sleeping bag. The aluminum stays and semi-rigid frame held the bag in place and also could serve double duty as a rifle rest taller than my bipod's legs.

Contents

With a backpack this big, it's easy to overpack. Extra room means you can carry more, but that isn't always positive. For a two-day scoped carbine class, I knew I could pack light, and I had plenty of room to spare. Ridgeline Defense sent students a final packing list a few days before the course, and the 5.11 RUSH100 could carry all that was required.

Clothing

Weather is always an uncertain variable. What you wear should allow you to change your body temperature accordingly — a notch up and a notch down. This shooting course lined up perfectly with Tropical Storm Fay; the forecast predicted scattered thunderstorms, humidity, and a high chance of rain on each day. Pair this with the

state bird of New Hampshire, the horse fly, and what that meant for me was packing long-sleeve shirts and pants for protection. I also wanted to leave room for a watch cap, gloves, neckerchief, and a spare set of socks. Rounding out clothing is a set of dedicated rain pants, gaiters, and rain jacket. Other considerations for the environment include bug dope and sunblock.

Rifle

The most important consideration for this pack was the scoped carbine it would contain. My rifle is a combination of an older (pre-'94 since I live in Connecticut) Eagle Arms lower with Geissele SSA-E trigger, Super 42 buffer, and a Bravo Company Kyle Defoor Spec Upper. This upper features a specific 1:7.7-inch twist barrel optimized for 77-grain Black Hills Ammo. It's a solid minute of angle rifle with that ammunition, and other ammo in that ballpark does well too. Due to the COVID crisis, I had a hard time acquiring enough Black Hills ammo, so I packed 75-grain Hornady Black ammo instead. The optic for this midrange class is the Trijicon 1-8 AccuPower in a GDI P-ROM mount. The only other accessories added to this rifle are a set of Troy BUIS, Streamlight TLR-1 HL, Blue Force Gear Vickers sling, and a Harris Bipod. A scoped AR-15 carbine is easily broken down and carried inside this pack. A makeshift divider can be fashioned from spare clothing, an old camping pad, or in my case, a folded shooting pad from Crosstac. With this rifle broken down and carried in the pack, I easily walked right into the local hotel each night without raising any concern.

Electronics

The benefit of using this particular pack for this course was the ability to organize with the multitude of pockets it comes with. I was able to separate my electronics, including a Kestrel, Leupold 650-yard rangefinder, and sensitive optics from my heavy and clunky metal water bottle and other items that could damage them. I also carried active ear pro. Electronics were carried in water-resistant Ziploc plastic bags along with a cotton rag to wipe any moisture from the optics.

Miscellaneous

Ridgeline's packing list included a rifle, a minimum of four 30-round magazines, ammo, a shooting pad, and support equipment. I also loaded my pack with basic daily use gear — granola bars and water, a small possibles pouch with emergency gear, a trauma kit, some firearms maintenance/cleaning equipment, flashlight, knife, and other kit. Each day, spare ammo was carried in stripper clips with a StripLULA loader. Generally, as you tack on

The author (6 feet and 215 pounds) wearing the RUSH100 pack for size reference.

Torrential rain and thunderstorms tested the willingness of the students and the water resistance of the gear the author carried.

more miles, a pack feels heavier, but when you burn through the ammo you carry, the opposite is true.

In the Field

In any martial arts or combatives training, you should always seek a better weapon and better position. What's better than a pistol? A rifle. What's better than a standing long-range shot? A more stable shot from a supported position. I used the RUSH100 backpack to carry all of my essentials for approximately 20 hours over two days. I had a surplus of room, and discovered I could remove the two outboard pockets and use them as internal storage organizers instead. For a course like this, that meant I could use them to separate short-range ball ammo from my longer-range precision ammo. As predicted, on day two, the skies opened up and poured, with lightning halting our training temporarily. The pack repelled water well, and the contents stayed dry. The lower separated compartment worked great to stow wet rain gear when the weather finally cleared in the final hours of the class.

The pack served a secondary purpose: to create more stability in the kneeling position behind barricades by straddling it like a saddle. This tip was one of many offered by our instructor from real-world experience using his ruck in the same way while deployed overseas. Another tip Rudy offered was using the pack, positioned straps-down with the opening toward the shooter in a prone position, as a gradual ramp to gain elevation and angle for shooting uphill. The training we were given worked well too. Rapid engagement techniques utilizing a 0.1 mil or 3 MOA hold at different ranges resulted in easy hits out to 400 yards with simple holds. The rifle worked extremely well with easy and fast controlled pairs with careful manipulation of the Geissele SSA-E trigger at close range and controlled careful shots at longer ranges. During the culminating events involving unknown distance target engagement from 15 yards out to 600,

The RUSH100 pack easily carried spare ammo, loading equipment, cleaning gear, electronics, and more during the duration of the Ridgeline Scoped Carbine course.

MAKE & MODEL
5.11 Tactical
RUSH100

WEIGHT
5.7 pounds

VOLUME
60 liters

MSRP
$250

URL
511tactical.com

Most rucks are shaped like a "ramp" that can be used to elevate your rifle.

the pack carried all I needed it to and the rifle responded as predicted with the DOPE we applied. At the end of the course, the pack easily swallowed up all my gear as it was policed and packed away for the drive home.

Of course, I didn't like everything about the pack — most of this came down to personal preference rather than design flaw. The waist belt buckle is only 1-inch wide; I'd prefer a more comfortable and secure 2-inch buckle. I also would've liked to see a compression strap on the waistband to pull the lower half of the bag closer to the body. The only other issue I encountered was with the layout of the zippers. I'd like to see an additional set on the main compartment to allow access to the side of the bag without "running" the zipper all the way around the track. Besides those little requests, I was pleased with the way it carried, held up, and organized my rifle gear.

Final Word

This bag and rifle are perfectly paired. From this point forward, I won't keep the bag loaded for a training course, but rather for a modern minuteman scenario where I need to travel discreetly to a family member's aid. I can ditch the spare clothing for just those environmental layers and have spare room for warmer gear in cooler months. I can keep this bag prepped near my gun safe, so all I'll have to do is grab the appropriate carbine for it. I never expected a global pandemic and civil unrest double whammy, but I can be better prepared for the next time something of this scale hits again. With the contents carried and skills learned, I can easily reach targets up to the "rifleman's half K" without issue. ⚏

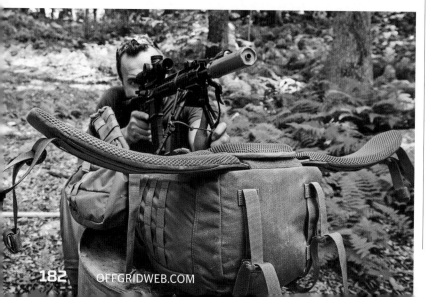

RECOIL TV
LIVE

A new podcast featuring RECOIL staff and subject matter experts giving their take on various topics including Firearms, Military, and everything relevant to the RECOIL lifestyle.

TUNE IN!

Hosted by
the staff of RECOIL

BROUGHT TO YOU BY

CARRY THE FUTURE®

AVAILABLE ON **RECOIL**TV
RECOIL.TV

Personal Security Detachment Bag

A Low-Vis Pack for Clandestine Missions
By **Joe Dawson**

ersonal Security Detachment (PSD) work isn't as glamorous as it sounds. The idea that you're always wearing a black suit with a curly earpiece hanging out of your ear like the Secret Service in the movies isn't accurate in most cases. The point is to offer close protection of a client or high-value individual. You don't want to look like a gang of heavily armed goons surrounding someone very important like the rings of the archery target encircling the bull's-eye. The more attention you bring to yourself, the riskier you make your unprotected movement in public areas.

During my time doing PSD work overseas, we had to protect quite a few high-value personnel. While armor plates and a pistol aren't necessarily hard to conceal, a carbine and a chest rig will make you stick out. In those situations where we were trying to be less conspicuous, we'd put an MP5 or similar PDW/SBR (Personal Defense Weapon/Short Barreled Rifle) in a backpack with a Rhodesian or similar LBE (Load Bearing Equipment) kit. This was an option we could deploy quickly if needed, but it let us blend in with any group of tourists simply walking around viewing the sights. These backpacks would be civilian in nature as to not draw attention with excessive MOLLE attachments and camouflage nylon.

Many of these events required us to sit and observe during a dinner or meeting that may last most of a day. If we were already carrying a backpack, why not use it to expand our ability to respond to violent threats, medical emergencies, or various daily inconveniences? While loading the backpack with required tactical gear took a lot of space, it could be loaded efficiently to minimize bulk. When I had to do this work years ago, we simply didn't have access to the enormous number of options we do today for backpacks and low-vis equipment.

The Bag

For my more modern take on this requirement, I started with a Vertx Gamut 2.0 backpack. I've had this specific bag for a couple years, and I use it every day. Its contents are typically set up in this specific configuration, but the PDW and chest rig are removed when necessary. The bag itself is 20.5 H by 11.5 W by 7.5 D inches and has an internal capacity of 25 liters. This bag is designed specifically for the carrying of a PDW and accessories while maintaining a very discreet external signature. The Gamut is built with a quick-access rear weapons compartment with a large pull tab. The bag can also utilize ballistic panels and complement any body armor you may already be wearing.

The Contents

The purpose of this bag is to bring a bigger gun than a pistol into the fight if needed. I chose to use a B&T APC9 Pro Pistol with brace, which fits perfectly with stock collapsed and a 30-round magazine inserted in the back compartment. I'd imagine similar guns like the MP5 or its clones, or a SIG Rattler or MPX, could also fit in a very similar fashion. The main compartment has a specific laptop (or armor plate) sleeve and multiple zippered pockets to keep all required equipment organized.

I loaded my internal main pocket with a beanie, light jacket, notebook, three pens, a Multitasker Twist, and a Haley Strategic DC3RM Micro with four additional 30-round magazines and assorted smaller items. The design of the bag allows rapid access to the weapons compartment, and only takes slightly more time to get the chest rig out. The idea is to deploy the bag's contents after using your sidearm to handle any immediate threats. Going from a pistol with 15+/- round magazines to a PDW with multiple 30-round magazines increases the defense capabilities of any protection detail in a high-threat environment.

I used the external pockets to stow quick-access items, so I won't need to open the main compartment. The Gamut features an external flap that can be opened and attached with two hooks to hold a jacket or helmet if needed, but I left it zipped up and used it for medical gear instead. I was able to insert a Dark Angel medical kit and a SOF-T tourniquet with room to spare for easy

MAKE & MODEL
Vertx
Gamut 2.0

MSRP
$220

URL
www.vertx.com

access. In the two external side pockets, I have another SOF-T, trauma shears, a Leatherman multi-tool, knife sharpener, two cigars, a torch, and a cutter. Those last items are for my positive mental attitude more than any tactical "need," obviously. I developed my love of cigars overseas, so it only seems fitting.

Finally, in the top smaller pocket, I keep mosquito repellent, sunscreen, a couple pens, all of my required chargers for cell phone and comms equipment, extra batteries, a small headlamp, and a handheld SureFire flashlight. Slide a Nalgene bottle on the outside and a couple Clif bars, and you're set for a full day of sitting around and ensuring someone stays alive. When fully loaded, the bag isn't light, but for what you're bringing to the fight — especially without causing mass panic in a public environment — this is a very capable option.

Closing Thoughts

Looking back at what we used in the past and what we're able to purchase, configure, and carry today is astounding. This bag and setup would've worked great for what I was doing in my past life, and hopefully the men and women currently serving in that capacity are able to use the best equipment for their given environment. There's something to be said about making do with what you have to accomplish a task, but if given the opportunity, always take the time to acquire the best tools for the job.

Reaping the Whirlwind

Hurricane Response Pack

By **Andrew Schrader**

hen I began my service in the Urban Search and Rescue (US&R) field back in 2014, I had joined for all the wrong reasons. I thought I'd be some kind of a cross between G.I. Joe and Indiana Jones. I imagined myself hanging off the back of a Chinook helicopter and smiling, serving America but mostly serving myself. I had a lot to learn.

During my time working as a Structures Specialist attached to the State of Florida's US&R Task Force, I've been privileged to deploy on rescue operations for four hurricanes and most recently the Champlain Towers collapse in Surfside, Florida. I've carried my gear in the whole series of 5.11 RUSH packs, starting with a big RUSH72 (55-liter size) and eventually working my way down to the RUSH12 (24-liter size) — a small and lightweight pack. I like it because it forces me to carefully consider everything I'm bringing, discouraging overpacking.

The Pack

The RUSH12 is my "12-hour pack" used for the 16- to 18-hour shifts that we actually end up working during a deployment. I grab this if I think I'll be walking all day (or in a helicopter, where space is at a premium). It's intended for supporting myself in an urban or suburban location that has been hit by a hurricane. My loadout is mostly just to make myself more comfortable, with minimal outside support. It's not intended to be a wilderness or desert setup — I assume I'll have access to food and water at some point. Normally, when we arrive somewhere that's been hit by a hurricane, it's not hard to find food or water. What most everyone wants is ice because it's hot and the power is out.

The Contents

There's a lot of empty space in this bag to start, and that's intentional. As the conditions dictate or change, I may add mission-specific items, and I want room to add without overstuffing the bag. When it comes to contents, my personal priorities center around maintaining communications and carrying appropriate personal protec-

tive equipment (PPE) — not just for my eyes and hands, but also for my skin. That includes things like Vaseline and sunscreen, for example.

I also do my best to stay comfortable and clean in an environment that's usually anything but. I carry some items that might be deemed non-essential — things that smell good and help me clean my body. My specific indulgence is MALIN+GOETZ travel-size soaps and moisturizer goodies. Yours might be a pair of earphones, to listen to music on your phone and be transported somewhere else for a little while. Or it could be a special snack that's impossible to find in the field. Whatever it is, use that indulgence to transport your mind somewhere else, even if it's just for a few minutes. Go to that space where you can recharge and gather your senses — or simply make sense of what you've just seen and experienced.

Outside Of Pack

➤ Gerber Suspension multi-tool: Lots of functional goodness packed into an inexpensive $28 package. I bought five of these, and I stash them everywhere.

➤ Line of Fire gloves: Keep them clipped to the outside, because when you really need gloves, you don't want to be digging through your bag to find them.

> I use Black Diamond MiniWire carabiners to attach whatever gear I need. Yes, I realize I don't need the thing that attaches my water bottle to withstand 4,000 pounds of tension. But on the day that — for some completely unforeseen reason — I need a "real" carabiner in a hurry, I'll be glad I didn't try to save $10 on these.

> Also outside the pack: morale patches from Thirty Seconds Out. It's important to keep some kind of sense of humor in absolutely humorless situations. If I'm not getting in an occasional laugh, my mind can go to a dark place very quickly. Fun patches help keep the mood as light as possible.

Exterior Back Compartment

> 2x Buff bandanas for sun protection: They don't weigh anything, and boy it feels good to swap out a sweat-logged one that's clean and dry.

> Costa del Mar sunglasses (I'll add a pair of Wiley-X goggles if I'm riding a helo or in a collapse-type environment).

MAKE & MODEL
5.11
RUSH12

MSRP
$100

URL
511tactical.com

Main Compartment

> North American Rescue IFAK with bleeding control plus non-emergency add-ons like tweezers, Dayquil, Afrin, and Advil.

> Garmin InReach GPS with satellite texting: I love redundancy when it comes to maintaining communications, especially after a hurricane when local cell service might be knocked out. It's nice to have an alternate means of reaching out, and the way the Garmin InReach syncs with your phone for messaging and contacts is absolutely seamless. Did I mention it provides GPS navigation as well?

> Battle Board green notebook keeper: I use this as a scratch pad to write down briefing notes, important addresses, and phone numbers. Any electronic device you're using to take notes, i.e. your phone, could die. It's nice to have a backup. Pro Tip: Use your cell phone to snap photos of each page of your journal before leaving basecamp. This way you've got the notes in two places. Redundancy!

> 3x Rite-in-the-Rain pens (1 black, 2 orange)

> Yellow Medium Rite-in-the-Rain pad, No. 373

> Red small shave bag by Garage Built Gear

> Duke Cannon Cold Shower Wipes: Because it's incredible what cleaning your face and neck can do for your outlook on the day.

> Small jar of Vaseline: You can rub it on any burn or skin damage, but mostly I use it to cut down on chafing. With that being said, since I've started wearing 2XU compression shorts as underwear, I don't think I've gotten a rash on any long humps. They're great, especially if you have to wade through water or work through a rainstorm and can't change into something dry just yet.

> Sun Bum Sunscreen: To be honest, I just love the way this stuff smells, and the moisturizers keep my skin feeling great. When I feel better, I work better. Sorry not sorry!

> ChapStick

Closing Thoughts

Seven years after joining Florida's Urban Search and Rescue Task Force, this pack has held up its end of the deal. I can think of a dozen things I would've suggested to my FNG younger self. Thing number one would've been to pack light — and the best way I know to pack light is to use a small pack which forces me to comply.

Leave a few cubic inches and ounces for indulgences in your own pack. Never underestimate the positive impact of taking the time to clean your face, or laughing with a buddy about a morale patch, or simply stashing an extra set of socks to be able to switch out to something clean and dry. I'll see you out there. ⠿

Wilderness
Wonder
Deep Woods Survival Pack
By **Patrick Diedrich**

For some, a trek through the wilderness means going to a nearby park within the range of cellular data, groomed trails, and posted maps. For others, it means quite the opposite. Venturing across areas without trails for extended durations is tough on mind, body, and equipment, and it's important to take gear that can stand up to punishment. Working as a forester, and volunteering for search-and-rescue incidents is demanding, and the Mystery Ranch Shift Plus 900 is perfect for those moments far from amenities. This pack has two components: the Shift is composed of the harness, fiberglass shelf system with easy access bottom compartments; the Plus is a modular bag with several compartments, including two easy-access, drawstring side pouches.

The Bag

Challenging terrain and the dense vegetation of remote areas can tear up gear quicker than black bears

tear through lunchboxes. There are places where the forest floor is so thick and tangled with undergrowth that a traveler may feel like they're swimming through finger-thick saplings rather than walking. Tangled bush like this will destroy inferior clothing and gear, but 1000D Teflon-coated material created with wildland fire crews in mind keeps the pack safely intact. Sturdy fiberglass internal framing lends the pack lightweight strength, and a telescoping yoke helps maximize comfort. These features optimize weight distribution and reduce physical fatigue. Pack modularity allows for the removal of unnecessary components as needed, and the fiberglass shelf of the Shift system allows for placement of a variety of chemical or water tanks.

Backpacks essentially all serve the same function, which is holding things of varying sizes and shapes. Having a shelf system and modular design is convenient for many reasons, but some of this pack's best features revolve around comfort and form factor. Its yoke, harness, and waist straps are some of the most ergonomic I've ever worn, and the narrow profile keeps the pack from getting snagged by vegetation. Using a waist strap to take the weight off shoulders and onto dedicated load-bearing joints is crucial to physical longevity, and not all straps are created equal. With wide waist straps and thick, breathable padding, the Shift holds the wearer from behind more comfortably than a worn-in Snuggie.

The yoke and shoulder straps have the same padding, further increasing the comfort.

In the Field

Although not ideal for extended backpacking or camping, it has enough space for the essentials when a rotation or resupply is expected. Firefighters use the bottom compartment for easy access to rapid-deploy fire shelters. I use it for waterproof items like ponchos, rain gear, and boot gaiters. Packing it in this way allows it to be set down in potentially wet conditions without having to worry about wrecking gear. For SAR operations, the Plus component can be added, which greatly increases carrying capacity. There's plenty of space for items such as first aid supplies, signaling equipment, a 3L Camelback, or tools for personnel recovery such as rope and emergency blankets. In addition to a water pouch, I always have a LifeStraw, and a high calorie survival meal. Having a high-quality knife is a must, and a folding saw has come in handy on several occasions when I find myself far from a gas-powered chainsaw.

Eye injuries are easy to come by when the undergrowth is thick, and my packing list includes several sets of eye-pro. Clear ballistic safety glasses for low or no-light conditions, yellow lens safety glasses for various inclement weather conditions, and a shaded pair of Wiley X Rx glasses for bright sunlight. Relying on technology, such as GPS/GIS or radio communications, I need enough electricity for the duration of the job. Using a waterproof Pelican case, I can safely store backup power banks, charging cords, and extra batteries. Light sources that I prepare include chemlights for trail or tracking markers, a 5.11 high-lumen handheld, and a Fenix Superraptor headlamp from Varusteleka.

Depending on the climate and weather conditions, the load out is adjusted before any operations take place. When the weather dips into freezing territory, some of the wet weather gear gets removed and replaced with a Varusteleka thermal cloak, and one of the side pouches is packed with a Massif Strato Low Loft jacket. Black Diamond spike traction devices have carried me across many icy situations. Depending on circumstances, such as working alone on a timber sale or a SAR incident, I may add extra emergency blankets and merino wool mittens to the main pouch of the Plus. For first aid and trauma care, my trusty military IFAK is connected to the MOLLE webbing of the waist strap, and a kit for abrasions and lacerations is added to the Plus.

Final Thoughts

People who have occupations or roles that take them into remote areas must stay maneuverable and be pre-

pared to take care of themselves. Unexpected weather, challenging terrain, and unpredictable wildlife can spring up at any moment. With the twist of an ankle, or sudden dip in temperature, preventing exposure and dehydration become high on the list of priorities while waiting for help to arrive. Thoughtfully planning out what gear to carry and what to carry it in can be a make the difference between surviving and thriving, but a pack intended for short-term use means that an extra precaution needs to be taken.

Of all the gear and preparations made before going to places where communications become difficult, the most important prep of all is letting someone know where you're going and how long you plan to be there. Sometimes I'll even leave a map of my location and a list of emergency numbers that my loved ones can call if they don't hear from me before the sun goes down. A successful remote operation is one in which you return, never having used your emergency gear; however, knowing that my survival gear is stowed in a pack that's up to the task provides immeasurable peace of mind. ⠿

MAKE & MODEL
Mystery Ranch
Shift Plus 900

MSRP
$315

URL
mysteryranch.com

Grand Odyssey

A Fireman's Take on an Extended Outdoor Pack

By **Scott Finazzo**

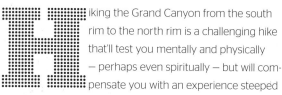

Hiking the Grand Canyon from the south rim to the north rim is a challenging hike that'll test you mentally and physically — perhaps even spiritually — but will compensate you with an experience steeped in unique natural beauty. At the end, it'll fill you with a feeling of accomplishment that's almost overwhelming. Most people who've hiked rim to rim will break it up over multiple days to lessen the physical burden and to take more time to enjoy the journey. That's the wise way to do it.

Three fellow firefighters and I decided we were going to take things a step further and hike rim to rim to rim — across the canyon and back. Not only that, but we did the initial south-rim-to-north-rim trek in one day, and then broke up the return trip over three days. This itinerary dictated we carry four days' worth of supplies on our backs from one rim of the Grand Canyon to the other, factoring in gear that'd account for snow and ice at the rims and triple-digit heat at the bottom of the canyon, with over 24 miles and 11,000 feet of elevation change between the two points.

The Pack

For this expedition I used an Osprey Kestrel 48. In my mind, a 48-liter pack is too large for an overnight hike, but too small for thru-hiking, so it seemed to fit our agenda. Osprey has a reputation of being relatively affordable and highly durable. I needed a pack that was tough and dependable. The backpack itself weighs about 3.5 pounds and has several features that were important to me. The Airscape ridged back panel that allowed my back to breathe, the multiple accessible pockets, side zipper access to the main compartment, and "stow on the go" trekking pole attachments were all key components that fit my personal backpack checklist. Additionally, the zippered waist strap pockets provided quick and easy access to smaller, commonly used items.

The Contents

I'm a firm believer in *you get what you pay for*, especially in the world of adventure and survival, but I also have to operate within my budget. This trip required me to balance high quality in some areas and affordability in others, all at the lightest weight possible. For certain pieces of gear, I spent more to get the quality I needed, and compromised a bit on others. In some aspects, I purposely packed items that added weight but benefitted my overall utility and/or happiness. It's most certainly a game of give and take.

The gear I packed:

> **Tent (MSR Carbon Reflex 1)**
> **Sleeping bag (Hyke & Byke 15-degree F650)**

- Sleeping pad (ThermaRest NeoAire Xlite)
- Trekking poles (Leki MCT 12 Vario Carbon)
- Pillow (RikkiTikki inflatable pillow)
- Headlamps (2) (Foxelli USB rechargeable)
- Hat
- Sunglasses
- Power bank (Getihu Ultra Slim Portable Charger)
- Jetboil stove
- Food (Mountain House meals, nuts, Goo packs, energy gel)
- Water (CamelBak plus 2 Nalgenes)
- Water Filter (Sawyer Mini)
- Coffee mug (GSI Outdoors Infinity Mug)
- Collapsible bowl (Sea to Summit)
- Long-handle spork (Morsel Spork XL)
- Toiletries
- Sunblock (Sun Bum SPF 50 and lip balm)
- Clothes (base layer/hat/gloves, convertible pants, sweat wicking underwear, socks, shirt)
- First aid kit (including Leukotape and climbing salve)
- Leatherman Micra
- Lighter
- Flip flops
- Garmin inReach Mini

As any backpacker will tell you, there's an art to loading your pack. Some items, such as the sleeping bag, are packed deep inside to reduce, as much as possible, their likelihood of getting wet. Other items are stored in the periphery for quick access. For this trip, my philosophy was based on functionality.

Main Compartment

The main compartment of my Kestrel 48 contained the bulk of the larger, essential items. My sleeping bag, which squeezes down nicely thanks to the compression straps, went to the bottom along with my sleeping pad and tent. I spent extra money on an ultra-lightweight tent, and it was worth every penny. The MSR Carbon Reflex 1 weighs in at a whopping 1 pound, 7 ounces. You barely even know it's there.

Next was my compression sack of clothes. I didn't pack a lot — a single change of clothing, two extra pairs of socks and underwear and base layers were the extent of my wardrobe options. Because the weather forecast was dry with a 0-percent chance of rain, I felt cautiously confident about leaving my rain gear in the car.

Next were my cooking items: a small compression sack of food and coffee packets, my lightweight coffee mug, collapsible bowl, a spork, and a Jetboil. I wasn't sure how hungry I'd be, but I knew that burning a lot of calories meant I had to put a lot of calories in, and I didn't want to

have to empty my pack if I was going to cook a meal. That proved to be more of a chore than I anticipated. I never really got hungry on the hike so I would have to remind myself to eat. The only other item I put on the inside of my pack was a heavily stickered water bottle that has been relegated to a single purpose — it's for when nature calls in the middle of the night and I don't want to leave the warmth of my tent. Its stickered decor is to ensure it's not confused with the other water bottle.

Exterior Pockets

The Kestrel 48 has a zippered lid compartment where I put my Garmin inReach Mini, first aid kit, a power charger, and my backup headlamp. I also put a lighter and my small bag of toiletries in this compartment. The zippered waist strap pockets were used to store items that could be accessed on the go without dropping the pack: my cell phone, a headlamp, sunblock, a Leatherman Micra, flavored electrolyte tablets, and energy snacks.

Finally, a segregated compartment on the bottom of the pack is where I kept some adverse weather options: a light jacket, a skull cap, gloves, and a pair of light flip-flops for evenings around the tent. The desert can freeze you out at night and unleash relentless heat during the day. Preparation for both was critical.

Closing Thoughts

This bag, with 3 liters of water split between an exterior bottle and a CamelBak, weighed in around 36 pounds. The first time I lifted it, fully loaded, I was surprised at how heavy it felt but then comforted with how natural it felt once on my back. Osprey does a superb job of providing options to customize how the load is carried on your back and hips. Outdoor enthusiasts will agree that one almost bonds with their gear when going toe-to-toe with the terrain and the elements. This pack gives me plenty of room without tempting me to fill it by offering excess space. It will be my go-to for many adventures to come. ⸬

MAKE & MODEL
Osprey
Kestrel 48

MSRP
$180

URL
www.osprey.com

Just What the Doctor Ordered

Medical/Truck Bag

By **Dr. David Miller**
Photos by **Stacie Kwacala**

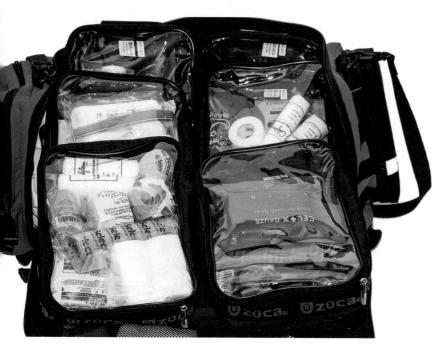

As a medical provider, I feel the need to carry the tools of my trade. From a first aid kit to my trauma kit to my truck bag, I think I have the right tools for the mission. Sometimes I'm called upon to place a bandage on an abrasion at the peewee baseball game; other times, I need to have my trauma kit ready at the range (especially when the guy next to me has his favorite new pistol blow up in his hands). Although it's impossible to have every tool for every incident, I can always improvise with the tools I have in this bag. This article will cover my medical/truck bag that travels with me everywhere my vehicle goes.

The bag I have is no longer available through 5.11 Tactical, although the company now offers a somewhat smaller 50-liter ALS/BLS Duffel Bag.

The Bag

I bought my 5.11 ALS 2900 bag seven years ago. It's a 72-liter bag with a shoulder strap and two straps to wear as a backpack. There's a main compartment that zips down on three sides. Inside the flap are a zippered

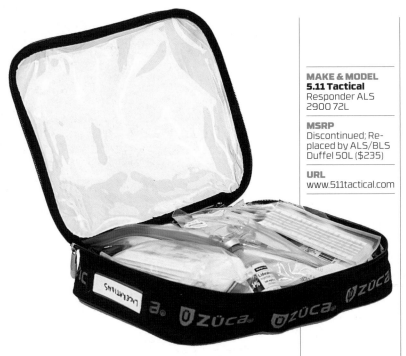

MAKE & MODEL
5.11 Tactical
Responder ALS
2900 72L

MSRP
Discontinued; Replaced by ALS/BLS Duffel 50L ($235)

URL
www.511tactical.com

ibuprofen, loperamide, ondansetron, acetaminophen, lip balm, and a tick twister.

> **Pouch 5, labeled Meds,** contains Proventil inhaler, glucose tablets, glucagon pen, EpiPen, lidocaine 1%, and Narcan.

> **Pouch 6, labeled Splints,** contains SAM Splints, tape, Kerlix gauze, and handkerchiefs.

The back zippered pouch contains Wagan Tech FRED lights, Mylar emergency blankets, cleansing wipes, and nitrile gloves. The side pouch contains an air horn, ethyl chloride, and a flashlight.

Final Thoughts

Since I purchased my ALS bag, 5.11 has gone through two different iterations. They've also moved to a more modular setup within the bag. I like my bag better than the current model — it's larger in capacity but can still be worn as a backpack. The pouches from Shiffler have made my bag much more manageable.

compartment and three pouches. The main compartment has dividers and two removable compartments that close with Velcro. At the back of the bag, there's another zippered compartment on the outside, which contains three subdivided spaces. On the outside of the bag to the left is another zippered compartment with two subdividers. There's PALS webbing on the outside of this compartment. The reflective tape also appears on the outside of the main compartment flap.

The Contents

Inside the main flap compartments, I have my sphygmomanometer, otoscope, ophthalmoscope, stethoscope, glucometer, pulse ox, and dental instruments. I removed the dividers and the removable compartments within the central part of the bag. I wanted to make this area easier to organize, so I replaced it with six modular vinyl bags (MobileAid Clear-View quick access utility pouches) from Shiffler.

> **Pouch 1, labeled GSW,** is my trauma kit that contains a CoTCCC-recommended TQ, HyFin Vent Chest Seal, Israeli dressing, decompression needle, nasopharyngeal airway, and Celox Z-Fold Gauze.

> **Pouch 2, labeled Dressings,** includes ACE wrap, Coban, rolled gauze, and 4x4 gauze.

> **Pouch 3, labeled Lacerations,** contains 4-0 Ethilon and 6-0 Prolene sutures, needle drivers, rat-toothed forceps, scalpels, skin stapler, Dermabond, lidocaine (1%), Steri-Strips, and 3ml syringes with 18- and 22-gauge needles.

> **Pouch 4, labeled First Aid,** contains Band-Aids, triple antibiotic ointment, burn gel, cotton balls, baby aspirin,

TWO-WHEEL ROAD WARRIOR

Get In and Out of Town With Your Equipment and Supplies Quickly and Silently

By Martin Anders
Photography by Michael Grey

Retaining mobility when a disaster on a grand scale strikes your town can be as, or even more important, than plans to stock up supplies and bunker down at home. When things are good, getting in, out, and around town is as easy as jumping in your transportation mode of choice — be it a car, truck, motorcycle, or even subway or bus — and simply going from point A to point B. But when roads are clogged, fuel is scarce, and the city's infrastructure is in disarray, moving about could get mighty tricky.

The most reliable mode of transportation is your feet. You can use them to traverse a multitude of terrain, and they require no additional forms of fuel other than what you already need to sustain your life. If your vehicle is rendered useless or the streets around you become impassable for some disastrous reason, you can probably still hike yourself out if need be. But relying on your feet to get you and your gear across long distances is a surefire way to turn them into hamburger meat. Because we like our feet the way there are, let's explore another human-powered alternative.

The bicycle runs on the same power as your feet, meaning that you don't need additional fuel to power it. Bicycles allow you to travel great distances more efficiently and allow you to be on the move quicker with heavier loads, while using less energy and having less impact on your body than if you were to go on foot. If there is a need to keep a low profile, which might often be the case, bicycles are a lot quieter than most motorized vehicles.

When properly equipped, the right bicycle can take you and your heavy survival gear, or possibly another passenger, over a number of types of terrain. If shit hits the fan while you are at work, a prepositioned bike could get you home faster than waiting for the roads to clear up. On the other hand, if you're bugging in and waiting it out in your prepared fortress, bicycles are a great way to scout the area rapidly and quietly while having a viable way to bring supplies back to home base. With basic tools and a couple of spares, your bike can always bring you and your gear to safety.

Although there are some really nice bicycles out there, you don't need to break the bank in order to get a two-wheeled escape plan going. There are plenty of used bikes you can pick up on the cheap from Goodwill, yard sales, Craigslist, pawn shops, and the like on which to base your silent escape rig. One of our staff members actually picked up a bike for $50 at a yard sale. He rigged his own carriers out of milk crates, scrap metal, and used backpacks to complete his get-out-of-town bike for less than $100. If you do pick up a used bike, make sure that it is inspected and serviced for safety at your local bike shop.

Like everything in life, what bike you get and how you set it up is all about what your individual needs are. Let's take a look at a couple of differently outfitted bikes and their accessories to get an idea of how you can configure a bike to best suit your needs.

The All-Terrain Scout

This setup is based on the Cogburn CB4 bike. With its oversized 3.8-inch-wide tires, the CB4 is an all-terrain fat bike capable of taking on some seriously rough roads and torn-up asphalt. Built to fulfill an all-terrain scout role, we wanted a bike that could zip around city-center all the way to the outskirts of town regardless of road conditions. It is capable of carrying back foraged food and supplies with its bags and single pannier as well as providing the rider with some defense and hunting capabilities with its mounted rifle.

It's equipped with disc brakes, wide track handle bars for confident control even with heavier loads, and pre-threaded attachment points all over the place for racks and carriers. We took advantage of those attachment points and added a few carriers and accessories that would help this bike fill a scout role.

1

MAKE & MODEL
Cogburn
CB4

FRONT AND REAR SHIFTERS
Shimano Deore 2 x 10 Speed

FRONT DERAILLEUR
Shimano Deore 2 x 10 Speed

REAR DERAILLEUR
Shimano Deore Shadow Plus 10 Speed

CRANKSET AND BOTTOM BRACKET
SRAM X5 GXP100, 175mm crank with sealed bearings, 22/36t gearing

CHAIN
KMC 10-speed

DERAILLEUR CABLE AND HOUSING
Jagwire stainless shift cables and full-length housing

CASSETTE
Shimano Deore – 10-speed, 11/36t gearing

WHEELS
Formula sealed-bearing hubs front and rear, Surly 82mm-wide Rolling Darryl rims, DT Swiss stainless steel spokes, built and finished by hand in the USA

TIRES AND TUBES
Surly Nate 26x3.8-inch tires, Surly Light Fat inner tubes

FRONT AND REAR BRAKE SET
Avid BB7 cable actuated disc brakes, 160mm stainless rotors, Avid FR5 levers

OVERALL LENGTH (LARGE FRAME, AS FEATURED)
74 inches

WEIGHT (LARGE FRAME, UNLOADED)
36 lb, 5 oz

MSRP
$2,200

URL
www.cogburnoutdoors.com

NOTES
To sum it up, the CB4 is a man-powered all-terrain vehicle. Its high-riding fat tire and wheel combination coupled with its wide frame give the rider a very capable and sturdy platform to traverse all types of terrain. It comes covered in RealTree Xtra camouflage and is bead-blasted so that the bike maintains a non-glare, low-profile look. The two-wheel disc brakes stop the bike quickly and confidently, while the 2 x 10-speed shifters change gears up and down smoothly. Accessory mounting points are found all over its frame, which is a huge bonus when we built up this example. It even has mounting holes for three water bottle holders — not found on most bikes. The bike is lighter than it looks due to its frame being made of high-quality heat-treated, double-butted A6N-6000AL tubing.

2 MAKE & MODEL
Blackburn
Mountain Bottle Cage

WEIGHT
2.4 oz

COLORWAY
Black (shown), silver, red, green, blue

MSRP
$5

URL
www.blackburndesign.com

NOTES
These bottle cages mount easily on any bike frame that has predrilled holes to accept them and securely hold most standard sport bottles.

3 MAKE & MODEL
Cogburn
Gear Carrier

WEIGHT
1 lb, 15 oz.

MSRP
$130

URL
www.cogburnoutdoors.com

NOTES
Although the Gear Carrier is designed to hold a rifle, bow, or fishing rod, it is capable of carrying a wide range of gear, thanks to its included positionable Quick Fist clamps. Along with the two 2-inch and one 1-inch Quick Fist clamps it comes with, the rider can easily employ rope, paracord, or bungee cables to secure other items such as firewood or other foraged materials. We found that the 2-inch Quick Fist clamps were too narrow to help attach long guns such as a shotgun or AR-15. Adding your own larger-diameter Quick Fist clamps would remedy that. The carrier itself is sturdy and covered in a matte-black powdercoat as well as mounting holes that allow for a myriad of mounting possibilities.

4 MAKE & MODEL
NiteRider
Mako Light System

HEADLIGHT BRIGHTNESS
150 lumens

HEADLIGHT MODES
High, low, flashing

HEADLIGHT RUNTIME
High - 20 hrs, low - 60 hrs, flashing - 120 hrs

TAILLIGHT RUNTIME
100+ hours

BATTERY TYPE
Headlight 2 x AA

MSRP
$60

URL
www.safarilandpatrol bikes.com

NOTES
The Mako Light System is perfect for those times when you need to be seen. It comes with a bright 150-lumen headlight that can keep you from riding at night into one of those pesky sinkholes and an LED taillight that can be seen up to 1 mile away. The headlight features side "gills" that light up red to make the rider more visible. The taillight emits light to its sides as well as to the rear for greater visibility as well. Multiple mounting options including a belt clip are included.

5 MAKE & MODEL
Topeak
Compact Handlebar Bag

CAPACITY
2 L

MAXIMUM LOAD
11 lbs

DIMENSIONS
8.7 in L x 5.1 in W x 7.1 in H

WEIGHT
1 lb

MSRP
$60

URL
www.topeak.com

NOTES
This handlebar bag converts to a fanny pack and is attached to the bike's handlebars with a quick-release mount. It keeps your essentials close at hand and is detachable so you can take them with you, right on your hip. The wings of the bag fold out in fanny pack form and feature hidden zippered compartments. It also includes a rain cover for those wet days on the road. Be careful not to overload handlebar bags as excessive weight on the handlebars can affect the bike's handling.

6 MAKE & MODEL
Blackburn
Barrier Universal Pannier

CAPACITY
17 L

MSRP
$100

URL
www.blackburndesign.com

NOTES
Blackburn's Barrier Universal Pannier features a waterproof roll-top design that makes it ideal to secure items that you need to bring back to basecamp. It features clear visibility panels on its sides, waterproof zipped exterior pocket, vertical compression straps, and lashing points. Its mounting fixtures can be custom fitted, making this pannier compatible with all standard racks. Its thick, tough skin and welded-seam construction are sure to give it a long, useful life on the road. When taken off the bike, the ends of the top clip together and form a convenient carry handle.

7 MAKE & MODEL
Novara
Novara Rack Trunk

CAPACITY
6.6 L

DIMENSIONS
12.5 in L x 6.5 in W x 5 in H

WEIGHT
12 oz

MSRP
$43

URL
www.rei.com/novara

NOTES
The Rack Trunk is a fairly standard, well-made bag that mounts on rear bike racks with four stout hook and loop straps. It is made of weather-resistant coated nylon, is padded, and the insulated main compartment protects contents and maintains shape. Its internal mesh pockets help keep everything in its place.

8 MAKE & MODEL
Salsa Cycles
Alternator Rack Wide

MAXIMUM LOAD
33 lbs

WEIGHT
1 lb, 11 oz

MSRP
$120

URL
www.salsacycles.com

NOTES
The Alternator Rack Wide is made for fat bikes such as the CB4. Its oversized tubular 6061-T6 aluminum construction fits over the extra-wide frame of fat bikes and includes longer struts for improved range of fit.

The Pack-Mule

This alternative setup is focused on the transportation of gear and supplies. Think of it as a pickup truck or cargo van version of a bicycle, if you will. This bike is set up with multiple racks, bags, panniers, and even a trailer that allows it to carry large loads in the event you need to get out of your place. If you do find yourself in a position where you need to move someplace else — and depending on the overall situation, you will probably want to take as many supplies and equipment as you can with you.

We based this example on a non-current model TREK FX, which is considered a hybrid bike. Hybrids are great for long rides due to their more upright seating position. Like we mentioned earlier, many used road-worthy bikes can be outfitted in much the same way at a fraction of the cost of a brand-new bicycle.

1 MAKE & MODEL
B.O.B.
Ibex Plus

MAXIMUM LOAD
70 lbs

CARGO AREA (APPROX.)
25 in L x 16 in W x 18 in H

WEIGHT
17 lbs

MSRP
$439

URL
www.bobgear.com

NOTES
As you can see, the Ibex Plus adds a whole lot more hauling capabilities to your bike. The trailer easily attaches to the bicycle's rear wheel using a quick-release system. B.O.B. offers multiple trailer options, but the Ibex stands out because it is equipped with a coilover shock that allows for 3 inches of adjustable suspension, greatly improving on- and off-road handling. We spoke to some bicyclists who have taken the Ibex over dirt roads and moderately rough terrain without trouble. It is constructed of 4130 chromoly steel tubing which makes it sturdy and is designed with a low center of gravity that keeps the weight off the bicycle frame for improved handling. The 70-pound hauling capacity will undoubtedly come in handy if you need to clear out of your bug out locale. The Ibex Plus model, as seen here, comes with a BOB DrySak, with PVC-coated nylon fabric that is tear-resistant and completely waterproof.

2 MAKE & MODEL
Ortlieb
Back-Roller Classic

COLORWAY
Black (shown), red, gray, orange, blue, white

CAPACITY
40 L

CARGO AREA (APPROX.)
16.5 in H x 12.6 in W x 6.7 in D

WEIGHT
4 lbs, 3 oz

MSRP
$180

URL
www.ortliebusa.com

NOTES
Ortlieb's pair of rear panniers are made of PVC-coated polyester fabric and close with a fold-over configuration, making them completely dustproof and protected from water splash coming from all directions. These panniers are incredibly rugged, to say the least. We like how they feature a quick-release handle at the top that allows them to be easily removed from the bike's rack. They include a shoulder strap that turn these panniers into shoulder carry bags when you need to load or unload them away from the bike. Inner pockets and large reflectors round out this great pannier option.

3 MAKE & MODEL
Ortlieb
Front-Roller Classic

COLORWAY
Yellow (shown), black, red, gray, orange, blue, white

CAPACITY
25 L

CARGO AREA (APPROX.)
11.8 in H x 9.8 in W x 5.5 in D

WEIGHT
3 lb, 8 oz

MSRP
$160

URL
www.ortliebusa.com

NOTES
Almost identical to Ortlieb's rear panniers, also featured here, the fronts are just smaller and capable of carrying 25 liters of gear. Adding gear on the front of your bike allows you to carry more supplies, but be careful to keep the loads on either side relatively equal in weight to maintain balanced handing characteristics.

4 MAKE & MODEL
Safariland
Bike Gear Bag

CAPACITY
6.9 L

CARGO AREA (APPROX.)
10 in L x 6 in W x 7 in D

WEIGHT
1 lb, 10 oz

MSRP
$65

URL
www.safarilandpatrol-bikes.com

NOTES
This bag was designed with input from both bicycle-mounted police officers and bike enthusiasts. It has a deceivingly spacious interior that encompasses a durable pocket for small items and a collapsible "false floor" for items you'd like to keep out of immediate sight. It is constructed from sturdy, water-resistant nylon materials, which are specifically blended to resist environmental changes. The top cover is equipped with exterior bungee drawstrings to quickly secure loose items. The top and sides each have zippered pockets for extra storage options.

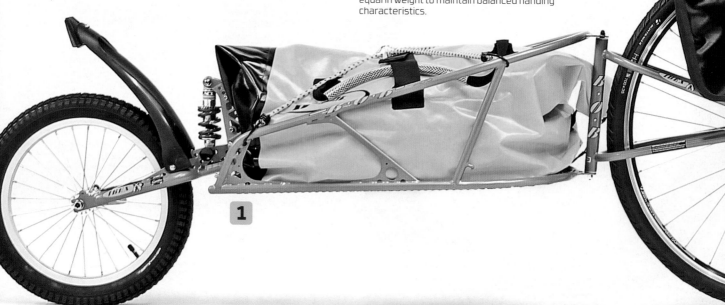

5 MAKE & MODEL
Timbuk2
Goody Bento Box
Top Tube Pack

CAPACITY
1 L

DIMENSIONS
6.7 in L x 3.9 in W x 2.8 in H

WEIGHT
5 oz

MSRP
$35

URL
www.timbuk2.com

NOTES
This bag attaches to your bike's top tube with hook and loop straps. The top external smartphone pocket is clear and retains touchscreen functionality. If not using a phone, paper maps can be tucked in it for weather-resistant reference. The generous interior can hold up a liter worth of items that you need to have access to during your ride. Sunscreen, lip balm, bike repair gear, or a knife — you won't have to choose since it will fit them all.

6 MAKE & MODEL
Topeak
Explorer MTX Rack

MAXIMUM LOAD
55 lbs

WEIGHT
1 lb, 6 oz

MSRP
$45

URL
www.topeak.com

NOTES
This rear rack is sturdy, easy to install, and a basic piece of kit for your bike if you intend on making it a mule. On it, you can mount a trunk type bag as well as panniers. To keep this piece lightweight, Topeak elected to make it out of 6061 T-6 hollow aluminum.

7 MAKE & MODEL
Planet Bike
PB Cage

COLORWAY
Silver (shown), various

WEIGHT
2.3 oz

MSRP
$5

URL
www.planetbike.com

NOTES
This aluminum bottle cage is available in 10 different colors and holds any standard sport bottle in place during your long trip to safety.

8 MAKE & MODEL
Racktime
Top-It

MAXIMUM LOAD
22 lbs

WEIGHT
1 lb, 3.2 oz

MSRP
$55

URL
www.ortliebusa.com

NOTES
A front rack is a must if you want to increase the load capabilities of your bike. On it, you can install front panniers as we did here. It also provides you extra space to mount yet another a bag — or, as in our case, we left it open to add whatever item we scavenge when on the road. This rack, like the others, does require threaded holes in your frame for proper installation, so do consult the manufacturer's website for installation information.

9 MAKE & MODEL
CatEye
HL-EL135 Front / Omni 3
Rear Bike Light Set

HEADLIGHT BRIGHTNESS
150 lumens

HEADLIGHT MODES
High, flashing

HEADLIGHT RUNTIME
High - 80 hrs,
flashing - 320 hrs

TAIL LIGHT MODES
Constant, flashing, rapid

TAIL LIGHT RUNTIME
Constant - 100 hrs, flashing - 150 hrs, rapid - 200 hrs

BATTERY TYPE
Headlight 2 x AA, Taillight 2 x AAA

MSRP
$30

URL
www.cateye.com

NOTES
We're going to bet that not all riding in a disaster-stricken situation will be of the stealthy assortment, so a set of lights on your bike will come in handy. Riding in the dark is a risky proposition, especially if other vehicles might be on the road. This CatEye light set runs on common batteries and is plenty bright enough to see where you are going — and allows you to be seen so you aren't flattened like a pancake on the highway.

Must-Have Accessories

Along with safety equipment such as gloves and a helmet for your noggin, we recommend taking a look at aftermarket seats if you don't find yours comfortable to sit on for hours on end. Also, to keep your bicycle on the road, and you on the move, we highly recommend a few tools and accessories to keep packed on the bike.

1 Hydration

There are plenty of hydration options on the market, including bottles and dedicated backpack-like carriers. Many bottles have special features such as Camelbak's Podium Chill, which is insulated and keeps water cool for hours. Clean Bottle is unique in that both the top and the bottom come off for ease of cleaning. Hydrapak's bottle can be collapsed down after the water is depleted and stored until it can be refilled.

№ MAKE & MODEL
Camelbak
Podium Chill 21 oz

$ MSRP
$12

⊕ URL
shop.camelbak.com

№ MAKE & MODEL
Clean Bottle
Original

$ MSRP
$10

⊕ URL
www.cleanbottle.com

№ MAKE & MODEL
Hydrapak
SF750 SOFTFLASK
Outdoor Collapsible
Bottle 750ml

$ MSRP
$21

⊕ URL
www.hydrapak.com

2 Tire Pump

Without air in your tires, your bike is as useful as a one-legged mule. That's why you should always carry a hand pump with you. Small, lightweight hand pumps are efficient and get you back on the road quickly. Remember there are two popular types of valves in use, Schrader and Presta. Make sure you get the right pump for the type of valve on your bike. If the pump can handle both types, then all the better.

№ MAKE & MODEL
Lezyne
Road Drive

$ MSRP
$45

⊕ URL
www.lezyne.com

✚ NOTES
The Road Drive is a lightweight hand pump that pumps up to 160 psi of pressure. Note that it is for use on Presta valves only. It comes with a mount that attaches to the same points as bottle cages.

3 Multitool

Bicycles are pretty standard as far as the tools that are required to work on them. Have a quality bike-specific multitool, and you won't need to search around for a metric hex or Torx wrench when you need it the most.

№ MAKE & MODEL
crankbrothers
Multi-17 Tool

$ MSRP
$27

⊕ URL
www.crankbrothers.com

4 Extra Tube

Some tire punctures can be repaired and some can't. Be sure you have a few spare tubes around; they're the cheapest insurance you can have to get moving after a flat.

№ MAKE & MODEL
Specialized
Standard Tube

$ MSRP
$13

⊕ URL
www.specialized.com

5 Tire Repair and Patch Kit

Most tire punctures can be fixed with a simple tire patch kit. Although not recommended, we've seen some tubes with more than five holes patched still rolling around just fine. When you're leaking air, you'll definitely want to patch it. Getting a kit with tire levers, such as the one by Park Tool, makes the job much easier.

№ MAKE & MODEL
Novara
Patch Kit

$ MSRP
$3

⊕ URL
www.rei.com/novara

№ MAKE & MODEL
Park Tool
Tire and Tube Repair Kit

$ MSRP
$6

⊕ URL
www.parktool.com

6 Bicycle Computer

Probably not a necessity for most, a bike computer can help you figure out exactly how many miles you have traveled, which may help with navigation and ETAs. Depending on the model, they also can tell you your current speed, average speed, distance traveled, time, air temperature, and more.

№ MAKE & MODEL
Sigma Sport
BC 5.12

$ MSRP
$25

⊕ URL
www.sigmasport.com/us

7 Saddle Pack

Looking for even more storage space? Look no further than right under your bottom. A bike's seat is called a saddle, and a saddle pack is a bag that sits right underneath your seat. They're great to squeeze every last cubic-inch out of your available storage space.

№ MAKE & MODEL
Avenir
Big Mouth Bike Bag - medium

$ MSRP
$15

⊕ URL
www.avenirusa.com

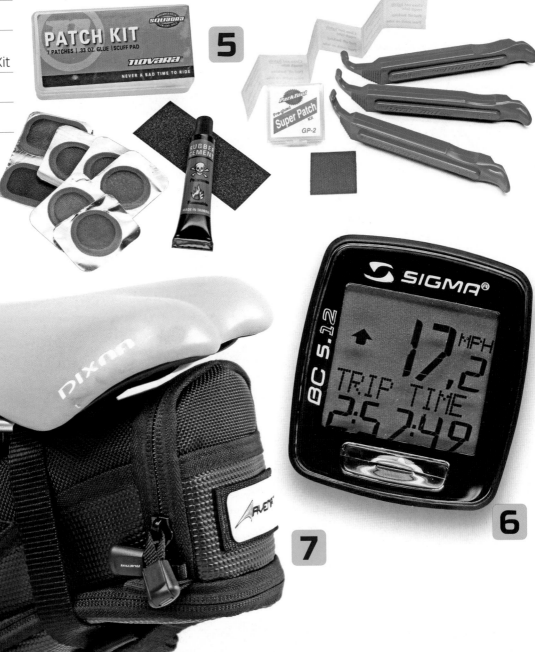

Choosing a Bicycle

Bicycles come in all different flavors, as do their riders, intended terrain, carrying load, and distance to be ridden. Picking the right bicycle can be tricky — and writing about how to pick the right bicycle can be even trickier. This topic can quickly become a 100-page dissertation, but we only have the space inside this little box, so we'll make it brief.

We are speaking in generalities here so you have a cursory idea of what to look for in a bike, but the experts at your local bicycle shop will be able to nail down the specifics of what bike will best fit your needs. Remember that fit is of upmost importance, so getting a bike that is the correct size for you along with being fitted to the proper seat height and handle bar adjustments is critical for riding comfort and efficiency.

Road Bikes

Good on pavement, road bikes are the sports cars of bicycles. They feature nimble handling, are built lighter, and are capable of greater speeds than other bikes when ridden on relatively smooth roads.

Mountain Bikes

Good on dirt and rocky roads, as well as rough roads with uneven pavement. Mountain bikes can be looked at as the Jeeps of the bike world. Many of them feature suspensions, some on the front only, and some with shocks front and back. If you are planning to ride on both soft surfaces such as dirt as well as pavement, a front suspension-only, or "hardtail" bike, is what you'll want. The idea of having a suspension in front and back might sound appealing, but the shocks on a bike make pedaling inefficient on hard surfaces — reducing speed, making the bike heavier, and sometimes even compromising the number of gear attachment points. They are great for complete off-road riding, however, providing more rear-wheel traction.

Hybrid Bikes

Hybrid bikes work well on everything from smooth pavement to gravel roads. They are generally built for comfort, ease of use, and sturdiness. Hybrids are heavier than typical road bikes, but feature heavier-duty wheels, wider tires, and a more comfortable upright-style seating position. Like mountain bikes, many hybrids offer front suspension options. We prefer this type of bike in urban settings to base a build around.

Fat Bikes

Fat bikes hail from the snow banks of Alaska and the deserts of New Mexico. They are essentially mountain bikes built with wider frames so they can accommodate extremely wide rims and tires. These "fat" wheels allow fat bikes to traverse a large range of terrain effortlessly and feel very stable to ride.

BE PREPARED.
UNDERSTAND THE LAW.
CARRY WITH CONFIDENCE.

Deadly Force, Massad Ayoob's best-selling title on concealed carry law, has been standard reading for responsible armed citizens for nearly a decade. This second edition continues his mission to educate gun owners on all aspects of lethal force laws. Ayoob covers legal, ethical and practical considerations of armed self-defense in layman's terms, a style that is the hallmark of his teaching methods.

This updated edition adds nearly 100 pages of new, no-nonsense commentary on headline-grabbing topics such as the Kyle Rittenhouse trial, the shooting of Ahmaud Arbery, and SCOTUS' landmark ruling on *New York State Rifle and Pistol Association v. Bruen*.

Also new to this edition is updated, detailed information on how to select the best attorney should you need one in the aftermath of a use-of-force event.

Whether you're new to concealed carry or just need a refresher on your rights as an armed citizen, *Deadly Force* is required reading!

"After forty years as a practicing criminal defense attorney, I know that what Mas says, teaches, and writes is the best, state of the art knowledge that you can get."

- Jeff Weiner
Former President, Nat'l Assn. of Criminal Defense Lawyers

Product No. R8161
ISBN 9781951115852

ORDER TODAY!

amazon.com   **GunDigestStore**   **BARNES&NOBLE**
BOOKSELLERS

OR CALL 920.471.4522

DECKED OUT FOR BUG OUT

This Toyota Tacoma Is a Daily Driver, Weekend Warrior, and an Escape Plan, All Rolled Into One

By Martin Anders
Photography by Mike Shin

If the city comes crumbling down around you and you have no choice but to bug out, what kind of vehicle would you choose to get out of town in? It sounds like a simple question, but reality makes it a lot tougher to answer than we'd like it to be.

Ask 10 people this question, and you're bound to get at least 10 different answers. Some might say an old carbureted truck, others swear by diesel power, yet others still would ride off on a motorcycle. Then there are those who would reach for their paddles instead (see "Bug-Out 'Yak" on page 88). Because everyone's situation and needs are different, there's no one-size-fits-all answer. What type of area you live in and the number of people in your household are just two in a long list of variables that determine what type of transportation you end up selecting.

For Mike Shin, choosing his daily driver (and just-in-case bug-out truck) was dictated by several factors. After a couple of outings over a few dirt trails in his previous ride, a two-wheel drive Nissan Xterra, Shin quickly realized that he needed a ride swap if he were to drive more aggressive routes. While the Xterra was great to run errands around town, it was not suited for the unpaved regions of the mountains and deserts of Southern California — the very areas he might need to bug out to one day.

Make and Model

Shin drew inspiration from go-anywhere Australian Outback-style 4x4s. One of his dream trucks was the venerable Toyota Land Cruiser Hardtop 150. He considered traveling to his wife's home country of Guatemala to drive one back, but soon realized that the logistics and legalities of owning such a vehicle in the United States was more work than he was willing to take on. Instead, he looked at more readily available stateside options. Shin quickly discovered the 2013 Toyota Tacoma Double Cab 4x4 TRD Sport Package and figured it would more than meet his requirements.

From Show to Go

The ball really got moving when Shin, a former employee at Toyo Tires, got the call to display his truck at the Toyo Tires booth at the 2013 Specialty Equipment Market Association (SEMA) Show being held in Las Vegas, Nevada, with the caveat that he build a show- and off-road-worthy truck out of his Tacoma in less than three months' time — and on his own dime. Considering the time and budget concerns, it was far from certain

An ARB Deluxe Bull Bar replaces the factory front bumper. The All Pro Off-Road Front IFS Skid Plate was added to armor up the vulnerable IFS third member and steering components. A weather-sealed Superwinch Tiger Shark 11500 Winch in the front bumper can pull up to 11,500 pounds of trouble with its 6hp motor.

that he would be able to pull this endeavor off. Even so, he was up to the challenge.

Engine

Its 1GR-FE model V-6 engine displaces 4 liters and runs on regular-grade fuel. That's good enough to churn out a factory-rated 236 horsepower and 266 lb-ft of torque. To help it breathe easier, an Australian-made Airflow Cold Air Induction System (ACAIS) snorkel was installed to force in air that is free of water and other contaminants. According to Airflow, the high positioning of the ACAIS' snorkel air inlet also allows for cleaner, colder air to be driven into the engine's induction system. Colder air contains more oxygen, helping to improve fuel efficiency and power.

To keep the entire system free flowing, Shin coupled the ACAIS with a custom-fitted MagnaFlow Race Series exhaust system. The fully stainless-steel cat-back exhaust system optimizes exhaust flow and is mounted just behind the factory catalytic converter. We noticed that it also gives the truck a refined yet throaty sound.

The high positioning of the ACAIS snorkel air inlet allows for cleaner, colder air to be driven into the engine's induction system, helping to improve fuel efficiency and power.

Differentials

This Toyota drives power to all four wheels with aftermarket ratio ring-and-pinion gears made by Nitro Gear and Axle, that are encased in the factory 8-inch front and 8.4-inch rear clamshell IFS differential housings. The stock 3.72 gear ratio is better suited for economy and the truck's standard 30-inch tires, but it doesn't cut it with the larger wheels and tires that Shin went with. Due to the increase in rolling mass of larger 33-inch tires, both power and fuel economy are lost with the factory setup. The new ring and pinion by Nitro Gear and Axle "lower" the ratio to 4.56, which better compensates for the larger tires.

ReadyLIFT's Off-Road Heavy Duty Steering Kit consists of heavy-duty aftermarket tie-rod assemblies that are suited for lifted trucks running larger tires.

Rays Gram Lights 57JX6 rims in 18x8-inch sizing are mounted with Toyo Tires' all-new Open Country R/Ts.

Suspension

The Tacoma was lifted 2 inches for additional ground clearance to get over natural and manmade obstructions. Shin opted for an Old Man Emu Lift Kit for the front that consisted of sets of Nitrocharger shock absorbers and coil springs. He matched the rearend with Old Man Emu Dakar Leaf Springs and shocks, as well. These suspension upgrades not only improve the ride, handling, and load-carrying capability of a heavily laden truck, but also decreases the chance of suspension-component failure. Because of the 2-inch height increase, an Old Man Emu Driveshaft Spacer kit was installed to reduce driveline vibration common to lifts on Tacomas of this type.

Shin further beefed up the frontend by installing a set of ReadyLIFT Off-Road Upper Control Arms. These arms are stronger than stock and feature zerk fittings that make regreasing its urethane bushings a breeze. Because the wheel and tire combination he's running is heavier than stock, he went with ReadyLIFT's Off-Road Heavy Duty Steering Kit to avoid possible parts breakage down the road. The kit consists of heavy-duty aftermarket tie-rod assemblies that are suited for lifted trucks running larger tires.

CBI Off-Road Rock Sliders help protect the doors and doorsills from impact with obstacles.

and rear wheels are CBI Off-Road Rock Sliders. These rock sliders help protect the doors and doorsills from impact with obstacles (fallen tree branches, boulders, etc.) and keep the body in pristine shape even if the sliders themselves are bumped.

A CBI Off-Road Trail Rider 2.0 bumper protects the rear. Because having extra fuel on hand is a bug-out essential, it's fitted with two 5-gallon Jerry Can fuel carriers and a spare wheel and tire. The tire carrier swings away, allowing for easy access to the tailgate and bed. It even conceals a fold-down camp table further increasing its usability. The bumper's higher undercut allows for the truck to clear steeper departure angles that the stock bumper can't.

Storage and Gear

Storage is always at a premium whether you're packing for a camping trip or trying to haul you, your loved ones, and your gear out of a bad situation. Shin wanted to maximize the organizational space of his truck bed with the use of a bed rack.

has become ubiquitous in the off-road world and is available for many makes and models of trucks.

Underneath, a laser-cut 3/16-inch steel All Pro Off-Road Front IFS Skidplate was added to armor up the vulnerable IFS third member and steering components. Running along the bottom of the truck body between the front

A CBI Off-Road Trail Rider 2.0 bumper with swing-away tire carrier protects the rear end. Tucked below the spare tire in the rear is a Hi-Lift X-TREME Jack which can be used not only for jacking the truck up to swap out a flat tire, but also for manual winching and clamping.

The All Pro-Off Road Expedition Series Pack Rack helped him do just that all without compromising the hauling capacity of the truck's bed. The Rack Pack allows him to carry an ARB Series III Simpson Roof Top Tent up top that comfortably sleeps two adults and an ARB Awning 2000 that deploys to the side, providing about 53 square feet of overhead coverage from the elements.

Keeping clean is a real morale booster — imagine being able to take a warm shower when bugging out. A Road Shower sits on the side of the rack and holds 5 gallons of water, heats up in the sun, and works by either having gravity push water out of its 55-inch length hose or alternatively, the tank can be pressurized with an air compressor or bike tire pump to provide a more powerful jet of water.

On the opposite side of the Pack Rack sits a Rotopax 2-gallon water container and a Rotopax First Aid+Preparedness Kit. The efficient kit contains everything from medical supplies and a shovel to toilet paper and zip ties.

To add even more storage area, Shin custom-mounted an ARB 52x44-inch Steel Roof Rack Basket above the

The All Pro-Off Road Expedition Series Pack Rack bed rack helps create organized storage space over the truck bed without compromising hauling capacity. A bevy of gear is attached to it, including an ARB Series III Simpson Roof Top Tent, ARB Awning 2000, and a Road Shower.

truck's cab using a fitment kit made for a Toyota Hilux. The roof rack basket allows for gear and other supplies to be stored as well as a high position for roof rack lights to be mounted.

Lighting

For better forward view in low light and blacked-out moonless nights, Shin decked his truck out with a wide range of lighting options. He went to The Retrofit Source (TRS) for a set of OEM-quality Morimoto FX-R Bi-Xenon HID projectors to retrofit his stock halogen lights. The reason for going with an HID retrofit is to improve light quality, as the factory halogens are generally pretty dim, especially when in off-road environments. The problem with sticking any cheap aftermarket HIDs in existing halogen housings is that they typically cast an uncontrolled beam pattern due to higher light output. This ends up blinding other drivers while giving the user only mediocre visibility.

Opting for OEM-quality HIDs results in a piercing beam that is controlled and distributed with a crisp and

These Rigid Industries 38- and 40-inch E-Series LED light bars are configured in a spot-and-flood-light combination.

Each of the 9-inch ARB Intensity LED Driving Lights that are mounted to the front bumper contain 32 LEDs, producing 8,200 raw lumens.

of 9-inch ARB Intensity LED Driving Lights to the front bumper. The flood and spot combination lights each contain 32 LEDs that produce 8,200 raw lumens and a spot reach of almost 1,000 meters.

Not to be outdone, the rear end was treated to a bank of LED lights as well. Rigid SR-M Back-Up lights, a Rigid SR-M Bed Light, and a Rigid Q-Series Camp Light mounted on the tire carrier round out the rear facing light fixtures.

Electronics

A Scan Gauge II monitors the vehicle's performance and is programmable to display information such as trip data, transmission temperature, fuel economy, engine speed, and vehicle speed, among other statistics. What's really useful too is that it is capable of displaying trouble codes, so you can troubleshoot problems.

focused cut-off beam pattern, delivering maximum visibility to the driver with higher light output that doesn't also blind oncoming drivers. To install the TRS-sourced HID projectors, Shin relied on a company called Essential Lites to do the painstaking work of retrofitting them into his factory headlights.

He continued by adding dual rows of high-mounted lights to the roof rack. Sitting on the top row is a Rigid Industries 38-inch E-Series LED Light Bar, which is configured in a spot and flood light combination. This combination is rated at 17,480 raw lumens and allows him to see a wide swath immediately forward as well as out to more than 1,300 meters ahead of the vehicle. If that isn't enough, a second 40-inch E-Series LED Light Bar sits just under the 38-incher. Also in spot-and-flood-combination configuration, this bar spits out 18,400 raw lumens of light up to a distance of 1,400 meters. For those keeping count, that's a range of almost 13 football fields.

As if he plans on exploring the eternal darkness of a black hole, Shin found a need to further mount a pair

Above: Ram Mount's versatile No Drill Laptop Mount can be configured to use with a tablet.

Top: A Scan Gauge II monitors the vehicle's performance and is programmable to display information, such as trip data, transmission temperature, fuel economy, engine speed, among other statistics.

Ram Mount Phone and No Drill Laptop Mounts help keep what otherwise would be loose electronics in place, even over the roughest of turf. The versatile No Drill Laptop Mount, as its name implies, requires no drilling for installation into your vehicle and, as seen here, can be configured to use with a tablet. Other than accessing electronic maps over his phone or tablet, Shin also carries an old-fashioned Thomas Guide (remember those?) and a compass for backup land navigation.

Never Done

Shin's Tacoma fits each of the roles he initially outlined quite nicely. It's a reliable daily driver that's a blast to take out for the occasional trail run. If push ever comes to shove, it looks as if this pickup will be a capable rolling urban escape plan as well. But automotive enthusiasts know that a project is rarely ever complete. When asked what the next step for his truck was, Shin mischievously smiled and said that he was done with it...somehow we're not so convinced.

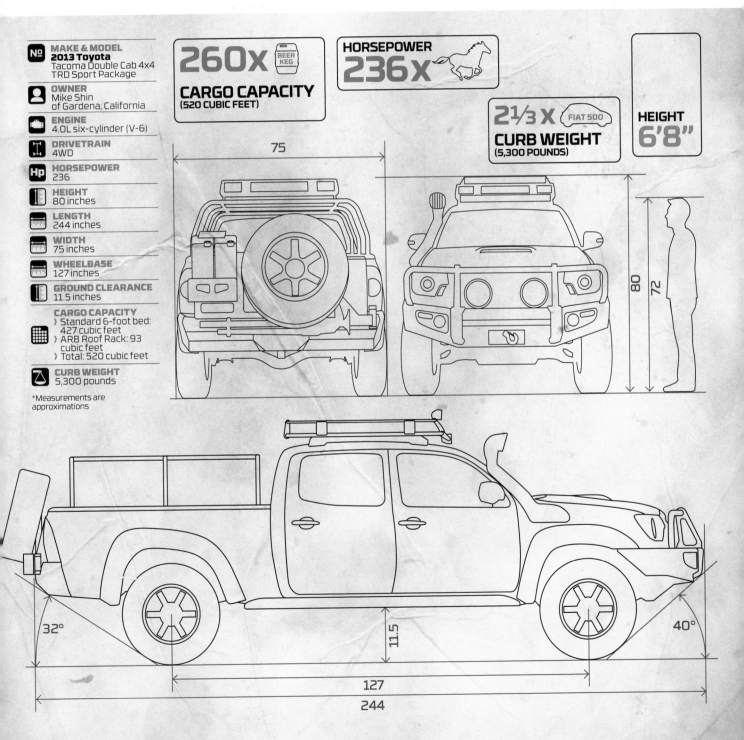

№ MAKE & MODEL
2013 Toyota
Tacoma Double Cab 4x4
TRD Sport Package

OWNER
Mike Shin
of Gardena, California

ENGINE
4.0L six-cylinder (V-6)

DRIVETRAIN
4WD

Hp HORSEPOWER
236

HEIGHT
80 inches

LENGTH
244 inches

WIDTH
75 inches

WHEELBASE
127 inches

GROUND CLEARANCE
11.5 inches

CARGO CAPACITY
› Standard 6-foot bed: 427 cubic feet
› ARB Roof Rack: 93 cubic feet
› Total: 520 cubic feet

CURB WEIGHT
5,300 pounds

*Measurements are approximations

260x BEER KEG
CARGO CAPACITY
(520 CUBIC FEET)

HORSEPOWER
236x

2⅓ x FIAT 500
CURB WEIGHT
(5,300 POUNDS)

HEIGHT
6'8"

75
80 72
32° 11.5 40°
127
244

BUG-OUT 'YAK

Dirt Roads Aren't Your Only Means of Escaping a Catastrophe

By David H. Martin

Come hell or high water, your best bet for slipping past urban threats with that 90-pound bug-out pack might just be a bug-out 'yak (BOY). Swift and wickedly silent, these low-signature kayaks are capable of carrying you plus your weight's worth in gear for days, all while vanishing without a trace. If you're not practicing your escaping or scouting with these shallow running craft, then your foolproof evacuation route is already landlocked — and for allowing that planning blind spot, fellow traveler, you deserve a good paddling.

Paddled solo, in tandem, or possibly strung together like a caravan of pack mules, BOYs bridge the water-surface mobility gap, serving as your conduit to safety when vehicles halt and roadways are impassable. To paraphrase an old saying, do not get caught up SHTF creek without a paddle.

Unlike larger craft (see OFFGRID's Summer 2014 issue for more on water vessels), the 'yak is man portable, capable of launching over rocks or a sea wall — especially with portage wheels (think two-wheeled dolly). No fossil fuels needed, and no engine to flood. No batteries, license, insurance, or registration. And there are few if any moving parts to maintain or corrode. Your BOY may be pre-staged at your home and camp, or strapped to your roof rack and locked with a bicycle cable, a torpedo-shaped plastic storage pod packed with gear below deck. A kayak can lead to a limitless source of drinking water, help you identify or scout for potential dangers, and be used for fishing or food gathering.

Types of 'Yaks

The recent BOY concept springs from the national explosion in recreational kayaking. These tough, accessible, and affordable reinforced polyethylene boats range from 12 to 16 feet or so. They're suitable for all ages, abilities, and family members. Recreational kayaks are generally divided into two styles: "sit-inside" open cockpit and "sit-on-top" seats that are molded into a decked or closed hull. Both have built-in floatation and some storage.

Our preference is the sit-on-tops by Confluence Outdoors with a fully enclosed deck, camo colors, and gasket-sealed storage hatches. When equipped with a flip-down rudder system, the foot pedals become our steering mechanism, helping the kayak track and preventing us from wasting energy on corrective paddle strokes while heading into the wind or the current. Gunwale rail system fittings hold adjustable tie-downs for customizing locations of additional dry storage bags, fishing-rod holders, anchor lines, and electronics.

With the hatches latched closed, the sit-on-top enclosed deck adds seaworthiness to the boat during rough waters and storms. These kayaks are self-bailing when punching through storms or waves because rain and water drains through built-in scuppers, a feature sit-inside boats lack in open waters.

Regarding carrying capacity, one 16-foot kayak classic, quiet hull Wilderness Systems Tarpon 160 we evaluated is rated for 375 pounds of load-out including the paddler. The stout Confluence Ride 13.5 model was rated for 550 pounds of capacity including paddler.

Pack Mules on Water

To see if the BOY concept would work for wives and kids, we recently gave a petite female friend some conditional paddling instructions and sent her on her way. She carried 100 pounds of gear balanced on her kayak for a few miles without undue strain. Trading her hiking staff for a double-bladed paddle, she was able to conserve her energy over several hours by resting and drifting between paddle strokes. Trying to carry that same load

You can fit a surprising amount of gear on a kayak.

A Brief History of Kayak Action

» "Kayak" comes from the Inuit word "qayak," a 2,000-year-old term for "hunter's boat." These early kayaks consisted of natural skins stretched over wood and bone frames.

» The World War II "canoe commandoes" of the British Royal Marines were immortalized in the 1955 British movie *The Cockleshell Heroes*, which is a fictionalization of their heroic raid on German ships in Nazi-occupied France.

» You'll find a faded black-and-white photo of two kayakers at the U.S. Navy UDT-SEAL Museum in Fort Pierce, Florida, serving as a reminder that not all surveillance missions take place in inflatable rafts.

» Medal of Honor recipient Thomas R. Norris is responsible for one of the most famous paddle missions ever while serving as a SEAL in Vietnam. When American airmen were downed over hostile territory, Norris and his South Vietnamese counterpart were able to rescue two pilots behind enemy lines on two separate nights by disguising themselves as local fishermen and paddling a sampan.

» Today, modern troops train using kayaks like the German Klepper faltboote (folding boat), which are formed by tautly fitting tough, coated fabric over wood and composite frames that are capable of deploying from a backpack. These kayaks feature airtight sponsons to remain afloat and below radar with low acoustic and thermal signatures. Even in the age of drone strikes, today's elite warriors still employ paddle strokes to conduct surveillance.

Waterproof Rigging

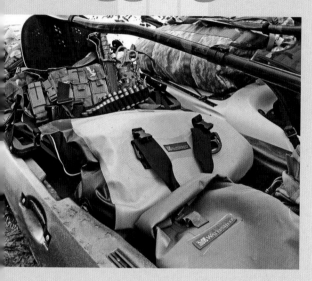

Saltwater destroys. It's ridiculously corrosive to steel and strips away at pretty much anything it touches. Even freshwater may be contaminated. So you have to waterproof your gear if you've chosen a bug-out kayak as your means of evacuation.

The key to waterproof rigging is breaking down your load by group and individually encasing essential components, then compartmentalizing each group in cases like a small Pelican hard case. For an amazingly watertight barrier and a silent-running approach, nothing surpasses the versatility of the line of Watershed Bags by Drybags. To handily secure that 12-gauge shotgun on deck and out of sight, go with the Watershed "Torpedo" case. Trim the boat for silent running with three or more duffels, backpacks, maritime survival bags, or the complete SOF backpacks (standard issue for U.S. Navy SEALs).

Encase heavily lubricated firearms separately from ammo. Outfit vulnerable electrical and optical pieces, illumination tools, cameras, batteries, power sources, and communications gear. Bag sub-groups, including licenses, documents, tools, and medical kit and prescriptions. Strap securely to the deck or stow below, but never trust even gasketed hatches to provide a watertight seal.

in a backpack on land would have crushed her within 100 paces. Yet, in her 'yak she still had strong legs at the end of the day.

To paddle efficiently, one can trim one's 'yak by adjusting the load fore and aft. The BOY offers recreational fitness paddling for your family and team members, but only if you load it properly. Build endurance and trust during trial runs near your home. Gauge your pace and shake down your gear along the way, putting into practice the theory of navigational chart and compass. Plot those courses on your handheld GPS unit, adding miles to your daily paddles at a walking pace.

Squared-away BOY watermen learn basic paddle strokes necessary to move the boat efficiently and without wasted motion. Work on the forward, reverse, and sweep strokes, as well as simple bracing or sculling moves. Practice draw strokes and rudder strokes to help build your confidence with a fully loaded kayak in open waters, tidal flows, and river currents. Find a coach and practice rescues. You may be the one called upon to go after an overboard team member, or to evacuate a child, relative, or pet using the kayak as a waterborne stretcher.

Alternative Escape Route

In the United States, flooding remains one of the leading causes of weather-related deaths. Surviving extreme

Below: For a waterborne escape plan, you'll need to do research and practice long before any impending emergency...and you'll need the right gear to help you navigate.

urban flooding may depend on your temporary access to kayaks pre-staged at home or on your vehicle with your family load out, combined with a specialized knowledge and practiced skillset to recognize the need to escape structures and navigate only those routes when safe to do so.

But even if it's not floodwaters contaminated with fuel, sewage, and debris, a disaster can still drive widespread chaos. With a population dependent upon prescribed paths, waves of panicked people following their on-grid mentality will guarantee gridlock on streets and highways. As order rapidly breaks down, roving preda-tor packs will recognize these chokepoints as ambush points to attack the immobile stragglers. Add blackouts, rioting and looting, fuel shortages, and communication breakdowns, and all bets are off.

In hard times, disconnecting from the grid may require reconnecting with the water. A kayak can provide a way out of danger when your car or even your bug-out truck can't. However, the safest distance between two points is not always the straightest.

Revisit your bug-out route, focusing on the blue lines that radiate outward toward your safe zones. Like the third plane on a three-dimensional chessboard, there

You've Bugged Out... Now What?

to weigh and tie down your boat, completely submerging your kayak at the water's edge, and a lot less trouble.

For temporary or late night rests during still-water stages, the BOYs are stable enough to be lashed together and cross decked with paddles, enabling small teams to stretch out at anchor for temporary shuteye. For overnight stays in standing water, two kayaks lashed side by side and cross-decked with scavenged planking make it possible with practice to erect self-supporting solo or two-man tents with rain fly.

When the all clear comes through your VHF, the "approach with caution rule" applies while paddling back to urban areas. Be prepared to portage your boat with the two-wheeled dolly you stashed at your launch point. Return super early during non-curfew hours, moving smoothly, swiftly, and decisively with photo I.D., a strong flashlight, concealed pistol, and paddle to re-stake your claim to your home...or to 'yak back to safety.

Sea kayakers can cover marathon distances in hours under flat-water conditions. When paddling a fully loaded bug-out 'yak (BOY), avoid strain, injuries, and detection by maintaining a steady but quiet stroke, gliding at a walking pace, paddling a few miles per hour until you reach your first way-point en route to base camp.

Ideally, you should try to reach high ground carrying a military-quality solo tent and rain fly like the Raider by Cato-ma. Weighing less than 2 pounds, these wonders are pure shelter, especially when combined with a lightweight sleeping bag like the Elite Survival Systems Recon II. At a minimum, the orange miniature space blanket sleeping bag and glow-worm SOL tent will work, even if highly visible.

To lay low during day or night, pull the kayak completely clear of the waters and bring it right into camp, anchor, paddle and all, so it will be there in the morning (or night) if flood waters and pirates follow you. Erase your trace, smoothing any 'yak drag marks in the dirt or mud that points the way to your camp. This is more secure than blowing the hatches and flotation

exists within our innermost cityscapes a serpentine labyrinth of water. Search for those little feeder creeks, bayous, sloughs, tributaries, and natural or man-altered drainage channels. Identity the intersections of roads and rivers near your home, business, or remote safety site. These are your BOY's on- and off-ramps. Once your home waters are mapped, plotted, and explored, your kayak becomes a rogue chess piece free from the confining black-and-white grid of asphalt and concrete.

Ninja Mode of Transport

Post-hurricane hostilities might require you to temporarily abandon your home or vehicle to adopt a defensive posture. A BOY provides an effective means of escape and evasion. After all, a 'yak leaves no tracks, gives off zero emissions, and is a tad quieter than a Hummer.

And unlike trekking on foot ('cause you're certainly not driving to safety), this type of boat allows you to pass through urban waterways with the ability to both quickly access and conceal any manner of long-gun, considered the ultimate tool for repelling plastic-boat pirates. Tandem paddle teams can place a scout bow-gunner or

Unlike a large RV or SUV, kayaks are effective at escape and evasion. They're relatively quiet, leave no tracks, and emit zero emissions.

tail-gunner outside your pack of paddlers, presenting a low-profile lethal combo.

But to stay discreet on the water, you'll have to train. Practice hand signals with your family and friends. Do not give away your silent advantage by excessively talking because sound carries over water. If your party must

Bug-Out 'Yak Gear Checklist

Having the right kit in a time of crisis can mean the difference between survival and starvation (or worse yet, a victimization by violent raiders). On a watercraft, having the right gear becomes even more important. Our author lists numerous options for what to pack in a bug-out kayak as a means to both inspire and inform those of you who are eyeing an aquatic evacuation plan.

❭ Aquatic Gear: 4mm Blue Line, folding sail, V-mast, 12-gauge flare pistol, hand-held flares, nautical charts, scale, solar calculator, anchor, lines, throwable buoy, plus sea anchor, double-bladed two-piece paddle on leash, spare paddle, snorkel, mask, fins, pole spear, and Hawaiian Sling

❭ Illumination: SureFire Maximus headlight, Petzl IR strobe, chem lights

❭ Navigation: Garmin Foretrex 401 GPS and spare Garmin 78sc, batteries, Ritchie Compass and spare

❭ Communications: Horizon VHF hand-held, GPS-enabled radio, emergency locator beacon, Spot phone

❭ Safety Gear: Flotation vest and whistle with Benchmade safety hook strap cutter

❭ Eye Protection: Polarized Wiley X sunglasses, Full Rx Wiley X Goggles

❭ Storage: CamelBak Linchpin hydration pack, YETI Roadie Cooler for medicine

❭ Tactical Gear: FirstSpear chest rig (with suppressor, MUT, SS KABAR, Dark Angel Kit, waterproofed, Medical Kit Below, medicine, stamps, documents, etc.)

❭ Clothing: Full MultiCam outer wear, boonie, two-piece storm suit and weather protective clothing, hat, gloves, face cover

❭ Footwear: Danner USMC boots, Altama Jungle Boots

❭ Weapons Gear: Spare magazines, cleaning kit, weapon-light batteries, ammo, Elite Bandolier, bow, arrows

❭ Shotgun: Remington 870 Marine Magnum, Stoeger 12-gauge Coach, Snake Charmer

rest, look for those side feeder creeks that offer a detour off the main water body, bay, lake, or river system.

Of utmost importance is your paddle selection. Do not scrimp or allow this to become an afterthought. Cry once. Reach for the advanced composite paddles, such as the Adventure Technology Fishstix with adjustable

length and angle, and woodland camo pattern. This paddle combines a bent shaft to reduce wrist strain and a feathery buoyant blade with serious bite. Let it become a part of you.

Once you've escaped the initial flooding or the resultant urban chaos, you can then take a stand on the high ground, hunker down until conditions improve, move to your next strongpoint, or return home. Like some of the best survival equipment, bug-out 'yaks come with this simple instruction: Just add water. ⠶

About The Author:

Bayou-born and hurricane-raised on the Texas Gulf, David H. Martin operates both Yippee Kayak Fishing (conservation-based angling instruction) and Myakka Kayaka (guided paddle tours) in Southwest Florida. He's also a NRA-certified firearms instructor and chief range safety officer, specializing in advanced defensive pistol, shotgun, and rifle. For more information, go to www.yippeekayakfishing.com.

> Rifle: Colt AR-15, Ruger 10/22 SS takedown, .177-cal. air rifle
> Pistols: SIG SAUER P556 SWAT Pistol, SIG SAUER P226 Navy 9mm, Glock 19
> Electronics: Mobile phone, camera, crank charger, solar panel
> Fishing & Gathering: Cuban yo-yo, light trolling rods, tackle, cast net, bait seine, spool line, hooks, sinkers
> Cooking: Coleman Peak stove, grill, skewer
> Toiletries: laundry soap, hand soap, ChapStick, cleaning solution, eye drops
> Camping Gear: Tent, rain fly, ground cloth, bug spray, repellent, bug suit,

> Water Management: Katadyn Vario Water filter, stainless cup, canteen
> Admin: Cash, weather writing pads, pens
> Repair: Steel cable, plastic tubing (kayak repairs/spares)
> Personal Items: Flask, Siesta Key Honey Spiced Rum, Zippo, cigars

hanging head net, gloves
> Tools: Binoculars, Zeiss Monocular, Casio G-Shock watch, Stainless steel sternum Spartan Blades knife, Glock folding shovel, machete, KABAR Kukri, Swiss Army Knife, pliers, filet knife, snares, fire-starter sticks, fuel, signal mirror

BUG-OUT BIKE

A Two-Wheeled Solution to a Cross-Country SHTF Problem

By Len Waldron
Photos courtesy of ReadyMan.com

As a father, he had it all planned out. Food, water, security...well, almost everything. Jayson Ross felt good about his preparations in the Mountain West region, but when his daughter chose to attend a college on the East Coast, her safety was suddenly out of his control. "If something bad happens really fast, I would never see her again," Jayson Ross says. "And I wasn't cool with that."

Ross has been a survivalist since childhood. He's spent most of his life training in hunting, fieldcraft, camping, firearms, scuba diving, athletics, and more. It's culminated in his cofounding ReadyMan.com, an online company that's made up largely of special-operation veterans and offers a wide range of survival training services through online videos and live courses. Yet, no amount of his equipment and skills could get his daughter home if a major disaster or social breakdown occurred. Not willing to accept that sort of loss, he began breaking down the challenges she might face in a 2,100-mile cross-country trek. Ultimately, Ross couldn't get past the near certainty that after a major event, roadways would be snarled with traffic and gasoline would be at a premium.

The only alternative was to build a well-equipped, lightweight, and maneuverable vehicle to carry his daughter forward when an automobile couldn't. In other words, he would have to build her a dual-sport motorbike.

Why a Motorcycle?

Ross's plan was to augment his daughter's Subaru Outback with a small trailer that carried two Suzuki DR200SE motorcycles and a specifically chosen load-out of complementary gear. The strategy he fashioned was for his daughter and a family friend in the area to, at the first sign of major trouble, hitch the motorcycle trailer and start heading west. If the catastrophe subsided quickly — no problem — return to school, but err on the side of getting out of Dodge.

Motorcycles aren't a perfect solution, but they do provide a number of significant advantages. First, they're efficient, particularly the small ones. Ross found that a 200cc engine got nearly 70 miles to the gallon. The combination of the long distance his daughter would have to cover and a likely shortage of gas made choosing a smaller engine a smart choice. In most cases, the next larger size of bike managed considerably fewer

miles per gallon and required a larger fuel tank to achieve an equivalent range. Additionally, the lighter overall weight made it a better fit for her smaller frame.

He chose the Suzuki DR200SE because it's a simple, versatile platform capable of both highway and off-road travel. The most likely scenario Ross envisioned was an interstate snarl with vehicles jamming the roads, stranding their operators in place, and putting them at risk of assaults and robbery. The motorcycles could be rolled off the trailer and ridden down the median or shoulders, around the traffic, and out of the danger area. While leaving the safety of the automobile would be a major decision, doing so on a bike would be an excellent alternative, with gear staged and packed for just such a contingency.

In any case, the bike beats walking by a long shot. But switching to the motorcycle changes just about every element of travel.

The riders would now be exposed to the elements, more vulnerable to external attack, and unable to rotate sleeping and driving duties. Travel post-crisis would now be as much physical as emotional. The simple act of balancing and steering the motorcycle over time would fatigue them, and interpersonal communication would be a challenge. With these obstacles in mind, Ross began adapting the Suzukis to maximize the range and survivability of their riders.

Motorcycle Outfitters

The first element to be enhanced was range and carrying capacity. That year's model of Suzuki came with a 2.5-gallon tank, which under ideal conditions puts the range at 175 miles. Ross wanted a minimum of 250 miles with a buffer to compensate for the added weight of equipment and fuel.

To increase the carrying capacity of the Suzukis, Ross installed the Kriega Overlander 60 system. The Overlander 60 is a frame-mounted rack that attaches without welding or cutting. Flexible and modular, the system allows for both pannier packs and fuel. The rack mounts above and behind the rear wheel, but clears both the frame and the exhaust. At 15 liters each, the Kriega packs ride forward of the fuel cans and just above the rear passenger pegs. Because they're below the seat and the rider's center of gravity, they don't significantly impact the handling characteristics of the motorcycle.

Behind the Kriega panniers, Ross added four 1-gallon RotoPax fuel tanks on either side of the rear wheels. Made of high-impact plastic, these tanks have a modular design that allows them to be mounted individually or stacked on a central mounting peg. The auxiliary tanks add an additional 275 miles of range to the fuel tank, providing nearly one-third of the fuel necessary for the trip — and this is after the automobile is abandoned. Refueling would be a necessity, but it wouldn't be immediate.

As functional add-ons, Ross added hand windshields on the grips and a small windshield. Short of the additional cargo and fuel, the motorcycle is largely stock.

Kitting the Bike

Deciding on how to divide gear between the rider and the motorcycle was a deliberate process. Ross decided on some redundancy with the kit carried on the rider (see the sidebar), but in the panniers he largely stuck to hard goods, bike support equipment, and items to deal with the changing external environment. For example, in addition to a helmet he staged riding leathers, gloves, hand and toe warmers, as well as dust and gas masks. For quick fixes he added a small tool kit, a knife, multitool, headlamp, and flashlight.

In a small backpack on the back of the bike above the rear fender, he staged field gear such as batteries, a medical kit with manual, a shortwave radio, a solar

Bug-Out Bike Gear List

The gear you select is essential in any preparedness situation, but it's especially true when you're trying to bug out on a motorcycle that's traveling at 75 mph or faster without a large windshield or steel doors. If your GTFO vehicle is a dual-sport bike, consider the following setup that Jayson Ross has established for his daughter's motorcycle.

On the Rider

- Backpacking backpack
- Tent with rain fly and footprint
- Rip-stop ponch (camouflage color)
- Sleeping bag (in compression sack)
- Small sleeping pad
- Light binoculars with harness
- Passport and/or ID
- $400 in cash
- Cellphone
- 1 Nalgene Water Bottle (full)
- Platypus Gravity Water Purifier
- Gortex Rain Parka
- Sunglasses
- Wind-up watch
- Toothbrush and toothpaste
- Tampons (if necessary)
- Single Kleenex pack (doubles as toilet paper)
- ChapStick
- Mechanix Gloves
- GPS and fresh batteries
- Maps
- Compass
- Fire-starter(s) and Bic lighters
- Sidearm
- Sidearm holster with magazine pouches
- 6 sidearm magazines
- 200 rounds of sidearm ammunition
- Folding AK-47
- 2 AK-47 magazines (loaded)
- 300 rounds of 7.62x39mm ammunition
- Fixed-blade knife
- Knife sharpener
- Leatherman multitool
- Petzel headlamp
- Tactical flashlight
- PVS-7 night vision google

In a Pack on the Bike

- Trauma medical kit with manual
- 2 Motorola two-way radios with batteries
- 8 extra AA Batteries
- 8 extra AAA Batteries
- Bath wipes
- 100-percent DEET insect repellant
- Travel Bible, playing cards
- 8 Kleenex packs
- Shortwave radio with line amplifier (if possible)
- Solar charger for shortwave and other devices
- JetBoil Stove and 2 canisters (one unopened)
- Compact cooking kit
- 1 Wool sweater
- 2 Pair of warm wool socks
- 1 Set of Polartec thermal underwear (top and bottom)
- 1 Long-sleeve shirt
- 1 Fleece jacket
- 1 Wool pants
- Thin beanie
- Neoprene facemask
- Hiking boots
- 8 MREs

On the Bike

- Suzuki 2013 DR200SE
- 4 RotoPax fuel cans and mounting hardware
- Kriega Overlander 60 Pannier Sets
- Happy Trails SU Side Rack (modified)
- Small windshields
- Hand windshields
- 2 Nalgene bottles
- Siphon
- Israeli gas mask
- Gas mask cartridges
- Leathers
- Helmet
- Motorcycle gloves
- N95 dust masks
- Battery trickle charger (to keep bike battery topped off/storage)
- 10 pairs of hand warmers/toe warmers
- Tool Kit (ratchet and screwdriver set)

7 Stealthy
Considerations for a Long-Distance Bug Out

Your bug-out plan might not require an escape route as lengthy or involved as Ross', but you may need to get to family or guide someone to your location. Here are a few items to consider:

1. Route Plan
Does your route avoid both choke points and population centers prone to social unrest? Will your vehicle get you across the terrain you might encounter (i.e. mountains, waterways, unimproved roads, etc.)

2. Weapons and Concealment
Do you have a means to carry your weapons in a manner that makes them accessible, but not obvious to onlookers.

3. Conflict Avoidance
Like your route plan, your mindset needs to be one of avoiding all contact with people.

4. Roadblocks
Never willingly approach a roadblock. Walking up to a roadblock is tantamount to surrendering everything you possess. There is never a reason to enter into a zone where you're knowingly covered by direct fire from multiple angles. Find a way around.

5. Gas is Life
As Mad Max taught us, be prepared to beg, borrow, or steal fuel to maintain your progress. (Keep in mind, you're still legally and morally accountable if and when law and order returns.) Carry both a simple siphon and pump to refuel as necessary.

6. Make a Communications Plan
Being able to talk with someone at your destination can make a massive difference to your morale, and poor morale is generally a death sentence. Cell phones, text messaging, and ham and short-wave radios may only work in some areas, but have a plan for multiple methods and means of communication.

7. Look, Listen, and Move
Make a small, chest-mounted pair of binoculars part of your essential kit. Binos that are accessible tend to get used more often. Knowing what lies ahead when you crest a hill, approach populated areas, or recon routes can make the critical difference between a conflict and safe passage.

charger, a JetBoil stove with fuel canisters and a small cook kit, extra cold-weather clothing, and MREs. The intent was to have essential items ready-to-grab and non-essential items ready-to-dump if the motorcycles had to be ditched.

Kitting the Rider

Deciding what kit to carry on the actual rider is a more serious and complicated question. Changing the weight of a rider changes not just the performance of the engine, but also the handling characteristics of the motorcycle. Because the engine is small and chosen for efficiency over power, weight is always a consideration. Ross also reckoned that on-foot bug-out equipment should not require sorting and packing. As such, the rider's backpack load-out closely resembles a hiker going on a backcountry trek.

While testing options for a personal backpack, it became clear the best option is a full frame backpack with a bombproof waistband. This helps to both secure the pack while operating the motorcycle, but also requires no changes or modifications if the bike has to be ditched and the rider has to continue on foot.

His daughter chose the REI XT 85 because it had the capacity to accommodate the required gear, and most importantly, it fit her. Ross chose an ultralight tent, fly, and footprint along with a compression sack-reduced sleeping bag and ground pad. To this he also added personal hygiene items, a Platypus water filter, a GPS, more batteries, light binoculars with a chest rig, cash, a pre-charged cell phone, passport or ID, Mechanix gloves, and a compass. The backpack was configured for his daughter and her companion. His daughter is an experienced backpacker and that definitely dictated some gear choices. So the backpacking gear was more customized than the more universal on-bike gear.

Armed With a Plan

Ross harbored no illusions about the necessity of carrying a firearm in a situation serious enough to warrant a cross-country bug out. But what to choose and how to stage it required some thought. He concluded an accessible, but semi-concealed waist holster was a must. For his daughter he chose a Glock 19 as she was trained to use it, and it was more likely than most other models to function under all conditions. He settled on 200 rounds of ammo divided between six magazines and a spare box stored on the bike.

Ross wasn't convinced having only a handgun was the answer, so he added a folding stock AK. Though the AK's reliability is well known, Ross had additional reasons for

choosing it. Traveling through potentially hostile territory on a motorcycle is no one's first choice, particularly because the rider has very little protection. Gone are the luxuries of body metal, steel frames, and the deflection of interior glass — and only mobility remains. The saddle of a motorcycle is not the place to initiate offensive action. Rather, Ross's strategy for travel and survival was to stay low profile, and avoid populated areas, danger, and conflict. While there are many short-barreled AR's out there, the buffer spring limits the degree to which they can be shortened. The AK can be folded and carried discreetly in the backpack, but drawn only during times of prolonged danger or for pulling security during bivouacs. Ross settled on 300 rounds with two pre-loaded magazines.

But the best arms and gear in the world mean very little without a well-contemplated and clearly understood plan for travel. Ross approached the route planning in a deductive and rational manner. His first step was to sim-

ply pull a Google map of the quickest route between his daughter's college and his home. His second step was to overlay population centers along the route. Ross planned routes around the densest counties and tried to avoid the major population centers by 250 miles whenever possible. This is much tougher in the East where cities and towns are both larger and more tightly clustered.

"It's tricky," says Ross. "There are small slots between populated areas and sometimes you have to go near or though places you wouldn't want to. Things get better west of the Mississippi, and particularly once you get past Des Moines." He then acquired detailed state maps of the route and planned primary, secondary, and alternate routes.

The plan for his daughter and her friend was to travel mostly at night. Their mindset would be one of escape and evasion. As two young people in unfamiliar territory, there is nothing to be gained from being spotted by anyone at any time. Though they could travel by headlamp or the motorcycle's headlight at night, they also were equipped with PVS-7 night vision goggles. Roadblocks would be avoided at all costs and stops in the open or during daylight would only be for critical items like fuel, water, and food.

Are motorcycles a great plan for a young family of five? Probably not. But if you have family, friends, or college students who could get caught hundreds or thousands of miles from hearth and home, this layered strategy of bugging out could be the difference between life or death. And, using some of the strategies Ross employed, motorcycles can be an excellent fallback when automobile travel becomes unworkable. ⁘

About The Author:

Len Waldron is a freelance outdoor writer and custom knife-maker from Bountiful, Utah. He became an Eagle Scout and attended Wake Forest University. Later, he served as an infantry officer in the U.S. Army and earned a master's in business administration. [Editor's note: Full journalistic disclosure — in between the time he submitted this story and this issue hitting newsstands, Waldron has since joined the ReadyMan.com team.]

Gas Sippers

A variety of options exist for nimble, efficient, and generally affordable alternatives when a single track is the only option. Here are some dual-sport motorcycles that could fit the bill.

	Suzuki DR200SE	Yamaha TW-200	Kawasaki KLX-250s	Honda CRF250L
Engine	199cc, four-stroke	196cc, four-stroke	249cc, four-stroke	249cc, four-stroke
Fuel Tank	3.4 gallons	1.8 gallons	2 gallons	2 gallons
Miles Per Gallon	68	78	70	73
Range	231 miles	140 miles	140 miles	146 miles
Weight	278 pounds	278 pounds	298 pounds	320 pounds
MSRP	$4,199	$4,590	$5,099	$4,999

BUG OUT BY AIR

When Chaos Strikes, is it Viable to Escape in a Plane?

By Neal H. Olshan

WARNING!
This article is meant to be a quick overview and is not a detailed guide on aviation, nor should it be construed as an endorsement to operate an aircraft without proper training and licenses. To learn more, consult with a reputable training school or instructor.

he TV reporter said all you needed to know in one sentence: "The governor is declaring a state of emergency and evacuation plans will be announced in the next five minutes." Strong winds from the Northwest are driving the flames toward a derailed train of tanker cars filled with volatile chlorine. A solid wall of flames stretches across the television screen and roiling clouds of thick brown smoke climb thousands of feet into the sky. Fire departments from all over the state have been unable to slow the fire's path toward the overturned tankers.

Your wife and two young children enter the room and stand next to you. Their survival will depend on your skills and decision-making over the next hour. You know what to do. You need to bug out now, and it's got to be by plane.

Without being told, each member of the family grabs their go-bags, and 10 minutes later you're entering the code that allows you into Sky Ranch Airport and to your bug-out aircraft: a 22-year-old Cessna 172. The preflight complete, you reach for the ignition key. Your wife puts her hand over yours and squeezes gently as the engine coughs to life, settling into the familiar rhythm. After a few heart-pounding minutes, you're in the air and cruising through 2,100 feet. You share a relieved look with your wife as you gently bank northeast toward your first destination, the mountain top airport 150 nautical miles north.

The preceding story, although fiction, has its basis in the stark reality of compromised land and water egress. Take this story's hypothetical opener: a chlorine tanker accident.

Chlorine is used in industrial and commercial products and is therefore commonplace. Depending on the concentration and the exposure time, this chemical can cause severe health problems and even death. At room temperature, chlorine is a gas that's heavier than air,

which means it'll linger in low-lying areas unless the wind picks up. The safest means of escaping its potentially fatal and widespread mist could very well be via an aircraft.

At this point, some of you might be asking, "What if I don't know how to fly?" or "Having a bug-out plane is stupid because it isn't realistic." Remember: If disaster has already struck, it's too late to develop a bug-out plavne strategy. Having an aircraft is an option that may take years to fully develop. But once you have it, it could mean the difference between saving your family and being stuck on the highway with thousands of other panicked drivers wishing you could grow a pair of wings. As they always say, "You can never have too many options when the SHTF."

Air Glossary

ADF: Automatic Direction Finder: Radio compass giving a relative bearing

ADT: Approved Departure Time

AGL: Above Ground Level

AIRMET: A type of weather advisory regarding turbulence, icing, and low visibility

AME: Aviation Medical Examiner

APP: Approach control

ARTCC: Air Route Traffic Control Centre

ASI: Airspeed Indicator

ATA: Actual Time of Arrival

ATIS: Automatic Terminal Information Service. Automatically recorded message transmitted on a particular frequency,

Winged Transport

If you're a regular reader, you know that OFFGRID delves into all manner of bug-out vehicles, from kayaks and snowmobiles to off-road rigs and mountain bikes. So, in this edition we shine the spotlight at aircraft as a survival option. Here's a look at the benefits and disadvantages of being a prepper pilot.

PROS:

❯ Best answer when getting distance between you and the event quickly is a priority

❯ Reduce limiting variables, such as traffic, road closures, unpredictable crowd behaviors (survival mob mentality), etc.

❯ Fly over disasters, hostiles, blocked roads, destroyed bridges, etc.

❯ Not stranded if the infrastructure can't handle the automotive traffic

❯ Ability to do fly-over reconnaissance prior to landing

❯ Access multiple destinations

CONS:

❯ Dependent on fuel

❯ Possibility of public airport closures (the best reason to keep your aircraft at a private airport)

❯ Governmental flight restrictions (e.g. Sept. 11 terrorist attack)

❯ Most small private aircraft are vulnerable to theft or vandalism due to poorly constructed locks

❯ Aircraft not parked in hangers are susceptible to weather events

❯ Cost of buying and maintaining an aircraft, and need for maintaining flight skills (whereas you drive your car or truck every day)

❯ The variable of flying in poor weather

❯ Limits of gross weight (baggage, supplies, etc.), depending on aircraft

INHALATION HAZARD CHLORINE
DOT-105-J-500-W

	STENCIL STATION	QUALIFIED	DUE
TANK QUALIFICATION	SGNW	1999	2009
THICKNESS TEST	CGRD	2005	2015
SERVICE EQUIPMENT	CGRD	2005	2015
PRD: VALVE 375 PSI	CANEXUS	2007	2015
LINING			
88.B.2 INSPECTION	SGNW	1999	2009
STUB SILL INSPECTION	SGNW	1999	2009

ABDX ABDX · LUB NO

1017 · 2

1017

2 INCH HF COMP SHOES

UNITED STATES OF AMERICA
DEPARTMENT OF TRANSPORTATION · FEDERAL AVIATION ADMINISTRATION
IV NAME
NEAL HUGH OLSHAN
V ADDRESS

VI NATIONALITY USA   SEX HEIGHT WEIGHT HAIR EYES
IVa D.O.B.   M   73   235   GRAY BLUE
IX HAS BEEN FOUND TO BE PROPERLY QUALIFIED TO EXERCISE THE PRIVILEGES OF
II PRIVATE PILOT
III CERTIFICATE NUMBER 4440
X DATE OF ISSUE 21 MAY
XIV
VIII   ADMINISTRATOR

Step One: Pilot's License

Let's say you've weighed the pros and cons, and you're game. Where do you start? Obtain a valid pilot's license (private, sport, or recreational) if you don't already have one. According to Federal Aviation Administration (FAA) guidelines, you can begin training at any age. However, you must be at least 16 to obtain a sport pilot certificate and 17 for a recreational pilot or private pilot certificate.

Here's a look at the main types of pilot's licenses and what it takes to obtain them.

❶ PRIVATE

Privileges:
❭ More than one passenger may be carried
❭ Flight outside U.S. airspace allowed
❭ Night flight allowed

Training Requirements:
❭ 40 hours minimum
❭ Pass FAA written exam
❭ Pass flight exam with an FAA examiner
❭ Requires FAA medical exam
❭ Average cost: $9,900

❷ RECREATIONAL

(Airplane and Rotorcraft)

Privilege:
❭ Only one passenger may be carried
❭ Night flight allowed, but only under the supervision of a certified flight instructor

Training:
❭ 30 hours minimum
❭ Pass the FAA written exam
❭ Pass flight exam with an FAA examiner
❭ Requires FAA medical exam
❭ Average cost: $7,700

❸ SPORT

(Airplane, Gyro, Weight-Shift-Control, Airships)

Privileges:
❭ Only one passenger may be carried

Training:
❭ 20 hours minimum
❭ Pass the FAA written exam
❭ Pass flight exam with an FAA examiner
❭ Requires FAA medical exam or a U.S. driver's license and self-certification
❭ Average cost $4,400

Step Two: Obtain a Plane

Once you've acquired your pilot's license, it's time to get an airplane that has the basic characteristics needed for a bug-out vehicle. Avoid a rental or club aircraft. Instead, consider a seaplane. It's quite possibly the most versatile bug-out aircraft available to the general public. The seaplane allows you access to runways, grass and dirt landing strips, lakes, ocean, and all manner of waterways.

Due to the inherent ruggedness and reliability of the Husky, Skyhawk, Caravan, and Beaver, all four models are ideal for bugging out to and from land, snow, or water. They also have several rather significant benefits not found in the newer aircraft: long production runs and availability of parts. These planes can be found used in greater quantities and at a lower cost. Here's a closer look at each one. See if one of them meets your needs.

De Havilland Beaver

This single-engine, high-wing Canadian bush plane has been used by military all over the world, from the U.S. Army to the Ghana Air Force.

CAPACITY:	One pilot, six passengers
CARGO:	2,100 pounds of useful load
LENGTH:	30 feet, 3 inches
WINGSPAN:	48 feet
HEIGHT:	9 feet
EMPTY WEIGHT:	3,000 pounds
GROSS WEIGHT:	5,100 pounds
POWER PLANT:	450hp Pratt and Whitney Wasp Jr. radial engine
MAXIMUM SPEED:	158 mph
CRUISE SPEED:	143 mph
RANGE:	455 miles
SERVICE CEILING:	18,000 feet
RATE OF CLIMB:	1,020 feet per minute

Air Glossary (CONTINUED)

containing current weather conditions, altimeter setting, active runways, etc., provided at airports with a tower (controlled).

AVGAS: Aviation Gasoline. Usually followed by the octane rating. Used by piston-engine aircraft.

Call sign: Phrase used in radio transmissions aircraft to identify an aircraft, before proceeding to actual instructions. An example would be "Motorglider 351 Hotel" or "Cessna 13 Whiskey."

Ceiling: Height above ground or water level of the base of the lowest layer of cloud.

Clearance: Authorization given by ATC (the tower, Air Traffic Control) to proceed as requested or instructed (for example: "Cleared for takeoff," "Cleared to land").

Crosswind: Wind perpendicular to the motion of the aircraft. The crosswind leg is also one of the many words describing the approach segments.

Density altitude: Pressure altitude (as indicated by the altimeter) corrected for air temperature.

DI: Direction Indicator. A gyro instrument, which indicates the magnetic heading of an aircraft.

Downwind: When flying parallel to the runway.

ELT or ELB: Emergency Locator Transmitter/Beacon

ETA: Estimated Time of Arrival

FAA: Federal Aviation Administration

FBO: Fixed-Base Operator. Supplier of fuel, maintenance, aircraft rental or sale, flight training, etc. at the airport.

FINAL: Final Approach is the part of a landing sequence in which the aircraft has made its final turn and is flying directly to the runway.

GND: Ground

Go-around: When an aircraft on final terminates its plans to land, gains altitude and begins the landing pattern again. ▶▶

GPS: Global Positioning System (Navstar).

Aviat Husky

In production since 1987, this rugged and dependable two-seater is one of the best-selling light aircraft designs of the past two decades. This high-wing utility plane is used for all sorts of functions, from pipeline inspection and glider towing to border patrol and anti-poaching missions.

CAPACITY: 1 pilot, 1 passenger
CARGO: 925 pounds of useful load
LENGTH: 30 feet, 6 inches
WINGSPAN: 35 feet
HEIGHT: 9 feet
EMPTY WEIGHT: 1,275 pounds
GROSS WEIGHT: 2,250 pounds
POWER PLANT: 180hp Lycoming O-360
MAXIMUM SPEED: 145 mph
CRUISE SPEED: 140 mph
RANGE: 800 miles
SERVICE CEILING: 20,000 feet
RATE OF CLIMB: 1,500 feet per minute

Cessna Caravan Amphibian

This rugged and proven aircraft can operate from terra firma or water — you can land on and take off from almost anywhere. The passenger capacity and ability to transport extensive supplies put this bug-out aircraft at the top of the list. Manufactured since 1998, it's the largest seaplane with a single engine.

CAPACITY: Eight, 10, or 14
CARGO: 3,230 pounds
LENGTH: 38 feet, 1 inches
WINGSPAN: 52 feet, 1 inches
HEIGHT: 17 feet, 7 inches
EMPTY WEIGHT: 5,555 pounds
GROSS WEIGHT: 8,750 pounds
POWER PLANT: 675hp Pratt & Whitney Model PT6A-114A
MAXIMUM SPEED: 175 kias
CRUISE SPEED: 159 knots
RANGE: 820 nautical miles
SERVICE CEILING: 20,000 feet
RATE OF CLIMB: 939 feet per minute

Cessna 172 Skyhawk

The Cessna 172 Skyhawk is a four-seat, single-engine, high-wing aircraft that first flew in 1955 and has been in production since 1956. More 172s have been manufactured than any other airplane in history. The availability of used aircraft in good condition is extensive.

CAPACITY: Two to three passengers (including the pilot)
LENGTH: 27 feet
WINGSPAN: 36 feet
CARGO: 446 pounds of useful load
EMPTY WEIGHT: 1,275 pounds
GROSS WEIGHT: 2,300 pounds
POWER PLANT: Lycoming O-360
MAXIMUM SPEED: 188 mph
CRUISE SPEED: 143 mph
RANGE: 800 miles
SERVICE CEILING: 20,000 feet
RATE OF CLIMB: 1,500 feet per minute

Step Three: Practice

Much like any other survival skill, flying a bug-out plane proficiently takes repetition. So once you have your license and your plane, practice, practice, and practice. And when you think that you have practiced enough, practice some more. Obviously, you can't learn how to fly from reading a magazine article. So we'll give you a brief overview of the basics.

Air Glossary
(CONTINUED)

Navigational system using orbiting satellites to determine the aircraft's position on the Earth.

IDENT: SQUAWK function of a transponder. When the "Ident" button is activated, an aircraft will briefly appear more distinctly on a radarscope and this may be used for identification or acknowledgment purposes.

IFR: Instrument Flight Rules for the operation of aircraft in instrument meteorological conditions.

ILS: Instrument Landing System provides horizontal and vertical guidance for the approach.

Knot (kt): Standard unit of speed in aviation were 1 knot equals 1.1515 mph

LAT: Latitude

Magnetic course: Intended horizontal direction, measured in degrees clockwise from magnetic north.

Mayday: The international radio distress call.

MSL: Mean Sea Level

NM: Nautical Miles

NTSB: National Transportation Safety Board

OAT: Outside Air Temperature

Payload: The combined weight of passengers and/or cargo.

POH: Pilot's Operating Handbook (aircraft's owners manual)

RPM: Revolutions Per Minute

RWY: Runway

SIGMET: Significant Meteorological Information. A type of weather advisory regarding severe weather conditions (thunderstorms, turbulence, icing, volcanic ash, etc.).

Squawk: To transmit an assigned code via a transponder.

Takeoff and Climbing

Complete your pre-take off checklist. Typically use one degree of flap and the elevator trim is adjusted to neutral. Now slowly advance the throttle, using the rudder pedals to steer the aircraft to the active runway and point the nose into the wind. Wait for the tower to say, "Skyhawk 6 Charlie Lima, clear for takeoff." The throttle is opened fully to start the takeoff roll. During this takeoff roll, the control wheel, or stick, is usually held in the neutral position, and the rudder pedals are used to keep the airplane on the runway's centerline.

As takeoff airspeed is approached, gently apply backpressure on the control wheel or stick and the plane's nose will begin to lift off the runway. Use the rudder pedals to keep the nose point straight.

When the airplane is clear of the runway, gently relax the control slightly, letting the nose drop slightly as you gain speed. As your airspeed increases, remember the best rate of climb for your aircraft (found in the aircraft operating manual).

Landing

First, find the airport — sometimes that's more difficult than it sounds. Check the wind direction at the airport by asking the tower controller the wind direction or look at the windsock on the airfield. At a controlled airport you must comply with the directions of the tower, and a controller will give you the runway information and tell you when to land.

At an uncontrolled airport, there is no tower. You announce your intentions, look for other planes, and when clear, land. Whether you are told which runway to land on or you make the choice, align yourself into the

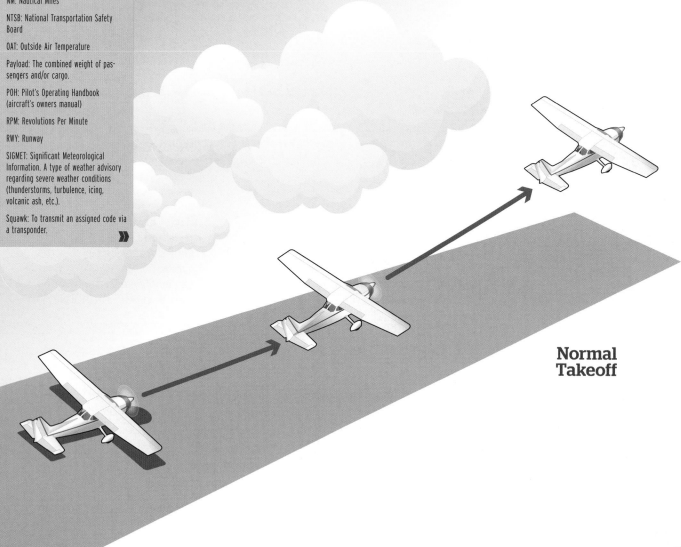

Normal Takeoff

wind and control your airspeed so that the needle in the airspeed indicator is in the white arc. This is a time to be careful and maintain the appropriate airspeed since the bottom of the white arc usually represents the planes stalling speed.

Run a "before landing" checklist, found in the aircraft manufacturer's operating handbook, prior to the final leg of your pattern. Maintain your glide slope angle by using the VASI (Visual Approach Slope Indicator) system installed along the runway. If you see a set of red lights over a set of white lights on the VASI system, you are on the proper glide slope. If the runway you are landing on doesn't have approach lights, you should be 300 feet above the ground 1 mile from the end of the runway and as you cross the runway threshold, smoothly bring the power to idle and smoothly pull back on the controls and flare (slightly nose up) and allow the plane to settle to the runway.

Once you've become proficient at the fundamentals, take it a step further and begin practicing for a potential bug out. Try these four exercises:

Checklist It: Keep a checklist in the office, house, and car. Discovering that you forgot an essential item after you're already strapped into the plane is of little use.

Preplan It: Find the best and fastest route to the airport from your home, work, and any other location were you go at least three times per week on a regular basis.

Drill It: Do a complete run-through at least once every three months with whomever is in your family or survival group.

Old-School It: Once in there air, pick an objective location and see if you can get there without a GPS and other advanced navigational aids. Hint: At times it may be as simple as following the highway and making the appropriate turn off — it's just that you're 4,000 feet above the ground.

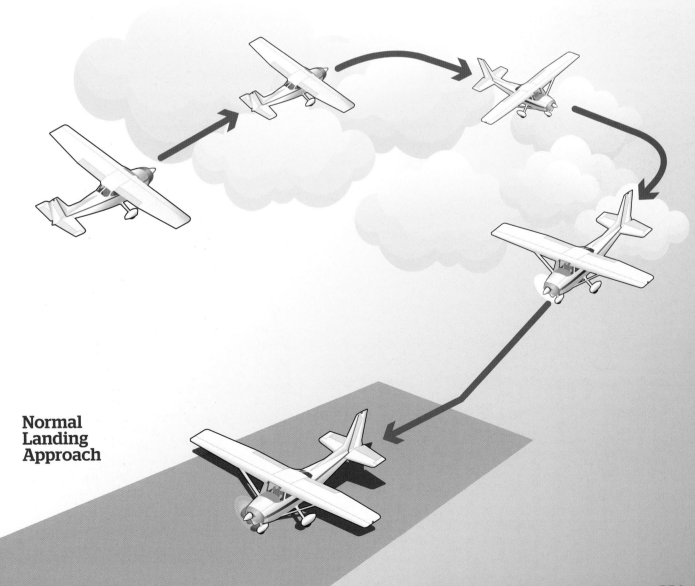

Normal Landing Approach

Air Glossary

STOL: Short Take-Off and Landing.

TAS: True Airspeed. Airspeed corrected for altitude and outside air temperature.

TCA: Terminal Control Area

Tailwind: Strong wind in the same direction as the motion of the aircraft.

Touchdown: Synonym for landing.

Transponder: A transponder is a wireless communications, monitoring, or control device that picks up and automatically responds to an incoming signal.

UNICOM: Privately operated radio service at uncontrolled airfields.

UTC: Co-ordinated Universal Time, formerly Greenwich Mean Time

VHF: Very high frequency. Radio frequencies in the 30-300 MHz band, used for most civil air-to-ground communication.

VOR: Very high frequency Omnidirectional Range.

Wake turbulence: Wingtip vortices generated behind a wing producing lift.

Waypoint: Reference point used for navigation indicated by latitude and longitude.

Wind shear: Refers to a rapid change in winds over a short horizontal distance that can cause a rapid change in lift, and thus the altitude of aircraft.

Zulu: Used worldwide for times of flight operations.

Aviation Adaptation

Whatever the cause, any disaster of significance will adversely affect the power and communications grids. That means your entire wiz bang — state-of-the-art communications and navigational devices will be useless, at least for a time. The world of convenience will be transported back to the 19th century.

Right now you are probably saying, "Yeah, but my glass panel and GPS have backup batteries. Wrong, all the backup batteries in the world will not be of any help if society's infrastructure begins to collapse. Tuning to your favorite radio station will be a waste of time if the station can't broadcast a signal. An electromagnetic pulse (EMP) burst will fry everything electrical and whatever survives will be worthless because satellites will be non-functional, ground-based NDBs (non-directional beacons), VORs (VHF omnidirectional range beacons), and TACAN (Tactical Air Navigation Beacons) will cease to function.

Within a matter of seconds you will be transported back to the days of the biplanes, when traveling from point A to point B involved following geographical landmarks such as roads, bridges, mountains, and lakes. Times when one's most important assets were common sense and self-reliance.

How about while you're flying? Are there specific altitudes you need to fly? Visual Flight Rules (VFR) will most likely be used if a crisis hits. The designated altitudes to fly at are 7,500 feet and 8,500 feet since the VFR state that traffic flying easterly should be at odd altitudes plus 500 feet (e.g. 7,500 feet). Westerly traffic utilizing VFR should be at even altitudes plus 500 feet (e.g. 8,500 feet).

Not every catastrophic event will be a chlorine tanker explosion fueled by a wildfire. And not every bug-out vehicle will (or should be) an aircraft. But if you're already a pilot, or have the means to become one, consider a plane as another card in your survival deck. ✖

SOURCES

Aircraft Owners and Pilots Association ➤ www.AOPA.org
Experimental Aircraft Association ➤ www.EAA.org
Federal Aviation Administration ➤ www.faa.gov
Seaplane Pilots Association ➤ www.seaplanes.org

About the Author:

Dr. Neal H. Olshan is a consulting psychologist, a pilot, a writer, and a fine art photographer, as well as the chief combat psychologist for LMS Defense. He is the developer of the Evolution of Mindset Training Program. Olshan is the author of six non-fiction books and wrote the novel *The Panama Escape* with his wife, Mary. **www.drolshan.com**

Aerial Go-Bag

The bug-out bag (BOB) may be as essential to your survival as the fuel in the aircraft's tanks. The first thing to remember is that although you are flying, nothing has to be TSA compliant. Each passenger should have his or her own BOB. There should be one bag for the aircraft that remains in the plane.

The BOB is a very important yet personalized necessity. Unlike on a motor vehicle or a boat, weight is of paramount consideration in an airplane. Weigh each bag and calculate into the total passenger and carry-on weight. This is extremely important as it relates to the plane's performance. You should inspect everyone's bags on a monthly basis using a checklist. Your family's BOBs should be stored in the same place and stored together. Some have used a hall closet or cabinet in the garage. Here's a closer explanation of what your bug-out gear should be.

ON YOUR PERSON

Whether you're flying commercial or private, make sure you're wearing cotton or wool (no nylon) and leather sole shoes or hiking boots. Pack a light jacket, a hat, and medication. Ask your doctor if you can get a prescription for a wide-spectrum antibiotic and an anti-diarrhea medication.

CAPTAIN'S BOB

For sake of clarity, the pilot's bag will be called the "Captain's BOB" and it's the responsibility of the pilot to verify that each passenger has their BOB. The Captain's BOB should contain:

- Sectional Charts
- Sectional Plotter
- Multiple forms of identification (passport, pilot's license, driver's license etc.)
- Carbon Monoxide Detector
- Aviation Transceiver with NOAA weather channel
- Handheld radio transceivers
- Pilot's tool kit
- Compass with mirror
- Poncho
- Hat
- Notepad with pen and pencil (preferably a pad that is designed to be used in rain or foul conditions)
- Spare prescription eyewear and sunglasses
- Fire piston (sparks for fires)
- Paracord 550 (50 feet)
- Headlamp plus spare batteries
- Long-sleeve shirt
- Socks and undergarments
- Leather work gloves
- Medical kit
- Life-Straw for water treatment
- Mylar blankets (one for each person on board)
- Vaseline-soaked cotton balls in container (starting/maintaining fires)
- Large Ziploc bag with toothpaste, medications, deodorant, dental floss Travel Kleenex Packets
- Sunscreen
- Tube of Vaseline Lip Therapy
- Hand sanitizer or wet wipes
- Extra batteries
- Assorted plastic bags (trash plus gallon and quart Ziploc bags
- At least $500 in cash and old/well used silver coins
- Two knives: one folding, one fixed blade
- Duct tape
- Leatherman type tool
- Aircraft Navigational Maps (Sectionals)
- Red marking pen or pencil for drawing route and adding changes
- Handgun and ammunition

FAMILY BOB:

The list here is a sample. Build your own go-bag based on your location, the age and health of passengers, and the potential weather.

- Quart Ziploc bag with toiletries
- Undergarments
- Two changes of clothes
- Hat
- Sunglasses
- Small flashlight
- Compass with mirror
- Three pairs of socks
- Gloves
- Compact water purifier
- Mini first-aid kit
- Wet wipes packets
- Ferrocerium rod fire starter
- Folding knife
- Mylar blanket
- Two large trash bags

Worst Bug-Out Aircraft

Given the parameters of a bug-out aircraft, there are certain aircraft that would not be appropriate for this type of mission. They're too small, too slow, have little to no cargo capacity, or have limited pilot and passenger protection, among other concerns. Avoid these types of craft when bugging out:

- Single seat self-launch gliders
- Hang gliders
- Paragliders
- Ultralight aircraft
- Hot air balloons
- Speed Parachutes

HOME ON WHEELS

Can Conventional RVs Work in a Bug-Out Scenario?

Story by Patrick McCarthy
Photos Courtesy of the Manufacturers

What makes a truly great survival vehicle? If someone asked you this question, you might reply with qualities like a powerful engine, high ground clearance, a huge payload of supplies, bright auxiliary lights, winches, push bars, and possibly even armor plating. Although we can certainly agree that all these features could come in handy, they also have a tendency to make the vehicle in question conspicuous — and in a survival scenario, that's the last thing you want to be. If your ride's appearance screams, "I'm prepared for anything," sooner or later someone less prepared will try to take it from you.

That said, consider a mobile survival platform that's common enough to blend in, spacious enough to be comfortable, and tough enough to use for years without repairs. Fortunately, there's a type of vehicle that's readily available and meets all these criteria — the recreational vehicle, or RV.

An RV will never be as stealthy as a motorcycle, or as capable off-road as a Jeep, but these homes-on-wheels are easy to find just about anywhere. Their living quarters provide plenty of room for gear and supplies, and best of all, anyone behind the wheel will end up looking more like a retiree on vacation than a hardened survival expert. So, don't discount that old motorhome in grandma's driveway just yet — it can be a real asset if you need to bug out.

A recreational vehicle is simply a motor vehicle with an attached living space. A wide range of vehicles can be considered RVs, from massive tour-bus-sized motor coaches to tiny pop-up trailers. There are three main categories of RV: motorhomes, trailers, and campers. Each class of RV has its own pros and cons to consider, so read on to determine which best fits your needs.

Courtesy of Winnebago Industries, Inc. Unauthorized use not permitted.

The first and most common type of RV is the motorhome. These vehicles are characterized by the powertrain and living quarters integrated together into a single package. Many motorhomes simply replace the rear section of a truck or van's body with living quarters, retaining the original chassis, engine, and driving position. These vehicles are known as Class C or midsize motorhomes, and can be identified by an extended section over the cab that often contains a bed.

The second category of motorhomes is the smallest, known as Class B (also called camper vans or conversion vans). These vehicles don't feature an extended section over the cab, resulting in a lower-profile roof. Often,

Class-B motorhomes are based on passenger vans, like the Mercedes-Benz Sprinter, Ford E-Series, or Chevrolet Express. The biggest upside to this design is its appearance — some Class-B motorhomes aren't easily recognizable as RVs, and therefore avoid unwanted attention in a survival scenario.

Finally, Class-A "integrated" motorhomes are built from the ground up, with driving position inside the living area. These mega-motorhomes are typically larger, feature a vertical windshield, and appear more similar to a commercial bus than to a passenger car. Features can include washer/dryer sets, expandable rooms, and even underside storage compartments for motorcycles or ATVs.

> The Winnebago View: Note the extended sleeping area directly above the vehicle's cab, this identifies a Class-C motorhome.

> The Winnebago Era, a Class-B motorhome based on a Mercedes Sprinter van. Notice the low-profile roof and lack of sleeping area above the cab.

As cool as that sounds, due to their cumbersome nature and noticeable appearance, Class-A motorhomes are better suited to transporting rock stars and celebrities than surviving the apocalypse. If you're behind the wheel of one of these giants, most onlookers will assume it has lots of desirable resources inside, and that's not a good thing in a dangerous situation.

∧ The Winnebago Grand Tour: Class-A motorhomes are the largest and most luxurious money can buy, and often feature amenities similar to a high-end hotel room.

From a cost standpoint, motorhomes run the gamut from tens of thousands to several million dollars. In a survival scenario, keeping a low profile is more important than having a fancy built-in jacuzzi or movie theater, so it's probably wise to avoid the more luxurious and expensive models. In addition, large Class-A motorhomes will be more difficult to maneuver and much more conspicuous on the road, so we recommend sticking to the smaller Class B and C motorhomes when SHTF.

∧ Here's the interior of the Winnebago Grand Tour. This palace on wheels will make you forget you ever evacuated your neighborhood...but it might not be the most practical for long-term survival.

PROS:

〉 The most common form of RV

〉 Spacious and luxurious with many available amenities

〉 Wide variety of sizes and configurations to choose from

〉 Moves under its own power, just hop in and hit the gas

CONS:

〉 The most expensive form of RV

〉 Larger models can draw unwanted attention and be difficult to maneuver

〉 May require specialty parts for repairs; most require diesel fuel

〉 Usually two-wheel drive with poor off-road performance (with the exception of expedition vehicles)

Photo courtesy of Jayco, Inc.

∧ Trailers are highly versatile and provide many options, such as the vehicle storage space of this Jayco Octane toy hauler.

The second type of RV is the travel trailer or caravan. Just as the name implies, travel trailers are living quarters that attach to a car or truck via a tow hitch, and can only move when towed. These are the oldest form of RV, dating back to the 1920s, and are relatively mechanically simple due to their dependence on a tow vehicle.

Travel trailers can be much smaller than a compact car, nearly as big as a city bus, or anywhere in between. Smaller trailers can be towed by an ordinary car, while the larger 30- to 40-foot trailers may require a purpose-built tow rig. For the purposes of survival, small and mid-size trailers shorter than 25 feet in length are ideal, as they can be towed by common pickups and SUVs.

Within the trailer category, there are several sub-groups to be aware of. Pop-ups, or expandable trailers, are handy for survival due to their low profile on the road and abundance of space when parked. Teardrops are small, aerodynamic, and lightweight (some can even be towed by a motorcycle). Toy haulers feature a fold-down rear ramp and storage space for ATVs or motorcycles. Finally, fifth-wheel trailers attach to an in-bed hitch (much like that of a semi truck) instead of a bumper hitch, resulting in improved on-road stability. However, fifth-wheel trailers are often larger and

∧ The Jayco Jay Series Sport, a compact pop-up trailer that also features pop-out expandable sleeping areas.

require specialized tow vehicles, so they may be less than ideal for survival.

The biggest advantage of a trailer is its ability to be disconnected from the tow vehicle. This enables establishing a home base far away from prying eyes, leaving the area in your vehicle to go on supply runs, and returning to your living quarters unnoticed. It's wise not to put all your eggs in one basket, and travel trailers make this easier than it would be in any other type of RV.

PROS:

❭ Can be easily disconnected from your vehicle

❭ Small, lightweight trailers provide excellent mobility

❭ Can be towed by a variety of cars, trucks, and vans

❭ More capable off-road than most motorhomes

CONS:

❭ Typically less luxurious and spacious than motorhomes

❭ Harder to move than motorhomes; requires a tow vehicle with a hitch

❭ May be difficult to maneuver for drivers with no towing experience

❭ Not all trailers have bathrooms or running water; may require an external generator for electricity

Expedition Vehicles

Taking the Path Less Traveled

Aside from the three classes of motorhomes listed in the main story, there's an important sub-group to be aware of: expedition vehicles, or off-road motorhomes. These vehicles are designed specifically with extreme conditions in mind, and often have heavy-duty suspensions, large tires, four-wheel drive, and other off-road-oriented upgrades. If you need to go just about anywhere, be totally self-reliant, and truly prepare for the worst, you'll want one of these monsters.

Expedition vehicles can fall into any of the above classes, and range from simple living quarters placed on the back of a lifted pickup truck to purpose-built behemoths with six- or eight-wheel drive. However, given this article's premise of staying inconspicuous, expedition vehicles may not necessarily be a wise choice. First of all, they tend to be much more expensive than a traditional motorhome and typically must be special-ordered from the manufacturer, so they're not easy to obtain. Secondly, they're definitely going to draw more attention than an ordinary motorhome as you roar down the road on huge mud tires.

So, in a bug-out scenario where you're heading into isolated wilderness for an extended period, an expedition vehicle would be ideal. However, in a situation where you may need to frequently use public roads or leave your vehicle exposed to gather supplies, these vehicles may cause more problems than they solve.

TYPE 3: Campers

Photo courtesy of Palomino RV, a division of Forest River, Inc.

The third type of RV is the camper. Also called slide-in, dismountable, or truck campers, these RVs are removable living quarters that sit inside the bed of an ordinary pickup truck. Campers benefit from the compact size of trailers, but feature even better mobility since they don't require towing experience — if you can drive a regular pickup truck, you can drive a truck with a camper. Like trailers, truck campers can also be removed from your vehicle temporarily, although it will take longer than simply unhitching a trailer. In order to dismount a truck camper, it must be jacked up using four corner jacks, then any turnbuckles or tie-downs must be disconnected before the truck can drive out from under the camper.

The type of camper you can use is typically determined by the type of truck you have access to. If you have a ½-ton short-bed truck with a gas engine, your options will be limited to smaller campers, but if you have a ¾- or 1-ton truck with a longbed and diesel engine, there will be many more choices available. Modern truck campers have most of the amenities of a comparable motorhome or trailer, including refrigerators, ovens, bathrooms, and showers. Some campers feature pop-up or expandable sections that provide extra space when parked and a lower profile on the road.

In a survival situation, an ordinary 4x4 diesel truck with a compact pop-up camper would be an excellent choice. This setup won't draw as much attention on the roads as other RVs, is highly capable off-road, and will provide more than enough space for two adults and their supplies. It won't be as spacious as a motorhome, or as modular as a trailer, but it's certainly a nice happy medium.

PROS:

❭ Easy to transport and highly maneuverable

❭ Extremely capable off-road when paired with a 4x4 pickup

❭ Can be removed from your vehicle, but not as easily as a trailer

❭ Features like pop-up tops can create a low-visual profile, not much larger than a bed cap or shell

CONS:

❭ Requires a pickup truck and must match the truck's bed length and weight capacity

❭ Less spacious than almost all motorhomes and most trailers

❭ Larger campers may require heavy-duty suspension and brake upgrades

❭ May be unavailable for small or light-duty trucks

△ An example of a truck camper, the Palomino Backpack Edition. Note the four corner jacks, which are used to mount or dismount the camper from the truck.

< A pop-up truck camper, the Palomino Real-Lite. The expandable top section provides enough height to stand, and additional space for sleeping quarters when raised.

Conclusions

Given these three categories of RVs, you must choose what's best for your location and conditions. For example, a large Class-A motorhome might be fine in the flat, sparsely populated Nevada desert. However, it would be a terrible choice for the densely packed streets of New York or Chicago, where a compact car with a teardrop trailer might fare better. If you need to survive in the tough terrain of the Sierra Nevada mountains, an expedition vehicle or 4x4 truck with a slide-in camper would probably serve you best.

You must also take into consideration the number of occupants and quantity of supplies you'll be transporting. A small trailer or camper might serve one person well, but if you have a large family, look into motorhomes or large trailers. Regarding supplies, extra gear can be strapped to your vehicle's roof, stored in the vehicle's cabin, or packed creatively in the living area itself. Much like building a bug-out bag or in-home emergency supply cache, you need to decide a time frame to plan for, and pack supplies accordingly.

Consider this guide a primer on choosing an RV for survival — there's still plenty to learn before you actually bring one home. Some might say the common RV is too obvious a choice for a bug-out vehicle, but we'd say it's an obvious choice for a reason. Someday, one of these versatile vehicles might make your life on the road a whole lot easier. ✖

UP SHTF CREEK WITH A PADDLE

Can a Bug-Out Canoe Be a Viable Transportation Alternative?

Story and photos
by Kevin Estela

New York City is home to approximately 8.5-million people. On any given day, the city has only a three-day food supply if the bridges and tunnels are cut off and resupply trucks are not able to get in. As history has shown, when crisis hits a city, people flee. For the surrounding suburbs, the strain on resources will prove unsustainable. Fortunately, urban crises have a finite life span and people will eventually return — but what can be done until then?

One option is to shelter in place and prepare for looting and civil unrest. Another option is leave the danger zone and return after things quiet down. Luckily for New Yorkers, just north of the Big Apple is the Adirondack State Park. It's home to 6-million-square acres of rugged land, some of which is so remote that access is limited to those with watercraft and the skills to navigate its winding channels.

Here's where the bug-out canoe comes into play. This scenario is not exclusive to the City that Never Sleeps. Metropolitans were established around major waterways, which can provide egress when streets and overland routes become chokepoints. From Puget Sound in Washington to the Okefenokee Swamp in Florida, there is a canoe bug-out location found in every state. If a bug-out is necessary, the panicked and unprepared will flood the roadways, turning freeways into parking lots. Preppers

without off-road rigs might hit the backcountry on foot, but a more effective means of escaping with a larger load is by water.

Weighing Your Options

"But aren't canoes too heavy and bulky for a SHTF scenario?" we hear you asking. Traditionally done with standard dual-capacity canoes, the carries and portages are often dreaded for good reason — hauling both a go-bag and a canoe can make overland travel painful and exhaustive. However, standard materials like canvas, leather, wool, and wood can be substituted with carbon fiber, Kevlar, sil-nylon, and Primaloft Insulation. And featherweight solo canoes — like the ones from Hornbeck Boats out of Olmsteadville, New York — allow you to cover a lot of ground, and water, with less effort.

There's a stereotype that people who paddle ultralight canoes are granola types who drive Subarus and eat vegan diets. But even the toughest, most-seasoned outdoor adventurer can appreciate how light this type of craft feels after a long carry. In fact, the British Special Air Service (SAS) have used small paddle-powered boats for warfare, and the portability and mobility of these solo canoes afford the user a level of stealth not found in other craft. The open design is an advantage over closed-cockpit boats providing easy entrance and exit in a hurry.

Modern canoes are lightweight, making them practical for recreation and bugging out.

With a well-thought-out route, any prepper can tap into existing supply stores, cache critical equipment, and spend an indefinite amount of time afield.

Gear 101

Before setting off though, there are some basic items no boater should be without. In addition to the gear carried in the daypack to address camp needs, this supplemental gear weight can quickly add up. However, if one is willing to make a significant investment in a featherweight canoe, spending slightly more on a quality paddle, life jacket, and dry bags shouldn't faze him too much.

Paddle: This style of canoe is best maneuvered with a double paddle (kayak paddle). At roughly $400, the Werner Paddles Kalliste is a top-of-the-line touring paddle. But, there is a distinct difference between using any heavy economy paddle compared to this ergonomic, all-day, double-bladed stick. For really tight channels, a single-bladed canoe paddle like the Werner Carbon

A quality water bag is essential for keeping your gear dry.

Bandit will make propulsion easier than a double-blade that could snag on low-hanging branches.

Life Vest: The ultralight boater should seek out a quality personal flotation device (PFD). The common type II — nicknamed "Mae West" for the busty actress of the 1930s — can work as a floatation device, but it is generally blaze orange, making visual camouflage difficult. Plus, there are better options for form and function. The type II isn't the best design for range of motion, and many modern life jackets, like those from Astral, are designed with canoers and kayakers in mind. Many are equipped with knife tabs and gear pockets for essential safety gear.

Water Bag: The canoe tripper should have a good supply of quality dry stuff sacks like those from Outdoor Research, as well as a water-resistant personal-security kit (filled with items for signaling, fire starting, etc.) within arm's reach. The UST Micro Survival Kit is a good way to start as it comes with an Aloksak waterproof bag, and the whole kit can fit in a PFD pocket.

Old-School GPS: Last but not least, a topographical map should be carried in a Ziploc bag. This map should be treated with Thompson's WaterSeal to provide an extra level of water resistance.

Bugging Out

When it's go time, the outdoorsman should move quickly but deliberately to load his canoe atop his vehicle. The basic bug-out gear can be tucked inside the canoe in storage to prevent disorganization and unnecessary searching when time is critical. Should roadways

be clogged and the designated put-in location be within reasonable and safe walking distance, it's not infeasible to park a vehicle and hoof it with an ultralight canoe over the shoulder.

Do Your Research: Waiting until after aliens have invaded is not a good time to figure out where to hit the water. Examine your escape route by physically scouting it out. In general, boat ramp signs found from state to state will give you an idea as to where there's a high amount of motorized boat traffic. These areas should be avoided. The ultralight boater can instead use any hiking trail that leads to water as his boat launch.

A good guide to canoeing in a given area will provide the macro details, while friendly discussions with locals encountered in country stores will fill in the minor details not found in print or online.

Entering the Water: Once at a convenient boat launch in a state or national park, the outdoorsman might have to sign in before traveling through the backcountry. Plenty of people "forget" to do this and don't disclose their destination, the number in the float party, or their length of stay. The waterways will take the paddler through different areas of varied occupancy and traffic.

Canoe Camping: Some campsites are fed not only by the water, but also by roads that allow RVs and trailered campers. Other campsites are primitive with no running water, electricity, or facilities — these are generally

A reliable bow saw can help clear branches and gather firewood.

Top 5 Tips to Keep the Hair Side Up

① Understand Primary/Secondary Stability

Boats have primary and secondary stability. Primary stability refers to the initial tendency of the boat to tip over when the boat is positioned upright in the water. Secondary stability is when a boat is riding on its side slightly and the tendency of it to continue over to capsizing or return upright. Many boats have "tippy" primary stability, but come into their own once they are on edge. This gives them a more responsive feel and improved handling.

② Turn into Wakes/Waves

When paddling a small solo canoe, every ripple in the water is felt. While the solo canoe is extremely fast through the water, it can be compromised by big water. Whenever possible, the paddler should turn the boat perpendicular into the wake or waves encountered. The boat has a longer surface to address the wave/wake lengthwise than it does widthwise.

③ Trim and Balance Properly

Solo canoes range in size from 9 feet on up. Depending on the design, the paddler will sit somewhere in relation to the centerline of the boat. The further back from the center, the more the paddler will need to offset the balance in the water with extra weight up front toward the bow. This practice is called "trimming." With proper trim and balancing the weight evenly between port and starboard, the boat will perform better in the water.

④ Avoid Overloading and Swamping

A properly loaded canoe should have no less than 3 inches of freeboard (the amount of space seen on the side of the canoe between the gunwales and waterline) visible. The more weight carried, the less performance a paddler can expect. Too much weight and the boat may swamp if overcome with a large wave or an accidental lean to one side.

⑤ Move Deliberately

Erratic movements and jerky-style paddling are leading causes of capsizing. Reaching over the side of a canoe, moving the center of balance too far to one side, will cause a boat to flip. Rushing paddling strokes and sweeps also leads to body movement inside the boat and creating instability. Moving deliberately, understanding the slower pace of a canoe, and staying calm will keep a canoe upright.

H$_2$O Ways: A water-bottle purifier allows the boater to dip and drink on the go. In cooler weather, boiling in a wide-bottomed pot is the preferred means of water purification as ceramic-filter elements can freeze, causing micro cracks that render the filter useless.

Gone Fishing: A takedown ultralight spinning rod with a small tackle box packed with flies, jigs, spoons, and spinners will put fresh panfish (bream, rock bass, perch, etc.) on the dinner plate nightly. [Editor's note: See "Teach a Man to Fish..." in our Summer 2014 issue and "Improvised Angling" in Issue 9 of *OG* for more ideas on how to catch dinner.]

Spice It Up: Though not a life-saving tool, a recommended item is a spice kit to fight off food boredom. While the Adirondack Park, for example, is filled with wild edibles that can supplement the fish and fur food taken from the woods, a spice kit containing salt, pepper, balsamic vinegar, honey, olive oil, and hot sauce (Sriracha all the way!) will take the bland out of your limited menu options.

Supply Runs: Since the canoes used for this ultralight bug-out are minimalist in size and carrying capacity, it will be necessary to resupply at some point. Look for roadside stores containing the basics for camp-like coffee, propane, insect repellent, canned goods, and camp provisions. Canoers generally stash their boats, securing them to docks with painter cords or pulling them on shore and out of sight.

Pre-Staged Cache: In an emergency, many of these stores will likely be emptied before you reach them. In the off season, these stores might not be open at all. However, if your bug-out plan is to canoe to a remote park, you should create and hide a sealed 5-gallon bucket cache of supplies well in advance. For example, flour, baking powder, and salt are all that are necessary to make backwoods bannock. These supplies and others deemed essential to long-term survival can be sealed,

∧ A large tarp with earthy colors makes for a quick and easy shelter.

Consider packing lightweight fishing gear with your bug-out canoe. You'll thank us later when things get desperate.

marked with a yellow placard on a tree facing out from the water.

The resources in the campsites will vary depending on the amount of use it sees. Campsites nearest canoe trail junctions and not far from civilization will be picked over, but as the sites extend deeper into the wilderness, more branches within arm's reach reappear, and signs of use are few and far between.

Clearing a Path: Speaking of branches and wood, to reduce your signature and presence in the park, a sturdy bow saw works more efficiently at creating less waste than a chopping tool like an axe or machete. If weight is a major concern, the saw blade can be carried on its own and a buck saw frame can be built off the land. If canoe camping is done in the late fall or early spring, a medium-sized axe will benefit the boater, providing the means to access the dry wood inside seemingly waterlogged firewood.

Basecamp Basics

In camp, a handful of dedicated kit items will make the extended stay more pleasant.

Shelter: A large area tarp, muted in color such as brown or gray that can blend into the foliage and rocks, makes shelter and living space an easy setup.

stored, and accessed when other gear known to the public has been depleted.

Conclusion

When crisis strikes and refugees are crowding the streets, the savvy ultralight paddler can escape quietly into the wilderness. The ultralight canoe provides sufficient storage for a bug-out kit and room for other gear acquired along the way. With steady paddling strokes, the ultralight canoe has almost no presence in the water with the exception of a few drips of water coming off the paddle on the recovery of each stroke.

As the city falls into chaos, the overwater route out of the city may be the best option to safety. With the right preparation, equipment, and mindset, the ultralight canoe could be the best bet to take you off the grid. ⠿

Stay Dry

A personal dry bag containing emergency essentials should always be carried close to hand while in a canoe or kayak. This bag may or may not be tethered to the paddler's personal floatation device and should be compact and light enough not to affect the buoyancy of the life jacket or range of motion while paddling. The Outdoor Research 5L Lightweight Dry sack is an ideal size and has sufficient water resistance for this application. The contents of the kit should be determined by purpose and reality.

Capsizing is a real threat to the open boater. Inside the personal dry bag, the paddler should carry an immersion kit. This kit should include various fire-starters that are easy to use with cold hands, as well as a flame source such as tinder or a candle. The open flame paired with a reflective blanket to trap heat will help mitigate the effects of hypothermia. These items should have priority placement at the top of the dry bag for immediate access.

A quality water-resistant white-light emitting flashlight should be carried. At night, this will prove useful for obvious navigation, but also to alert larger boats, should they be encountered, of your presence. Signaling devices such as a floating mirror and whistle should accompany this light for daytime use.

Miscellaneous items including a small roll or card of duct tape, spare cordage, high-calorie energy bars, and minor first-aid items should take up some of the extra space in this bag. The rest of the space should contain a spare key for your vehicle, your identification, wallet, and everyday-carry items.

Tricked Out

The author's bug-out canoe of choice is the New Tricks from Hornbeck Boats — a family owned company that's been building boats in Olmstedville, New York, for more than 40 years.

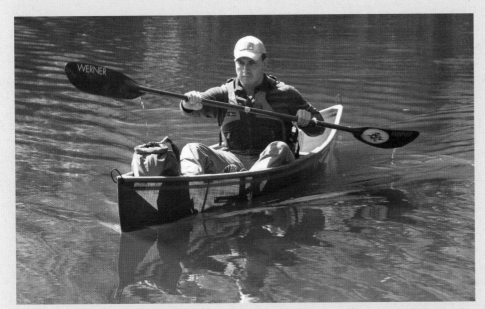

MAKE & MODEL:
Hornbeck Boats
New Tricks

WEIGHT
15 pounds

LENGTH:
12 feet

BEAM:
24.5 inches

PROFILE:
Mid

MATERIALS:
Carbon/Kevlar construction with rot-resistant Pennsylvania cherry wood trim

FEATURES
Polyethylene foam seat, custom-installed adjustable aluminum foot braces

MSRP
$1,695

URL
www.hornbeckboats.com

THE ROAD LESS TRAVELED

Tips on Prepping Your UTV for an Emergency

By **John Schwartze**
Photos by **Mark Saint**

he dreaded, high-pitched buzz of the Emergency Broadcast System simultaneously came across my phone and television. I was finishing my coffee and bracing myself for Friday morning rush-hour traffic, but realized there was something unusual about this broadcast. I was so used to hearing the word "test" after these alerts began that I initially ignored what was being said. As the message continued past its usual duration I realized things were about to get hairy real quick.

A massive chemical spill had occurred at a railway junction less than two miles from my home. The broadcast was unclear about the contaminants being released into the air, but what I knew for sure was that staying here was dangerous. It was time to beat feet. Since the freeways were gridlocked due to time of day and others surely looking to bail after hearing the broadcast, I determined that the best thing to do was to drive my UTV (Utility Task Vehicle) away from the direction of the accident using an escape route I'd plotted a while back. I grabbed my backpack, strapped down some other ancillaries as fast as I could, started up the UTV, and split like a bat out of hell toward my bug-out location.

This is Only a Test ... This Time

Although the aforementioned prompt is fictitious, it's meant to get you thinking about your means of transportation and evacuation plans if you were faced with a similar situation. The train crash mentioned was based on the Graniteville, South Carolina, rail disaster in 2005 where tanker cars hauling chlorine ruptured after a collision, releasing poison gas into the atmosphere. It was considered by many to be the worst chemical accident in U.S. history. Nine people were killed, several hundred were injured, and thousands were forced to flee their homes. Had winds been stronger, the death toll would've undoubtedly risen.

According to a Department of Transportation report, *Train Wreck and Chlorine Spill in Graniteville, South Carolina* by A.E. Dunning and Jennifer Oswalt, "The emergency response community has recognized a need to reduce the chaos of the type experienced in Graniteville. Poor communication between agencies and lack of clear decision-making authority exacerbated the disaster. Responders disagreed over how to evacuate the town, and this disagreement resulted in inaction. While the Reverse 911 system worked, the timing and decision making of the evacuation actions rendered the system only marginally effective. Responders couldn't quickly and positively identify the hazardous material or the proper procedure."

What does this tell you? As we've said in RECOIL OFFGRID before, sometimes you only have yourself to rely on. Unfortunately, in instances like this, hazardous materials are often transported through rural areas that are ill-equipped to deal with such a large-scale incident.

When you combine that with bureaucratic bungling, sometimes it's better to preplan rather than risk your life waiting for rescue personnel who could be hours away to handle the situation. That being said, how do you plan to evacuate if fleeing on foot may not be realistic?

Getting Out of Harm's Way

Here we're exploring the use of a UTV (also called a side-by-side) during bug-out for several reasons, including the number of advantages it offers over a conventional vehicle. We won't get into criteria for selecting a temporary or permanent bug-out location, as that's a whole other list of priorities to cogitate on. This article is more focused on what transportation you'll use to get there and related considerations to make when traveling off-road.

There's no right or wrong answer when it comes to the method you use to evacuate, but there's no perfect solu-

Maintenance: The more features you have on a vehicle, the more things can break. You won't care about the convenience of cruise control or parking sensors during an emergency. A UTV's simplicity makes it desirable since it's devoid of the abundance of electronics most standard vehicles are becoming dependent on. UTVs are built for durability and easy maintenance or repair in the field.

Size/Signature: Not only does its smaller size and design enable a UTV to traverse unforgiving topography and obstacles, but it also increases your ability to remain hidden if necessary. It's much harder to conceal a larger vehicle when parked, as well as the footprint it leaves behind. Having a smaller vehicle will draw less attention to your escape route. While you may be concerned about the noise UTVs make versus a car, there are plenty of mufflers and exhaust systems you can use to minimize sound output.

Modifications: The aftermarket support for UTVs is huge. Tons of companies offer modifications for your UTV's drivetrain, suspension, lighting system, cargo storage, fuel capacity, and other features. One can easily upgrade a stock UTV to support a heavier payload or haul a trailer. It all depends on what your intentions are and how much weight in people or supplies you intend to carry. But rest assured that consumers have plenty of choices to improve upon the vehicle's existing capabilities. Many require only basic tools and knowhow to install.

Where Are You Going?

Although many bemoan the range and carrying capacity of UTVs as being limited compared to standard vehicles, that may not necessarily be a deal breaker if you've preplanned your escape routes and destinations. The first determination you should make is whether the range of a UTV you're considering is conducive to your destination. For instance, if your bug-out location is 100 miles away, can you get there on a full tank of gas with plenty of margin for emergency detours? How will that range be impacted by the amount of people and supplies you're loading? Research the range, fuel capacity, and payload capacity of the vehicles you're considering.

Determining possible routes out of the area shouldn't be something you put off to the last minute. Unless you already have a bug-out location in mind, find some suitable spots that are reachable in a UTV. Plan alternate routes and revisit them every few months to confirm they've remained unfettered. Better yet, test them out with your UTV, preferably loaded up with supplies to ensure they're as accessible as you think they are when you're fully laden. Continued urban and suburban development has a way of throwing up obstacles and

tion either. While every vehicle has strengths and weaknesses, consider that various catastrophes may render surface streets and highways impassable. Here are some things to keep in mind if you're in the market for a UTV. Your initial intentions to buy an off-roader may be strictly recreational, but let's examine how it could also double as a very practical escape vehicle.

Why a UTV?

Mobility and Access: Remember that gridlock mentioned earlier? The UTV can get places a standard car or truck can't. When the usual roads and highways are inaccessible or jammed with commuters, you may find yourself wishing you had an alternative to your daily driver. If you're forced to cut through firebreaks, access roads, horse trails, or other off-road thoroughfares, a vehicle designed specifically to negotiate that kind of terrain could prove invaluable.

Keeping current maps of the areas you need to travel through during an emergency is essential in the absence of GPS or a cell signal.

changing topography from when you initially scouted out access to a locale that works for your purposes. You might return to an escape route you'd planned out six months ago only to find much of the property has been built up, which forces you to rethink the whole strategy.

What Should You Bring?

Your load-out, and the weight thereof, will be just one of the factors that affect fuel consumption. The range ratings for vehicles are measured on flat surfaces, so rough terrain, other passengers, and how heavy your right foot is are variables that make it difficult to determine the total range you'll get out of an off-road vehicle. If you have friends with UTVs, borrowing theirs would be another way to help get an accurate idea of the range before you make that initial purchase. Do some test runs loaded up with the supplies you plan to bring so you have an accurate baseline of the fuel consumption. That will help determine how much extra fuel you should carry.

Fuel Storage: Aside from possibly adding a secondary tank, RotopaX or Cam Cans are great ways to store additional fuel or water on the vehicle and take up a bare minimum of space. Due to the additives and compounds found in modern pump gasoline in the U.S., assume

fuel will begin degrading within a year or so to the point where it loses much of its volatility and gums up with resins. This may clog fuel lines and pumps. Even with stabilizers added, gasoline supplies should be rotated at least every six months if you plan to cache any fuel.

Maps: Remember those? Local automotive stores and online retailers are great resources for maps. These will show off-road trails that your smartphone's map app or GPS might not clearly identify (assuming you'll even have reception). You can also visit MyTopo.com for USGS Topo, satellite, and even lake maps. Replace your maps every year or so to ensure you have the most up-to-date versions available.

Tools: Bolt cutters or a small breaching saw will come in handy if you have to cut through locks, chain-link fences, or barbed wire to save your skin. A toolkit consisting of wrenches, a ratchet and sockets, screwdrivers, locking pliers, zip ties, duct tape, epoxy, and a multi-tool should be enough for the repairs you may encounter during a breakdown. Many UTVs come with toolkits designed specifically for that vehicle. Aftermarket accessories such as a winch, Hi-Lift jack, and MaxTrax ramps can help you bail yourself out if you get stuck on a remote trail.

The rest of your supplies are only limited by your

imagination. Carrying a tent, stove, cooler, flashlights, first-aid kit, binoculars, clothing, radio, fire-making supplies, power supply, and firearms/ammo is really up to the user. Assemble your desired contents and start Tetris-ing them onto the vehicle to figure out the best configuration to economize space and to get an idea of how much weight they'll add.

Do Your Homework

A golf cart is not a UTV, so don't think it's a suitable vehicle for driving on anything other than nicely manicured lawns. If you own a large piece of property and use construction or ranching-style vehicles to get around and perform menial tasks, don't assume these will work for bug-out purposes either. Visit trusted manufacturers, test-drive as many as you can that are within your budget, ask about their warranty programs, and spend some time getting off-road training from certified instructors. Driving a car on surface streets is vastly different than

driving an open-cockpit vehicle like a UTV through rough terrain during an emergency, especially if you have no prior experience.

Also, ask yourself if you can save weight by taking off anything that you feel is unnecessary for your intentions (and consider if removing those items will void your warranty). Spare tires or features meant to protect your suspension like glide plates should not be sacrificed to save weight. Spend some time changing parts yourself and outline some practice situations that would simulate problems you might encounter in an emergency. Extraction in water crossings, deep sand, mud, and low-light conditions are all great ways to become familiar with how the vehicle handles and what to do to mitigate potential obstacles. The more time you spend getting the feel for a UTV's capabilities, the better off you'll be if you have to make a quick departure. For a full review on the Yamaha Wolverine X4 SE seen here, check out Issue 37 of our sister publication, RECOIL. ⠗

Don't wait until an emergency arises to scout out potential bug-out locations. Do your homework on suitable places to hold up well in advance.

BUG-OUT GONE BAD

Surviving the Loss of Your Disaster Gear

By Tim MacWelch
Illustrations by Ced Nocon

If you believe you are prepared for everything, here's a little reality check to easily illustrate how your best laid plans can go straight to hell. Let's say you've spent months of study and selection (not to mention hundreds of dollars) to assemble the finest bug-out bag ever conceived. Now let's say that you had to evacuate your city due to some kind of calamity, such as a dirty bomb or other radiological event. Your world went from normal to nightmarish as you listened to that emergency radio broadcast stating that your home is now uninhabitable, perhaps forever. And if you thought things couldn't go any more wrong, here's the part when the worst day of your life gets even more horrific — you lose your bug-out bag. Now everything is gone.

It doesn't matter how it happened. Maybe someone pulled the pack off your back in the press of evacuees. Or maybe it set off a Geiger counter at a checkpoint and the authorities wouldn't let you proceed with the bag. The punch line to this cruel cosmic joke is the simple fact that you've just lost every piece of carefully chosen gear that was meant to sustain your life. While minimalists and primitive technology experts may keep their footing in the familiar territory of survival without supplies, this type of scenario would be (and should be) terrifying to the average person. So what do you do now?

Distance Yourself and Prioritize

The No. 1 priority in a bug-out scenario is to reach a safe distance away from the hazard. This will probably have to occur by foot, since most highways would be impassable to vehicles due to the post-disaster gridlock, assuming you had a vehicle in the first place. With your supplies gone, you will be in desperate need of the survival essentials you once carried. Security, shelter, first aid, water, fire, food, and communications are at the top of your list of priorities to stay alive, once you reach a safe distance from the danger that sent you packing. How do you source these survival basics from scratch? Our ancestors managed to pull it off in the wilderness on a regular basis, but it's a crude and painful shock for the modern person to find themselves flung back into this ancestral, hand-to-mouth lifestyle. But, don't lose hope. Trust me, you can survive this way by handling your survival priorities, one by one.

Gain Security

Once you have distanced yourself from the bug-out-inducing disturbance, security will be a very high priority. Since you no longer carry your bug-out bag, chances are good that the knives and other weapons are gone, too. If you find yourself unarmed in a disaster survival scenario, the weapons for personal security and hunting will be primitive at best.

At the onset of any survival situation, you can start off by finding a hardwood stick, a length of pipe, or some similar item to act as a club or bludgeon. This can be used as a baton for self-defense, and it can be thrown as a "rabbit stick" to dispatch rabbits (obviously), squirrels, pigeons, or any other small game. The best approach for throwing this stick is to swing it sidearm and release the stick so that it spins through the air like a helicopter blade. This generates enough force to shatter the eggshell-thin skull of a small animal, and the width of the spinning stick allows you a little margin for error on your aim. This amount of impact can also be discouraging to larger predatory creatures (people).

Another major point of security is to be off the radar of those who may harm you. In a very hostile survival setting, with looting, robbery, rape, and murder, avoiding detection can be your best form of security. Hide as best as you can. Find a place to barricade yourself until things calm down and make sure that you draw no attention

to yourself, unless it is to seek rescue or assistance from likely search personnel.

Find Shelter

Your clothing will be your first line of defense from the elements now that your other gear is out of the picture. You'd be fortunate if you were wearing performance fabrics that wick away sweat and help to regulate body temperature. But, regardless of your wardrobe selection, you can enhance the shelter value of almost any clothes with an easy technique. If conditions are cold, you can add insulation to your clothing by stuffing grass, leaves, crumpled newspaper, Styrofoam, or any other type of insulating material into your clothing. These materials create a better layer of insulation between your skin and the environment. Yes, you will look like a fool, and you'll be uncomfortable, but you'll also be warmer than you were.

If this isn't sufficient, you can build a full-sized shelter or shanty from sticks, boards, debris, and vegetative materi-

After a crisis hits, your No. 1 priority is gaining security. Distance yourself from the danger and find an improvised weapon for self-defense and hunting small game.

als. Create a rigid frame from broken sticks, lumber, or branches, based on a long pole for a center beam. Heap a huge pile of material over this stick skeleton, and add some plastic into the roof to create a windproof and water-resistant layer. Then fill the interior with more vegetation or insulation for the bedding, and burrow down inside. If you make this kind of shelter with all natural materials, you'll have a naturally camouflaged shelter. In sketchy bug-out circumstances, the less people who can spot you, the less they will bother you. This junk-pile style of shelter can also be adapted when using a vehicle as a shelter. Whether it's your own car or an abandoned vehicle, use it as a waterproof and windproof shelter base, then fill it with insulating material if you find it to be too cold.

Render First Aid

Medical skills come through training prior to the medical emergency, not by flipping through a first-aid book after someone is hurt. Your medical assessments and treatments may not require much equipment, depending on the nature of the injuries and illnesses. But, what these assessments and treatments will require is knowledge, experience, and adaptability. If you should get caught without your medical gear, you'll find that medical knowledge and improvisation will now be your strongest assets.

While no amount of creativity and know-how will match the right meds and clean dressings, there are a number of ways to render medical help to yourself and others. A great place to begin your training is by taking a first-aid class with your local branch of the Red Cross. This type of preparation gives you one of the most important skillsets that a person can acquire (medical); and the odds are good that throughout your life you'll use your first-aid skills far more than any other survival skills.

Find Water

The importance of safe water in adequate amounts can never be overstated. In high heat with dry, windy conditions, a person can die of dehydration within one day's time. Water can be very difficult to find in hot, dry climates like that. But, thankfully, fresh water is a little easier to come by in the rest of the world. Ground water, precipitation, and even water from vegetation can provide you with viable sources, but they are not without risk. The ground water in particular can be choked with pathogens that cannot be seen by the naked eye. Without a practical way to disinfect the water, your survival situation could move to a whole new level of danger if you consume biologically contaminated water or contract dysentery. A global killer, water-borne illnesses can aggravate dehydration and malnutrition, sapping the body's energy reserves and leaving a person immobilized before they eventually die.

Catching rainwater is a great way to source clean water, unless you are downwind of a radiological event. And for once, it's a good thing that people litter worldwide. A cast-off glass bottle or metal container will make a serviceable vessel to boil water, rendering it safe to drink, if you can build a fire to heat the water. If you cannot make a fire, or don't want to attract attention, solar disinfection can be an option in sunny weather. Find a clear water bottle with a lid, fill it with the clearest water you can find, and place it in direct sunlight for six to eight hours. This is not 100-percent effective for disinfection, but the sun's UV rays kill most normal pathogens in water.

If all else fails and you are unable to boil the water, you'll have to take a gamble and drink the best-looking water available. This may make you ill, but at least you'll stay alive longer than going without any water. It's a far better choice to be alive and ill than to be dead and pathogen-free. If you can get to medical assistance at some point, your water-borne illness can likely be cured, but what they can't cure is death.

Build a Fire?

This survival priority is vital to water disinfection, warmth, light, cooking, signaling for help, and tool manufacturing, to name just a few tasks. You may survive for a while without fire's benefits, but don't expect to prosper. This is the one place where redundancy can be an absolute game changer for your survival. You may have had several different ways to make a fire in your lost bug-out bag. That doesn't matter anymore. What matters is that you have one lighter in your pants pocket all the time. Or you have a spark rod built into the paracord bracelet that you never take off.

The point is that you always have a way to make fire on your person and you practice fire building under adverse conditions. It is relatively easy to kindle a fire on a dry, pleasant day, but the time you will need fire the most is the time when it is wet, cold, and windy. These are the types of conditions during which you should train yourself in fire building, but at times like that, you should be smart enough to realize that some conditions are impossible for fire building.

Communicate

This broad category includes one-way communications, two-way communications, and general distress signals. These are hardly the blood-pumping survival skills that people enjoy practicing, but they are your ticket to

Learn These Skills

3

There are many lifesaving skills that you may need to employ in an emergency. The ones that are the most useful and necessary will depend on the nature of the situation, but here are the top three skillsets that can be performed with little to no gear and are the most likely to increase your chances of survival.

UNARMED FIGHTING

Don't be a victim; be a victor. Learn some form of unarmed combat by taking martial arts and practicing them. Everyone is entitled to their opinion on the very polarizing world of martial arts and the idea of the "best" martial art will vary a lot. For our purposes, the best martial art is the one practiced at a dojo near your home or work, so that you can get in there and practice often.

MEDICINAL PLANTS

There are also numerous plants found worldwide that can be used as antiseptics, styptics, laxatives, analgesics, and for other medicinal uses. Yarrow, dandelion, burdock, plantain, and many other common "weeds" have made their way across the globe due in no small part to their highly medicinal properties. Before you go plastering potentially medicinal leaves all over yourself, know that all facets of medical training, including wild plant medicine, require prior training through a reputable business or organization.

FORAGING

You don't have to be a wild food expert to find a meal in the city park. Wild food is unbelievably abundant, even in urban and suburban environments. A reputable book on wild edible plants, or a hands-on class, can get you started on the path to find free food everywhere you go. (See page 150 in Recoil issue #8 for more on nature's salad bar.)

be rescued and your means of gathering information. Without the technology to communicate in a modern way, the communications part of our low-tech survival skillset will be relegated to calls for help, whistling, signal fires, smoke signals, general distress signals, writing notes and signs, and talking with other survivors. Speak to people who you feel comfortable approaching. Find out what's going on and try to get messages out to friends and family outside the effected disaster area.

Find Some Food

Something to eat may be the first thing on our minds while working our way through an emergency, but it's usually a low priority in most survival situations. Most people will find that their bodies will begin devouring fat reserves and then muscle tissue within a few days of fasting. This process can continue for several weeks in the average person, until they are finally too weak to move.

Though wild food is abundant in most parts of the world, it's best to only eat things that you can positively identify. The animal kingdom is an easy place to start. Healthy-looking birds, mammals, and reptiles are safe and nutritious, when cooked well-done. There are a few odd animals and parts that are to be avoided, like Gila monster lizards and polar bear livers. Just skip the nuts and berries unless you know what you are doing — beyond all shadow of doubt.

Keep Up Your Morale

Your bug-out has gone badly. Many things have happened that were way beyond your control. You tried to be prepared for these types of emergencies; you even had a nice BOB, but you still had your ass handed to you. When all your material goods are gone, the only things that you can really own are your attitude, your survivor mentality, and your morale. You are the only person in charge of your thoughts and feelings and the subsequent actions they lead you to take. Do whatever you have to do to maintain your morale, while continuing to face reality and staying on top of the emergency as best you can. Remember, people can survive with almost nothing. You are living proof that your ancestors survived (for a while, anyway).

About The Author

Tim MacWelch has been a survival skills and outdoor writer for numerous publications over the past 10 years. He has also been a professional wilderness survival instructor for the past 17 years and teaches classes year-round in Virginia. MacWelch has personally trained members from all branches of the U.S. Armed Forces, along with State Department, DOD, and DOJ personnel. He also offers a wide range of training to the public. For information about his school, visit **www.advancedsurvivaltraining.com.**

TIME TO BOOGIE

A Tactical Tracking Expert Reveals the Keys to Bugging Out Without Leaving a Trail

By Freddy Osuna
Photos by Luis Chacon Photography

While the exact cause of the crisis is not certain — an unpopular trial verdict, the loss of the power grid? — the aftermath is quite clear: complete infrastructure collapse, mass rioting and looting, and violence on a most epic scale. And it's heading your way. Waiting out the impending doom at home just isn't a safe option anymore. Let's face it...your primary residence is compromised.

"Time to boogie, Joe," says the familiar voice in your head. Immediately, you communicate with your loved ones not at home via text message and leave a secret visual marker at the front of your residence — this lets your clan know to begin the primary bug-out timeline you've all memorized and practiced. And you've taught them to acknowledge these messages with a pre-designated response.

Bug-Out Timeline

Bug-out signal to initial movement	Movement to hole-up site	Hole-up site to rally point	Rally point to observation point	Observation point to basecamp
1 hour	4 hours	2 hours	2 hours	1 hour

As planned, the timeline begins upon acknowledgment of the signal. You figured it would take one hour to get your supplies and leave the house. You planned for three alternate modes of travel: 2WD vehicle on roads,

ATV by backcountry trails, and on foot through sole-busting brush. Due to the nature of the disaster at hand (near complete lawlessness), you determine that the path of least human interaction is best and decide to go off-road immediately. Your house backs up to state land, which is a vast desert terrain with minimal 2WD access.

So, at hour one, you have your ATV loaded up and out of the garage in a hurry. As you ride away, you hear distant gunfire from multiple large-caliber, fully automatic rifles, which you estimate is down the street from your home. "They're too late," you chuckle as you open up the throttle.

But then you slow down, remembering the tracks you are leaving behind. "Complacency kills," the voice says. You heed the collective wisdom of all the teachers and mentors you've had in the life and know that you must begin anti-tracking immediately. If those gun-toting opportunists come across your tracks a day or even a week from now and are able to follow them, you might compromise your camp's position and the safety of all who are sheltered there.

Ninja Escape and Evasion

Anti-tracking methods are used to confuse, delay, and dissuade a threat who's pursuing you. These are passive measures that are to be employed constantly wherever

Bugging out in the backcountry? Veg will be your edge. There's more to disappearing into your surroundings than just wearing camouflage patterns. Break up your outline by wearing local vegetation.

As you bug out, be aware of the environment you disturb. You'll leave a clear trail behind you if you don't prop up trees you've knocked over.

your trail might be discovered or easily followed. It would be disastrous if all the money, time, and sweat equity you put into preparing for a successful bug out were wasted because you were too easily tracked.

In this story's opening scenario, our hero, Joe, has a total weight (ATV included) of about 900 pounds, translating to a lot of destruction on the ground and deep definable tread patterns. His boots are a non-typical high-quality hiking boot with an uncommon tread pattern supporting his 180-pound frame, which shoulders 100 pounds of kit. From his method of transport to his footwear selection, he has clear target indicators (i.e. anything a man does or fails to do which reveals his presence to the enemy) that are unique to him and easily identifiable to even the most novice trackers. So what does one do when faced with the situation of needing to be somewhere in a specified time, while trying not to be followed?

I'll share some considerations that will always apply to any situation in which your trail could lead to your undoing, and how our hero, Joe, has been trained to deal with them. There are three factors of priority in relation to minimizing your signature on the ground upon bug out:

▼	▼	▼
What you're taking	**Where you're going**	**How you're moving**

What Joe Takes

Hopefully your long-term survival plan afforded you the ability to travel fast and light upon emergency evacuation. If you have a tracker on your trail who knows what he's doing, then fast and light is what you are going to need to be. A good tracker can deduce how fast you're moving and estimate how far you can move within a given timeframe to determine where you may be. (Think Tommy Lee Jones hunting for fugitives.)

"Damn it, Joe! Ounces equal pounds, and pounds equal pain."

Traveling light affords you agility. And having agility affords you the ability to take the route of most resistance, which is counterintuitive to what most people want to do during a bug-out situation. By doing this, you will severely hamper a tracker's ability to anticipate where you're going. You will also force him to go through the same terrain, which he may not be prepared for, or to go around and attempt to pick up your trail further ahead — which can be a tall task at times.

"Do your homework, Joe. It's the hard right versus the easy wrong."

Joe will move quickly by ATV, but leave an obvious trail. Because of this fact, he will gain distance away from his starting point as swiftly as possible. Once at a safe distance, he will button hook (moving into a position from a 90-degree angle and then back out from the direction he came) and cache the ATV in the thickest, nastiest terrain he can find. Then, he will brush out the vehicle tracks for a considerable amount of distance. While he's brushing out tracks he will wear foot coverings that hide his tread pattern and give the illusion of aged tracks, if anything at all. Now he's on foot and has significantly reduced his signature and gained vital agility.

Where Joe's Going

During preparation, you must thoroughly analyze the terrain along your bug-out route. The best way to do this is by going there in advance, before disaster strikes, to hike your chosen route by foot, taking thorough notes along the way of key terrain features that you may be able to use for rest, observation, ambush, communication, or to cache supplies.

How might a hostile tracker use these key terrain features against you? How much concealment does this route provide while moving during the day? Are there significant obstacles on your route that work for or against you?

Joe has learned the habits of nocturnal and diurnal creatures along this route because these creatures will display behavior that a tracker reads to anticipate danger. He will also use the ground type to his advantage. When feasible, he will walk to the sides of trails instead of on them, and he will walk on rocky ground instead of on soft soil. He will walk in water along streams when available. He will be attentive to every step he takes, because he knows it only takes one footprint for a good tracker to determine if you're his prey.

A good tracker can not only identify you by the treads of your Nikes, but will also decipher which way you're heading, how fast you're traveling, and whether you're carrying anything. Naturally, if you're trying not to be followed, you don't want to leave footprints. But short of having a helicopter or hover-board, you'll inevitably leave a trail of Nike Swoosh marks – unless you have foot coverings.

"There is no such thing as tough, only the trained and untrained."

How to Track a Tracker

As a teacher of this craft, I am often requested to provide a class specific to anti/counter tracking. My first response is this: If you wanted to defeat a sniper, what would you do? You would hire another sniper.

If you want to learn how to defeat a tracking threat, I suggest you learn how to track first. There are many schools across the United States that can teach you how to track both man and beast. Once you learn how to track, the anti-tracking techniques you come up with will be limited only by your own imagination. **⚏**

About The Author:

Freddy Osuna is the owner and primary teacher at Greenside Training LLC of Benson, Arizona. As a former USMC infantry squad leader and scout sniper/chief scout, Osuna is now providing some of the most innovative tracking training in the United States. His résumé includes being lead instructor for the U.S. Army Combat Trackers Course at Fort Huachuc and serving as combat tracking subject matter expert for the USMC's 2nd Marine Division.

Greenside Training provides training to military and law enforcement agencies worldwide and will be providing courses open to all in Southern Arizona throughout 2015. Osuna and Jon Boyd are the authors of Index Tracking: Essential Guide to Trailing Man and Beast. Osuna is now writing his second book that he promises will change the way people view tracking in America (release scheduled for summer 2015). Greenside's goal to lead you to discover an awareness of your world you never thought possible, then weaponize it on the battlefield, the streets, a hunt, or in the boardroom.

Go to **www.greensidetraining.com** for more info.

How Joe Moves

Joe's movement is determined by two main considerations: speed and security. He moves only as fast as he can clear every covered and concealed position in front of him. Without the assurance that his next step is safe, he cannot proceed any further.

He has certain benchmarks to reach within his bug-out timeline, so efficiency and safety is key here. A trained tracker is sensitive to his environment. Joe's senses of vision, scent, sound, touch, and taste are aligned with his intuition, meaning that he senses more than most people

Whether fleeing on wheels or feet, you'll need to mask your tracks or make them disappear altogether. Grab a tree branch with a lot of leaves and brush out your tracks to confuse, delay, or deter any bad guys following you.

"Look, listen, and smell before you move, Joe."

because he has been trained to.

Joe will ultimately survive the initial fallout of this disaster and will do so without compromising his long-term survival location. He will thrive as a good student of his teachers. He will monitor every piece of dirt that yields a footprint in the immediate vicinity of the basecamp, giving early warning of possible threats. If needed, he will also track high-protein meat and provide for his people.

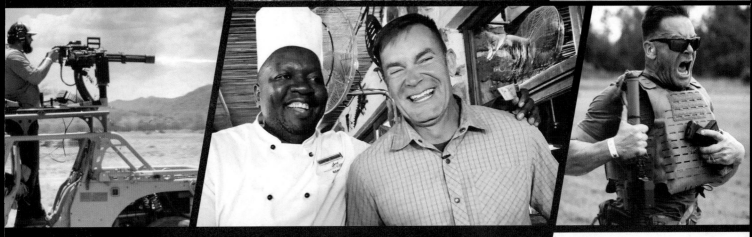

RECOIL TV

DOWNLOAD THE FREE APP TODAY!

RECOIL TV

Navigate between a variety of channels

By signing up you agree to our terms of service & privacy policy

RELEVANT.
HONEST.
UNFILTERED.

RECOILTV IS THE PREMIER AUTHORITY FOR THE FIREARMS NEWS AND MEDIA YOU WANT AND DESERVE.

RECOILTV is a **2A** friendly streaming platform created to entertain and inform you on the latest guns and gear associated with the firearms lifestyle.

PRESENTED BY:

 BCM®   vertx   INFORCE   PULSAR   SIGHTMARK®

RECOILTV is available on: Download on the App Store   Download on Apple TV   GET IT ON Google Play   Roku   fire tv   Chromecast

➔ WWW.RECOIL.TV

BUGGING OUT WITH BABY

We Take a Hard Look at What It Really Takes to Prep for an Infant

Story by Dave Merrill
Photos by Dave Merrill and Chris Hernandez

We love stories and movies about a lone survivor. A single man in the apocalypse, roaming the ruined world on a dual-sport bike. Maybe there's a canine sidekick. He is always getting into adventures, and while he's not a bad guy, he'll often do bad things for the right reasons. He's the stoic badass underdog it seems every American man wishes he could be.

But you know what he rarely has? Children. In the few stories where there are children, they're always at a useful age and can largely act independently. I don't blame publishers for this. There's not a whole lot of badass gun-fighting action going on when you're changing diapers or cooing them to sleep, and it's hard to keep a baby alive on a dual-sport.

So, what does our swashbuckling hero do when he has an infant? This is something that I've had to figure out for myself.

Even a quick trip to the grocery store, something that was so cavalierly performed as a bachelor, has turned into an affair that requires more time, thought, and consideration than ever before. A venture *anywhere* now requires logistics and safety checking akin to a pilot going through a preflight checklist. There is a little human with you who cannot survive on its own, likely made from half of your DNA, for whom you are responsible. Now imagine it's a disaster scenario — the potential complications ramp up very quickly, and your learning curve gets considerably steeper.

If you are not currently a parent or never intend to be one, you can still get something out of this article. You may find yourself among friends or family members with infants or small children when the worst happens. Plus, condoms could break — if you can find any in a post-apocalyptic world.

The innocent victims of any large-scale disaster or mass movement of people are infants, and it isn't their fault. You can't verbally reason with them or have a discussion because they can't even control their

^ From left, the author's bug-out bag, the baby's BOB, and the baby carrier.

bowels, let alone understand language. They're needy, complicated, and entirely unprepared for any situation — hell, many of them can't even fall asleep by themselves. To make matters worse, parents and caregivers of small children can be easy targets for predators.

The raw fact of the matter is that many children die. Sometimes it's just a bad roll of the dice, but all too often it's due to a failure of preparation by the guardians. We prepare because we don't want to rely on outside agencies to see us through. We prepare because historically it gives us a higher chance of survival. So, let's go through some of the lessons learned, often by examining the failures of others.

The Baby Bug-Out Bag

Right after buying canned ravioli and terrible ramen noodles, one of the first things people try to square away when they start seriously considering prepping is their bug-out bag (BOB). If you're a parent, the good news is that you probably already have at least the skeletal architecture of a BOB for your kid — you just call it something else: the diaper bag.

In fact, just adding some additional items (many of which you may already have in there) and weatherproofing can make it a complete baby BOB, when combined with the contents of your own.

In my house, the major sticking point for the baby BOB was exactly what kind of bag to use. I wanted something that was tough and modular, and so many of the dedicated baby bags are cheap to the point of being disposable. The ability to carry it independently or as an add-on to my own bug-out bag for easy carrying was mandatory. I ended up with an assault pack from Tactical Tailor. Originally designed to be worn on the back or attached to a plate carrier, the shoulder straps can be

stowed internally and there are provisions to attach it to another pack via Fastex clips.

Weatherproofing is important. Even if you have a waterproof bag, packing like components together in Ziplocs or similar not only keeps water out, but helps organize the bag.

Ultimately, you may end up with several bags of different sizes. A larger one for a vehicle where space and weight is less of a concern, and an essentials bag if you have to ruck it.

Clothing

Infants, being so small, are far more subject to the environmental changes than adults are, so clothing has to be well thought out. It doesn't have to be cute (though my wife disagrees), but it absolutely does have to be utilitarian. Warm clothes for cold weather, and light clothes for hot weather. Children grow rapidly, so while for your own personal BOB you may have a set of X clothes for summer and Y clothes for winter, it's more complex with a baby. Instead of swapping clothes out seasonally, you have to do it every couple of months. Thrift store clothing is perfectly suitable for this application and buying a size up is advisable.

Baby clothes are small, and even smaller if you use a vacuum sealer. This is good, as even the newest parents learn that babies can soil their clothing rapidly.

Blankets and warming layers are often needed even in hot weather. What isn't used for physical warmth can double as a sunshade. If your kiddo is uncomfortable, you'll definitely hear about it, and so will others around you.

Diapers & Sanitation

Like clothing, diapers come in different sizes as your kiddo grows. As such, they need to be changed out regularly. Even if you use cloth diapers at home, you're probably going to want some disposables in the diaper bag. My infant BOB is full of nighttime diapers. While they are marginally more expensive, they'll keep the baby drier for a longer period of time. You don't want have to worry about storing soiled diapers or about cleaning until you have to.

Depending on how long of a scenario you're planning for, at some point you may have to worry about cleaning. In a pinch, just about anything absorbent will work as an impromptu diaper or wipe. I have wet wipes and cloth wipes. You may want to include a biodegradable soap or powdered sanitizer for longer-term prepping.

Specific medical and grooming needs are up to you. A fever reducer, teething medication, nail clippers, and other such items fall into this category. As an example, I have one of those disgusting Snotsucker nasal aspirators in there. She gets stuffed up? I snake the snot right out. The joys of parenting.

Food and Water

Having water — and the ability to make potable water — is essential in any disaster, but it's of even higher importance if you are traveling with an infant. Babies easily become victims of dehydration through dysentery; diarrhea is the top killer of children in developing nations. Though when you're changing a diaper it may seem like there's

Marsupial Carry Options

Improvised Wrap: From a pillowcase with duct tape to a torso carry with a beach towel, a quick Internet search will yield a plethora of improvised baby carriers. Knowledge on how to safely and securely carry your baby or small child in an improvised carrier could save their life in an emergency. The example shown here was crafted from three cotton T-shirts.

Soft Structured Carrier: Typically made of canvas, a soft structured carrier (SSC) is a durable pack built to withstand heavy use. The buckles and straps are easy to adjust for multiple wearers, and the ergonomic support makes these carriers comfortable for both you and your child. This is the author's preferred carry option. Shown here is a KinderPack **(www.mykinderpack.com)**.

Ring Sling: The ring sling is great for situations in which you need to get the baby quickly up and wrapped. With the ring sling you can carry from newborn to toddler age, however, extended wear with a heavier baby can quickly become uncomfortable. The example shown is from Cassiope Woven **(www.cassiopewoven.com)**.

Woven Wrap: Although it carries a steep learning curve, a woven wrap is the most versatile baby carrier. It can be used to comfortably carry babies from infant to preschool age, and can even carry an injured adult in a pinch. A wrap can also be used as a blanket or a hammock. This is the author's wife's preference. Shown here is from Oscha Slings **(www.oschaslings.com)**.

an endless supply of liquids in there, it actually doesn't take much to put a baby at risk.

Even if your infant is exclusively breast fed (my wife calls it "EBF"), you're still going to need a lot of water. Why? Well if momma gets dehydrated, she can lose her breast milk. Very quickly you could have both a hungry baby and a sick companion. Not exactly the trouble you want when you've already left home due to an emerging disaster. For the situation that my wife's milk dries up, or if she isn't there because she's succumbed to injury or been carried off by a zombie biker hoard, I keep a supply of premixed formula in the bag. There are single-serving powdered options you may wish to consider as well.

TV commercials and ads in baby magazines would have us all believe that your little monster needs specially formulated colored goop that comes in a squeeze bag

> Those tactical packs have buckles for a reason. Here the author connects his go-bag to his baby's bug-out bag.

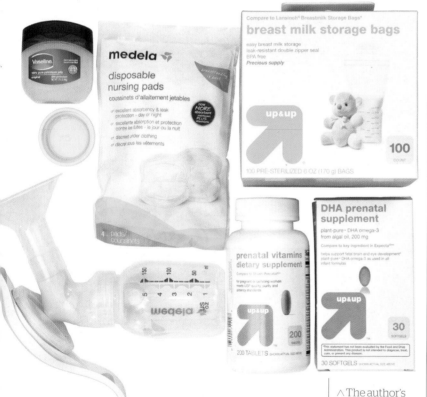

∧ The author's bug-out breast-feeding kit.

or glass bottle with a side of rice cereal. This is nonsense. With little exception, your baby can eat the same things you do, provided they're smashed or masticated small enough. If push comes to shove, I'll chew a piece of meat or other food first like a momma bird.

Transportation

If you're in a car, this is a no-brainer. The real trouble starts when you have to ruck it. Sure, you can just carry the baby. And your arms will get tired. And you won't be able to negotiate many obstacles. And you'll never have your hands free.

There are dedicated baby framed backpacks out there, mostly catering to the outdoors crowd. I found a few problems with these: First, the amount of gear you can carry in addition to the infant is dismal. Good luck getting anything more than what you'd need for a simple day hike. Secondly, with the baby on your back, you can't wear an additional backpack. Nor can you monitor them. And you're going to get puke all over your head at some point. Ask me how I know this.

I found carrying the baby on a front carrier or using baby wrapping to be the best method. Your hands are free, you can wear a backpack, you can still access your weapons (concealed or otherwise, though your carry configuration may have to be modded), you can monitor your child, and you can keep him or her warm and protected from the environment.

My go-to is a KinderPack. The ride height is comfortable, makes for great visibility, and it's easy to take your infant in and out.

If you look at pictures of tribal women in *National Geographic*, it looks like they just obtained some cloth and went to town. And sure, you *can* do that, but your results won't be as secure or safe. What can look so haphazard is actually carefully crafted. Believe it or not, there is a whole quasi-cultist subculture of baby wearing in the United States. They have forums, meet-ups, Facebook groups, and potlucks, all centering around physically wearing your baby. This is a resource you should pursue for your prepping. Even toddlers and beyond can be carried safely when they're tired if you have the right gear; think of it like a piggyback ride where you don't have to use your hands.

Stealth Mode

The catch-22 of having an infant: When it's more important than ever that you don't attract attention to yourself, you have a ticking time bomb of noise. Your baby will cry and scream. You can't blame them, it's the only surefire communication tool they have. But invariably there are times you need to be extra quiet. You'll probably know the best way to keep your baby happy, but warm and fed makes for the quietest baby.

< Attaching a pacifier and toy to your emergency gear can go a long way when silence equals survival.

About the Author

Dave Merrill is an Eagle Scout, U.S. Marine Corps veteran, and avid outdoorsman. Spending time in the backwoods canoeing and backpacking sparked his initial interest in survivalism at a young age. This attraction was hammered into enthusiasm by witnessing the effects of catastrophe first hand in developing nations. Dave is also a moderator on the forum for Zombie Squad (www.zombiehunters.org), a multinational non-governmental organization focused on promoting personal preparation for disasters. And, yes, he's well aware the zombie theme has worn out its campy welcome.

Pacifiers can go a long way, just be sure to dummy cord them to your rig, lest they be lost. While a favorite toy is ideal, you probably can't keep that in the BOB for prep purposes, so try to keep a favored toy in there. My daughter will want the mutant dragonfly-bee thing named Hamilton, but Elephonté Bellafonté the elephant is in the bag.

Depending on the age of your child, a nice thick lollipop may also work. You don't want something they'll choke on, just something to work on when needed. Additionally I keep a teething ring in the bag.

Have a Team

Having a team makes everything easier. [**Editor's Note:** *For more on group survival, see "It Takes a Village" in Issue 7 of* OG.] Since this isn't a pulpy survival novel set in the 1980s, your most likely team member will be a spouse or roommate — and not a bunch of experts at a Rawles ranch. The chance of survival with just you and an infant decreases exponentially the longer you're away from civilization. The ability to take turns caring for an infant while another provides security is a force multiplier, and it only increases with capable and supply-flushed people. But ...

The idea that you can live off the land and out of your pack forever is pure fantasy. If you haven't figured it out by now, the chain of logistical needs for an infant is long. You'll have to seek civilization sooner rather than later if you have an infant. You don't need to last indefinitely, but you want enough to get out of Dodge and get somewhere else on your own terms. ⁙

OLD-SCHOOL NAVIGATION

What to Do When Your GPS Goes Down

By **Ryan Cleckner**

 ow hard can it be? After all, if you want to go "up" on a map, you just follow the direction that your compass is pointing, right? Well, it's actually a bit more complicated than that.

There are three different "norths" — true north, magnetic north, and grid north.

True north refers to the very top of the globe (the North Pole), magnetic north is where the north-seeking arrow of your compass points, and grid north is the direction the vertical grid lines on your map point. Why are they different, and how does this affect your ability to navigate accurately? Follow along to find out.

True North and Magnetic North

True north and magnetic north are different because, despite what many believe, the North Pole isn't magnetic and your compass doesn't point there. Instead, your compass points to a giant ore deposit in Northern Canada. Therefore, depending on where you're standing in the world, your compass may actually point off to the side of true north.

For example, in parts of Tennessee and Alabama, magnetic north and true north are in line with each other so there's no perceptible difference between the two at that location.

However, the variance gets worse the further east or west you are. For example, in parts of Georgia, your compass will indicate a few degrees west of the North Pole. In Maine, your compass will be a staggering 16 degrees west of true north.

Going the other direction produces opposite results. In Louisiana, your compass will point a few degrees east of True North, and in Alaska, your compass might point a whopping 25 degrees to the east of true north. So if you're in certain parts of America and want to walk to the

True north (top of globe/earth) versus magnetic north (where your compass points). Compasses don't actually point at the North Pole; instead they point at Northern Canada.

Geographic North Pole

Magnetic North

These lines show how magnetic declination varies across the United States. The lines curve because a map, as shown, is flat but the Earth isn't.

North Pole by following "north" on your compass, you'll never get there.

To make this more difficult, magnetic north actually shifts. Year to year, the location to which your compass points changes slightly. Therefore, it's important to know the current values for your specific location. It doesn't move much, so if you use information from last year it may not make much of a difference. But if you use data from 10 years ago, it may be enough of a change to cause you to miss your mark.

The difference between true north and magnetic north for a given location is called magnetic declination, measured in the number of degrees of variation and the direction (east or west). More on declination in a bit.

Grid North

Grid north refers to the orientation of the gridlines on a map and often diverges quite a bit from true north and magnetic north.

Why don't the gridlines on a map point to true north? Well, let's start with a fact that may upset some diehard conspiracy theorists — the Earth is spherical. If you've ever tried to cover a bowling ball with postage stamps (don't ask), you'll know that a bunch of square shapes don't fit nicely on a sphere, especially toward the top and bottom. The same is true with trying to create a bunch of square representations (maps) of our Earth. Therefore, to keep our maps square, we have to fudge a bit on the orientation of gridlines.

The current system used for U.S. Geological Survey (USGS) maps is called Universal Transverse Mercator (UTM). That's just a really fancy way of referring to the layout and number of gridlines on our globe. This methodology is very similar to the Military Grid Reference System (MGRS) used by the U.S. Armed Forces.

The UTM concept is metric-based, in that grids are

Pattern of Magnetic Declination

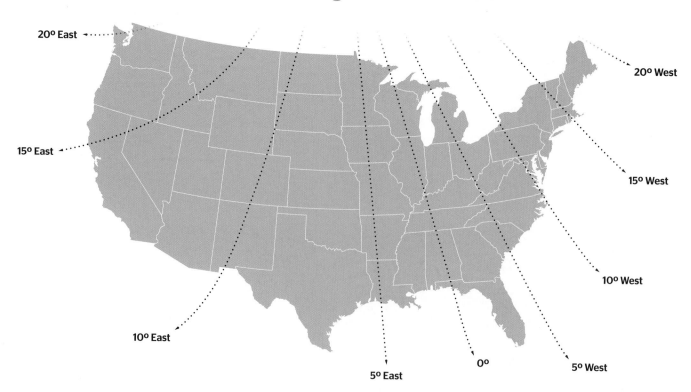

20° East
20° West
15° East
15° West
10° West
10° East
5° West
5° East
0°

broken down into tenths to determine a location on the map. Once you've learned it, it's an incredibly powerful system that can utilize varying numbers of digits to signify different levels of accuracy. For example, a four-digit grid number refers to a square kilometer (1,000 meter square), while a 10-digit grid number is used for accuracy down to 1 square meter.

Understanding and using this system could easily be a subject for its own article, so we'll leave it at that for now.

Why Should You Care About the Three Norths?

Well, if you look on a map and see a fresh water source or road you need to reach directly above your current position, it's essential to know which north is "up" and how to make your conversions to get there.

Although we refer to these as the "Three Norths," it's really the three types of directions or azimuths. An azimuth is the direction of an object/location from an observer represented in degrees. Whereas, a bearing is the direction you're traveling. For example, "I confirmed that the water tower was behind me at an azimuth of 90 degrees before I continued on my bearing of 270 degrees."

It's common to refer to an azimuth as "measured" when it was determined a map, and "shot" when it was determined from using a lensatic compass. Shooting an azimuth is accomplished by aiming at a visible landmark through the sights of a lensatic compass, much like you would with the iron sights of a gun. For example, "I measured an azimuth of 45 degrees from the map. I confirmed the direction of the hilltop by shooting an azimuth of 45 degrees."

Shooting an azimuth with a lensmatic compass.

For example, there's 90 degrees (east) on your compass (magnetic 90 degrees), a right turn from true north (true 90 degrees), and straight to the right on your map (grid 90 degrees).

That isn't meant to confuse you or make it sound excessively complicated. Instead, it's important to picture three different orientations of an entire 360-degree circle. Each circle's north points to a slightly different location, and it's important to know which system someone is referring to when they tell you to travel 5 kilometers with an azimuth of 180 degrees. If you're in Acadia National Park in Maine and they gave you a grid north azimuth and you use a magnetic azimuth, you'll end up almost 1.5 kilometers away from where you intended.

Declination

When using a map and compass, it's often necessary to convert between a grid azimuth and a magnetic azimuth. Although we introduced the concept of the deviation of magnetic north from true north, it's not very common to convert between them. The two norths you'll likely be most concerned with are grid north and magnetic north because those are the two norths that correspond with the tools in your hand — the map is a grid while your compass is magnetic.

When converting from one to the other, you must either add or subtract the difference in degrees depending on whether magnetic north appears to the left or right of grid north from your current position.

On USGS maps, you'll find a declination diagram at

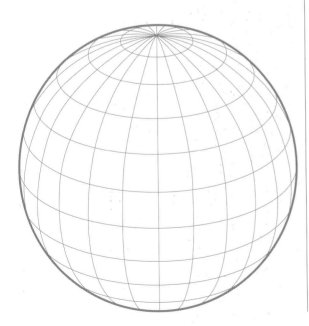

Square maps might work around the equator, but notice how the shape changes closer to the poles.

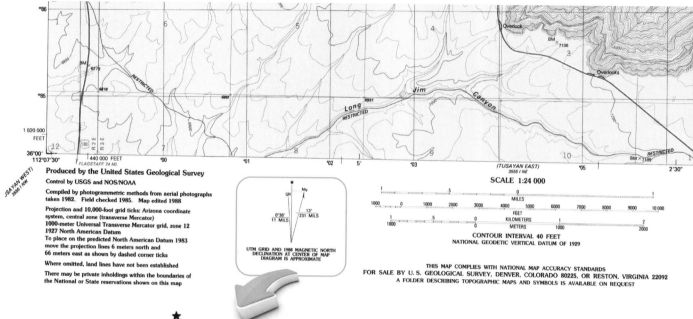

Produced by the United States Geological Survey

Control by USGS and NOS/NOAA

Compiled by photogrammetric methods from aerial photographs
taken 1982. Field checked 1985. Map edited 1988

Projection and 10,000-foot grid ticks: Arizona coordinate
system, central zone (transverse Mercator)
1000-meter Universal Transverse Mercator grid, zone 12
1927 North American Datum
To place on the predicted North American Datum 1983
move the projection lines 6 meters north and
66 meters east as shown by dashed corner ticks

Where omitted, land lines have not been established

There may be private inholdings within the boundaries of
the National or State reservations shown on this map

UTM GRID AND 1988 MAGNETIC NORTH
DECLINATION AT CENTER OF MAP
DIAGRAM IS APPROXIMATE

SCALE 1:24 000

CONTOUR INTERVAL 40 FEET
NATIONAL GEODETIC VERTICAL DATUM OF 1929

THIS MAP COMPLIES WITH NATIONAL MAP ACCURACY STANDARDS
FOR SALE BY U. S. GEOLOGICAL SURVEY, DENVER, COLORADO 80225, OR RESTON, VIRGINIA 22092
A FOLDER DESCRIBING TOPOGRAPHIC MAPS AND SYMBOLS IS AVAILABLE ON REQUEST

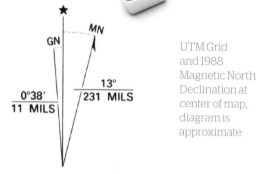

For this example in the Grand Canyon, grid north ("GN") differs from true north (the star) by 38 minutes and from magnetic north ("MN") by another 13 degrees. Grid north is what you'd see on your map, and magnetic north is what your compass would indicate.

UTM Grid and 1988 Magnetic North Declination at center of map, diagram is approximate

the bottom of the map. This diagram will represent the difference between each of the three norths from the center of the map on a certain date. Be sure to check the date! If it's too old, you should look up the current declination numbers for that map.

Here's an example from an older map of the Grand Canyon. From this diagram, we can see that our compass would point to magnetic north a little over 13 degrees to the right of "straight up" on the map (grid north). True north is represented by a star.

Note that the difference between magnetic north and grid north in this diagram is 13 degrees and 38 minutes (slightly over half a degree because there are 60 minutes in a degree). It's 13 degrees from magnetic north to true north and then an additional 0 degrees and 38 minutes from true north to grid north.

For this example, I wouldn't worry about the additional 0 degrees and 38 minutes. After all, I'd be planning to walk across terrain — I'm not surveying property lines. However, it's important to note because it is a significant figure on some maps. Let's just assume an even 13 degrees for the rest of this example.

Conversions

From any azimuth using this map, there'll be a 13-degree difference between the azimuth on the map and an azimuth shot with your compass. There are a few mnemonics to help you remember when to add or subtract the difference (we'll give you an example shortly). Also, some compasses have tools that help account for declination.

If you'd like to set the declination in your compass, follow the instructions for your particular model compass. By doing this, you can offset the direction the compass points in relation to where the magnetic needle points. This can be handy for many; however, there are good reasons to convert declination in your head and to leave the settings on your compass alone.

First, you'll never forget your settings on your compass and accidentally use an old/incorrect declination setting. Second, many compass features involve perfectly orienting a map, aligning a compass edge for your path, and then aligning the needle within certain marks as a guide for your azimuth. This is a good way to use a map and compass. In fact, it's probably the most recommended and taught method. However, I like to use a map and compass "on the go" and don't always want to stop and spread everything out.

Also, I like to employ advanced techniques, such as intersection and resection, that require a good understanding of what's going on. Using rotating bezels and guide marks to help you with your path are handy, but they often remove some of the important basics, such as understanding how to convert azimuths and what you're actually doing.

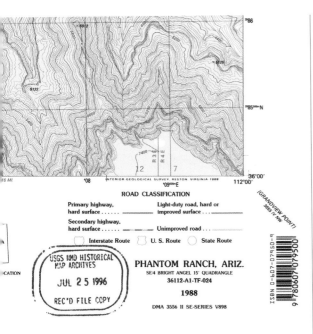

ROAD CLASSIFICATION

Primary highway, hard surface	Light-duty road, hard or improved surface . . . .
Secondary highway, hard surface	Unimproved road . . .

☐ Interstate Route ◯ U. S. Route ◯ State Route

PHANTOM RANCH, ARIZ.

SE/4 BRIGHT ANGEL 15' QUADRANGLE
36112-A1-TF-024

1988

DMA 3556 II SE-SERIES V898

ISBN 0-607-07950-9

A great mnemonic to convert for declination is "LARS," which stands for "left add, right subtract," because it's simple and doesn't require you to know whether you're in an area with easterly or westerly declination (more on that next).

To use the LARS mnemonic, you simply look at, and use, the declination diagram on the bottom of your map. If you have a magnetic azimuth at the Grand Canyon and you want to convert that to a grid azimuth, place your finger on the magnetic north arrow and note that you'd need to move your finger left to get to the grid north arrow.

Using LARS, we know that going to the left means "add" — therefore we add the 13 degrees to convert from magnetic north to grid north. To convert from grid to magnetic, we'd move our finger to the right so we'd subtract the 13 degrees.

Let's jump to an example to see how this works and also to see a real-world example of when you might need to do this.

Grid to Magnetic: Imagine that you know your position on the map, and you'd like to walk to a road intersection on the map that measures 35 degrees from your position. As you now know, you can't just find 35 degrees with your compass and walk that way because you'll be 13 degrees off-course … but which way? We have a measured grid azimuth of 35 degrees, but we need to shoot a magnetic azimuth for our compass. On this map, we move to the right to get from Grid North to Magnetic North on the declination diagram so we use the LARS mnemonic and know that we have to subtract the 13-degree difference for this location. We end up walking

a bearing of 22 degrees with our compass to get to a point on our map 35 degrees from our location.

Magnetic to Grid: Now imagine that you're sitting on a hilltop and see something in the distance. You use your compass and determine that the object is 270 degrees from your position, but you'd like to see where the object is on your map. Because you used your compass, you now have a magnetic azimuth and you need to convert to a grid azimuth. On our example map, your finger must move to the left as it transitions from the magnetic to the grid north arrows in the declination diagram, therefore using the mnemonic LARS tells us to add the 13-degree declination to our magnetic azimuth to get our grid azimuth of 283 degrees.

Another popular mnemonic is "west is best, east is least." The trick here is to add the difference (best) with westerly declination and subtract it (least) for easterly declination. There are two reasons why we don't recommend this one.

First, you need to remember that the declination is east on the west half of the U.S. and west in the east. Yes, you read that right. Second, you need to remember that this is only for converting from grid to magnetic (and not the other way around). The modified mnemonic "from map to field the proper yield is east is least and west is best" can help you recall this conversion, but even then, it's ripe for confusion.

Drop the GPS

This may have been a lot to absorb. Apologies if it was. However, we hope that this encourages you to learn more about the critical skill of land navigation with a map and compass. ⠿

Acadia National Park, Maine. The difference between magnetic north and grid north is 16.5 degrees; failing to account for this on a 5km trek will make you miss your target by 1.4 km.

GN

MN

1.4 km

16.5°

5 km   5 km

About the Author

Ryan Cleckner is a former special operations sniper and sniper instructor. Currently, he's a firearms law attorney, best-selling author, university lecturer, Trigger Words podcast host, and entrepreneur. He runs RocketFFL, which helps people get an FFL and stay compliant, Mayday Safety, a software/app company that helps protect schools and other organizations, and his newest project, online firearms courses at GunUniversity.com ➔ RyanCleckner.com

Traveling Cross-Country Safely
With Kids, Guns, and Pets

By **Mel Ward**

ROAD
WARRIOR

hile you may not be Mad Max driving the last V-8 across the wasteland, traveling long distances through unfamiliar places comes with inherent risks. For instance, many of you may be familiar with the story of James Kim, a TV personality whose vehicle became immobile in inclement weather during a holiday road trip. He died of exposure after deciding to leave his family in the car to go search for help in rural Oregon.

You may have also heard about the case of Denise Huber, whose car was found abandoned on the side of the freeway in 1991. Years after her disappearance, her body was discovered in a freezer in another state. It's believed that Denise pulled over with a flat tire and her killer approached her under the pretenses of offering help before abducting and murdering her.

Aside from the traditional dangers presented by hundreds of miles of high-speed driving, there are less obvious ones you'll want to think about and plan for, as our road trip experiences have illustrated. We'll discuss where we're going, how we're getting there, what to take, and where to stay. We'll talk maps, apps, and safety as well as a host of other topics to keep you protected on the road — whether you're traveling a few hundred miles or a few thousand.

Recently, I completed my second coast-to-coast crossing. As a parent, I found myself confronted with a plethora of challenges presented by traversing 3,500 miles from Washington State to North Carolina in two vehicles with a wife, five children, two dogs, and everything we owned packed into a 16-foot box truck. The following considerations are based on the lessons my family learned while traveling across the country.

Preplanning

Preplanning the trip consists of gathering information on routes, driving schedule, accommodations, and vehicle inspection. I want to know where I'm going, how I'm getting there, what kind of pace I need to maintain to make it happen, and feel assured that my vehicle is good to go before we roll out. Much like my days in Afghanistan, we found ourselves surrounded by locals at temporary stops in strange towns, and not everyone we met along the way may have had the best of intentions toward us.

A homeless guy screaming at his dog at a gas station at 10:30 at night in Las Cruces, New Mexico, can be either an annoyance or something entirely unpredictable. So, while you fill up your tank with your entire world

in the car and a mental breakdown 10 feet away, your decision to deal with him or avoid the situation entirely should've been made before you left your driveway. Let's do some planning and avoid these types of situations altogether.

Route Planning

Fire up the Google machine and take a look at your intended route. And I don't mean simply inputting your start and end points. Google or Apple — or whichever dystopian tech conglomerate is currently ruling your digital life — will likely take you on the most direct route, but not necessarily the smartest or safest. You want to get an overview of where you'll actually be staying or stopping along the various points of your journey. The way I like to do this is a good, old-fashioned paper map (laminated if you can find it).

Incredibly, you can actually unfold these and lay them out on a table and see the entire country and its various roadways without pinching and zooming on a 6-inch screen while going blind. Though redundant, it's rather like insurance — you rarely use it, but it's invaluable when you need it. This road warrior recommends the latest Rand McNally spiral-bound Road Atlas. It covers the entirety of the United States and can be had for around 15 bucks. For another option, Michelin — yes, the tire company – also makes a nice atlas that features GPS coordinates to parks as well as information on events and festivals in your area of travel.

Undoubtedly, you'll use some type of navigation mobile app. That's fine. Something I learned was to make sure everyone on the trip is using the same one. This is critically impor-

Often overshadowed by the crippling convenience of route-planning apps, traditional paper maps have a lot of info to offer and never have to be plugged in.

Of course, digital GPS is an excellent real-time resource to keep you on track and notify you of changing traffic or weather conditions.

tant if you're caravanning in two or more vehicles. While my wife drove her Suburban, I drove the rental box-truck. Being an Android guy, I was using Google Maps. Her being an Apple devotee used whatever navigation sorcery was loaded onto the iPhone. Turns out different map apps do things slightly differently and can (and will) cause issues along the way. Pick one app and ensure all drivers use it. Waze is a good one. It offers driver-updated road and traffic conditions among other bits of relevant information, such as warnings about obstructions on the road and speed traps. It's free and available on both Android and iOS.

When planning the route, look at potential areas of concern. For us, one leg of our trip took us down to Tucson, Arizona. Part of my concern for that leg was its proximity to the U.S.-Mexico border. After our visit, we had choices that included dropping down to El Paso and using Highway 62 to head east. Instead, we chose to give the border a wider berth and stick to more northerly routes. This isn't to say El Paso is unsafe — it's simply a mitigation technique. I have had friends tell me stories of areas along the border (on the U.S. side!) that are simply not smart to travel on or near due to heightened criminal activity. Cartels are known to zealously guard their trafficking routes into the U.S. Tactics include emplacing men in OP's (Observation Post) to monitor activity in their territory as well as the use of snipers for area denial. So why risk it?

Speaking of risk, let's mitigate some more of it by getting familiar with crime in and around our areas of travel with LexisNexis. Lexis-Nexis provides all kinds of tools to allow businesses and individuals to prioritize safety. Their Community

Crime Map is the one I like to refer to when traveling. It's a lot like looking at Google maps, but it provides crime data for your area of interest. Passing through a major city? How many car-jackings or muggings have occurred there over the last week or month? LexisNexis can show you that and a whole lot more. Visit LexisNexis at CommunityCrimeMap.com and get familiar with this incredible and free resource.

Driving Schedule

Do not wing it. I did this, and it didn't work. We ended up stuck on the road more than once driving way too late into the evening. Remember what mom said: Nothing good happens after midnight. Further, many hotels won't let you check in past a certain time, or if they do, they may already be booked up. Sticking to a schedule will also help prevent fatigue. Driving tired can be just as dangerous as driving drunk. A schedule ensures you're not on the road too long trying to make up lost time.

Figure out how far you need to travel each day and come up with a road schedule that'll allow you to make it happen. Up at 0600. Depart at 0700. Drive eight hours. Hotel reservations for the evening. Boom, done. The bigger your family, the earlier you'll need to be up. You can easily get "trapped" on the road with no lodging availability and a car full of tired and angry kids. Avoid this by preplanning a driving schedule and sticking to it.

Keep your tank filled by identifying your fuel stops ahead of time. I like to use Google Maps to search ahead for gas stations along my planned route. You can add them as stops along the way depending on your schedule and vehicle range. Gas Buddy is another great option. The free app allows you to filter for your station of choice by brand, amenities, etc. It also features user reviews and its data is crowd-sourced and constantly updated.

Accommodations

Have your hotel booked in advance. Guess who else is traveling during the summer, weekends, and holidays? Every red-blooded American on the continent, and they all need a place to stay. Places will get booked up, so don't get screwed by assuming they'll have a vacancy. Book in advance. I'd rather pay the fee for missing my check-in, should our plans change, than get stuck sleeping in a rest stop. Trust me. I did it, and it sucks.

If at all possible, don't let cheap rates on accommodations drive your decisions on where to stay. I noticed a demonstrable correlation between a hotel's cost and the part of town it was located in. Spend a little more on the rate to be in a nicer area surrounded by nicer folks. Unsurprisingly, seedy motels tend to attract seedy

Despite the stress and perils of multi-state road trips, they can also be an educational bonding experience for younger children and a chance for quality time with your spouse.

characters. Cross-reference crime rates using the tools we mentioned previously to find an area that's relatively safe.

When traveling with your family you're soft and vulnerable. Remove this vulnerability by not being in areas where it's likely to be exploited. Also, use Google Street-View, or a similar tool, to take a look at your chosen hotel's location. You can pan around 360 degrees and get an idea of the surrounding area. If your hotel is flanked by liquor stores, smoke shops, payday loan centers, and bail bond offices, you may decide to stay elsewhere. While your map app is open, this is also an excellent time to make a couple notes on where the nearest major hospital is relative to where you'll be staying as well as the local "doc-in-a-box" urgent care clinic in cases of minor scrapes and bumps.

Further considerations for accommodations should include which floor you're staying on in your hotel. Staying at a hotel may be relatively mundane, but it isn't always — we learned this in Pendleton, Oregon. We had just pulled up to the hotel after many wearying hours of driving. As we arrived, so too did the local fire department with lights and sirens blaring. Apparently, something electrical was misbehaving in the hotel and caused a full-on evacuation of the premises that lasted over an hour.

Despite it not being a five-alarm fire, it did get me thinking about what I would and wouldn't be able to do if it had turned into a serious incident. Watching the people mill about outside in the dark showed me that those on the bottom floor not only got out first, but they got out fast. In many hotels the ground floor has at least four exits. All you have to do is get into the hall and pick a direction. With my youngest son in a wheelchair, this is a part of our everyday logistical calculations. Stairs aren't really an option for us, and during a fire, elevators are a bad idea. So, wherever possible, we try to get a room on the first floor. Whether you're dealing with young children and strollers, or actually need to evacuate as we witnessed, a ground-floor room makes a lot of sense.

Finally, if you're traveling with pets like we did, plan your accommodations accordingly. Some hotels will allow you a small pet or two, but larger dogs might pose a problem. Call ahead and find out about the pet policy of the hotel you're looking to book.

Check out www.BringFido.com to help figure out where you and your four-legged children are welcome.

Road Warrior Quick Tips

❯ Shady truck-stop bathroom? Try using the urinal farthest from the door. Distance equals time to react.

❯ Stay off hotel Wi-Fi. Your 4G cell service should be plenty of data to get you through. Using free hotel Wi-Fi to send or receive secure information is potentially dangerous. Public Wi-Fi networks are targets for hackers to breach and exploit. With today's cellular data speeds "free Wi-Fi" isn't worth the risk. Treat all unfamiliar networks as though they're tracking your online activity. Public, unsecured networks are prime targets for anyone looking to intercept passwords and other valuable data.

Vehicle Inspection

Modern family vehicles are amazing machines — they're safer, more comfortable, and more capable than ever before — but they still need maintenance. My wife's Suburban has performed like a champ all the years we've owned it just with regular maintenance. But before we hit the road for a short or long haul, I make sure we schedule a tune-up/inspection or perform one ourselves.

Basic inspection should at least cover the following: fluids, air filter, fuel filter, battery, plugs and wires, hoses and belts, tire pressure, tire tread and condition, markers and headlights, and a spare tire inspection (including the jack, tire iron, and associated tools). Also, check to see if your particular vehicle has any outstanding safety recalls and get those issues corrected before you travel.

Have children in car seats? If you do, now is a perfect time to ensure proper installation of their car seats. Your local fire department will normally offer a free inspection/installation to make sure the job is done right. Otherwise, make sure you follow the directions stipulated in the car seat's manual. For more on pre-road trip inspections, car seat installation, and other automotive safety subjects, take a look at www.dmv.org/how-to-guides/pre-trip-maintenance.php. To see if your vehicle has any outstanding safety recalls check www.nhtsa.gov/recalls.

You don't have to be your own mechanic, but at least have a plan for roadside breakdowns and have a rough idea of where the next major town is that can offer repair services.

Gear

When considering what to bring, I break it up into the following subcategories: first-aid, recovery equipment, and vehicle sundries. It's important to update your first-aid kit before a long haul. I keep a fairly well-stocked kit for bumps and bruises in our family vehicle. I didn't replenish it after our last few road trips, and it bit me in the ass. Toward the end of our trip, my 2-year old daughter was promptly bit in the face by her great-grandmother's very skittish Chihuahua. It was a very shallow, but wide-open laceration to her cheek, and I really needed a butterfly bandage (which I didn't have) to close it temporarily. We ended up getting what we needed, but the lesson was painfully learned: I should've had it ready to go in the first place.

First-Aid

I have a two-part solution package for carrying first-aid while traveling. First and foremost, I want to be able to stop, or at least control, major hemorrhages regardless of how far we are from advanced care. Second, I want to be able to deal with all the mundane cuts and bruises that are much more likely to be the order of the day.

For major trauma, I carry and recommend North American Rescue's Bleeding Control Kit. This kit includes

...eeding Control laminated instruction card — I ...uggest keeping this with the kit so even an un-... person can follow the steps and properly apply ...aid. I also supplement my kits with additional gauze ...erlix, if you can find it) as well as ACE wrap bandages and HyFin chest seals. The kit comes with the latest C.A.T. Tourniquet, but I'd recommend buying several more of these TQ's on hand in case a car accident yields more than one life-threatening bleed. They're inexpensive, and worth every cent should they be needed.

Now, if you supplement your kit as I have, you might find it won't all fit inside that handy red pouch the kit comes with. No sweat. Find yourself a slightly larger IFAK (individual first-aid kit) or any travel-size go-bag to neatly store all your trauma items. Mark the bag with one of those travel tag bag identifiers, a Velcro first-aid cross patch, or just some duct-tape that clearly labels the bag "first-aid." Finally, make sure your family knows where it is and what's in it. If you have a big family like I do, consider doubling or tripling up on the items in the kit in the case of multiple, simultaneous injuries. Larger squad-sized trauma bags can be had from North American Rescue that are more robustly stocked for MASCAL situations.

On the mundane but more common side of first-aid, any sizable kit that features lots of Band-Aids, Neosporin, bandages, and so on will generally fit the bill. You can order these online like your trauma kit, or they can often be found for fair prices at stores like Costco or Sam's Club. Also, I like to keep this as a separate kit from my trauma stuff so don't combine them. I don't want my teenager pillaging my trauma gear for a Band-Aid or conversely, my wife looking for a tourniquet in the "bumps 'n' bruises" bag.

Before you close the hatch on all that first-aid gear, throw a couple cases of water in the back somewhere as well, particularly if you're traveling during the summer. It's nice to have for washing out cuts and scrapes, topping off a radiator, or simply keeping kids and pets hydrated in hot, desolate areas. We faced down some long, dry stretches of road in New Mexico and Arizona with nary a gas station in sight and the water came in handy.

For more information on classes, techniques, and kits, check out www.bleedingcontrol.org.

Recovery Equipment

If you want to go a step further, you can do what I did and put together a basic off-road recovery kit as well. I chose to build my own kits for my vehicles, but companies like Warn and ARB also make some really nice (albeit more expensive) kits that include everything you'd need to get yourself unstuck.

Medical supplies are an important part of trip planning, especially if you'll be crossing long stretches of interstate between towns. Whether you come across a severe car accident or suffer a few bumps and scrapes, having some supplies on hand could go a long way to easing the pain.

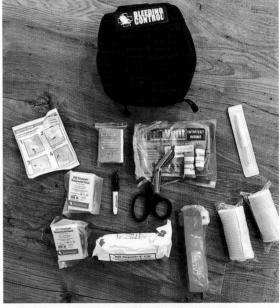

The author has chosen to supplement a pre-packed first aid kit with additional supplies that seem to come in the highest demand.

Simple hand tools and some tow straps or heavy chains can be improvised into a lot of useful trouble-savers. It never hurts to have this capability.

These kits include things like recovery straps and chains, shackles, snatch blocks, and heavy-duty gloves. I also throw shackle hitches in my kits for additional attachment points if your vehicle is equipped with a trailer hitch receiver. Toss in a couple road flares and a shovel as well, and you're set. If you build your own kit like I did, drop all this gear into a nice nylon tool bag from a company like Husky. You can find these bags in various sizes at Home Depot for $15 to $30.

A good jack is also absolutely critical. In many situations, the bottle jack your vehicle comes with can be rendered useless. I prefer a Hi-Lift-style jack because it has so many additional uses beyond just jacking up a vehicle. It can act as a come-along, clamper, or spreader, and there are several awesome accessories available that further expand this tool's capabilities. They're inexpensive and should last a lifetime. Hi-Lifts also come in various sizes and can fit in your trunk. So just because your family vehicle is a sedan and not an overland monster-machine doesn't mean you can't upgrade your jack to something that can handle virtually any situation.

Finally, consider a set of recovery boards. These can be as simple as throwing some scrap plywood in your trunk to give your tires purchase when stuck in sand, snow, or mud. This can often be the fastest and easiest way out of a sticky situation. Plywood scraps will do, but if you have the coin, I'd suggest a set of purpose-built recovery boards like MaxTrax MkII's. They aren't cheap, but their quality and utility easily exceeds their price. Take a peek at them on Amazon.

Add to this arsenal a roadside assistance plan like a AAA membership and you should be all set. Major insurance companies like USAA also offer roadside assistance if you're a customer so be sure to ask your insurance agent if you're covered and how to access their services. These days many vehicle manufacturers like Lexus feature complimentary roadside assistance. Check with your vehicle manufacturer or dealership. If your vehicle features a service like OnStar, ensure its function prior to traveling.

Other free, or low-cost services can be had through your cell phone carrier, believe it or not. Carriers like Verizon offer roadside assistance services so be sure to check with your provider for cost and options. Whichever roadside assistance option you choose, now you're covered. You can call for towing or, if the situation dictates, you at least have the basic tools to try and recover yourself or someone else. If you want to learn more about off-road recovery and how to use some of the tools listed above, give www.offroadre-coveryguide.com a look.

NEXT SERVICES 72 MILES

...e Sundries

...ngly believe we need to at least be able to deal with ...ids, dead batteries, and flat tires while on the road. ...se are common issues, but easily remedied if we have ...e right gear with us. Grab a milk crate and put a quart of your vehicle's motor oil, a bottle of brake fluid, transmission fluid, power steering fluid, and a gallon of coolant and put it in the trunk or the back of your SUV or truck.

Next make sure you have some jumper cables, and I'd also recommend one of those handy little jump-starter batteries like a Micro-Start or NOCO Genius Boost. They're small, portable, very powerful, and worth every penny. Many of them can also be used to charge cell phones and other portable USB devices.

Jacks and spares we covered in the previous section, but if you have the room, carry a full-sized spare with you. Donuts are for coffee. If we have to change a flat out on the highway, we can be ready to stay on schedule with a full-size spare rather than just ready to go to the nearest gas station on a donut. The next time you get new tires, keep one of the old ones for this purpose. An inexpensive spare wheel can be found on Craigslist or at a local scrap yard (be sure it's the appropriate size and bolt pattern). One last tire-related item: If you're traveling during winter, make sure you have a quality set of snow chains or traction cables for your tires. Cheap sets will break. Look for a brand like Security Chain Company.

That'll cover the basics for emergencies. Now let's address a few additional items to have in your vehicle to make life easier.

Toilet paper. The good stuff. I'm serious. Throw a roll in a Ziploc bag and put it in a backpack. There are still stretches of highway out there where bathrooms are as scarce as honest politicians. In that bag with the toilet paper, throw a pack of baby wipes in next to it, whether you have babies or not. Baby wipes are mission-essential equipment. I've never fought a war without them.

We're also going to need things like flashlights, a headlamp, extra batteries, power banks for cell phones, and necessary medications, etc. On the subject of medications, ensure you have more than you need. In the case of my son, only certain pharmacies are able to fill his prescriptions so we have to account for this when traveling by taking extra in case we're on the road longer than we planned.

For flashlights, I prefer the kind equipped with magnets or hooks or some other method of attachment. A handheld light is fine, but it's likely if I need my light, I also need to be doing something else with my hands simultaneously like changing a tire at night or topping up a radiator. Home Depot or Lowe's carry an arsenal of

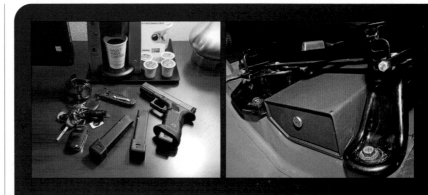

Traveling With Firearms

Our travels often include firearms, whether it's a concealed handgun in the waistband, a rifle stowed in the trunk, or – in the case of this author's road trip – every weapon you own being transported on a cross-country move. No matter the case, there are some important safety and legal considerations for traveling with guns. The consequences of ignoring these issues could be dire – arrest, imprisonment, theft, or even your own guns being used against you and your loved ones.

We delved into these issues in a web-exclusive supplement to this article. You can read it now at offgridweb.com/transportation/traveling-with-firearms.

these inexpensive work lights. Grab a headlamp, also in the same store, and you're ready for night ops.

Cell phones are great, but coverage can vary. When caravanning, use a good set of hand-held radios for communication between vehicles. Companies like Cobra offer family packs of four radios that feature several miles of range, are rechargeable, and can also use non-rechargeable batteries. The ones we have also have a NOAA weather radio mode so you can listen to weather information if available. These are also great to have in the vehicle if your road trip will feature any hiking or camping destinations along the way.

Satellite phones from companies like Inmarsat or Iridium are potential options as well. They offer pre-paid or monthly plans often managed by a third-party company like Bluecosmo. They can be expensive ($600-$1,200 USD or more) depending on the manufacturer and model, but in the event that cell coverage is absent, or cellular networks are overloaded in the case of a localized emergency, a sat phone in your go-bag could be the day-saver. The waters start to get deep when considering satellite networks, LOS (line-of-sight) considerations, etc., so be sure to do your research before investing. I found the reviews on Amazon to be helpful in zeroing in which phone would be best for our family.

Throw all this kit into the bag with the TP and wipes and you should have a pretty good start on the basic sundries to keep your family happy and hygienic even in the absence of modern amenities and services.

Defensive Driving

According to the National Highway Traffic Safety Administration, there were 37,133 lives lost on U.S. roadways in 2017 alone. When you're putting in 3,500 miles of continuous driving over nine days, you're bound to have some close calls. What this trip really emphasized for me was that sometimes the best defense really is having the best defense.

In Arkansas, we pulled out onto I-40 East. I was ahead in the rental truck; my wife entered the highway a minute or two behind me in her Suburban. A semi-truck

travelling in the opposite, westbound lane overturned, entered the median, and began sliding toward her. The tractor-trailer ground to a halt before fully entering her eastbound lane, but it came so close to her that it threw dirt and debris across her windshield as she passed.

She had two hands on the wheel and the road had her full attention. She was driving defensively and alertly and used just enough of her lane to swerve around the chaos coming at her while not endangering others around her. Most of our family was in the truck with her, and she avoided that potentially lethal incident by being switched-on and not making a bad situation any worse with panicked over-corrections.

The incident made the local news as those types of events often do, but our family wasn't part of the story thanks to my wife.

On this subject, I'd like to say driving defensively is a lost art, but that'd imply there's some sort of elusive mastery of the skill few can attain. There's no art to it. It simply requires focus. Driving defensively is driving alertly and safely, plain and simple. The road, your vehicle, and the vehicles around you get your full attention. Expect others around you to do foolish things like veer into your lane, brake suddenly, or run stop signs. If you're thinking about these things while driving, instead of trying to post to your Instagram, you're already several precious fractions of a second ahead of any potential situation.

Most of the accidents I see on the road these days are rear-end collisions. This tells me people simply aren't paying attention and are following too closely, often while speeding. You need to maintain at least a 2-second gap between your car and the one in front of you. Impatiently tailgating other cars won't get you to your destination any faster, but it might earn you a trip to the hospital. Anticipate traffic slowdowns around bends or as you approach intersections. Be thinking about what you'll do if that car in front of you slams on its brakes right now. Where is my "out?" In other words, where can I

Situational Awareness Around Your Vehicle

Driving defensively can help keep you safe behind the wheel, but what about when you pull over for a meal, fuel fill-up, bathroom break, or overnight stop? You can't afford to leave your defensive mindset and observational skills behind the second you step out of the driver seat. To learn more about how situational awareness should be incorporated into your road trip plan, read our second web-exclusive supplement article at offgridweb.com/transportation/situational-awareness.

safely steer (not suddenly swerve) to avoid the collision? The shoulder? The other lane? Is it clear?

These are the types of mental calculations we make every second on the road, but they require the majority of your attention, not the minority. Six million car accidents take place in the U.S. each year, according to the NHTSA. Nearly half of them are rear-end collisions. Start paying attention to your driving. With numbers like these, it's likely those around you are not.

Read more on defensive driving at www.dmv.org/defensive-driving/defensive-driving-101.php.

Conclusion

This may sound like overkill for a road trip, but when you place your entire family on a set of four tires barreling down the highway at 75 mph into unfamiliar places full of strange people, you really are leaving the wire. You're leaving the safety and security of the known and trading it for the completely unknown. You had damn well better think about all the what-ifs that lie out there along those dark roads. We traveled 3,500 miles over nine days coast-to-coast with our entire family in tow. We avoided potential danger areas. We chose nicer hotels to stay at to avoid bad areas of town. We ensured we were obeying the laws of each state and jurisdiction we passed through as it pertained to our firearms. We used technology to help guide us, but we didn't rely on it. We brought gear, first-aid supplies, and equipment for all the just-in-case moments a lengthy road trip odyssey can present. We made sure our vehicles were maintained to avoid surprises. We didn't do it all perfectly, but we did our best to cover a lot of "what-ifs."

We did all these things because we know — as you now should if you didn't already — that many of the situations we prepared for are not actually questions of "if," but of "when." Are you ready?

RECOIL OFFGRID

SUBSCRIPTIONS ARE
DAMAGE
RESISTANT

ORDER TODAY and your magazines will be shipped to you in a #4 LDPE 100% recyclable polybag along with a protective privacy insert **to keep your investment safe**.

SUBSCRIBE TODAY:
WWW.OFFGRIDWEB.COM

RECOIL OFFGRID
P.O. Box 433326
Palm Coast, FL 32143-3326

ELECTRONIC SERVICE REQUESTED

OFG OUT9

RENEW ONLINE:
renew.offgrid-mag.com

When crisis comes to your door, will you **BE PREPARED?**

Get RECOIL's sister publication, RECOIL OFFGRID, delivered right to your door six times a year! It's a fresh approach to urban survival and emergency preparation — with in-depth buyer's guides, honest, rigorous product reviews, and survival techniques from the country's top specialists. Want more? Mobile optimized, fully interactive, and featuring our trademark combination of pull-no-punches writing and easy-to-read design, OFFGRIDweb.com is loaded with expert advice, tips, and techniques to enhance your emergency response skillset. It's where prepared citizens, survivalists, and those who want to be in the know come to stay ready. Experience it for yourself and live confidently in an uncertain world.